A Guerrilla Odyssey

Modern Intellectual and Political History of the Middle East
Mehrzad Boroujerdi, *Series Editor*

A Guerrilla Odyssey

Modernization, Secularism, Democracy,
and the Fadai Period of National Liberation
in Iran, 1971–1979

Peyman Vahabzadeh

SYRACUSE UNIVERSITY PRESS

For a listing of books published and distributed by Syracuse University Press,
visit our Web site at SyracuseUniversityPress.syr.edu.

ISBN: 978-0-8156-3243-6

Library of Congress Cataloging-in-Publication Data

Vahabzadeh, Peyman.
  A guerrilla odyssey : modernization, secularism, democracy, and the Fadai period
of national liberation in Iran, 1971–1979 / Peyman Vahabzadeh. — 1st ed.
    p. cm.
  Includes bibliographical references and index.
  ISBN 978-0-8156-3243-6 (cloth : alk. paper)
  1. Iran—Politics and government—1941–1979. 2. National liberation movements—
Iran—History—20th century. 3. Guerrillas—Iran—History—20th century.
4. New Left—Iran—History—20th century. 5. Sazman-i Chirik'ha-yi Fada'i-i Khalq-i
Iran—History. 6. Chirik'ha-yi Fadayi-i Khalq-i Iran—History. 7. Islamic modernism—
Iran—History—20th century. 8. Islam and secularism—Iran—History—20th century.
9. Democracy—Iran—History—20th century. I. Title.
  DS316.6.V34 2010
  956.704'3—dc22   2010003484

Manufactured in the United States of America

To the future generations of activists

Peyman Vahabzadeh is an assistant professor of sociology at the University of Victoria in British Columbia and author of *Articulated Experiences: Toward a Radical Phenomenology of Contemporary Social Movements* (2003). His papers, essays, poems, short stories, criticism, reviews, and interviews have been published in English, Persian, German, and Kurdish.

Only the origin of what is matters: something that my gaze cannot confront except in an attenuated form. . . . All the rest is reflection among reflections, me included.

—ITALO CALVINO, *Mr. Palomar*

Contents

Illustrations

Acknowledgments

THIS BOOK would not have been possible without the support of many individuals throughout my long and painstaking research. I thank Ali Akbar Mahdi, Warren Magnusson, Marilyn Gates, and Murray Smith for various ideas that surface in parts of this book. I also thank the anonymous reviewers of the manuscript for their suggestions. Special thanks go to Cosroe Chaqueri (K. Shakeri), the editor of Edition Mazdak, for providing rare documents and communicating his knowledge about the history of the Iranian Left. I also acknowledge Mastureh Ahmadzadeh, Mehdi Fatapour, Abbas Hashemi, Behzad Karimi, Parviz Navidi, Farrokh Negahdar, Mashallah Razmi, Mariam Satwat, and other (former) activists who agreed to answer my questions about different aspects of the history of Fadaiyan.

I am also grateful to the late Ahmad Vahabzadeh, Ali Reza Feizabadi, Babak Amir Khosravi, Maziar Behrooz, and Nader Naji, who sent me copies of documents pertaining to the early years of Fadaiyan. I thank Jasper Benjamin Goldman and Hossein Fazeli, who worked as research assistants, respectively, at Harvard University's Widener Library and Columbia University Libraries, as well as Natalie Gidora and Ehsan Faizabadi for help with the appendixes. Likewise, my gratitude goes to the University of Victoria Library Inter-Library Loans Division for their efforts in obtaining sources. Ehsan Faizabadi provided assistance with the photos. Last but not least, I acknowledge and thank Karin Renee O'Leary, who provided meticulous editorial assistance to the final draft of the manuscript.

I acknowledge the Social Sciences and Humanities Research Council of Canada (SSHRCC) Postdoctoral Fellowship (2001–3). I also thank the Office of Vice-President Research and the Dean of Faculty of Social Sciences at the University of Victoria, as well as the late Ellen Gee, chair of the Department of Sociology and Anthropology at Simon Fraser University, for providing a travel grant to visit archives of the Iranian Left in Paris in 2001. I thank Mary Selden Evans, executive editor, and Mehrzad Boroujerdi, series editor, at Syracuse University Press for their support and encouragement. Parts of chapter 6 were formerly published in the *British Journal of Middle Eastern Studies* (34 [1], April 2007) and *Iranian Studies* (40 [3], June 2007).

Finally, this book materialized through the loving support of my longtime companion, Giti, and our son, Emile, who always encouraged me through my years of academic vagrancy and underemployment. My words fall short in expressing my love and gratitude toward them.

Notes on Translation

BECAUSE MOST of the published accounts that I used for this study have never been presented to the Anglophone world, the unenviable task of providing the reader with English translations of the Persian texts fell to me. In translating some Persian polysemic words, I chose to accede to their contextual meanings by introducing the word's etymological significance or historical context, or simply by inserting the Persian words in parentheses. In transliterating names of persons or places, or certain Persian words or concepts, I followed the simple rule of approximating the sound of Persian letters to those in the English alphabet. The only exception pertains to those Persian or Arabic proper names that have a certain norm of spelling owing to their appearance in English (e.g., Mohammad, Muslim, Mahmoud). For simplicity's sake, I disregarded the distinction between long and short vowels in Persian. I eliminated the typographical ciphers and diacritics that are used to designate Persian letter-sounds involving scanning and accentuation. I have used the apostrophe to mark the vowel *ayn* in the middle of some Persian words (e.g., Sa'id) but simplified that rule in one case only (Sho'aiyan). I have dropped the apostrophe when the *ayn* appears as the first vowel of the word (e.g., Ali or *Elm*).

My main objective in translating excerpts from the texts relating to this research is to negotiate between a readable English and the writing styles and idiosyncrasies of the authors of these texts, because I hold that the style of writing captures, at least partially, the nuances in a discourse as a subset of language that locates, conditions, and makes possible the articulation of the subject matter.

Finally, in referring to "the OIPFG," I mean to denote the original Fadai Organization between 1971 and 1979. All earlier or later changes to the name of the group—the People's Fadai Guerrillas (PFG, the original designation), the Organization of People's Fadai Guerrillas (OPFG, the mid-carrier name of the group), and Organization of Iranian People's Fadai Guerrillas (OIPFG)—fall under this acronym. I also frequently use "Fadaiyan" (the Persian plural of "Fadai") or the Fadai Guerrillas in addition to PFG, OPFG, or OIPFG. One revolution and several schisms later, and to this day, certain factions still call themselves the OIPFG. For clarification's sake, I have tried to specify these later groups by extra notation.

Introduction to a Belated Study

Set this cage ablaze, release the birds and the messengers
So that the smile of freedom, the grapes of joy, grow with the sunrise
—from a popular Fadai song (lyrics by M. HOMAYUNPUR)

THE FAST PACE of unfolding events that followed the 1979 Iranian Revolution, and the tremendous social and political issues it caused, resulted in a certain neglect on the part of scholars to study the various contributions of Fadaiyan to the contemporary political discourse in Iran. The fate of the Fadai Guerrillas seems to have been sealed by the 1979 Islamic Revolution: its discourses, social projects, activities, and objectives, as well as the identity that the Fadai movement bestowed upon urban, secular Iranian dissidents between 1971 and 1979, receded into the popular revolutionary movement. Therefore the history, the life, and the theoretical works of the Organization of Iranian People's Fadai Guerrillas (henceforth the OIPFG, or Fadaiyan, the plural of Fadai) were subsumed under the social and political events that took place between the 1953 CIA-engineered coup d'état, which ended twelve years of pathbreaking national liberation and democratic movement in Iran, and the Revolution of February 1979. Thus the Fadai movement did not receive the analytical attention it deserves and was mainly discussed in relation to other studies (Abrahamian 1980; 1982, 480–89; Alaolmolki 1987; Behrooz 1999, 48–71; Boroujerdi 1996, 34–42; Halliday 1980; Mirsepassi 2000, 159–79; Fayazmanesh 1995; Zabih 1986, 113–33).[1]

---

1. Ironically, the only book-length study of the OIPFG was recently published in Persian by the state-sponsored Political Studies and Research Institute (Naderi 2008). This book, in 984 pages, is based on the SAVAK archives. While offering new information about the OIPFG, the book

This book shows that through the construction of a discourse of national liberation, the OIPFG came to define nearly a decade of recent Iranian history and politics by breaking new possibilities in action and thought and catalyzing a significant secular-Left intellectual and cultural movement. Fadaiyan produced an unparalleled amount of comparatively original theoretical works, and spurred society into a phase of violent polarization, *ironically* in order to achieve political openness. This study shows that despite the intentions of its founders, the OIPFG was never fully a unified organization with a clear, let alone pure, ideological base. The present work illustrates that the OIPFG was founded upon a plurality of diverse, even conflicting, interpretations, influences, and principles that never allowed the group to achieve its idealized unity as represented by the organizational fetishism endemic to Communist parties. The study's nuanced reading of the writings of Fadai theorists problematizes the existing monolithic interpretations. A discourse analysis of the theories of Fadaiyan illustrates that this urban guerrilla group was in fact obliquely enlivened by a democratic impulse that was cloaked under the revolutionary discursive mantle of the time (i.e., Marxism-Leninism and the guerrilla theories of Ernesto Che Guevara and Carlos Marighella). By pointing out the inner dynamics, and the apparent impasse, of conventional revolutionary theories, this book argues that the revolutionary discourse created a "constitutive paradox" as revealed in the life and works of Fadaiyan.

Conducting this study was arduous, slow, and demanding. Putting together the bits and pieces of the fragmented history of an underground and secretive group was not easy. Under the custodianship of authorities in Iran, the security documents pertaining to the group still remain closed to independent scholars. Thus I had to glean scattered documents, communiqués, books, pamphlets, and other publications of the group, which took several years to complete. I also had to read comparatively the works on recent Iranian history, memoirs, and other related publications that might contain some information about Fadaiyan. I

---

also contains unsubstantiated claims and unsupported interpretations, and as such, it cannot be regarded as an impartial study. Naderi's book follows an earlier one, published by the Iranian Ministry of Intelligence, which contains selected and annotated security reports relating to activists and activities of the OIPFG (CSHD 2001). These books intend to discredit non-Muslim opposition against the Shah. In this respect, one must point out the neglect of many surviving OIPFG activists and leaders of various Fadai splinter groups in producing their own versions of the OIPFG history.

always needed to read between the lines of the official OIPFG documents. To complete the picture, I needed to interview a number of activists of the period. While most would answer my questions, some refused. Some interviewees showed remarkable courage in speaking of the events about which they had knowledge. I quickly found out that there were subjects that certain interviewees liked to discuss, yet there were other matters that some interviewees gently dodged, as if reluctant to release information or bound by a vow of secrecy. Human research ethics directed my conduct when engaging in such interviews, so I had no interest in causing psychological discomfort for my research participants. As a result, at times I had to contain my eagerness to get to the bottom of things. Because the topic of this study is a controversial one, I imagine that my attempt at arriving at an impartial and objective view of Fadaiyan in this book will garner me enemies, and friends, from all sides. My hope is that this study will provide greater knowledge of the life and times of Fadaiyan and will set the groundwork for further study. No one will ever be able to write the definitive story about the past.

THE QUESTION OF APPROACH

My intention here is to *contextualize* the emergence, activities, and theories of the OIPFG between 1971 and 1979. This period witnessed the adamant efforts of the Fadai Guerrillas in materializing their original mandate: to instigate a popular and national movement that would overthrow Iran's monarchy. As such, this book does not focus on what became of Fadaiyan after the Revolution, except when certain postrevolutionary events were relevant for understanding the pre-1979 guerrillas. The "guerrilla period," as this period is commonly called, raised a number of issues of universal and cross-cultural concerns about political life under a repressive autocracy based on a peripheral-dependent economy. This period also offered a radical method—armed struggle—as the means for igniting the national liberation movement. A small but bold underground group, the People's Fadai Guerrillas stood at the forefront of this unprecedented shift both in theory and in action.

The current investigation is partly historical, but it does not presuppose the object of historical narrative to be motivated by universal, purposive rationality. Likewise, this study does not hide behind the insight conveniently granted by hindsight (however inevitable this may be at some points). To avoid objectifying

Fadaiyan, I will allow them to speak in their own terms, and not in terms of our expectations or disappointments with their policies or performance. By removing such expectations we allow the past to speak to our present conditions. This book does not simply evaluate the accuracy of the OIPFG's theories; rather, it focuses on the hidden and oblique contributions of Fadaiyan to political theory and to an understanding of the Iranian conditions. This caveat said, however, I offer critical engagements with particular past actions of Fadaiyan in order to depict a complete image of the group.

What sets this work apart from the existing, limited studies of the OIPFG is its radical phenomenological approach. The merit of this approach lies in its understanding of social phenomena based on their specific relations to the historical contexts of their advent. From this point of view, *social and political movements are points of attempted (re-)institution of society.* Thus they cannot be simply evaluated in terms of success or failure. Nor can they be assessed according to the scholar's normative measure(s), or according to the preset standards of theoretical frameworks (like Marxism).[2] Instead, social movements are understood in relations to the openings they instigate in the political constellation of society as well as the closures that inevitably follow such openings (Vahabzadeh 2003).

Given the objectives and the theoretical concerns of this work, an evaluative analysis of the rise and fall of the OIPFG would simply prove insufficient. Therefore *the conceptual removal of historical demands and rationality of goals should include those demands that originally gave rise to the movement and motivated Fadaiyan,* as represented in the body of literature that can be called theories of national liberation. Indeed, the OIPFG constructed an original body of social and political works seldom paralleled in the contemporary Iranian Left. This book shows how major OIPFG theorists constructed a discourse of national

---

2. Disregarding the spirit of Fadaiyan, for instance, Abrahamian calls the "central thesis" of Fadaiyan to be "astonishingly simple: guerrilla warfare and more guerrilla warfare" (1982, 486). On the other hand, Fayazmanesh refutes the theories of Fadaiyan because they deviated from Marxist principles. He identifies Marxism-Leninism and dependency theory as two sources of Fadaiyan's theories and argues that Fadaiyan failed to present themselves "as a viable alternative . . . to influence the path of economic development in Iran" (Fayazmanesh 1995, 98) because they could not properly understand Marxism-Leninism. Assessments like this cannot properly situate Fadaiyan within their generational zeitgeist.

liberation, how their critics problematized or enriched this discourse, and how those within the actual organization received it. Understanding the Fadai discourse of national liberation is essential to the understanding of an era of political life in Iran, and we clearly see, after three decades, how *historical eras render certain ways of acting and thinking intelligible and plausible.* Indeed, I will argue that within the rebellious zeitgeist of the 1960s and 1970s, the OIPFG borrowed conceptual elements from three political and intellectual discursive fields: (a) postcolonial self-affirmation and national liberation movements; (b) the Cold War and polarization of the world; and finally (c) the Latin American revolutionary wave that challenged the Leninist blueprint.

The merit of my hermeneutical endeavor is that it allows a new reading of the theories of the group, an interpretation that is not bound by the assumptions of the theorists themselves. This interpretation will render such theories intelligible and relevant to our lives today. The arch principle of this hermeneutical approach is its nuanced reading of the OIPFG texts, a reading sensitive to diction, narrative strategies, and subtexts, as well as to the specific historical situations that gave rise to them. I will show in this book how the diverse internal of Fadaiyan had been cloaked by their illusive unitary external.

With the fall of the Berlin Wall and the subsequent tremendous political changes, today we need to reread the works of these theorists beyond their own political mandates, ideological frameworks, and theoretical assumptions, and release them from the prison of dogmatic referentiality, presumed ultimacies in positional justifications, or factional appropriation. Yet most important, I free these theorists from the theoretical oblivion they have been subjected to in the past three decades and examine them against the possibility of whether they have something worthwhile to offer to our time. This book offers a more complete depiction of the OIPFG, although no one can ultimately claim to offer an exhaustive history. Therefore, my work calls for further studies of the group's suppressed, overlooked, or concealed histories.

THE QUESTION OF METHOD

The radical phenomenology of Reiner Schürmann makes up the principal framework of my study and informs my method. Schürmann (1987) develops an epochal theory that displays how certain modes of acting and thinking become possible, even necessary, in certain periods. The hegemony of certain principles over action and thought distinguishes one era from another. For Schürmann, history is not a unilinear accumulation of events affecting one another in causal ways or according to universal or rationalistic logics. Rather, epochs are bound by the hegemony of certain constellations of Truth that hinge on certain ultimate referents before these founding referents recede into a prolonged period of impoverishment. Such hegemonies allow us to speak of distinct eras like ancient Greece, the Renaissance, or the sixties. In each one of these eras certain modes of praxis became possible and were justified by appealing to some theoretical higher ground. Radical phenomenology enables us to identify such ultimacies and in so doing to remove them from our theoretical gaze.

Key to my approach in this study is the concept of "ultimate referentiality," a derivation of Schürmann's concept of "ultimate referent." Schürmann uses the concept of "ultimate referent" to identify the reign of certain concepts over certain epochs in the history of metaphysics. I use ultimate referentiality to deconstruct the fundamental assumptions about the constructed ultimacy of social ground in sociological analysis, revealing the theoretical approaches that subsume all modes of action and knowledge under an assumed higher and seemingly unshakable ground. Hegemonically, an ultimate referentiality creates a community of analysts, social scientists, and activists who share a subscription to a mysteriously endowed ultimate and rational ground (Vahabzadeh 2009).

Ultimate referentiality operates simultaneously on two different, but corresponding, levels: in theory and in the "real." Its double movement reinforces the presumed inevitability of an ultimate ground and thus conceals its assumptive nature. As such, theory designates a domain as a point of moorage in the "real" where all inquiry about the subject matter of the study is (supposedly) satisfied. Thanks to the referential appointment of theory, the "real" ultimate ground stands on its own and is deemed the ultimate realm of verification of theoretical postulates. Thus the *institutive role of theory in imposing norms upon reality* is sent into oblivion: theory is held as a higher realm of inquiry whose truth can be verified only against the very reality that theory has constructed.

As pertains to this study, sociology largely treats social movements as indicative of social crises and as revealing deviated norms of social practice that must be addressed, corrected, and brought back to their rational status. Relative deprivation and J-curve theories presuppose the presence of rational actors who resist, to varying degrees, their exclusion from economic activity. In fact, theory demands the actors to respond in a calculable way to perceived "if-then" scenarios. One can clearly observe how the frames of economic change and the norms of (revolutionary) practice are already set by a theory that reduces the possibilities to only the scenarios for which theory can account. As such, theory sets the norms for practice while pretending to follow the changing patterns of practice. *The ends of practice, founded by theory, determine the origins of practice,* or put simply, the origin is already determined by the end.

The removal of ultimate referentiality will free analysis from theoretical expectations. In our case, it will free our gaze from evaluating the success or failure of the Fadai movement based on the degree of "authenticity" of reading, or on applying revolutionary programs like Marxism-Leninism. I step back from the ideological and theoretical demands that governed theories of Fadaiyan, while acknowledging the fact that its theorists wrote from within the prison of leftist-sanctioned theoretical impositions.

This book will take a further step by applying a *genealogical critique* of the Fadai discourse of national liberation through a *discourse analysis* of their theories, memoirs, journals, exchanges, pamphlets, manuals, and communiqués. Given that a genealogical critique is not bound by normative judgments, and because this critique reanimates the possible pasts in the present, it provides counterintuitive insights into the connection between the lives of the activists and their theories. A genealogical critique disassembles theoretical essentialism and referentiality and allows a nonessentialist reading of Fadaiyan's works. My genealogical critique will illustrate that the Fadai discourse of national liberation contained a theory of democracy that was muted by the imposed ideological jargon. Finally, a genealogical critique will bring to the fore the inescapable haunting of a plurivocal origination, an origin that emerged in manifold ways, which subverted the unitary pretense of the OIPFG's dominant narratives and history. Specifically, this book will reveal that the OIPFG was never a unified group and that it contained many alternative narratives and diverse roots.

My deconstructive endeavor requires that I treat the OIPFG texts as inevitably incomplete, open-ended, or understated. In rereading the OIPFG texts with a deconstructive gaze, this book is indebted to the deconstruction of the Marxist tradition by Ernesto Laclau and Chantal Mouffe (Laclau and Mouffe 1985; Laclau 1996; 2005). A deconstructive reading demonstrates that, at least in the Iranian case, the discourse of national liberation implicitly pointed at its own *imminent exhaustion* that eventually gave way to various democratic discourses of today.

Last but not least, I will analyze the OIPFG as a clandestine guerrilla organization as well as the core of a larger social movement. The Fadai armed struggle was the articulation of a nationwide movement for independence and democracy. The rise and demise of the OIPFG is an example of how social movements are products of the eras that capture their political imaginary, giving them an identity and a language of resistance. As these eras wither, so do the discourses to which they gave rise. Yet discourses do not simply vanish. Instead, many of their constitutive elements resurface in the nascent discourses. For instance, democracy, a major component of the national liberation discourse, has outlived the latter and become the dominant discourse of our time. This book argues that although the Fadai discourse of national liberation in the 1970s was informed by Marxism-Leninism and Latin American militantism, it obliquely enabled struggles for democratizing and expanding civil society in Iran.

THE ROAD AHEAD

Chapter 1 follows the historical path that culminated in an armed guerrilla movement, tracing the "guerrilla period" back to the CIA-engineered coup d'état of 1953 that overthrew the nationalist premier Dr. Mohammad Mosaddeq. It provides a glimpse into the militant predecessors of Fadaiyan. Chapter 2 specifically narrates a thematic history of the OIPFG by sketching the conditions of the emergence of armed cells that later formed the People's Fadai Guerrillas. This chapter details how Fadai guerrillas changed Iranian political life and in turn experienced major shifts in their own theories and practices.

These two mainly historical chapters are followed by the analytical chapters. Chapter 3 offers discourse and content analyses of Bizhan Jazani's theory of national liberation and armed struggle. Jazani produced several critical treatises rarely equaled by Iranian social and political theorists. Chapter 4 analyzes the works of two of the founders of Fadaiyan: Massoud Ahmadzadeh and Amir Parviz Puyan, whose ideas became the guiding theory of the PFG after its formation in 1971. This chapter concludes by analyzing the post-1979 debates between supporters of Ahmadzadeh and those of Jazani. Chapter 5 displays the varied and conflictual plurality of ideas among the Fadai theorists by analyzing the debates between Fadaiyan and three other underground groups. These debates raised issues that were quickly suppressed or disregarded by Fadaiyan, fearing the debates would threaten the group's allegiance to revolutionary Marxism. Chapter 6 offers a reading of selected works of Mostafa Sho'aiyan, who briefly joined the OIPFG before he was expelled from the group because of his disagreements with the Fadai leaders and his critique of Leninism.

These theoretical chapters are followed by a sociological analysis in chapter 7, which surveys the cultural and social impacts of the Fadai movement to illustrate the extent of moral and intellectual support that Fadaiyan received in the 1970s. The selfless guerrillas became sources of inspiration for many writers, artists, and intellectuals of the decade because the name "Fadai" never designated a small, urban guerrillas group, but connoted the high hopes of an entire rebellious generation. Chapter 8 argues that the centrist ideology and organizational life of Fadaiyan in fact replicated the state-centrist regime of Iran. Using a Foucaultian approach, this chapter investigates the technologies of resistance used by the OIPFG.

Chapter 9 concludes this study by revealing the "constitutive paradox" of national liberation, arguing that the assumption of a privileged agent of history and the state as an agent for liberation precluded the Fadai theorists from adequately developing theories of democracy, secularism, expansion of civil society, and the recognition of a plurality of actors.

Finally, the appendixes provide additional information about various aspects of the OIPFG's history.

A Guerrilla Odyssey

1

Iran in the 1960s

Repressive Development

> We are the last to have struggled politically through the Constitutional
> means. We expect the judge to convey this point to his superiors . . .
>
> —MEHDI BAZARGAN, quoted in Nejati, *Tarikh-e siyasi-ye*
> *bistopanj saleh-ye Iran* [The twenty-five year political his-
> tory of Iran][1]

FOLLOWING A DECADE of sociopolitical development in relative liberty, the
CIA-engineered coup d'état of 1953 removed the popular-nationalist premier, Dr.
Mohammad Mosaddeq, crushed the oil nationalization movement, and restored
the absolute monarchical rule. The return of the ousted Shah, Mohammad Reza
Pahlavi, from his short-lived exile in Baghdad and Rome marked the beginning
of a new era: political modernization, originally initiated through the Constitutional Movement of 1906–11, was suspended, as the Shah practically suspended
constitutional provisions that allowed the nation to rule itself. Between 1925 and
1941, Iranians had experienced an enforced process of laic, institutional modernization that was commanded by the founder of the Pahlavi dynasty, Reza
Shah. The Anglo-Soviet invasion of Iran in 1941 paradoxically brought a period
of self-assertion and nationalism and ended the dictator's rule (owing to Reza
Shah's propensity toward Nazi Germany). With the exile of Reza Shah by the

---

1. In 1979, as the leader of the (Islamic) Freedom Movement of Iran, Mehdi Bazargan was
appointed the premier in the provisional government by Ayatollah Khomeini, and was involved,
in an uneasy way, in establishing the Islamic Republic in Iran before the fall of his government in
1980. Toward the end of his life, Bazargan led, in the 1980s, the only tolerated, but badly treated,
opposition group in Iran.

Allies, new parties burgeoned in the political scene, labor unions expanded, and ethnonationalist movements found momentum, particularly in Azerbaijan and Kurdistan. This period provided the first significant opportunity, after the Constitutional Movement, for Iranians to engage in the practical and self-didactic process of political modernization. By 1950, the ten-year experience of relative political openness had resulted in a heightened sense of nationalism embodied by Mosaddeq and his uncompromising defense of Iran's right to self-determination. Mosaddeq's conflict with Mohammad Reza Shah over the Shah's constitutional powers led to the premier's removal from office. The subsequent uprising of July 20, 1952, in support of Mosaddeq forced the Shah to reinstate the defiant premier and to concede to the constitutional limitation on his power. Mosaddeq made history by becoming the only premier to be also the commander in chief. Intent upon ending the concession of the Anglo-Iranian Oil Company and upholding the constitutional power of the people's representatives, the national liberation movement in Iran could no longer be contained.

The coup was engineered to put a stop to such a pioneer postcolonial movement. Its success was a devastating blow to the future of political development in Iran. Not only did the coup bring back royal dictatorship, it established the influence of the United States over all major decisions regarding Iranian economic and political development. The coup also demonstrated the incompetence of the leadership of the pro-Soviet Tudeh Party of Iran (Hezb-e Tudeh-ye Iran). Having formerly confronted Mosaddeq's National Front, the Tudeh Party had suddenly made an about-face after the July 1952 uprising and supported the premier. However, the Tudeh leadership failed to call upon its enormous membership for street confrontation with the coup forces. Nor did it call on its 600-strong, covert Officers Organization (Sazman-e Afsaran), which consisted of high-ranking military officers and commanders of units and regiments, to stage a counter-coup. Instead, in the aftermath of Stalin's death in the Soviet Union and the perceived weakness of the new leadership of the Socialist bloc, the Tudeh leadership fled to the Soviet Union, leaving the pro-Tudeh military personnel and the Party members at the mercy of the regime. Following the coup, Mosaddeq was captured, tried in a military court, and given a three-year prison term plus lifetime house arrest in Ahmadabad. The National Front, the heterogeneous coalition that Mosaddeq led, was quickly dismantled by the military, its leaders were imprisoned, and Mosaddeq's foreign minister, Dr. Hossein Fatemi, was executed. By 1957 the coup regime had brutally crushed the last dissident circles. More important, it cauterized the collective memory of a new generation of political activists that rose in the 1960s with an unforgiving attitude toward the Tudeh Party, often viewing the Tudeh's indecision as tantamount to treason.

The 1953 coup must be understood in the context of the Cold War and its ramifications for the Third World. At issue was the expansion of capitalism to undeveloped societies where Socialist ideas could potentially challenge the international hegemony of the United States and its allies. Following World War II, the Marshall Plan was implemented to rebuild war-stricken Western Europe and then began the campaign of "development" in former colonies, a development that euphemistically concealed the neocolonial capitalism under the guise of political and economic humanism. Given the international context, one way to "guide" the Third World in economic modernization was through foreign investment. "Developing" countries, the doctrine held, could pace faster in their road to a capitalist economy if they accepted the aid packages and prescriptions of Western overseers (see Escobar 1995).

In Iran, the repression of nationalist and Socialist oppositions, the establishment of the dreaded SAVAK (security agency) in 1957, and the consolidation of power in the hands of the Shah were all parts of the initial step at securing Iran's allegiance to the United States. By the late 1950s, the Shah launched development projects that mainly aimed at building the institutional means and the necessary infrastructure for state-owned corporations. Facing funding shortages, he turned to the United States and the World Bank for loans, but the Kennedy administration demanded structural reforms. To initiate the reforms, the ruling Democrats favored Dr. Ali Amini, Iran's ambassador to Washington, as the premier. In 1960, the Shah had allowed the two "rival" state-run parties and the Second National Front candidates to run for the Twentieth Majles (Parliament). Embarrassed by election irregularities and the dismissal of two successive handpicked premiers, the Shah finally conceded to Amini's premiership despite his evident dislike of him. Enjoying U.S. support, Amini forced the Shah to dissolve the Twentieth Majles and to exile the notorious head of SAVAK, General Bakhtiar. He also started negotiating with the Second National Front and introduced land reform. His clash with the Shah over military expenditure, however, led to Amini's dismissal in 1962. The Shah took over the reforms, now presented in the six-point "White Revolution." Between 1960 and 1963, Iran rejuvenated with new hopes for change as people witnessed a heightened return of the student movement and the National Front. However, because of its utterly reformist attitude, the Second National Front failed to attain Mosaddeq's approval (under house arrest) and alienated university students. Land reform and women's suffrage angered Shi'i clerics, seminary students, and traditional bazaar merchants. The Shah's heavy-handed suppression of religious opposition led to the bloody clash of June 5, 1963, and to the exile of Ayatollah Ruhollah Khomeini, a vocal cleric popular among traditional sectors. With all opposition brutally repressed, the reforms were carried out and expanded, the Shah soon regained absolute control, and Iran received the much-needed loans (Keddie 1981, 159).

The 1960–63 period brought about a close affinity between repression and development in Iran, and "repressive development" became prevalent for the next fifteen years. Benefiting the ruling elite, it was characterized by autocratic plans and technocratic implementation of projects while blocking political participation. Brokered by the Shah and the state, modernization increasingly pulled Iran into the periphery of capitalist metropolitans. The result was a mutant giant: the emerging or expanding classes (the working and the bureaucratic classes as well as intellectuals and experts) were deprived of the necessary institutions for political participation. Those affected by modernization were ironically excluded from decision-making (Mirsepassi 2000, 74). Stated differently, "The shah's state and the Iranian intelligentsia each posed a problem for the other. The state relied heavily on technocrats and bureaucrats to manage its rapidly expanding industrial machinery. At the same time the technocrats' demand for an increasing voice in government matters was a source of worry for the state" (Boroujerdi 1996, 32). The Shah, in his usual arrogant fashion, consistently defended repression as a prerequisite for modernizing Iran: "To carry through reforms, one can't help but be authoritarian," he announced. "Especially when the reforms take place in a country like Iran, where only twenty-five percent of the inhabitants know how to read and write. . . . If I hadn't been harsh, I wouldn't even have been able to carry out agrarian reform and my whole reform program would have been stalemated" (Shah in interview by Fallaci 1976, 275). His tone reveals the social arrangements endemic to a "rentier state" financed by its monopoly over the sale or lease of natural resources (Iran's oil) and foreclosures on mechanisms of accountability. "The state's main relationships to Iranian society were mediated through its *expenditures*—on the military, on development projects, on modern construction, on consumption subsidies, and the like," observes Theda Skocpol. "Suspended above its own people, the Iranian state bought them off, rearranged their lives, and repressed any dissidents among them" (1994, 244). This is how modernization embraced Iran.

Political repression in Iran after 1963 forced a new generation of activists to face the question of sociopolitical participation as a necessary component of economic development. In the absence of formal political venues, new circles of university students congregated on campuses in Tehran and Tabriz. Two militant groups, the Organization of Iranian People's Fadai Guerrillas (OIPFG) and the Organization of Iranian People's Mojahedin (OIPM), both trace their emergence back to the "point of no return" in 1963 when the last hopes for peaceful and legal revival of democratic movement vanished (Jazani 1978; Ahmadzadeh 1976; Puyan 1979; OIPM 1979b; Abrahamian 1980, 4; Abrahamian 1982, 482; Alaolmolki 1987, 218; Behrooz 1999, 33–34). Both of these groups spent the rest of the 1960s planning and organizing. In the meantime, Iran witnessed short-lived insurgencies. A brief account of these early attempts sheds light on how and why Fadaiyan succeeded in staging a guerrilla movement in Iran.

EARLY MILITANT ATTEMPTS

Two simultaneous elements led to the idea of guerrilla warfare: the *national element* was derived from the particular conditions of early 1960s Iran, and the *international element* was inspired by the new revolutionary models in China, Cuba, and Latin America. Both of these elements originated with the Iranian opposition abroad.

As regards the national element, the idea of armed struggle emerged among the activists of the National Front Abroad as they observed the failure of the Second National Front to win the support of Mosaddeq and to craft a unified strategy against the regime. The reformist High Council of the Second National Front and its "Patience and Awaiting Policy" alienated the National Front Student Organization (Matin 1999, 173–74). Thus a new, radical political trend developed at the Second Congress of the National Front in Europe (in Meinz, West Germany, August 15–20, 1963). Two experiences informed this trend: that of the rebellious sixties as the age of global conflict between the oppressed and the oppressors, and the growing belief that peaceful struggle in Iran had reached an impasse. The congress held that since the Shah "has shut down the possibility of legal struggles for the Iranian people, we ask the Iranian people to turn to more radical and fundamental methods of struggle" (quoted in Matin 1999, 175).

With respect to the international element, two landmark events transformed the landscape of the Third World Communist movements in the 1960s. First, the rise of the Maoist model (revolution led by a Communist peasant army) inspired activists in Asia and Africa where because of limited industrialization the working class did not have significant political presence. Second, the Cuban Revolution of 1959 demonstrated that a group of dedicated intellectuals could act as the agent of revolution. These intellectuals staged rural guerrilla warfare, and in the process of expansion they created liberated zones, recruited members, and organized peasants and the urban masses. Despite their reference to Lenin, both the Chinese and the Cuban revolutions undermined the Leninist principles of the ripeness of objective and subjective conditions of the revolution: presence of the vanguard party and the "red" workers' networks (see Lenin 1932; 1935). For the new Iranian Left, China and Cuba reignited the hope that was lost with Tudeh's tragic failure in 1953 and new momentum for reinstating the Left back into the country's political landscape.

National Front activists in Europe should be credited as the pioneers of guerrilla warfare in Iran. Cosroe Chaqueri (K. Shakeri), a founding member of the Confederation of Iranian Students–National Unity (CISNU) and member of the National Front, was arrested in 1961 in Mexico on his way to Cuba. A year later, as an emissary of the new National Front High Council in Europe, he met with the Egyptian ambassador in London, who later informed him that President Gamal Abdul Nasser was willing to assist Iranian revolutionaries in overthrowing the Shah, bringing the National Front to power, and releasing Mosaddeq. Chaqueri traveled to Iran to discuss the matter with the Second National Front leaders and met with Dr. Mehdi Azar, the Front's secretary of foreign relations. Azar informed Chaqueri that the National Front activities in Iran were bound by the Constitution and so he could not approve of any relations with foreign states. He also said that the National Front Abroad would be free to act based on its own discretion, so long as it was clear that the Second National Front (in Iran) was not implicated. The promised Persian radio broadcast did not materialize when Egyptian authorities insisted on editing the contents of Persian programs. In the spring of 1964, Chaqueri traveled to

Algeria and met with President Ahmad Ben Bella, who also promised support. The next meeting of the National Front delegates coincided with political crisis in Algeria, and the delegates returned to Europe empty-handed shortly before Ben Bella was overthrown (Matin 1999, 198–201). At the same time, National Front activists in Germany published Che Guevara's *Guerrilla Warfare* in their periodical *Iran-e Azad* (in 1963 and 1964) (Matin 1999, 183). This book soon found its way into Iran and influenced the first Fadai theorists, including Massoud Ahmadzadeh.

Meanwhile, Muslim students and activists outside Iran embarked on preparations for armed movement as well. In 1962, Ali Shari'ati, Mostafa Chamran, and Ebrahim Yazdi printed pamphlets on guerrilla warfare and secretly sent them to Iran. At the same time, activists of the Freedom Movement of Iran (Nehzat-e Azadi-ye Iran) in Paris went to Algeria for military training. In December 1963, Freedom Movement members Chamran, Yazdi, and Sadeq Qotbzadeh went to Egypt to receive training and aid, but Shari'ati rejected collaboration with the Egyptians and refused to join them. In 1964, Chamran took charge of the organization based in Egypt until the Egyptians closed down his office in 1966 (Matin 1999, 200–201).

Setbacks, however, did not impede activists in Europe and those in Iran from pursuing the idea of armed struggle. Here is a brief summary of some of the main attempts in the 1960s.

The Revolutionary Organization

This group originates with the growing dissent within the Tudeh Party ranks in exile in 1963, when a faction sprang out of the Tudeh in Europe, partly owing to their disagreement with the leadership of Iraj Eskandari and Reza Radmanesh, and partly owing to the Sino-Soviet split. The dissenters had pro-Chinese tendencies and, according to Maziar Behrooz, absorbed 90 percent of the Tudeh activists (1999, 40). Calling the Tudeh leadership "reformist," the dissenters held a "preparatory conference" in a Munich café in February 1964 (Rezvani 2005, 63; Khanbaba Tehrani 2001, 132). Inspired by China and Cuba, they emphasized the necessity of armed struggle and defended new revolutionary models while condemning the Soviet Union's domineering sway over Third World movements. In their First Congress in 1965, held in Tirana, Albania, the group called itself the Revolutionary Organization of the Tudeh Party of Iran (ROTPI; Sazman-e Enqelabi-ye Hezb-e Tudeh-ye Iran). They believed that Iran was still feudal and precapitalist (or a semifeudal-semicolony economic formation), despite the land reform. "Based on this analysis, the ROTPI came up with a blueprint of the Chinese revolution for Iran and concluded that in fighting against the Iranian imperial regime, the vanguard organization should work among the peasants, create a people's army, and besiege the urban areas from rural bases" (Behrooz 1999, 40). Following the First Congress but prior to the formation of a new party, the leaders decided to send volunteers to China or Cuba for military training and a group to Iran to assess the conditions. Prominent figures of this group were Parviz Nikkhah, Bizhan Chehrazi, and Sirus Nahavandi, who secretly entered Iran in 1964 and started the first cells (Matin 1999, 201–5, 234). On April 9, 1965, an Imperial Guard private, Reza Shamsabadi, opened fire at the Shah at the Marmar Palace in Tehran. The Shah escaped death and Shamsabadi was gunned down on the spot. Subsequent investigations revealed connections between Shamsabadi and a new recruit of an ROTPI cell named Ahmad Kamrani. It was clear that Shamsabadi had acted on his own initiative given that Nikkhah and others had already rejected the idea of assassinating the Shah (Jazani 1979a, 155). The group was raided and fourteen individuals were arrested in relation to the assassination attempt. With the international campaign of the CISNU, the appeals court commuted death sentences of the arrestees to life imprisonment (Matin 1999, 218–25; Rezvani 2005, 53, fn). Nikkhah's courageous defense statements in the military court immediately elevated him as a heroic figure. Five years into his life sentence, however, he had a change of heart, recanted on a TV broadcast, was awarded clemency by the Shah, and was later given a position in the state-controlled national television. Appearing as the regime's intellectual figure, he garnered the resentment of the revolutionaries: he was arrested after the Revolution and sentenced to death (Matin 1999, 225, fn.1, 350, fn.2). Nahavandi and the surviving members of the ROTPI formed the Liberation Organization of Iranian Peoples (Sazman-e Azadibakhsh-e Khalqha-ye Iran). Nahavandi became a collaborator upon his arrest. SAVAK staged an escape for him in 1972 so that he would lead his group as a SAVAK sting operation, which eventually led to the deaths of several members and mass arrests of about two hundred in December 1976 (Hadjebi-Tabrizi 2004, 303–4; Rezvani 2005, 199–202).

The Qashqai Uprising

The Qashqai nomads of Fars Province (central Iran) have been involved in political unrests since 1960. Bahman Qashqai (a nephew of tribal chiefs Nasser and Khosrow Qashqai) had studied medicine in England in the early 1960s and held nationalist, pro-Mosaddeq views, but he was influenced by the ROTPI. He returned to Iran to utilize his tribal status in order to stage an uprising among the Qashqai. Contrary to a popular source (Jazani 1979a, 159–60), Bahman did not have organizational links with ethnic Qashqai ROTPI members Ata and Iraj Kashkuli. In fact, Bahman returned to his tribe on his own initiative, but he was joined by the Kashkuli brothers, who were trained in Cuba (Shokat 2002, 93; Khanbaba Tehrani 2001, 142; Rezvani 2005, 132–34) and who had encouraged him, in the early 1960s, to start the uprising (Matin 1999, 235; Shokat 2002, 93; Khanbaba Tehrani 2001, 113; Kashkuli 2001, 45–57). In any case, Bahman only managed to create a band of several dozen tribal warriors. He spent 1965–66 in sporadic clashes with the government forces in the region (Jazani 1979a, 159–60; Kashkuli 2001, 46–66) before the military suppressed the uprising. Bahman was executed in 1966 and the Kashkuli brothers fled Iran (Matin 1999, 235; Khanbaba Tehrani 2001, 113–15).

Islamic Nations Party

Originating in the late 1950s, the two-hundred-strong Islamic Nations Party (Hezb-e Melal-e Eslami) was a short-lived network of cells of ten, whose leaders were inspired by guerrilla warfare and in particular by Che Guevara (Martin 2000, 69). The Islamic Nations Party consisted of middle-class individuals, mostly high school teachers and university students, and it operated as an independent secret group before the entrance of Ayatollah Khomeini into the political scene in 1963.

The aim of the group was "justice in both Socialist and Islamic terms" (Martin 2000, 66). The founder of the group, Seyyed Mohammad Kazem Mousavi Bojnurdi, was born into an Iranian family in Iraq and went to Iran to continue his education. In the heyday of the Second National Front, Bojnurdi and six others founded the Islamic Nations Party based on four principles: Islamic belief, principality of the Koran, solidarity with Islamic nations, and belief in revolution.

The Party expanded rapidly in the aftermath of June 1963 unrest by recruiting younger students without former political affiliations or police records. After 1963, members increasingly leaned toward armed resistance. Returning from a visit to Iraq, Bojnurdi brought two firearms to the group for its planned bank holdups and kidnapping. The accidental arrest of a rank-and-file member, however, led the security forces to a list of 140 members of the Party. In the group's sole standoff, Bojnurdi opened fire on the police before he was arrested along with other leading members (Jazani 1979a, 163). In 1965, the military prosecutor announced fifty-seven arrests in conjunction with the Islamic Nations Party. Heavy prison sentences were handed down to most of the members and Bojnurdi's death sentence was later reduced to life in prison (Matin 1999, 227).

Association of Allied Islamic Societies

Heyatha-ye Motalefeh-ye Eslami was originally a bazaar-based network of merchants, clerics, small businessmen, and workers. It provided the logistics for an Islamic mobilization through its centralized planning of religious processions (see Martin 2000, 152). Some members of Fadaiyan-e Islam, who had survived the group's annihilation by the regime in the 1950s, had been involved in the formation of the Association. The Association formed a military wing to deliver armed attacks (Martin 2000, 69–70). Modeled after Fadaiyan-e Islam a decade earlier, the Association carried out the assassination of Premier Hossein Ali Mansur on January 20, 1965, because he had been involved in the Shah's White Revolution and had legislated the diplomatic immunity of American military personnel (known as *kapitolasion*). The assassin, Mohammad Bokharai, and three others (Saffar Harandi, Sadeq Amani Hamedani, and Morteza Niknezhad) were sentenced to death, and nine other members received prison terms (Matin 1999, 193).

The Damghani-Rad Group

Dr. Manuchehr Damghani and Behruz Shahdust Rad were both politically active during the 1960–63 upheavals. After the return of dictatorship, they formed a group to try the Chinese model of a peasant revolutionary army. They purchased a farm outside the town of Torbat Heydaryyeh (in the province of Khorasan). Rad rented a farm in Varamin, south of Tehran; and Damghani, a physician, started a cell in Kurdistan (Jazani 1979a, 168). In 1968, a strange incident exposed the group. Lost outside Torbat Heydaryyeh, a Literacy Corps conscript private saw a man in the distance and called to him in desperation, but the man simply vanished from where he stood. Later the private reported the incident to the gendarmerie and the gendarmes found an underground tunnel that led to the group's farm (Sho'aiyan 1976a, 41–42). During the search, the authorities found the group's hunting rifles and cassette tapes of Radio Beijing Persian Programs. Rad, Damghani, Mansur Rahmani, and others were subsequently arrested. On account of their remorsefulness, twenty members of the group were later released without charges and five others, including Damghani and Rad, received prison terms (Jazani 1979a, 198–99).

The Kurdish Uprising

In the early 1960s, Esmail Sharifzadeh and Seraji were members of the Tehran Committee of the Democratic Party, a group of Kurdish university students in Tehran. In 1963, Ebrahim Eshaqi, a leader of the Democratic Party of Kurdistan, initiated a fund-raising campaign by finding individuals sympathetic to the Party's cause. His agent in Iran, Mo'tasam Hesabi, who was actually a SAVAK agent, managed to infiltrate the Kurdish student network in Tehran, and subsequently more than two hundred supporters of the Kurdish cause were arrested. Sharifzadeh and several others fled to Iraqi Kurdistan.

In June 1964, the growing tension between two rival Kurdish warlords in Iraq, Mulla Mostafa Barezani and Jalal Talebani, led to armed clashes between them. Barezani's militiamen forced Talebani and his men to seek asylum in Iran. While sheltering Talebani and his followers, the Iranian government convinced Barezani to release his captives in return for Iran's support for him in his campaign against the Iraqi regime. In Iraq, Sharifzadeh did not cooperate with Barezani and instead formed a new group to fight the Iranian regime (Jazani 1979a, 171–77). Meanwhile Sharifzadeh made contacts with the Cadres splinter group of the ROTPI. In 1967, Kourosh Lashai, a medical doctor, was delegated by the ROTPI to Kurdistan, where he spent six months with Sharifzadeh (Rezvani 2005, 223). Meanwhile another Kurdish insurgent, Mulla Avareh (Mohammad Shalmashi), led armed operations against the regime. Lashai observed that Kurdistan was not ready for an armed peasant uprising (Matin 1999, 254–55). Nonetheless, when some members of the ROTPI entered Kurdistan to join the Kurdish militants, it was already too late (Rezvani 2005, 175–76, 179, 224). Prior to this time, Sharifzadeh's group had made contact with local peasants as well as with Ali Reza Nabdel (who later joined Fadaiyan) in Azerbaijan (Razmi 2008), but Sharifzadeh's Maoist ideas deterred Nabdel from pursuing further contact. In the winter of 1968, the group sent its first operative teams into Iranian Kurdistan to initiate armed struggle, but a collaborator in the group had already tipped off the authorities and the regime militarized the entire region in anticipation of guerrilla attacks. Members of Sharifzadeh's team and three others lost their lives in a clash with the military near the Kurdish town of Baneh. Within a week, Mulla Avareh, a progressive peasant and poet, and his men were also killed in armed clashes with the military (Jazani 1979a, 171–77). The Kurdish uprising was effectively put down.

The Palestine Group

The network of dissident individuals later known as Guruh-e Felestin formed in 1960–63 out of three small groups of mainly university students. Prominent among them was Shokrollah Paknezhad, a law graduate who had joined the Iranian Nation Party in 1960. He was once arrested in 1965 when the police discovered in his home a copy of Che Guevara's *Guerrilla Warfare*. Paknezhad was released after a few months. In the mid-1960s, he left the Iranian Nation Party in disagreement with its leader, Dariush Foruhar. In the meantime, he met Hossein Riahi, Rezvan Ja'fari, Massoud Bathai, Behruz Sotudeh, and Nasser Kakhsaz. Later, in prison, some of them met with Ebrahim Anzabi and Mohammad Reza Shalguni from the second constitutive group. They also met Hedayat Soltanzadeh, who had Marxist leanings. The third group included student activists Ahmad Saburi, Navvab Bushehri, Salamat Ranjbar, and Mohammad Mo'ezzi. These three groups gradually converged until 1968, but never consolidated into a unitary group. They did not have any clear strategy except that they believed in armed struggle. The members mainly had pro-Chinese leanings, to the extent that in 1969 the group sent Ja'fari, Sotudeh, and Bathai to Afghanistan to explore the possibility of sending members to China for military training. When the Chinese turned them down and they returned to Iran, the idea of joining Palestinian militants found momentum. In late 1969, Saburi met with General Bakhtiar, the former head of SAVAK, in exile in Iraq, and sought his assistance in smuggling members out of Iran. Bakhtiar referred Saburi to Abbas Shahriyari, a former member of the Tudeh Party and an able SAVAK agent, trusted by Tudeh's Central Committee and Bakhtiar alike. Shahriyari led a SAVAK sting operation by running a network of Tudeh activists called the Tehran Organization (Tashkilat-e Tehran) to entrap dissidents. As a result, all members of the Palestine Group (except Riahi, Ja'fari, and Sotudeh) were arrested while trying to cross the border into Iraq. Paknezhad's bold defense statements, published in Europe, earned him a heavy prison term (Jazani 1979a, 169–71). However, one of the main figures of the group, Saburi, remorsefully appeared on national television (Ghahremanian 1999, 234–44). While in prison, a number of members of the Palestine Group, including Shalguni, rejected armed struggle. After the Revolution they were joined by other activists and founded the Worker's Path (Rah-e Kargar), a Marxist group that soon renamed itself the Organization of Revolutionary Workers of Iran (Sazman-e Kargaran-e Enqelabi-ye Iran).

A NEW ERA, A NEW BEGINNING

In the aftermath of the Shah's repressive development, Iranian activists woke to a decade in which, in an observer's words, "for a time, everything was possible; . . . this period, in other words, was a moment of universal liberation" (Jameson 1988, 207). Revolutionary fervor was in the air. The world witnessed a resurgence of national liberation movements, from Front de Liberation Nationale in Algeria, the Palestine Liberation Organization (PLO), the PAIGC in Guinea, and Qavam Nekrumeh's Pan-African movement, to full-fledged liberation wars in Vietnam, Cambodia, and Dhofar (Oman). The summary execution of Ernesto Che Guevara in Bolivia in 1967 created a worldwide wave of revolutionary solidarity that even reached Western societies, including Germany's Socialisticher Deutscher Studentenbund (SDS). Revolutionary movements in the periphery coincided with the emergence of new social movements in the civil rights and women's movements in the United States, the 1968 student and workers' uprising in France, and the democratic movement in Czechoslovakia and the Prague Spring; these events created an unique global ambiance of revolutionary change. The early attempts at launching guerrilla warfare in Iran must be understood in terms of the possibilities for action that the historical moment revealed in the particular context of Iran.

However, a meticulous observation reveals a curious irony: *the theoretical imagination of the above groups in fact worked to the detriment of their coveted movement.* Maoist-inspired groups paid dearly to find out that Mao's program could not work in the conditions of Iran. Iranian peasants only reluctantly trailed the urban movements. In the case of Kurdistan, tribal networks allowed limited peasant support; however, rival Kurdish warlords (Talebani and Barezani) exploited these networks as a means to acquire concessions from the Iranian state. The primacy of tribal relations in fact indicates the lack of political awareness among Kurdish peasants, which explains the isolation of Kurdish revolutionaries like Sharifzadeh. Moreover, in the case of the Qashqai uprising, the absence of political awareness (despite the tribe's rebellious history) impeded a full-fledged uprising. The Association of Allied Islamic Societies and the Palestine Group did not have a clear strategy and were terminated before arriving at one. In short, the militant attempts of the 1960s could not affect the three factors that Bizhan Jazani names as decisive factors: the progressive movement, the people, and the regime (Jazani 1978, 46). As such, they were unable to alter the political landscape of the country.

Later in the 1960s, the Maoist and Cuban models revealed theoretical and practical impasses. The Cuban model based on the guerrilla-peasant alliance lost momentum in 1967: "Che's *foco* theory subsequently was discredited in Latin America; those who attempted to implement it failed miserably. In Peru in 1965, Héctor Béjar's insurrectionary foco met defeat, and two years later Che himself was killed while attempting to follow this strategy in Bolivia" (Becker in Che Guevara 1998, xii–xiii). The futility of applying the Cuban "miracle" to other societies became apparent, and with certain exceptions, Latin American intellectuals shifted their attention from rural to urban guerrilla warfare. The Tupamaros in Uruguay, the Monteneros in Argentina, and the MIR in Chile exemplify the urban wave that had Carlos Marighella as its theorist (Marighella 1971). Against the background of failed Maoist groups and the shifting revolutionary paradigm in Latin America, the failure of the Siahkal operation (chapter 2) forced the early Fadaiyan to learn their lesson quickly. Key to the successful rise of Fadaiyan was their experience of the repressive conditions of 1960s Iran, which convinced them of the necessity of armed struggle *without* simply duplicating the existing models (see Pakdaman in Rahnema 1997, 185). The founders of the PFG were situated in a particular generational rift with severed ties to the leftist tradition of Iran. In the absence of a movement to represent, this generation searched for its social constituents in urban areas, especially among the young, idealistic, and aspiring university students. By the mid-1970s, the urban guerrilla model too had lost its plausibility. But between 1971 and 1979, Fadaiyan succeeded in repoliticizing Iranian society and catalyzed the collective consciousness necessary for the 1979 Revolution. The subsequent chapters will highlight Fadaiyan's operational and theoretical efforts in launching a national liberation movement. Although what they had hoped for did not materialize, the *problematique* of liberation gave birth to a movement that was deeply concerned with finding a way to complete the deferred task of political development in Iran. To detail this process, a historical overview of the OIPFG is in order.

2

Organization of the Iranian People's Fadai Guerrillas (1971–1979)

> The new struggles for the liberation of the Iranian people, which set out through a realistic understanding of the historical forces of the contemporary era and an objective analysis of these forces in our homeland, has placed our movement in the rank of national liberation movements of the peoples across the world.
> —OIPFG's introduction to Dehqani, *Hamaseh-ye moqavemat* [The epic of resistance]

THIS CHAPTER OFFERS a detailed history of the OIPFG in eight sections. The reader will notice that the chronology of the OIPFG history is halted at two points by thematic sections that review aspects of the group's history that do not readily surface in its official documents.

THE FORMATIVE GROUPS

In April 1971, in the wake of a series of armed operations in Tehran and Tabriz, the People's Fadai Guerrillas announced its foundation through a series of communiqués. Soon the Fadai Guerrillas shone in one of the darkest nights of dictatorship in the history of modern Iran, an era of political repression, bloody confrontations, social polarization, high hopes, heroic deeds, international campaigns, and intellectual movements. Grasping the significance of Fadaiyan is impossible without attending to the social and political context of their advent.

Fadaiyan emerged as two different groups crossed paths while attempting to revive politics under repressive development. Named after their founders, these formative groups were the Jazani-Zarifi Group (later called Group One) and the

16

Ahmadzadeh-Puyan-Meftahi Group (later named Group Two). Let us first situate these formative groups.

The Jazani-Zarifi Group

Born in 1937, Bizhan Jazani joined the Tudeh Youth Organization at the age of ten and became a student activist. His father was a leftist military officer active with the Azerbaijan Democratic Party (which governed the autonomous province of Azerbaijan for about a year). He had fled to the Soviet Union after the violent occupation of Azerbaijan by the Iranian military in November 1946. Bizhan did not see his father again for almost a quarter-century, until his father visited him in prison. Jazani was arrested following the 1953 coup but was conditionally released after a few weeks. In 1954, he was arrested again and spent a year in prison, where he became disillusioned with the Tudeh Party as he observed the exposure, arrests, and execution of members of the Party's clandestine Officers Organization, as well as the public recantations of Tudeh leaders Morteza Yazdi, Mohammad Bahrami, and Nader Shermini. Between 1955 and 1959, the young Jazani formed a small activist circle. When the Second National Front reemerged in 1960, he was a social science student at the University of Tehran, and he became an elected student representative to the Second National Front. He also served as a member of the University Student Committee and a founding member of the influential publication of the National Front Youth Organization, *Payam-e Daneshju* (The student courier). These positions won him an unsought reputation as a student leader, which resulted in his repeated arrests between 1960 and 1963. In 1963 he graduated as the top student with an Honors degree.

In March 1963, as the regime tightened its grip on the opposition, Jazani, Manuchehr Kalantari, Dr. Heshmatollah Shahrzad, and Kiumars Izadi founded the nucleus of the group that later evolved into Group One. Previously Jazani, Kalantari, and Izadi had been active with the National Front Student Organization while Shahrzad was a key student activist who had spent time in prison. The four comrades decided to separate open activities from underground activities and to organize their recruits in three partitioned units: (1) those who participated in student activities and in the publication of *Payam-e Daneshju*; (2) the "auxiliary elements," or potential candidates for recruitment into the third unit; and (3) the largest unit of militant activists who prepared for armed struggle. This last unit had its own command cell as well as logistics and operations teams, specializing as the "urban team" (*tim-e shahr*) and the "rural team" (*tim-e kuh*; literally "the mountain team"). Ali Akbar Safai Farahani, Mohammad Saffari Ashtiyani, Aziz Sarmadi, Ahmad Jalil Afshar, Mohammad Chupanzadeh, Mash'uf (Sa'id) Kalantari (Jazani's maternal uncle), and Hamid Ashraf were recruited for the clandestine teams. The members had already adopted Marxism-Leninism and engaged in internal discussions about armed struggle.

The group's preparation was painfully slow. Izadi, commander of the urban team, soon grew weary of the group's endless internal discussions and slow development, so in the spring of 1965 he proposed that the group should prepare its first operation. "Our duty is to kindle a light in this darkness through our self-sacrifice. Our action means our self-sacrifice (*fada shodan*)," he reportedly argued. Calling his suggestion "adventurism," others argued that guerrillas must never engage in an operation that would jeopardize their very existence. In protest, Izadi left the group that rejected "collective self-sacrifice in the first move" (Anonymous 1976b, 18).

Hassan Zia Zarifi was born in the Caspian town of Lahijan in 1939. As a Tudeh supporter, he was first arrested in 1956 but released shortly afterward thanks to the influence of his father, a respected entrepreneur. Zia Zarifi later became a law student at the University of Tehran and a leader in the National Front Student Organization between 1960 and 1963. He was arrested several times for participating in student protests and was once hospitalized for injuries he sustained in a rally. He was twice elected the student representative to the Congress of National Front but was barred from attending the Congress because of his leftism. Upon graduation, Zia Zarifi was drafted into the army as a conscript officer.

In 1965 Zia Zarifi was introduced to and joined the Central Cadre (CC; Kadr-e Markazi) of Group One. Zia Zarifi knew Abbas Surki, who had been arrested in 1960 for creating an underground circle named the Warriors of the Tudeh Party (Razmavaran-e Hezb-e Tudeh). Surki had shown remarkable courage under interrogation. In the past, Surki had sporadic contacts with Jazani as well. In the CC, Zia Zarifi nominated Surki for recruitment based on Surki's claim to have weapons, ammunition, and a network of 120 militants. These incredible resources encouraged Jazani to approach Surki, but it turned out that Surki had no such resources. Nevertheless, Surki and Zarrar Zahedian joined the guerrilla unit of Group One, while a few others, including Nasser Aqayan (a SAVAK agent), joined the second, auxiliary, unit.

In 1966 the group concluded that the land reform had weakened the revolutionary potential of the peasants, so the group shifted its focus from the country to the city as the base for armed movement. The group's earliest text, later published as the *Thesis of the Jazani Group*, is believed to be a summary of the discussions that took place during the mid-1960s (Anonymous nd, 21–22). During these years until the 1971 Siahkal operation, members of the group compiled three book-length rural studies (on land reform, agricultural corporations, and Caspian fishermen); essays on the 1953 coup, the party, and unity; and two book-length treatises. Among these, *What a Revolutionary Must Know* (Safai Farahani 1976), backdated 1969 with Abu-Abbas-Ramas (Safai Farahani's alias in Palestine) as its author, was published and distributed after the police raids of the summer of 1970 (Anonymous 1976b, 50). Jazani's widow, Mihan, who smuggled several of his writings out of prison, reports that Jazani secretly gave her the monograph of this book during a visit in Qom Prison in 1970 (Jazani 1999, 67), an account confirmed by an original member of the group as well (Negahdar 2008).

By the mid-1960s another founding member of the group, Manuchehr Kalantari, called the group's agenda and abilities unrealistic. This new disagreement resolved when Kalantari agreed to leave for Europe to function as the logistics person while receiving treatment for his illness (Kalantari later published the writings of Jazani in London in the *19 Bahman Teorik* series). But the group was still caught in internal rifts. In 1967, Dr. Shahrzad had serious confrontations with Jazani, Surki, and Zia Zarifi in the CC because he had presented them with several cases of dubious conduct by Aqayan, who was then the head of the auxiliary unit. Instead of seriously considering Shahrzad's allegations, the CC expelled him, even denying his request to stay on as a rank-and-file member. The group soon paid a heavy price for its negligence, because Aqayan was indeed a SAVAK agent.

Surki asked Aqayan to bring him the two handguns he had cached for the group. After tipping off SAVAK, Aqayan handed Surki the weapons on January 9, 1968, three days before the group's first planned operation (a bank robbery). After this rendezvous, Surki went to meet with Jazani, and the police arrested them both just as the handguns changed hands. The arrest was part of security preparation as the 1971 extravagant celebration of 2,500 years of the Persian Empire was underway. Abbas Ali Shahriyarinezhad (alias Eslami, henceforth Shahriyari) was a top SAVAK agent who was a trusted member of the Tudeh Party. On SAVAK instructions, he had established the Tehran Organization (Tashkilat-e Tehran) of the Tudeh Party in the mid-1960s, and enjoyed, for several years, the unconditional support of the exiled Tudeh general secretary, Reza Radmanesh. For several years the Tehran Organization attracted leftist activists only to turn them in to SAVAK (see Kianuri 1992, 445–49, 453–60). In earlier years, Shahriyari had recruited Aqayan to infiltrate Jazani's group. This is how SAVAK found out about the group's imminent operations and intercepted Jazani and others.

Several members including Farrokh Negahdar, Qasem Rashidi, Shahrzad, and Izadi were arrested. Zia Zarifi managed to hide in the residence of Iraj Vahedipur, a member of the Tehran Organization, but he was arrested on February 15, 1968, along with Jalil Afshar. At this point, however, five members of the group who had remained at large (Safai Farahani, Mohammad Chupanzadeh, Sa'id Kalantari, Mohammad Saffari Ashtiyani, and Mohammad Kianzad) decided to join the Palestinian resistance. They asked Shahriyari to arrange for them to cross the border into Iraq. SAVAK's plan was to trap Kalantari because he was perceived to be the group's leader. Shahriyari arranged for the first party, Safai Farahani and Saffari Ashtiyani, to safely cross the border. Once on Iraqi soil, the two were captured but were serendipitously released when a coup d'état brought the Ba'ath Party to power on July 17, 1968. They joined the Palestinians, and Safai Farahani trained (under the alias Abu-Abbas-Ramas) and later commanded a post in George Habash's People's Front for the Liberation of Palestine. Tipped off by SAVAK, the border patrol captured the second party, Kalantari, Chupanzadeh, and Kianzad, on July 13, 1968.

In total, fourteen members of the Jazani-Zarifi group were eventually charged: nine from the CC, three from the first unit, and two former members. Aqayan and members of the auxiliary unit were not charged. The trial began in February 1969. Thanks to the efforts of Manuchehr Kalantari in London, Amnesty International sent observers to the court proceedings. The Confederation of Iranian Students–National Unity (CISNU) had also launched an international campaign to save the prisoners. In the presence of human rights observers during the trial, Jazani, Surki, Zia Zarifi, and Shahrzad each described the brutal tortures they had endured, showing the scars or burns inflicted by SAVAK interrogators (Jazani 1999, 53). In the end, thanks to the campaigns of Kalantari and the CISNU (Matin 1999, 267), the military court handed down heavy sentences: a fifteen-year prison term for Jazani; ten years for Zia Zarifi, Surki, Sarmadi, Zahedian, Shahrzad, and Jalil Afshar; and shorter prison terms for Sa'id Kalantari, Rashidi, Negahdar, Mohammad Kianzad, Kurosh Izadi, Kiomars Izadi, and Majid Ahsan. The appeals court ratified the verdict of the first court (Jazani 1999, 55).

A noteworthy incident after the second trial was the failed escape attempt by four members of the group that resulted in a bitter conflict between Kalantari and Jazani. While in Qasr prison in central Tehran, Kalantari, Chupanzadeh, Sarmadi, and Surki discussed an escape plan with Jazani, and when Jazani strongly disapproved, they decided to proceed without him. The attempt failed because of Surki's heart condition during the escape, and the four were captured. The failure upset Kalantari, who had always been critical of Jazani for trusting Zia Zarifi owing to his alleged links with the Tudeh Party (Same' 1999, 138–39; Ghahremanian 1999, 192–93; Amui 2001, 316–17; CSHD 2001, 35–39; Navidi 2008). Following the incident and to prevent them from regrouping, the detainees were assigned to prisons across the country.

According to one source, by the winter of 1968, only three members of the group had remained in Iran (Ashraf 1978, 7). During 1967–68, these survivors began contacting other circles. Ghaffur Hassanpur, a conscript officer at the time, played a vital role in reorganizing the group. He contacted, without success, the Palestine Group as well as the SAKA (Sazman-e Enqelabi-ye Komonistha-ye Iran [Organization of the Revolutionary Communists of Iran]). Likewise, another member of the group, Mehdi Same', contacted members of Tufan, but they refused further liaisons. Meanwhile, Rahim Sema'i recruited Mehdi Eshaqi in Shiraz from a cell named Setareh-ye Sorkh (Red Star). Nasser Seyf Dalil Safai and Esma'il Mo'ini Araqi joined the group at this time. As the group grew again, it planned an offensive against the regime, an operation that became the defining moment of the subsequent decade of Iranian politics, to which we will return later.

The Ahmadzadeh-Puyan-Meftahi Group

The origins of Group Two are traced back to the Second National Front. In the city of Mashhad, the hometown of Massoud Ahmadzadeh Heravi (1947–1972, henceforth Ahmadzadeh) and Amir Parviz Puyan (1947–1971), the Second National

Front was active in the early 1960s, enjoying the support of students, bazaar merchants, and shopkeepers. At that time, Muslim Student Societies had appeared in the universities and were under the influence of the Freedom Movement of Iran, the liberal-Muslim wing of the National Front. With the National Front's decline owing to the lack of a viable political program, by 1962 Muslim clerics emerged at the forefront of the struggle. Massoud was the son of Taher Ahmadzadeh, a well-known nationalist and a prominent opposition leader in Mashhad.

In 1963, while in his senior year of high school, Puyan became involved in a religious-political circle that was soon disbanded by the police. His early activities brought him two-and-one-half months in prison. In 1965, Puyan moved to Tehran to study in the Faculty of the Social Sciences at the University of Tehran. In 1967, Ahmadzadeh moved to Tehran to study mathematics at Ariyamehr Industrial University (Nejati 1992, 383). Abbas Meftahi (1945–1972) came from the Caspian town of Sari. In 1962–63, while a student at the Sari Technical School, Meftahi's teacher, Safai Farahani, had introduced him to Marxism. In 1963 he was admitted to the prestigious School of Technology at the University of Tehran. Even though he was a Marxist at this time, he performed his Muslim daily prayers. Between 1963 and 1967, Meftahi became acquainted with the students of Tehran Polytechnic: Dalil Safai, Kianzad, and Hassanpur from the revived Jazani group. Meftahi also came to know Kazem Selahi. He was introduced to Ahmadzadeh and Puyan in 1965, and they started a reading circle. Puyan had already adopted Marxism in 1966 but Ahmadzadeh turned to Marxist ideas a year later.

Although it is widely believed that in the winter of 1968 Puyan, Meftahi, and Ahmadzadeh vowed to start an underground militant group, in fact only the first two formed the group (Hamidian 2004, 28). It was only later that the three of them acted as the CC and searched for trustworthy friends to recruit. They embarked on a systematic study of Marxism-Leninism and were generally indifferent to student activism, which is surprising given that virtually all of the group's recruits were university students.

However, with the new wave of unrest in Iranian universities, the group emerged out of its cocoon to find itself confronted with the key question of its generation: *activism*. By 1968–69, the group rejected the Maoist assessment of Iranian society as semifeudal-semicolonial and turned to Latin American revolutionary literature. Members read Che Guevara, Régis Debray, and the works of Tupamaros. That Group Two did not arise from the Iranian Marxist tradition had its advantages, as the fresh start allowed the group theoretical flexibility instead of ingrained dogmatism. The relations between the membership and the CC were relatively democratic and all cells participated in the discussions regarding strategic decisions. In the spring of 1968, Ahmadzadeh and Puyan started the Mashhad branch of the group by recruiting their friends. With the formation of the CC, Majid Ahmadzadeh, Kazem Selahi, and Javad Selahi were recruited.

Independent from the events in Mashhad and Tehran, five Azeri cultural figures and activists—Ali Reza Nabdel, Samad Behrangi, Behruz Dehqani, Kazem Sa'adati, and Manaf Falaki—had already formed a cell in Tabriz in the winter of 1966. This cell later became the PFG's Tabriz branch. These intellectuals edited a literary weekly named the *Friday Special* of *Mahd-e Azadi*, which lasted for a year before it was banned. In 1967–68, the cell had reached the conclusion that armed struggle was the necessary response to repression. In early 1968, Puyan met in Tabriz with the prominent writer Samad Behrangi, whom he knew earlier through cultural and literary activities, and Behrangi introduced him to Behruz Dehqani. In August 1968 when Puyan went to Tabriz to jump-start the Tabriz branch, he heard Behrangi had drowned in the River Aras. Behrangi's critical pedagogy had already made him a SAVAK target. This motivated prominent writers Gholam Hossein Sa'edi and Jalal Al Ahmad to announce Behrangi's death as a SAVAK conspiracy, although they were aware of its accidental nature.[1] The dissident generation needed a martyr so badly that it readily accepted this fabrication.

---

1. Samad Behrangi was born in Tabriz in 1939 and graduated from the two-year teacher-training program in 1957. Until his death in the River Aras in August 1968, he taught in the villages of Azerbaijan. He published children's stories, Azeri folklore, and critical pedagogy, and translated contemporary Turkish literature into Persian. The myth of Behrangi's martyrdom (by SAVAK conspiracy) resulted from an intentional distortion by Jalal Al Ahmad, who spread the word that at the time of his death, Behrangi was in the company of an "unidentified officer" (by implication, a police agent). The mysterious officer was no one but Behrangi's comrade from his Tabriz cell, Hamzeh Farahati. It was not until 1991 that Farahati revealed the circumstances surrounding Behrangi's drowning. He reported that Dehqani, Nabdel, and Sa'adati, as well as Al Ahmad, Sa'edi, and Puyan knew the truth. As Farahati recalls, "They all consented to announce Samad as a martyr . . . on the

In 1969 the cell became the Tabriz branch of Group Two (Nabdel 1977, 12–14). Dehqani, Nabdel, and Falaki formed the CC, and along with Kazem Sa'adati they recruited others mainly from the University of Tabriz (Karimi 2001). In 1969 Puyan contacted Sirus Nahavandi of the Liberation Organization of Iranian Peoples, but the negotiations between the two groups failed. A second contact between them in 1970 also led nowhere. In 1968, Meftahi created the Mazandaran branch, and in 1969 he started a new branch in Tabriz, partitioned off from the earlier cells. Further recruitments took place in 1970 in Tehran and Tabriz. Within a year the group grew to an extent rarely seen in an underground organization.

Despite its surprising expansion, the groups did not yet have a clear political platform. Debates among the membership hinged on whether or not the group should engage in armed struggle. By early 1970, the group finally reached the conclusion that armed struggle was the only means for political presence in Iran. Puyan's polemical essay *The Necessity of Armed Struggle and the Rejection of the Survival Theory* emerged as a persuasive summation of the internal debates. He argued in favor of shifting from political to military forms of struggle (see chapter 4). The internal circulation of the essay had a major impact on consolidating the group's agenda. At this point, members who did not agree with the new objectives left the group. Armed struggle was adopted in the form of urban guerrilla warfare. The group's leaders were influenced by Carlos Marighella and Régis Debray, as is evident in Ahmadzadeh's *Armed Struggle: Both Strategy and Tactic*. However, the leaders handled the transformation of student circles into an urban guerrilla network rather heedlessly and in haste (unlike Group One). The structure of the group did not change to match clandestine activities. This neglect gravely endangered the group as only a handful had escaped SAVAK raids by the summer of 1971 (Anonymous 1976a; Anonymous nd, 28–30).

---

condition that there should be no mention of me, only of that 'officer'" (Farahati 1991, 12; Farahati 2006, 153–66). In a special issue of *Arash* literary journal dedicated to Behrangi, the conspiracy story was popularized. According to Farahati, in the 1970s many, including Fadaiyan, knew the truth, but Behrangi was irreversibly glorified as a Fadai martyr, and his famous children's story, *The Little Black Fish*, had become a Fadai manifesto. Despite the revelation, Samad's brother, Asad Behrangi, still insists on conspiracy (Behrangi 2000).

TOWARD THE HISTORIC MOMENT

By 1968 the two formative groups were occupied with (re-)organizing and preparing for armed struggle. However, police imposed serious setbacks on both groups between 1968 and February 1971. The three surviving members of Group One, Hamid Ashraf, Ghaffur Hassanpur, and Eskandar Sadeqinezhad, regrouped after the 1967 arrests. Thanks to their efforts, by the fall of 1968 the group had eight members, and by the end of 1970, twenty-two individuals were organized in mountain, urban operations, military logistics, communications, and technical-engineering teams (Ashraf 1978, 93). Weapons were obtained in Iraq or supplied by George Habash (Hassanpour 2007, 171). To finance their operations, the teams robbed the Vozara Branch of Bank Melli in July 1970 and Iran-England Bank in September 1970, acquiring the equivalent of US$25,000 and US$55,000 respectively. The group targeted the Caspian region to launch its first operation, an area that Safai Farahani and others had previously mapped as expert mountaineers.

The choice of the Caspian region for launching guerrilla warfare came from the group's assessment of the "revolutionary potential" of the people of the area, a region that enjoys a reputation for its people's political consciousness and leftist tendencies. The region was home to the uprising led by the radical democrat Mirza Kuchek Khan and the birthplace of the Soviet Socialist Republic of Iran during 1920–21, but the movement ended in tragedy when the young Bolshevik government in Russia betrayed it (Chaqueri 1995; Sho'aiyan 1976e). The Alborz range partitions coastal Caspian from Tehran Province, keeping most of the precipitation on the northern side of the range, creating wooded highlands north of the Alborz. Farmers, peasants, cattle herders, nomads, fishermen, industrial workers, and government employees live in a densely populated coastal line, with villages and towns proximally situated.

The "Siahkal Resurrection"

Finally, on September 5, 1970, the mountain team left for the Caspian region. The six members of this team were Safai Farahani (commander), Mehdi Eshaqi, Rahim Sema'i, Abbas Danesh Behzadi, Jalil Enferadi, and Hadi Bandehkhoda Langarudi (Nayyeri nd, 63). Their weapons had already been delivered and hidden in the forest. Over the next few months, Mohammad Ali Mohaddes Qandchi,

Houshang Nayyeri, and Ahmad Farhudi joined the group. Reportedly, another member was lost in a winter storm (Ashraf 1978, 99) or froze to death (Anonymous 1976b, 38), but SAVAK documents suggest that Iraj Salehi (the member in question) quietly fled the mountains and returned to Tehran, only to be arrested later based on the interrogation information extracted from the captured guerrillas (Rohani 1993, 291).

As the guerrillas were secretly training in the Alborz, the tightening grip of the police almost eradicated Group One. On December 6, 1970, SAVAK's arrest of university student Abolhasan Khatib, Hassanpur's roommate, led the police to Hassanpur, whom SAVAK had already known about through an arrested member of the Palestine Group (Heydar 2001, 27). Hassanpur's arrest on December 13, 1970, sent the group into hiding. SAVAK immediately televised a briefing about the recent arrests in which the role of the arrestees was trivialized. SAVAK's tactic deceived Hassanpur's comrades, causing them to underestimate the danger and let down their guard. After seventeen days of horrendous torture leading to his death, Hassanpur eventually gave up some information. On January 30, 1971, Mohammad Hadi Fazeli, Sho'aeddin Moshayyedi, and Esma'il Mo'ini Araqi, and then Dalil Safai and Eskandar Rahimi were arrested. All in all, three were arrested in Gilan, five in Tehran, and two elsewhere in the next few days. By this time, SAVAK knew all the group's secrets (see *Kar* [OIPF-M] 1995, 5). Saffari Ashtiyani, Sadeqinezhad, Manuchehr Bahaipur, Rahmatollah Peyro Naziri, and Hamid Ashraf went into hiding. At the heights of the arrests on February 4, 1971, Ashraf personally met Safai Farahani to alert him to the police raids. Facing the impending eradication of the group, Safai Farahani decided to launch the planned operation within three days. The mountain team now had nine guerrillas including Ahmad Farhudi, a wanted man from Group Two who had joined in January 1971.

Unaware of the capture of Iraj Nayyeri, who was a village teacher and the mountain team's logistics person, the team sent Bandehkhoda Langarudi to the village to inform Nayyeri of the imminent operation, but the villagers captured Bandehkhoda Langarudi. He fired in the air, to no avail, but the echoing gunshots informed his company of his capture. The guerrillas came out of the forest on February 8, 1971 (19 Bahman 1349 in the Persian solar calendar) to force his release. They seized a van and drove to the Siahkal gendarmerie post that evening, but after capturing the post, they discovered Bahdehkhoda Langarudi had already been removed to the Gendarmerie Headquarters in Lahijan.

Official OIPFG accounts hold that the team seized weapons, stopped a passing bus, spoke to the people, and distributed leaflets before heading back into the mountains (Anonymous nd, 39). Parts of the handwritten leaflet, signed the "Armed Revolutionary Movement of Iran," reads as follows:

> Brothers and Sisters, Fellow Countrymen! The Oppressive regime and its foreign masters have weighed heavily on the shoulders of this nation for a long time. They loot [our] forests, seas and other natural resources under the name of nationalization. They buy tea leaves [from you] for cheap and sell it at a high price; they impose heavy taxes on the people's basic needs . . . Long live the solidarity between village dwellers and urban revolutionaries. (quoted in Naderi 2008, 198)

One account reports that all personnel defending the post were killed and that the team also shot Akbar Vahdati, the civilian allegedly responsible for the capture of the two guerrillas, and another account holds that they executed the subcommander of the post (*Zamimeh Nabard-e Khalq* 1975, 2; *Kar* [OIPFG] 1980b). Ashraf reports that the team killed two individuals (the second commander and a civilian, probably Vahdati) (1978, 101). In light of recent, partial publication of interrogation records, however, these reports turn out to be only partly true.

The team carried out the attack in haste. The eight militants seized a Ford van and temporarily held its passengers in the woods under the guard of Mohaddes Qandchi. They drove to a nearby forestry post and left Sema'i and Eshaqi in the woods. They had orders to attack and disarm the forest rangers stationed there when given the signal. Safai Farahani, Farhudi, Houshang Nayyeri, Danesh Behzadi, and Enferadi drove to the gendarmerie post. When they failed to overpower the officers inside, they opened fire, killing an officer and a civilian and injuring another officer. In the mayhem that ensued, Safai Farahani mistakenly shot and injured Nayyeri. In their haste to leave, they seized ten weapons without taking ammunition, and forgot their leaflets and explosives inside the post. When the second team did not hear the signal (the first team was supposed to blow up the post), they did not attack the forestry post either. The guerrillas regrouped, returned the van, released the hostages, and left for higher elevations (Rohani 1993, 293–95; Naderi 2008, 191–99).

Officially, it is also reported that between February 8 and 26, 1971, the guerrillas engaged with a formidable military might. Weary of the persistence of an underground militant presence, the Shah sent the entire Gilan Gendarmerie Regiment, hundreds of police forces, and several helicopters to suppress the eight guerrillas. He placed Lieutenant-General Oveysi, the commander of National Gendarmerie, in charge of the operation and sent his own brother, Gholam Reza Pahlavi, to supervise the counterinsurgency operations (Ashraf 1978, 105). After several clashes with the government forces, the mountain team split into two squads. Safai Farahani, Enferadi, and Hushang Nayyeri moved down from the mountain, only to be captured by unarmed, frightened villagers of Chehel Sotun.

The second team, under Farhudi's command, engaged with the army. In the last battle around Mount Kaku, Sema'i and Eshaqi carried out suicide attacks on gendarmerie forces (Anonymous nd, 40). Farhudi and Danesh Behzadi were taken prisoner, while Mohaddes Qandchi broke through the siege and fled. These accounts are also partially true. It was chiefly the freezing temperatures and exhaustion that defeated the Siahkal team. The team managed to hike to Kaku heights without any incident by February 17, 1971. Safai Farahani, Enferadi, and the injured Nayyeri went down to get Nayyeri to the city for treatment. Cold and exhausted, they landed in the village of Kalestan to get food. Having heard of the attack of the "bandits," the villagers invited them in, and then captured and viciously injured them before turning them over to the authorities. Mohaddes Qandchi, who had fled earlier, was captured by a villager in utter physical exhaustion eight days later. Located by the helicopters, the remaining four decided to surrender, but the frightened gendarmes opened fire, killing Eshaqi and Sema'i, and only then did they capture Farhudi and Danesh Behzadi. The government announced that six officers and one civilian were killed and ten officers were injured (Rohani 1993, 296–303; Naderi 2008, 199–221).

State-sponsored publications (Naderi 2008; Rohani 1993) have used these interrogation records to depict the Siahkal team as a band of demoralized militants. However, the captured militants must be commended for leaving their hands-on accounts of the incident, which show the messy nature of such operations and point out the sad fact that most of the guerrillas were actually captured by the peasants for whom they had fought. What is important, however, is the unforgettable political impact of the Siahkal operation. To maintain the image of Iran as the "island of stability" at the eve of Imperial Celebrations, the Shah ordered the arrestees to be swiftly tried in the military court. On March 16, 1971, thirteen guerrillas were executed: Safai Farahani, Farhudi, Mohaddes Qandchi,

Dalil Safai, Bandehkhoda Langarudi, Fazeli, Mo'ini Araqi, Moshayyedi, Rahimi, Danesh Behzadi, Houshang Nayyeri, Enferadi, and Hassanpur (who died under torture). Iraj Nayyeri received a life sentence (Anonymous nd, 41; *Kar* [OIPFG] 1980b). Of the twenty-two members, only five survived the police raids in this period (Ashraf 1978, 106).

The swift eradication of the militants who had prepared for prolonged guerrilla warfare and the creation of the *foco* raised doubts about the applicability of a Cuban-style revolution in Iran. Ashraf refers to a tactical error on the part of the mountain team: "'the theory of the regional impact of operation' replaced 'the theory of the general impact of operation,'" he notes (Ashraf 1978, 104). This error resulted in a lack of mobility that enabled the troops to pinpoint the militants. Moreover, as shown, the guerrillas, being urban intellectuals, obviously had an idealistic notion of the peasants. The capturing of many of them by frightened peasants shows that they did not exercise the basic principles of guerrilla warfare that they had read in Che Guevara's *Guerrilla Warfare*.

According to Mostafa Madani, at first only a small number of activists heard of the Siahkal operation. It was actually the execution of the thirteen arrested guerrillas that brought public awareness of the operation (*Kar* [OIPF-M] 1995, 2). Once the news spread, student protests in universities began, often ending in confrontations with the police as the students came out to support the guerrilla movement. In April 1971 police raided universities across the country and arrested over one thousand dissident students. By October the student support for the guerrillas caused universities to lose their status as a sanctuary, and units of the newly established University Guard invaded campuses indefinitely. By this time most dissident student circles were determined to join the guerrillas (Heydar 2001, 27).

The Siahkal operation was a parochial operation. Its defeat was never deemed strategic; on the contrary, Siahkal marked a symbolic triumph. Later Jazani called the operation an "armed propaganda" and a spark in darkness for three reasons. First, attacking a military post was an unequivocal assault against an omnipotent regime; second, the operation invoked the popular memory of Kuchek Khan's uprising a half-century earlier; and finally, the state of emergency measures imposed on the province of Gilan left the impression that the guerrillas were more powerful than the regime had reported. This impression was reinforced when a team of surviving members assassinated Lieutenant-General

Farsiu, the military judge who had handed down the death sentences of the Siahkal militants.

Hamid Ashraf and Eskandar Sadeqinazhad reorganized the surviving members into two teams. It was one of these teams that carried out the assassination of Farsiu in April 1971 (Ashraf 1978, 12–13). Of the urban team, Mahmoud Mahmoudi, Mohammad Ali Partovi, and Mostafa Hassanpur were arrested later. "Thus, a clandestine struggle transformed into a social movement and was recognized as an effective and growing element in determining the conditions of society," observes Jazani. "Such a transformation signified the birth of the armed revolutionary movement. The strategic significance of Siahkal rests in this transformation" (1978, 49). The legendary narrative of Fadaiyan placed the operation in a socially tangible heroic discourse and gave birth to a popular term, *rastakhiz-e Siahkal* (the Siahkal Resurrection). Siahkal baffled the Islamic opposition as well, and Ayatollah Khomeini condemned it as an act that reinforced the colonial regime (Rohani 1993, 314). The symbolic significance of the guerrillas' presence in Iran's 1970s political scene elevated Fadaiyan as social and cultural heroes, linking them to social, political, cultural, and artistic movements (see chapter 7).

Of course, the Siahkal operation brought serious consequences for the detained members of Group One. Originally, SAVAK had concluded it had destroyed the group, but it later uncovered the link between the Siahkal teams and the Jazani-Zarifi group. In 1969 Hassanpur had visited Zia Zarifi in Rasht Prison. During the visits, Zia Zarifi had provided information about his group, and Hassanpur had suggested an attack on Rasht Prison to release Zia Zarifi, which the latter rejected. With Hassanpur's arrest, the police discovered two letters from Zia Zarifi to Hassanpur that outlined Group One's activities (see Zia Zarifi 1979, 2). It is also said that a police raid found a forged birth certificate bearing Zia Zarifi's photo (Navidi 1999, 168). Certain of the connection of the two groups, SAVAK brought back members of Group One to Qasr Prison, and Bizhan Jazani and Zia Zarifi were interrogated and tortured. Mihan Jazani was also detained and Jazani himself was transferred to Evin Prison until 1973 (see Jazani 1979a, 5–11).

Toward Unification

Safai Farahani was Abbas Meftahi's instructor at Sari Technical Secondary in the early 1960s. After Meftahi entered the University of Tehran in 1963, he regularly socialized with Tehran Polytechnic student Nasser Seyf Dalil Safai. After the return of Safai Farahani from Palestine in the early summer of 1970, the group gave him Meftahi's contact information. Unaware of Meftahi's activities, Safai Farahani asked him to join the mountain team, an invitation that Meftahi refused. Clearly the two groups were not aware of one another. In the late summer of 1970, after the mountain team had already left for the Caspian region, decisive contacts took place between Ashraf and Ahmadzadeh, who began negotiating the possible unification of the two groups. One outcome of these meetings was the assigning of Farhudi from Group Two to the mountain team as he was a wanted man.

The two groups continued negotiations and initially united in January 1971 (Heydar 1999, 251), but some issues still kept them apart. Most notably was a theoretical disagreement: Ashraf believed in both urban and rural guerrilla warfare while admitting the lack of resources and personnel to organize urban teams. So he viewed Group Two as the backbone of the urban teams within a unified organization. Ahmadzadeh, on the contrary, emphasized urban guerrilla activity. In the course of negotiations, the two reached a compromise and agreed on having both urban and mountain cells, but Ahmadzadeh insisted that the mountain team should delay its operation for two months so that the urban teams could prepare for operations (Ashraf 1978, 97–98). Of course, the circumstances described above did not grant the groups the luxury of time. As for the international Socialist divisions, the two agreed on maintaining neutrality from both China and the Soviet Union (Heydar 1999, 247).

After the execution of the Siahkal guerrillas, Group Two carried out small operations in Tehran and Tabriz. Also, on April 7, 1971, a team of Group One led by Sadeqinezhad assassinated Lieutenant-General Farsiu in retaliation for the execution of their comrades. In response to these attacks and assassinations, SAVAK distributed posters containing photos of nine of Iran's most wanted "saboteurs" (*kharabkaran*) with a reward of about US$ 15,000 (1,000,000 Rls) for information leading to their arrest (see Anonymous nd, 35; Dehqani 1974, 2; Hamidian 2004, 428).

Meetings continued between April 6 and 11 until the two groups finally merged. The negotiators agreed that they had common ideology and policy while acknowledging disagreement on issues pertaining to application. Yet they envisioned that the process of revolutionary action would resolve such divergences (Anonymous 1976a, 25). The People's Fadai Guerrillas (PFG) announced its emergence at this time through thirteen successive communiqués. The first PFG communiqué reads

> Where there is oppression, there is resistance. . . . We are the children of the toiling masses who taught us how to achieve freedom and a decent life by shedding their blood in the past hundreds of years. . . . Guerrilla warfare has now begun. . . . The heroic assault of self-sacrificing guerrillas on the Siahkal Post in Gilan clearly shows that armed struggle is the only path to the freedom of Iranian people. By attacking the Qolhak Police station and execution of the murderer [General] Farsiu, we, People's Fadai Guerrillas, have shown that we would continue the heroic struggle of Siahkal. (quoted in *Kar* [OIPF-M] 1995, 8)

The CC of the Fadai Guerrillas (Ahmadzadeh, Puyan, Meftahi, Ashraf) met for the first time on May 17, 1971, a couple of days after a successful robbery of a bank on Eisenhower Street in Tehran. Following the instructions of Carlos Marighella, the CC planned to create partitioned assault teams, and members were summoned to Tehran to form the new teams. Three operational teams, one publication team, and one technical team were established with Ashraf's team remaining intact (Ashraf 1978, 15–16, 22–23). The CC also decided, following Meftahi's suggestion, to create a new mountain team, but it never materialized (Ashraf 1978, 47–49). Before the next meeting of the CC on May 31, 1971, Puyan was killed in a shoot-out with the police.

After Ahmadzadeh's arrest in June 1971, a new CC consisting of Ashraf, Meftahi, and Majid Ahmadzadeh (Massoud's younger brother) was formed. After only three meetings, Majid Ahmadzadeh, and the next day Meftahi, were captured. Consequently, the entire organization was practically dismantled as members lost contact with their team leaders. In mid-August 1971, Hassan Noruzi, Asadollah Meftahi (Abbas Meftahi's younger brother), and Ashraf met at the outskirts of Tehran and formed a new CC with Ashraf, Noruzi, and Dr. Changiz Qobadi (Ashraf 1978, 75–77). The tightening grip of the police did not leave room for any operations. Just a few weeks into its life the PFG was already desperately on the defensive.

From the beginning, Fadaiyan remained watchful toward absorbing other militant Marxist cells. In the early 1971, Homayun Katirai from the People's Ideal Group (Guruh-e Arman-e Khalq) contacted the Tabriz branch of Group

Two. The shared views of the two groups led to their vow of unification. The People's Ideal Group was originally formed in the town of Borujerd in 1965–66 by a dozen young men, mostly workers, who became intrigued by revolutionary literature. The People's Ideal Group was a typical Fadai group, almost indistinguishable in zeal and character from Ahmadzadeh's group (Fatapour 2001a). After the Siahkal operation, Nabdel and later Meftahi contacted Katirai. In their last meeting, Katirai took copies of the first communiqués of the PFG for distribution and announced that his group would join Fadaiyan after the completion of their planned robbery of the Aramgah Branch of Bank Melli in February 1971. But two members of the People's Ideal Group were arrested during the holdup, and within a few days SAVAK arrested the remaining members, all of whom were sentenced to death.[2]

The Incongruent Origins

The People's Fadai Guerrillas emerged out of the convergence of two very different groups. One obliquely had its roots in the Tudeh Party (Group One) while the other rose out of the Second National Front (Group Two). They each brought their own worldviews to the PFG. As we will see, these origins haunted the OIPFG in the years to come. One can observe these differences in the course of negotiations between Ahmadzadeh and Ashraf. Ahmadzadeh exercised authority over Ashraf, who was the only member of Group One to enter the CC of the PFG. A meticulous reader can glean in Ashraf's *The Three-Year Summation* implications that he was sometimes kept in the dark about the cells organized by Group Two (1978, 65).

While we should not exaggerate these differences, we must recognize that they represent the internal disagreements as a reality of the group's life. The OIPFG emerged out of divergent origins and converging practices, so the compromise that unified the formative groups cannot be regarded as an exercise of internal democracy. This is evidenced by the fact that the internal diversity of the

---

2. Members of the People's Ideal Group, Homayun Katirai, Bahram Taherzadeh, Nasser Karimi, Hushang Targol, and Nasser Madani were executed in 1971, and Hossein Karimi was murdered under torture (Anonymous nd, 83–86).

rank-and-file members was constantly hindered, however unsuccessfully, under Ashraf's leadership. Chapters 3 and 4 will show that the theory-based internal differences led to factionalism among Fadai prisoners who held allegiances to the theories of either Ahmadzadeh or Jazani.

THE PEOPLE'S FADAI GUERRILLAS AND ITS OPERATIONS

Aside from the PFG, the radical Muslim Organization of Iranian People's Mojahedin (OIPM) also launched its guerrilla operations in August 1971. By the summer of 1971, Fadaiyan had sustained serious setbacks while trying to escape the tightening grip of the police. The year 1972 was marked by the state's promise to eradicate guerrilla warfare. Yet the guerrillas persevered and carried out operations to mark their presence that underscored what they called the "hollow might" of the regime.

Between March 1971 and March 1972, the PFG lost forty-two members. In the same period, about three hundred individuals were arrested in relation to Fadaiyan. In "Some Hasty Glances," Mostafa Sho'aiyan notes that most of them were captured without armed resistance (in 1976a, 52; article individually paginated). After heavy assaults on the group in the spring and summer of 1971, only two operational teams and eight cadres remained at large (Heydar 1999, 248). The militants were desperate for money and resources needed for their planned disruption, in October 1971, of the Shah's celebration of 2,500 years of the Persian Empire. They managed to blast some power lines, causing blackouts in parts of Tehran as the celebration was televised (Ashraf 1978, 52). Other operations in 1971 included the bombing of the Iran-America Cultural Centre and the robbery of a Bank Saderat branch in Tehran (Ashraf 1978, 65). In the spring of 1971, the PFG sent three members to Palestine and they brought back weapons and ammunition (Ashraf 1978, 62–63).

The Fadai Guerrillas recruited members from the student movement and from the cells modeled after them. As urban guerrilla warfare intensified, in February 1972 the regime created the Anti-Terrorism Joint Task Force (Komiteh-ye Moshtarak-e Zedd-e Kharabkari) to coordinate the operations of armed and security forces. University students frequently clashed with the University Guard, and that led to the mass arrests of student activists by the end of the spring (Fatapour 2001c). Fadaiyan's strictly partitioned teams were now vertically linked up to the higher rank while all lateral contacts were blocked. In the guerrillas' bases, rooms partitioned with curtains kept militants (new, in transit, or fugitives from raided teams) in cell-like spaces, preserving their anonymity. While the operations of 1971 mostly focused on the group's survival, as bank holdups demonstrate, the year ended with Fadaiyan's proven ability to carry out such operations as blowing up sonar bombs at the state rallies (OIPFG nd-a, 39, 51).

By 1972 the PFG was a leaner, but more efficient, group. Ashraf and Noruzi were the leaders, each having at least three years of experience in underground activities. Born in 1946, Hamid Ashraf joined the Jazani-Zarifi group in 1963 and entered the University of Tehran to study mechanical engineering in 1965. In 1966, Ashraf was assigned to the mountain team, but after Jazani's arrest he moved up to the CC of the group in the fall of 1968. He handled the communications between the urban and the mountain teams during the Siahkal operation and went underground in 1970. A sharp and able militant, he broke through police and SAVAK lines fourteen times in the last six years of his life (OIPFG 1979b). Born in 1946, Hassan Noruzi was a worker whose father was a Communist railroad worker who had died while derailing a military train in 1945. Noruzi participated in several operations and was once wounded but managed to escape. He commanded the team that blasted power lines during the Imperial Celebrations. In 1972, he was reportedly surrounded by sixty security agents but still managed to escape. Ultimately he was killed in a shoot-out in January 1974 (*Nabard-e Khalq* 1974c, 68–69; Anonymous 1976a, 60–68).

In 1971–72 the Fadai prisoners significantly outnumbered the Fadai militants at large. The (pro-)Fadai prisoners in Tehran prisons had therefore established a clandestine prison network (*tashkilat-e zendan*). Collective communes, a tradition among political prisoners in Iran, were established. In these communes, all responsibilities and personal property were communally shared, and for a short period, sketches of Marx, Engels, Lenin, Ahmadzadeh, Puyan, and Meftahi decorated the walls of the cells (Navidi 1999, 124). Many prisoners called prison a "liberated zone" as prison had become a sanctuary for theoretical studies and a source of recruitment for the guerrillas outside. In 1971–72 Jazani and his comrades were ideologically in the minority, as most Fadai prisoners supported Ahmadzadeh's thesis of the "objective conditions of the revolution." After 1973, Jazani began recruiting new members for the PFG (Heydar 1999, 261, n.6).

By 1974 the relationship between pro-Ahmadzadeh and pro-Jazani factions in Qasr Prison had become critical (Same' 1999, 139).

In 1973 the PFG made a turnabout and launched an offensive that confused the regime. At this time Ali Akbar Ja'fari, Behruz Armaghani, and Mehdi Fazilatkalam served in the CC along with Ashraf and Noruzi. After Noruzi's death, Ashraf and Ja'fari became the key figures, joined by Hamid Momeni as the group's theorist. The PFG established networks in Mashhad and Isfahan, and smaller cells in Sari, Qazvin, Tabriz, and Shiraz. In 1975 new internal bylaws (*asasnameh*) of the group were drafted, and they designated a Supreme Council as the organization's highest body. Reports conflict on whether the Supreme Council ever actualized (Heydar 2001, 29, 31; Abdolrahimpur 1999b, 277). The ill-fated meeting of June 28, 1976, in which the top ten Fadai Guerrillas were killed shows there existed a larger body of leadership than the small, earlier CCs. But with or without the Supreme Council, specific leaders like Ashraf, Ja'fari, Momeni, and later Armaghani actually shaped the OPFG's policies.

In 1973 Fadaiyan entered a process of unification with a clandestine group within the CISNU, which later called itself the Group for Communist Unity (GCU; see chapter 5). Later in 1975, the relationship between the two groups became strained, as the GCU accused Fadaiyan of Stalinist-style purges of its members. In 1975, Ashraf sent Mohammad Dabirifard (Heydar) abroad to establish the much-needed logistics support network independent of the GCU. In London he contacted Manuchehr Kalantari (from Group One and publisher of *19 Bahman Teorik*), who closely cooperated with him. Soon, however, contact with Iran was lost because of the demise of the OIPFG leadership (Heydar 1999, 262, n.11). Fadai couriers Mohsen Nurbakhsh and Mohammad Ali Khosravi Ardebili regularly smuggled heavy loads of weapons and ammunitions (supplied by Palestinians or Libya, or purchased from smugglers) into Iran via the Iraqi border (until the 1975 Algiers Treaty between Iran and Iraq) and later via Turkey. At the same time, Fadaiyan succeeded in having their literature broadcast by Radio Mihanparastan (Radio Patriots), based in Iraq and operated by Hossein Riahi, a surviving member of the Palestine Group (Same' 1999, 148, n.30).

The first issue of Fadaiyan's official periodical, *Nabard-e Khalq* (the people's combat), was published in April 1974. The group's original 1971 name, the People's Fadai Guerrillas (PFG), changed to the Organization of People's Fadai Guerrillas (OPFG) in 1974. Later in early 1975, because of increased liaison between

Fadaiyan and the revolutionary movements or states in the Middle East (Libya and the Democratic Republic of Yemen), the Organization of Iranian People's Fadai Guerrillas (OIPFG) became the group's official name. No emblem marked Fadaiyan's publications in 1971. In early 1972 Faramarz Sharifi designed an emblem that later underwent a series of modifications by Ali Akbar Ja'fari and Kiomars Sanjanri until 1975, when a hammer and a sickle completed the insignia of Fadaiyan (Dehqani 2004, 17; Heydar 1999, 261n4).

Fadaiyan on the Offensive

The three-year period of expansion of the PFG started in the spring of 1973 and ended with the nearly total eradication of the OIPFG in June 1976. In this period, the guerrillas assassinated capitalist tycoon Mohammad Fateh Yazdi (August 1974), SAVAK interrogator Major Niktab (December 1974), Khorasan Province SAVAK Assistant Director Hossein Nahidi (1975), commander of the Ariamehr University Guard Major Yaddollah Noruzi (March 1975), SAVAK agent Abbas Shahriyari (March 1975), and an alleged collaborator, Ebrahim Nushirvanpur (May 1975). They had also identified residences of SAVAK interrogators Bahman Farnezhad (Dr. Javan) and Bahman Naderipur (Tehrani), and planned to assassinate them (Heydar 2001, 31). Other operations included the bombing of Lahijan Gendarmerie Attachment on the anniversary of Siahkal, Soleymaniyyeh Gendarmerie Post in Tehran, Babol Police Headquarters, Rudsar and Khorasan Province Governorship buildings (February 1975), Khorasan Provincial Department of Labour (April 1976), and the Gendarmerie Headquarters in Tehran (*Zamimeh-ye Nabard-e Khalq* 1975, 1–2, 14–15; *Nabard-e Khalq* 1976, 78, 87, 117–18; *Nabard-e Khalq* 1975a). In solidarity with taxicab drivers, Fadaiyan bombed several traffic police booths in Tehran, which led to the removal of the booths (*Nabard-e Khalq* 1976, 87). According to one account, between August 1974 and March 1975 alone, Fadaiyan carried out ten operations (Heydar 1999, 252), aside from street battles with police and security forces.

The impact of Fadaiyan's operations on the regime cost them dearly: systematic use of clinical torture for extracting information from prisoners intensified. Fadai and other militants preferred to commit suicide upon arrest, usually by swallowing cyanide capsules, rather than facing torture. Upon capture, high-profile militants were hideously tortured for prolonged periods of time. Jazani was tortured for months. Brutal beatings hospitalized Zia Zarifi for two weeks, and Ahmadzadeh spent two months in the hospital and underwent several operations. He managed to show his "toasted" back to the international human rights observers who had attended his trial. Human rights lawyer Nuri Albala described what he saw: "The whole of the middle of his chest and his stomach was a mass of twisted scars from very deep burns . . . his back was even worse" (in Nobari 1978, 148; Anonymous 1976b, 109–10; see also Rejali 1994). Many died under torture. Moreover, the assassinations of SAVAK informant Shahriyari and interrogators Niktab and Noruzi caused SAVAK to retaliate in kind (Hassanpour 2007, 181–83): on April 19, 1975 outside Evin Prison in northern Tehran, a select group of SAVAK agents murdered Jazani, six members of Group One (Zia Zarifi, Sarmadi, Surki, Sa'id Kalantari, Chupanzadeh, and Afshar), and two members of the OIPM (Kazem Zolanvar and Mostafa Javan Khoshdel), all serving their long sentences. SAVAK claimed they were shot during an escape attempt and SAVAK documents alleged that Jazani was leading the OIPFG from inside the prison (CSHD 2001, 50–53). With his growing intellectual influence on Fadaiyan, Jazani's loss was heavily felt.

Armed Propaganda

The forceful reappearance of Fadaiyan by 1974 was partly the result of an abundance of cash from their supporters in Iran and from the CISNU activists in Europe. Financial security removed the need for dangerous bank holdups. Killing Lieutenant-General Farsiu (the only assassination in the first two years) was clearly an act of revenge. But the subsequent assassinations came with a double message: each one aimed at winning the support of a specific group of people, while warning the security agents of the guerrillas' punishing presence. Popular support among intellectuals and students led Fadaiyan to shift their operations beyond military or state targets.

Fadaiyan's blueprint for guerrilla warfare consisted of two main components: first, the execution of an operation on a carefully selected target, and second, the construction of a narrative around the operation for propaganda purposes. This blueprint was derived from the notions of "armed propaganda" (*tabliq-e mosallahaneh*) of both Ahmadzadeh and Jazani. Armed propaganda created the discursive means that separated Fadai operations from blind terrorist attacks and transformed military actions into social and political manifestos. The symbolic presence of the guerrillas transmuted their operations into a political discourse open to public debate, conflicting interpretations, and reconstruction of the events. In Momeni's words, "politics is the content of struggle and military [operation] the form of struggle" (1979, 30). As the discursive and symbolic presence of the guerrillas dominated Iranian politics (between 1973 and 1976), it created a binary political situation in which every social movement was forced to ally itself with one of the two opposing camps. To highlight this situation, let us consider a few selected high-profile operations.

(1) On August 11, 1974, a Fadai team gunned down Mohammad Fateh Yazdi, an Iranian tycoon who owned the Jahan Chit textile factory. The OPFG justified this "revolutionary execution" based on his alleged involvement in the bloody suppression of the striking Jahan Chit workers by Karaj gendarmerie forces on March 6, 1971, which left several workers dead or wounded. Following the assassination, the OPFG launched a communication campaign to declare its solidarity with the workers: "By executing Fateh Yazdi, the Karaj bloodsucking capitalist, who had caused the death of over 20 frustrated, striking workers, our Organization embarked on supporting the workers' movement" (*Zamimeh-ye Nabard-e Khalq* 1975, 11). Moreover, Fadaiyan emphasized their symbolic presence in Iran and offered an interesting reading of the event:

> We knew that the massacre of Jahan Chit was regarded as the symbol of the crimes of the regime against the working class of our country, and our success in politicizing the event would clearly expose the regime's fascistic methods in dealing with the rightful grievances of the working class and is considered a crucial step toward calling working-class attention toward its vanguard. Therefore, an armed operation in relation to the Jahan Chit massacre is a tactic toward the massification of armed struggle. (*Nabard-e Khalq* 1975a, 1)

Reportedly, Tehran university students raided the Fateh Foundation in Tehran to show their support and the OPFG reported the workers' celebratory reception of the news (*Nabard-e Khalq* 1975a, 2, 66–81, 83–84). However, many Fadai members, especially those in prison, regarded the killing of a civilian entrepreneur an act of desperation (Fatapour 2001a). The assassination proves the fundamental limitation of guerrilla warfare in establishing relations with the working class, let alone organizing it. Evidently it was a miscalculated attempt to extend the OPFG's influence beyond its intellectual constituency.

(2) On December 30, 1974, a Fadai team killed SAVAK interrogator Major Niktab. The assassination clearly proved to police and SAVAK agents that they were vulnerable and under the surveillance of omnipresent guerrillas. The operation also signified solidarity with political prisoners, victims of torture, and families of fallen militants (*Nashriyeh-ye Dakheli* 1975b, 30). The divisiveness of these symbolically charged operations led to the polarization of society, which impeded peaceful and reformist opposition against the regime.

(3) On March 3, 1975, a team of Fadaiyan shot Captain Yaddollah Noruzi, the commanding officer of the University Guard stationed at Ariamehr University. The OPFG should be regarded as the militant branch of the leftist student movement of the 1970s, and the assassination of Noruzi was meant to strengthen Fadaiyan's solidarity with the university students (*Zamimeh-ye Nabard-e Khalq* 1975, 3–4).

(4) On March 5, 1975, a Fadai team gunned down Abbas Shahriyari, a former member of the Tudeh Party who was recruited by SAVAK to run a sting operation in Iran. He was responsible for the arrest of members of the Tudeh Party, the Palestine Group, and Group One in the 1960s. Once exposed by the revolutionaries, he made public "confessions" on a staged television show in 1970 (his face was not shown on TV). Then he eclipsed into obscurity under an assumed identity, working for private companies and living a quiet life. The Tudeh Party had published Shahriyari's photo in *Mardom* (no. 103, December 1973). Reportedly, it was by sheer accident that a Fadai member identified Shahriyari on the street (although his appearance had been altered), and he was soon tracked down (Fatapour 2001a). This assassination signified that no agent, however skillful, could escape the retribution of the guerrillas, and it made a mockery of SAVAK's inability to protect its loyal agent. Fadaiyan used the operation to launch a campaign against the Tudeh Party. The book *The Revolutionary Execution of Abbas Shahriyari* contains details of Shahriyari's activities and a long polemical rejoinder to the Tudeh's letter to the OPFG in which the Tudeh had called armed struggle futile and defeatist. In the book, the Fadai author conjoined the resented image of Shahriyari with the Tudeh Party, and in so doing separated the armed movement from the history of the Iranian Communist movement. That is why Fadaiyan are celebrated as Iran's "new Communist movement," or *khat-e do,* the "Second

Line." The text insisted that because Iran was a police state, armed struggle was the political struggle par excellence (OIPFG 1975a, 98–99). The Tudeh leaders "want to dominate and influence the armed movement so that they can utilize it in their political collusions and for the purpose of cutting a deal with the regime" (OIPFG 1975a, 136). One can clearly discern the text's eerie message: the "execution" of a SAVAK agent with dubious links to the Tudeh leadership was also the symbolic execution of Tudeh opportunism. Fadaiyan asserted themselves as the new generation of Iranian Communists that had emerged, like the phoenix, out of the ashes of the Tudeh. By dehistoricizing their movement, the 1970s revolutionary generation symbolically severed links with the Tudeh Party. History works in mysterious ways, however: the ghost of the Tudeh that the early Fadaiyan wished to exorcize eventually returned to Fadaiyan in the early 1980s, and with a vengeance.

New Turns

As Fadaiyan continued to astonish both the people and the regime with their perseverance, a quiet undertow gradually altered, at least in theory, the original objectives of the group. Ahmadzadeh's theory of strategic armed struggle had dominated the inceptive years of the PFG, but by 1974 the group was joined by the advocates of Jazani's idea that armed struggle was a tactic toward political struggle and popular movement. Early pro-Jazani Fadai cadres included Farhad Sediqi Pashaki, Masrur Farhang, and in particular Behruz Armaghani, who joined the CC of OPFG after his release from prison (Fatapour 2001a; Dehqani 2002, 15, 27). In the spring of 1974, the leadership began distributing some of Jazani's writings in teams. Later that year, though, the internal debates over the existence or lack of the objective conditions of the revolution did not yield any policy shift, but the leadership decided not to distribute the new printing of Ahmadzadeh's *Armed Struggle* (Heydar 1999, 251–52).

Fadaiyan's turn toward political activism did not simply stem from the role of new political cadres like Armaghani. Mahdi Fatapour, who was in charge of the student activities of the PFG and directly in contact with Ashraf, reports that as early as 1973 he and Ashraf had discussed new ideas pertaining to the creation of student and political wings. He is uncertain about whether Ashraf's initiative was approved by the CC or simply his own. In any case, the plan was soon abandoned. Fatapour notes that until Jaf'ari's death in April 1975, there had been a rivalry between the pro-Jazani (Ashraf and Armaghani) and the pro-Ahmadzadeh leaders (Ja'fari and Yasrebi) to the extent that each individual directed his teams according to his own beliefs. By 1975 Jazani's ideas dominated the OPFG but Ahmadzadeh's ideas also had supporters (Fatapour 2001a). A close reading of the group's publications between 1974 and 1976 shows theoretical fluctuations between Jazani and Ahmadzadeh as well as sporadic praises for Stalin and Mao (see *Nabard-e Khalq* 1974a; 1975b). What is more, the "internal diversity" of Fadaiyan must be viewed as mainly limited to the leadership. Rank-and-file Fadai cadres generally remained quite uneducated theoretically, as they arose from a "practice-oriented generation" (*nasl-e amalgara*).

In 1974–75, when theoretical shifts in the OPFG were imminent, the CC made a surprising, and ultimately naïve, effort to obtain support from the Soviet Union. Ashraf instructed Dehqani and Hormatipur (who were based in the Middle East) to contact the Soviets. According to Hassan Masali, who was involved in the process, the contacts took place in total secrecy. Dehqani and Hormatipur sought the assistance of (allegedly) two members (Masali was one of them) of Setareh (renamed Group for Communist Unity, GCU). Despite clear GCU anti-Soviet policy, the GCU member(s) cooperated in the mission.[3] As a result, Hormatipur, Dehqani, and Masali met with Soviet agents (aliases Victor and Alexander) in Beirut, Rome, Sophia, and Damascus. The Soviets' attitude toward Third World revolutionary movements was based on creating Soviet satellites, and only on the perceived possibility of victory of such movements would the Soviets support them (Kuzichkin 1997, 264–65). So the Soviet agents consistently postponed Fadaiyan's request for money, weapons, or political support. In turn, they asked the OPFG to provide military intelligence and reports on Iran's social and political situation. Although one account holds that Ashraf rejected the Soviets' demands (Masali 1985, 53), and despite the Fadaiyan's self-acclaimed gesture of being "independent" Marxists, there is a controversial letter allegedly

3. Masali's involvement in this affair produced discontent among his GCU comrades. According to Masali, two members of the GCU were involved in the contacts with the Soviets. Several years later, however, his former comrades claimed that no Setareh member other than Masali was even aware of such contacts, given that Setareh's anti-Soviet principles did not allow them to engage in such dealings (OCUA 1987, 117–27).

from Hamid Ashraf to Ashraf Dehqani that indicates Ashraf accepted the Soviets' condition (Masali 1985, 84; Rohani 1993, 323; CSHD 2004, 435–38, 442–44; Hassanpour 2007, 196–97; Naderi 2008, 932–34). SAVAK claims to have obtained this letter from the West German police, who had found two letters during a raid on Dehqani's temporary residence in Frankfurt. These letters were published in Iran's newspapers in 1976. Because independent scholars have not examined the authenticity of these letters, they must be viewed with caution, as SAVAK is known to have altered documents for its public opinion campaigns.

The Fadai Guerrillas were not unknown to the Soviets: they had been supported by pro-Soviet revolutionaries, among them the Palestinian leftist George Habash, Libyan leader Muammar Kaddafi, and the Democratic Republic of Yemen. Even earlier, when the mountain team sent Saffari Ashtiyani and Houshang Nayyeri allegedly to Palestine to acquire weapons and ammunition for the Siahkal operation, it is known that they actually received support through an Iranian KGB agent in Iraq named General Mahmoud Panahian (Rohani 1993, 289; Razmi 2008), an error on the part of the two that was later criticized by Safai Farahani (Naderi 2008, 332).

In any case, with the eradication of the OIPFG leadership in the spring of 1976, the affair with the Soviets came to an end (Masali 1985, 52–53). Some Fadai activists view the contact simply as a part of Fadaiyan's seeking international support (from Habash, Libya, and Yemen) and thus not contradictory to their resolve to maintain a nonreliance policy (Abdolrahimpur 1999b, 280; Abdolrahimpur and Karimi 2001, 40; Fatapour 2001a). In contrast, Masali (1985) publicized this affair for the first time in the mid-1980s to show it as a sign of Fadaiyan's alleged Stalinism and hypocrisy.

The Political Dilemma

The OPFG's new policy of organizing the working class indicates a theoretical shift. Until this point, a few workers who joined the group were quickly transformed into full-time revolutionaries. Fadaiyan molded their worker recruits after their intellectual notion of self-sacrificing revolutionary. The Fadai workers provided the OPFG with useful occasions for tokenism, as the OPFG glorified its "working-class martyrs" at every opportunity. But the fact is that most Fadai workers actually belonged to the working class through family background or some past employment in labor sectors.[4] This indicates that Fadaiyan claimed to represent a class that did not actually take part in the struggle launched in its name. So the OPFG needed to collapse the distinction between class origins and class belonging in order to claim the coveted working-class character. Ideological blinds impeded Fadaiyan from acknowledging their intellectual basis and character. Fadai cadres were often assigned to work as laborers as a way of gaining knowledge about life among the masses, or paradoxically, as a disciplinary measure. Such occasional pilgrimages of the intellectual to the shrine of the "toiling masses" are indeed superficial, but these "visits" attest to the deep, class-based social rift that set apart two different realities of Iranian society, an effect of repressive development. In any case, keeping the Organization alive outweighed the task of organizing the masses.

In 1973–74, the OPFG concluded that it was necessary to systematically participate in the workforce and contact workers (*Nashriyeh-ye Dakheli* 1975b, 26). The attempt to create niches among workers must be understood in its theoretical context: by 1974, the OPFG leadership viewed armed struggle to have entered its second stage. In one of his last prison writings, Jazani identified three stages of the revolutionary movement: in the first, the guerrillas stabilize armed struggle; in the second, they win the moral and material support of the masses; and in the final stage, armed struggle breaks out of its guerrilla cocoon and becomes "popular" (*tudehi shodan*), leading to revolutionary war (Jazani 1978, 16). Jazani specifies that in the first and second stages, armed struggle remains the feat of intellectuals (Jazani 1978, 36–37; see Jazani 1979c).

Furthermore, an equally important factor in turning toward political organization was an organizational impasse. Already by 1974, the OPFG faced a structural problem as it recruited more members than an underground organization could absorb. To reach out to supporters, they applied Jazani's concept of

4. *Nabard-e Khalq* names the following individuals as Fadai workers: Jalil Enferadi, Javad Selahi, Kazem Selahi, Behruz Dehqani, Eskandar Sadeqinezhad, Asghar Arab Harisi, Mohammad Taqizadeh, Manaf Falaki, Ahmad Zeybaram, Iraj Sepehri, Hassan Noruzi, and Yusof Zarkari (1975, 86–88). One simple observation shows that several of the above in fact were not workers when they joined Fadaiyan: Dehqani and Falaki were involved for several years in cultural and educational activities, and Zeybaram was a librarian before joining the PGF. Fadaiyan seem to emphasize the "class origins" of these activists instead of their place in the labor sector.

organizing armed struggle in tandem with the immediate demands of the people as manifested through spontaneous movements (OIPFG 1975a, 92–93), a concept that implies that armed struggle alone cannot instigate popular uprising. This was a dilemma that could not be overcome, but only postponed. By 1975, the "practice-oriented" (*amalgara*, or in Ahmadzadeh's word, "*peratisian*") generation that founded the PFG had understood the need for a solid strategy, which in turn necessitated a robust theory. The leadership moved to create a study group with Ashraf, Momeni, and Armaghani as its prospective members (*Kar* [OIPF-M] 1998a, 7).

The creation of a political wing, which Jazani called the "second leg" of armed movement, promised a way out of this impasse. The intended political expansion of the OPFG was not only a theoretical requirement but also a dictate of practice. The leadership proposed a three-part restructuring plan: first, full partitioning of all units and teams; second, distribution of responsibilities across partitioned units and the expansion of leadership; and finally, increasing the group's capacity to incorporate new political tasks or organize workers (Heydar 1999, 253). Three different views existed within the OPFG on this restructuring: one did not think political reorganization was necessary; another approved of Jazani's idea of creating two partitioned wings, military and political; and the last recognized the necessity of political activity but saw it as a function of both armed operations and activity among the masses (Heydar 1999, 253–54).

The OIPFG literature on the political wing almost entirely defines political involvement as presence among workers. Despite the fact that the OIPFG was a student organization, or perhaps because of it, the Fadai Guerrillas showed an unjustified disregard for their presence among students and intellectuals. This tendency, of course, indicates the propinquity of Fadaiyan to the student movement, a proximity that blinded Fadaiyan to their potential as leaders of Iran's secular-Left movement. The OIPFG took the student movement for granted, always ready and available. Looking back in history, one finds Fadaiyan's attitude toward the student movement rather insulting: their ideological preoccupation with the working class and their revolutionary zeal-impeded Fadaiyan from partaking in democratic tasks (see chapter 7). The OIPFG specifically instructed students to organize themselves in clandestine guerrilla-style cells, carry out propaganda against the regime, recruit potential militants, and seek contacts with the OIPFG (*Payam-e Daneshju* 1975, 16–65). By expanding politically, Fadaiyan did not seek to push the limits of restricted political space in Iran that prevented intellectuals from winning the hearts of the masses; instead, they sought to "infiltrate" social groups and organize them in underground, and now "political," cells. In short, their notion of political activity was only an extension of their guerrilla organization, and thus ultimately parochial.

Preparing for the new political wing was slow, as the OIPFG was caught up in its everyday challenges. In the fall of 1975, one issue of *Nabard-e Khalq for Workers and Toilers* was published, but its publication ceased as the Fadai Guerrillas were headed for a battle of life and death in 1976 (Abdolrahimpur 1999b, 278; see also *Nabard-e Khalq* 1978). Before attending to that, though, we need to review the OIPFG's relations with other militants.

THE OIPFG AND OTHER UNDERGROUND GROUPS

A fact that is often ignored in regard to the history of the OIPFG is that *there was never one Fadai group but many*. Fadaiyan could not have survived without being continually replenished by small, self-motivated militant cells of students and intellectuals. While the role of these small cells in reinvigorating the PFG can hardly be exaggerated, unearthing the extent of their contribution remains the historian's overwhelming challenge, as the OIPFG documents make only sporadic and vague allusions to such cells, except for the high-profile groups like the People's Ideal.

Urban guerrilla warfare enjoyed an interesting situation: it created a symbolic realm in the public discourse of dissent, a realm in which guerrilla activities produced greater social presence than the original acts. This metonymic effect of guerrilla warfare arose primarily from the pervasive repressive measures. The state was so restrictive that any political activity outside state-run politics echoed louder than it originally sounded. This totalizing closure magnified the effect of attempted political opening by the guerrillas like the way a speck of light in total darkness leaves disproportionate glare. The shadowy presence of the guerrillas elevated them to a mythic status: rumors held that the Siahkal guerrillas were more numerous than the regime had captured, and the assassination of Farsiu proved just that. Once state-run newspapers announced his death, Puyan mysteriously surfaced in different places. The extent of training and resilience of Fadaiyan both in prison and outside was also frequently exaggerated in public discourse.

While ideology did not allow Fadaiyan to perceive their symbolic presence, they intuitively realized that the Fadai Organization could be actually enhanced if it expanded beyond its organizational walls. Hence the PFG advice: "The Marxist-Leninist groups that could not contact the People's Fadai Guerrillas should operate under the name 'People's Fadai Guerrillas' (with a suitable addition)" (*Nashriyeh-ye Dakheli* 1975b, 37). If the Fadai presence could be extended beyond the organization, then not only would the regime find itself facing a formidable and omnipresent adversary, but the people would also find the prospect of the final battle closer. Moreover, the early designation "People's Fadai Guerrillas" (with no reference to an organization) was a response to the necessity of survival while implying that the PFG functioned as an umbrella group. Indeed, as Mostafa Sho'aiyan pointed out, adding the word "Organization" to the Fadaiyan's official name betrayed the group's original intent (Behrooz 1999, 63; see chapter 6). The OPFG intended to either "absorb these groups and directly train and organize them," or provide them, through official publications, with the experiences of Fadaiyan (*Nabard-e Khalq* 1974c, 8). Indeed, by virtue of starting armed struggle in Iran, the OIPFG always considered itself as the core of a future national liberation front, a hegemonic core that would unify the Left and persuade others (Muslim or nationalist) to support and eventually accept the leadership of the Left in the struggle against the Shah. As Fadaiyan grew stronger, the OIPFG saw itself as the pivot of the revolution (*Nashriyeh-ye Dakheli* 1976, 79), and it developed a sectarian attitude that impeded collaborative relations with other full-fledged groups.

Fadaiyan's attitude toward the People's Democratic Front (PDF) was arrogant, opportunistic, and mostly a reaction against the PDF's maverick theorist and prolific writer Mostafa Sho'aiyan. In July 1973, after the PDF cells were raided by SAVAK, the loss of several key members prompted the survivors to join the OPFG. After insisting on the internal distribution of his book, *Revolution,* Sho'aiyan was blocked, isolated, and then simply jettisoned from the OIPFG, while the rest of PDF members stayed with Fadaiyan (see chapter 6).

The OPFG's relationship with Setareh (later the GCU) went more smoothly. Setareh was a small, clandestine network of Communist intellectuals and students in Europe with anti-Stalinist tendencies. The façade organization of Setareh was the National Front of Iran–Middle East Division. In 1973, after the two groups agreed on a process of unification (*tajanos*), Setareh was dissolved and its members began to work directly under the OPFG representatives in Europe and in the Middle East. Over the past years, Setareh had built up relations with various movements or states in the Middle East, relations that greatly benefited the OPFG. The process of unification also produced several volumes of debates on the Socialist camp (see chapter 5). By 1975, however, when members of Setareh were informed of Stalinist-style purges within the OPFG (see below), they abandoned the process of unification.

The relations between Fadaiyan and the Muslim Mojahedin-e Khalq (OIPM) demonstrated mutual support and respect, despite ideological differences. Ardeshir Davar, who had connections with Meftahi, facilitated the first contact between the two groups (Ashraf 1978, 49). In 1971, Mojahedin agreed that militant Muslims and Marxists could cooperate (*Nashriyeh-ye Dakheli* 1976, 100), and the two groups maintained regular contact with one another throughout the first half of the 1970s. In several instances, Mojahedin helped cutoff Fadai cadres to rejoin the PFG. Ashraf Dehqani escaped from Qasr Prison with the assistance of the families of Mojahedin prisoners, and her escape caused the arrest of fifteen family members of Mojahedin (Hadjebi-Tabrizi 2004, 354). Similarly, in 1974, Sediqeh Rezai, who had lost three brothers, all members of the Mojahedin, escaped from prison with the help of Fadaiyan and later joined the Marxist Mojahedin (Nejati 1992, 421). Similar friendly attitudes informed the relations between the prisoners of the two groups and were expressed through an agreement (Same' 1999, 149, n.41). With a majority of Mojahedin turning Marxist and splitting from the rest of the group (in a bloody "coup") in 1975, it seemed that the prospect of unification of the militant Left was near. However, Fadaiyan soon found themselves negotiating, without success, with a group that had no respect for the OIPFG's perceived hegemony and was by any standard nothing short of Stalinist (see chapter 5).

Another case involved a group named after its founder, Dr. Hushang Azami Lurestani (henceforth Azami). Azami's group consisted of intellectuals and activists who, in June 1974, started Cuban-style guerrilla warfare in the mountains of Lurestan Province. His group attacked gendarmerie posts in the region, and in July 1974 they were besieged but broke through the lines of the armed forces. Survivors of this group briefly joined Fadaiyan in the aftermath of this incident. Azami was personally in touch with Group One before the 1967 arrests, but his contact with the OPFG was new. Azami returned to the mountains of Lurestan, despite Ashraf's disapproval, while some members of his group, including Mahmoud Khorramabadi and Siamak Asadian, stayed with Fadaiyan. Dr. Azami was killed in May 1976 in unclear circumstances (Kamalvand 2002; Heydar 1999, 264, n.17; Same' 1999, 145–46, n.11).

In contrast to these cases that failed to unify the militants, the Fadai Guerrillas enjoyed the unconditional support of smaller, action-oriented, militant circles. Fadaiyan's symbolic presence had quickly produced a new space for, and a modality of, action. Were it not for the invigorating incorporation of small militant circles, the PFG would probably never have survived its first year, let alone expanded by 1974, and yet its expansion was a blessing that turned into a curse.

One of the first groups to join Fadaiyan in prison was Setareh-ye Sorkh (Red Star). A group of young, radical intellectuals, the Red Star was intercepted by SAVAK before undertaking any serious activity. For a short time in 1971, Setareh-ye Sorkh had the highest number of prisoners among leftist groups, and their notable prisoners included Abdollah Qavami, Ali Shokuhi, Mohammad Ahmadian, and Habtollah Ghaffari, who participated in the debates in Tehran and Shiraz prisons. Most Red Star members ultimately joined the PFG in prison, while others rejected armed struggle and eventually formed Rah-e Kargar in 1979 (Fatapour 2001a).

Another group to join Fadaiyan was founded by Martik Qazarian, Nezhatosadat Ruhi Ahangaran, and several others (in 1972). Ruhi Ahangaran was a top female militant who took part in the assassinations of Fateh Yazdi and Major Niktab. She was promoted to key positions within the OIPFG until her death in 1975 (*Nashriyeh-ye Dakheli* 1975b, i; *Nabard-e Khalq* 1976, 109–11). Little is known about Hamid Reza Hezarkhani and his group that joined the PFG (*Nashriyeh-ye Dakheli* 1976, 80). There was also a circle of about fifteen Ariamehr University students that joined Fadaiyan sometime in the early 1970s, and notable among them were Hossein Qalambor, Turaj Heydari Bigvand, Farzad Dadgar, and Tahereh Khorram. In 1976, many members of this group imposed the first split on the OIPFG's new leadership.

ON THE VERGE OF ANNIHILATION

In 1975, the OIPFG experienced an unprecedented expansion. The theoretical shift toward Jazani's ideas and thereby political activities, uneasy, inconsistent, and fluctuating as it was, responded, at least in part, to the organizational impasse of the OIPFG. The group abandoned the spectacular operations that defined its presence for most of 1974. The institution of a political wing required strategic planning. The leadership finally acknowledged the weakness that it had long denied by privileging practitioners over theoreticians. It was clear now that the movement needed theorists and strategists. In the winter of 1976, the leadership decided that Ashraf, Momeni, Armaghani, and Farhad Sediqi Pashaki should form a theoretical group (Abdolrahimpur 1999b, 279).

However, it seems that instead of offering a bold critique of the past, Fadaiyan justified their theoretical shift based on a strange continuity with the past and as such they missed the opportunity to have a long-lasting impact on Iranian political life. In an extensive editorial in *Nabard-e Khalq* (June 1976), Ashraf announces the OIPFG's theoretical shift toward Jazani's theory of "armed propaganda" (*Nabard-e Khalq* 1976, 1–19, 129–40) and asserts that Jazani offered a culmination of all hitherto guerrilla theories. As proof, he argues that in the first stage of armed movement, in the past five years, the guerrillas sought to: (1) impose armed struggle as the antithesis to the Shah's dictatorship; (2) put an end to various "patience and waiting policies" of the National Front and the Tudeh Party; (3) provide means of organizing the progressive forces; (4) organize dissident groups (of students and intellectuals); and finally (5) expand armed propaganda (*Nabard-e Khalq* 1976, 4–5). The emphasis was on the notion of "armed propaganda," but Ashraf tries to arrive at the necessity of political activity not from a critical engagement with the concept of "armed propaganda," but strangely, as an expansion of it. "To bring the [armed] movement to the masses," he writes, Jazani's "theory teaches that we must launch operations that illuminate the goals of the armed movement for the masses of people in an objective, practical, and tangible way. . . . Therefore, *operations with clear objectives* must be put on our agenda" (*Nabard-e Khalq* 1976, 13; emphasis in original). Jazani's thesis of armed propaganda means that military operations should have clear political messages, and Ashraf announces that this was the source of inspiration behind the operations of 1974–75 (*Nabard-e Khalq* 1976, 14, 16). After carefully stitching together the premises needed by his conclusion, he explains, "We must attend to the fact that as an integrated, precise, and scientific concept, armed propaganda is a modified form of 'political exposure' [*efshagari-ye siasi*] in our society. . . . In other words, '*armed propaganda is the pivot of all forms of struggle of our people*'" (*Nabard-e Khalq* 1976, 134; emphasis in original).

One can clearly see that the conclusion does not derive from the premises. While it cannot be denied that "armed propaganda" has a certain theoretical affinity with political activity, by abandoning the concept of "armed propaganda" Fadaiyan could have grasped politics properly. A Fadai activist of the time suggests that by 1976, many of the members no longer believed in guerrilla warfare (Abdolrahimpur and Karimi 2001, 40). Eventually, though, the discussion came to a halt during the gory spring of 1976, and Fadaiyan did not make the shift toward Jazani's ideas until 1977.

The precipitate expansion of the OIPFG inevitably led to security breaches. To pinpoint Ashraf, SAVAK had upgraded its counterterrorist trainings, increased unmarked patrols in cities, tapped telephone lines, and held surprise midnight neighborhood searches. Bylaws were enacted that increased intelligence, including one requiring landlords and rental agents to report the identity of their tenants and clients to local police stations. Although Fadaiyan had shifted away from strident operations, in early 1976 many street battles inflicted significant casualties on the OIPFG membership. Notable among these earlier casualties were two leading members, Hamid Momeni and Behruz Armaghani. Sixteen Fadai cadres were killed on May 15, 1976, and five on May 17. During these weeks, Ashraf broke twice out of besieged Fadai bases. One of his legendary escapes and battles lasted half a day, during which he was intercepted by the police, killed several officers and agents, and stole a police vehicle to finally escape without a trace. Eventually, on June 28, 1976, military personnel and security forces surrounded the meeting place of the OIPFG High Council in Mehrabad Jonubi in southwest Tehran. In a battle that lasted for several hours, Ashraf and nine other leaders in the house were killed. To show their victory, the state-run television broadcast a photo of Ashraf's body, and SAVAK showed the same photo to prisoners (Negahdar 1997, 148). In three months, SAVAK had destroyed 80 percent of the Tehran branch (Abdolrahimpur 1999b, 281), although this estimate seems exaggerated given that the Tehran teams that later became the Monsha'ebin (about ten members) remained intact (see *Kar* [OIPF-M] 1996, 7–8).

The official OIPFG line holds that SAVAK tapped the telephone lines Fadaiyan often used for quick messaging. This explanation first appeared after the May 1976 assaults and before Ashraf's death (*Nabard-e Khalq* 1976, 180, 184; *Kar* [OIPF-M] 1998a, 7; Masali 2001, 160). Fadaiyan believed that phone calls under twenty-three seconds could not be traced, but such a notion was tragically erroneous, as SAVAK had a center in Tehran to systematically tap phone lines (Hassanpour 2007, 234). SAVAK got the first lead when security forces found a codebook on Bahman Ruhi Ahangaran upon his arrest. Subjecting him to tortures that eventually led to his death, SAVAK extracted the code and traced the teams and the location of their houses (Hadjebi-Tabrizi 2004, 119; Hamidian 2004, 276; CSHD 2001, 63, 81). The eradication of the OIPFG leadership indicates the state's changing counterinsurgency tactics in 1975. By tapping phone lines, SAVAK no longer needed to intercept the guerrillas. Instead, surveillance continued until SAVAK uncovered the network of teams. Meanwhile, political prisoners were moved to the notorious Evin Prison in Tehran, and their visiting privileges were suspended to cut them off from the outside world. Prisoners were no longer released after serving their sentences.

With the loss of OIPFG leadership, horizontal contacts between surviving partitioned units and cells proved impossible. According to one activist, only two cadres in Tehran survived (Qasem Siyadati and Abbas Hashemi) (Hashemi 2001a, 43). Scattered rank-and-file members of different teams were out of money, searching desperately for a place to stay and for ways to contact their surviving comrades. Mashhad and Isfahan cells remained untouched but isolated. The prospect of reviving the Fadai Guerrillas now seemed extremely remote. But here one can observe one of the ironies of the history of the OIPFG: *the resilient Fadai activists persevered and survived; what did not survive, however, was the intelligibility of guerrilla warfare.*

REVIVED INTO THE REVOLUTION

The loss of leadership proved to be a decisive turn, as it epitomized the failure of guerrilla warfare, an issue that Fadai leaders had evaded for six years. Now the formidable task of retrieving lost contacts, discovering isolated cells, and finding the Fadai delegates in the Middle East fell on the shoulders of rank-and-file cadres. In the late summer of 1976, Hassan Jan Farjudi, Ahmad Gholamiyan Langarudi (henceforth Gholamiyan), Saba Bizhanzadeh, and Qorban Ali Abdolrahimpur met at Khajeh Rabi Shrine outside Mashhad, and by default they formed the new CC of the OIPFG. Jan Farjudi was assigned the task of reorganizing the group (Abdolrahimpur 1996, 8).

Aside from the members who simply returned to normal life and never contacted Fadaiyan again, there are reported cases of members in teams who opted out of the Organization. In sharp contrast to the early 1970s (see below), there are cases in which team leaders assisted the resigning members to leave the OIPFG by erasing their traces (Ahmadzadeh 2001; Satwat 2002).

More significant, though, was the coalescing and then departure of a splinter group after the assaults (see chapter 5). The teams that were later called the Monsha'ebin (the splinter group) made up a major OIPFG unit in Tehran, containing about ten members (a quarter of the total cadres of Fadaiyan at the time), some of whom were experienced militants. Back in 1974, these teams had strongly reacted against the OIPFG's occasional admirations of Maoism. They had also developed sharp criticisms of guerrilla warfare from a Leninist viewpoint (see OIPFG [Splinter Group] 1977), and one of them, Turaj Heydari Bigvand, had written a critique that specifically targeted Jazani's theory. As the differences between these members and other Fadaiyan became apparent, so did the lack of internal democracy in the OIPFG. The leadership void catalyzed ideological differences and brought organizational grievances to the surface. The new leadership circulated audiotapes containing the Monsha'ebin's positions and asked the splinters to remain within the OIPFG and circulate their ideas, a gesture unthinkable under Ashraf. However, pointing out the lack of organizational democracy and the earlier purges, the Monsha'ebin refused the offer and left the OIPFG (Fatapour 2001a).

On a different ground, the new CC made desperate efforts to find the lost contacts with their comrades in the Middle East. Dabirifard (Heydar) also made attempts from abroad to find his comrades in the country. In the summer of 1976, Mohsen Nurbakhsh went back to Iran for a rendezvous arranged through the Marxist Mojahedin, but he was later killed in a shoot-out with the police (Heydar 2001, 27–28). Another attempt in the spring of 1977 also failed because of the arrest of the leading Fadai of the time, Jan Farjudi. Subsequently, Dabirifard and another member created a new base in Turkey, closing down OIPFG bases in Beirut because of the civil war and in Syria because of shrinking resources. Concurrently, the ideological conflict between pro-Ahmadzadeh (Dehqani and Hormatipur) and pro-Jazani (Heydar) Fadai representatives abroad intensified, reaching a critical point. In the wake of June 1976 assaults, Heydar met with Hormatipur and Dehqani for the first time later that summer. He was informed in this meeting that Setareh had withdrawn its support for the OIPFG. Cassette tapes containing the positions of Setareh referred to organizational, not theoretical, issues (Heydar 2001, 27–28). In 1978, following the resumption of contacts between members in Iran and abroad, the OIPFG leadership instructed each rival faction (pro-Ahmadzadeh and pro-Jazani) to send delegates to Iran for negotiations. Three pro-Jazani members (including Heydar) went back to Iran, but the pro-Ahmadzadeh faction declined to send delegates. A few months later, Mohammad Reza Ghabrai went abroad to negotiate with the pro-Ahmadzadeh dissenters but without results (Heydar 2001, 28; Heydar 1999, 267–68, n.37). Meanwhile, Dehqani and Hormatipur published their pro-Ahmadzadeh works as official OIPFG publications without the authorization of the new leadership.

The soul-searching that inevitably followed the loss of leadership in 1976 found expression in discussions around the viability of guerrilla warfare. The Monsha'ebin's departure reflects an honest response to the problems of guerrilla warfare and the undemocratic structure that was euphemistically called "democratic centralism." Abdolrahimpur remembers three approaches to this crisis: a large minority, represented by the Monsha'ebin, clearly named armed struggle as the culprit and advocated joining the Tudeh Party. Another sizable minority, led by Gholamiyan, sought to return to vigorous armed struggle based on Ahmadzadeh's thesis, while a small minority, under Jan Farjudi, defended Jazani's notion of armed struggle as a catalyst for political activities and the organization of labor (Abdolrahimpur 1996, 8).

In the months to come, it was Jan Farjudi who played a key role in propagating Jazani's theory among Fadaiyan. Jazani's book *War Against the Shah's Dictatorship* was published by the group, despite the disapproval of Gholamiyan. In March 1977, Jan Farjudi was arrested and murdered under interrogation. Given his position, he had a vast knowledge of the teams, and although one account claims that he cooperated with the police (Naderi 2008, 872), it is clear that since no major security raids took place after his arrest, he had withheld key information. Saba Bizhanzadeh, the first woman in Fadaiyan's CC, was also killed in a shoot-out in April 1977. Together, such losses, the split, and disillusionment with guerrilla warfare reduced the group to about twenty members in 1977 (Fatapour 2001a).

The post-1976 OIPFG leadership only provided organizational directives, as it did not have the authority to maneuver Fadaiyan politically (Ahmadzadeh

2001). Many disenchanted members who had nevertheless stayed on pressured for democratic input, so internal debates consumed much of the organizational energy. As a result, the new leadership was not able to issue a single political communiqué until December 1977 (Abdolrahimpur 1996, 8). But the communiqué of December 6, 1977 (on the anniversary of University Student Day or 16 Azar) was a decisive one: it announced Jazani's ideas as the guiding theory of the OIPFG. The idea had been discussed in the summer of 1977, and the three leaders (Abdolrahimpur, Ghabrai, and Gholamiyan, the latter reluctantly) had assigned Abbas Hashemi to prepare a draft for the communiqué (Abdolrahimpur 1999b, 282–83). Interestingly, these leaders were later informed by Dabirifard (Heydar) that the pre-1976 leadership had already adopted Jazani's views and moved toward implementing them.

As if referencing the OIPFG's 1976 military defeat, the communiqué assessed the early Fadaiyan's adoption of Ahmadzadeh's thesis of the objective conditions of the revolution to be an error, one that induced Fadaiyan to conceive of armed struggle as short-term. As guerrilla warfare took off, the "leadership comrades" became so entangled in the everyday survival of the group that they "did not critically engage with the early theories" (*Payam-e Daneshju* 1977, 25). The 1976 assaults caused this theoretical problem to surface, leading to the adoption of Jazani's ideas. To justify Jazani's liberation "war against the Shah's dictatorship" and thus toward a democratic revolution (*Payam-e Daneshju* 1977, 47, 51), the communiqué referred to Lenin's two-tiered notion of the revolution as democratic and Socialist (Lenin 1935). It concluded that it was necessary to transform the OIPFG into a political force. In hindsight, of course, the naïveté of this position is hardly ignorable: the strategy clearly lacked an understanding of the long-term social and political activities of the Shi'i forces among the people.

With further loss of key members such as Ghazal Ayati and Saba Bizhan-zadeh in the spring of 1977, Gholamiyan, Abdolrahimpur, and Ghabrai, and later Qasem Siyadati, formed the CC (Fatapour 2001a). Already in 1976, the new leadership had resolved not to recruit any new members because of the fear of further SAVAK intelligence. By 1977–78, with pressure from U.S. President Jimmy Carter, who emphasized democracy and human rights, the Shah allowed certain reforms to the Iranian political landscape, starting with the dissolution of the state-run Resurgence Party. Those political prisoners who had been kept in prison beyond their sentences were released. Slackened restrictions quickly resulted in the revitalization of the student movement. In the spring of 1978, the OIPFG reestablished the Tehran Branch, which by the summer of that year included three teams (Ahmadzadeh 2001; Satwat 2002).

At this point, the leadership decided to increase the OIPFG's political presence through "special recruitment" (*ozvgiri-ye vizheh*) of the recently released veteran Fadai prisoners known for their theoretical competence. Mastureh Ahmadzadeh, Mehdi Fatapour, Akbar Sanaye Dustdar, Ali Reza Akbari Shandiz, Hadi Mir Moayyed, Mohammad Reza Behkish, Hassan Tavassoli, Farrokh Negahdar, and later Jamshid Taheripur and Behzad Karimi were among the special recruits who gradually went underground (Ahmadzadeh 2001; Fatapour 2001a; Satwat 2002). The choice of these particular individuals indicates that their recruitment was not ideologically based. The recruitment, however, immediately created a dual leadership: an existing organizational leadership (*rahbari-ye tashkilati*) and an emerging theoretical authority (*rahbari-ye siasi*). In the existing CC, Ghabrai and Abdolrahimpur supported the newly recruited cadres, while Gholamiyan expressed discontent about the inclinations of some of them (Satwat 2002; Hamidian 2004, 217–18).

Just as Fadaiyan emerged out of the student movement of the late 1960s, so for their revival the student movement was an indispensable factor. In the early 1970s, the PFG had created its phantom student body, called the "Militant Students" (*Daneshjuyan-e Mobarez*), which was not actually an organization but only a designation to assert the PFG's presence on university campuses. The next generation of pro-OPFG activists, Raziaddin Taban and Mansur Farshidi, tried to maintain the presence of the "Militant Students" but were both arrested in 1975. The third generation of the "Militant Students," Mahmoud Vahidi and Sa'id Kurd, rejected armed struggle and later joined the Maoist Sazman-e Razmandegan (The Organization of Combatants) while continuing to use the name Daneshjuyan-e Mobarez. By the mid-1970s, Fadaiyan's influence over students had significantly faded, and by 1977 most leftist student leaders no longer supported the OIPFG. Interestingly, many students joined the Monsha'ebin (Fatapour 2001a).

But the situation quickly reversed in the summer of 1978: heightened revolutionary spirit and the OIPFG's increased presence led to Fadaiyan's decisive return as the most influential leftist organization on Iranian campuses (Fatapour 2001a), as the revival of the student movement in turn reactivated the OIPFG (Ahmadzadeh 2001). Revolution was in the air in January 1979 with the possibility of open expansion of dissident organizations, which led to the emergence of the student affiliate of the OIPFG, the Pishgam (Vanguard) Student Organization (Sazman-e Daneshjuyan-e Pishgam) (*Kar* [OIPF-M] 1998b, 7).

As revolutionary fever traveled through the country, the OIPFG found itself in a perplexing situation. The Fadai leadership treated the rising waves of protest with caution or disbelief. Some even saw it as a SAVAK conspiracy to create mayhem that would legitimize a heavy-handed suppression of the people (Satwat 2002). First, in April 1978, Abdolrahimpur (1999a, 7; Fatapour 1999, 8), and then, after the Black Friday of September 8, 1978, Fatapour argued that the objective conditions of the revolution were ripe, but with the opposition from Gholamiyan and Siyadati this analysis did not yield any specific policy (Fatapour 2001a; Fatapour 1999, 8). On November 3, 1978, Tehran, all major Iranian cities, and numerous towns were hit by a destructive unrest during which banks, government offices, and liquor stores were trashed by protestors. On this day, the OIPFG's pathbreaking communiqué entitled "Let Us Believe in the Uprising" brought Fadaiyan in line with the revolutionary wave. The communiqué, written by Farrokh Negahdar (Negahdar 2008; Negahdar 1999, 10), did not sit well with Gholamiyan, who only reluctantly mimeographed it (Satwat 2002). The communiqué was distributed among thousands of protestors on November 5, 1978. As the communiqué reached other Fadai cells, Gholamiyan was severely criticized for its distribution without the prior approval of the leadership (Satwat 2002). The revolutionary whirlpool, though, soon convinced everyone that the communiqué was of great significance, despite the lack of collective and democratic process in adopting such an important position. The rigidly partitioned structure could no longer support expanding connections with the students, participation in street rallies, and the increased need for coordination among the guerrilla cells. The OIPFG had to "come out" now.

In the decisive shift toward political activity, the Fadai leaders searched and later found self-created circles of supporters among workers, with whom they had lost contact after 1976 (Abdolrahimpur 2001, 7; Mahdizadeh 2001, 9; see chapter 7). Still, the OIPFG's presence among workers was negligible. Aside from a number of bank robberies that Fadaiyan did anonymously in 1976–77 (Hamidian 2004, 279), the pattern of OIPFG's guerrilla strikes in this period indicates a positive correlation with the rise of revolutionary movement in the country. These include bombing of the Iran-America Cultural Association in Tehran on

December 28, 1977 (Fadaiyan's first operation after June 1976) in protest against President Carter's visit to Iran, and bombings and attacks in Tehran, Qom, Mashhad, Tabriz, and Isfahan between mid-1978 and the February 1979 Revolution. Fadaiyan also assassinated Colonel Zamanipur in Mashhad and fired at military officers during a rally in Tehran on December 23, 1978 (OIPFG 1979a, 14). In the days before the Revolution, Fadai militants occasionally engaged the military forces that had opened fire on protestors.

With the Shah's fateful departure on January 15, 1979, and Ayatollah Khomeini's victorious return from exile on January 31, the country came under a dual government. Premier Shapur Bakhtiar and the military ruled the country, trying to introduce reforms and contain demonstrations, while the Revolutionary Council and its premier designate, Mehdi Bazargan, utilized the popular movement to assert their terms of transition of the government in their secret negotiations with the Americans and the Iranian military.

Serendipitously, the OIPFG held a crucial leadership meeting on February 10. Abdolrahimpur, Ghabrai, Gholamiyan, Siyadati, Rahim Asadollahi, Negahdar, Fatapour, Akbari Shandiz, Taheripur, and Mir Moayyed attended the meeting held in Fatapour's secret residence on Taj Street (Abdolrahimpur 1999a, 7; Fatapour 1999, 8). During the meeting, Negahdar proposed the creation of a four-tiered leadership consisting of political, organizational, military, and communications-democratic activities teams with twelve individuals in these teams together forming the new CC. Negahdar predicted that a "broker government" (*dowlat-e mohallel*) would replace Bakhtiar with Bazargan, who would then lead the provisional government. For the transition to take place smoothly, he analyzed, the revolutionary leaders would have to promise the United States that they would preserve the military intact. Based on their radicalism, Fadaiyan decided that they should pressure the leaders of the Revolution into breaking off their deals with the Americans. The meeting, however, was abandoned in haste and the leaders rushed into the streets (Fatapour 2001a).

On the anniversary of the Siahkal operation on February 8, 1979, the OIPFG had scheduled a demonstration but it was canceled. Fadaiyan announced another rally on February 10 starting from the University of Tehran. On the night of February 9, the Imperial Guard had attacked an air force base in East Tehran to suppress units of renegade air force technicians, the *homafaran*. The mutinous homafaran clashed with the Imperial Guards, so a curfew was imposed beginning at 16:00 on February 10. By 15:00, the office of Ayatollah Khomeini had not yet announced his position in regard to the curfew, and people in the streets were told by pro-Khomeini patrols to go home. Fatapour and Same' were in charge of the OIPFG rally, and when the crowd reached Ferdowsi Square in central Tehran by noon, they called on the demonstrators to defend the rebellious homafaran (Same' 1997, 8; *Kar* 1980b, 7–8). Armed Fadai guerrillas and hundreds of their supporters rushed to the battle scene. At this point, the renegade officers opened the base's arsenal to the public, triggering an uprising. Thousands of armed people attacked military bases, police, SAVAK, Gendarmerie Headquarters, prisons, and radio and television stations. The armed popular uprising decisively terminated the Pahlavi regime by the next day, forcing to an end the negotiations between Ayatollah Khomeini's followers and the imperial military and Americans.

On the evening of February 10, the OIPFG established its first office in its birthplace: the School of Technology of the University of Tehran. The decisions to support the homafaran and to establish an office (which put an end to the OIPFG as an underground group) were not taken by the OIPFG leadership (Fatapour 2001a). The communiqué of Fadaiyan, announcing the end of monarchy, was broadcast from Radio Tehran on the evening of February 11 (Fatapour 1999, 8). During the uprising, Fadai cadres Siyadati and Abolqasem Hamedanian, as well as several supporters, were killed (see *Kar* [OIPF-M] 1994; *Kar* [OIPF-M] 1999, 5–10).

Thus the Fadai Guerrillas whose presence defined almost a decade of Iranian political life eventually came to play a significant role in the overthrow of the Shah's regime. The Revolution came: it was swift, with the staggering participation of the people and a drive that nullified backroom dealings of its leaders. The people's liberation was finally realized, except it did not happen the way the founders of Fadaiyan had expected it. The Revolution displaced Fadaiyan's conception of the Iranian people's liberation. The OIPFG's response to the new situation goes beyond the scope of this book, but I will offer a brief sketch of the postrevolutionary Fadaiyan. Before that, however, we must attend to an aspect of the OIPFG history that one cannot find in the group's official documents or narratives.

THE INTERNAL PURGES AND OTHER ISSUES

Increasingly and in recent years, disturbing reports about the internal affairs of the OIPFG have surfaced. As if bound by a vow of secrecy, some surviving members deny the existence of such reports, while others feign ignorance. Yet a few principled activists have come forward with what they know. As expected, former members sometimes dub these reports SAVAK fabrications or anti-Left propaganda by the Islamic Republic.

The 1967 death of Samad Behrangi shows how in a polarized society dissident intellectuals could be consumed by political interests instead of committing themselves to truth. In trying to implicate SAVAK in Behrangi's untimely death, as we saw, Sa'edi and Al Ahmad propagated a falsified story and created a "martyr." The saddest part of the story is not even sacrificing truth for political gains but rather the fact that many activists did know the truth but chose to conceal it. Those who maintained public silence on such issues must deal with their own conscience. My point here, though, is to show the devastating effect of political binarism on social memory.

It was Hassan Masali (1985) who first publicized the issue of purging three deserting Fadai members in the mid-1980s, a commendable act given the controversial nature of the matter. More recently, Maziar Behrooz brought up the issue with an account that raised the number of purged members to four. Accusing Fadaiyan of Stalinism, he portrayed the purges as ideologically motivated (1999, 66–67). While the response to Masali's report was silence, Behrooz's stirred up controversy, and several Fadai members of the time, now in exile, came forward and professed their knowledge about the purges.

The Purges

A Tehran Polytechnic student, Ebrahim Nushirvanpur was recruited for Group One by Hassanpur in 1969. Although he participated in the formation of the mountain team, he refused to become a professional revolutionary in 1970. He was arrested in 1971 and publicly recanted on national television in April 1972, after allegedly revealing the group's secrets to the police. He was later working for the state-run oil company as an engineer when an OIPFG team, headed by Nastaran Al Aqa, gunned him down on May 21, 1975 (*Nabard-e Khalq* 1976, 103–8; *Nashriyeh-ye Dakheli* 1975b, 44; Anonymous 1976b, 46; CSHD 2001, 101–2). Certain members (probably the Monsha'ebin) objected to the assassination of Nushirvanpur to the extent that the leadership had to defend its decision. So in the *Internal Bulletin,* the leadership described the operation as a deliberate "warning to such [weak or doubtful] elements so that they would think twice before joining the ranks of the militants" (*Nashriyeh-ye Dakheli* 1975b, 30). Given that he had knowledge of the mountain team and given that the mountain team actually succeeded in launching the Siahkal operation, logically we can deduce that he did not reveal key information to SAVAK. Nushirvanpur was arrested on February 1, 1971 (Naderi 2008, 626–27), along with others, on the second day of SAVAK raids of the group based on the confessions of Hassanpur, who had been arrested on December 13, 1970. Nushirvanpur was released about six months later. While the OIPFG communiqué accuses him of having exposed the mountain team to security forces (*Nabard-e Khalq* 1976, 105–6), we have Ashraf's own 1972 account that traces the arrests back to the key information provided by Hassanpur during three weeks of torture that led to his death (Ashraf 1978, 99). Nushirvanpur had a change of heart and defended the regime in prison (Hamidian 2004, 91–92), but his assassination was a sheer act of vengeance, and it displayed the Fadai leaders' impoverished judgment.

Another case, obscured until recently, pertains to Oranus Purhassan, who must have joined Group Two in 1970. Soon after he heard his team's plans for a mountain team, he quit and went into hiding. Fearful of his former comrades' revenge, he has lived in obscurity ever since and even security forces had a hard time tracking him down (Naderi 2008, 377–79). Although Ashraf admits that it was not Purhassan who exposed the mountain team, Purhassan's action caused a debate in which Ashraf insisted on killing him as a traitor while Ahmadzadeh rejected the idea (Ashraf 1978, 69).

The circumstances surrounding the purging of Abdullah Panjehshahi are now reasonably clear, and Behrooz (1999, 68) should be credited for exposing it for the first time. An Isfahan team commander, Panjehshahi was called to Mashhad sometime in May 1977 and murdered by Gholamiyan. His murder was not, as Behrooz asserts, ideologically motivated, that is, over his affiliation with the Monsha'ebin (1999, 68) or his rejection of armed struggle (Naderi 2008, 820). Rather, it is now known that Panjehshahi was in love with a female comrade, Edna Sabet. Apparently, on one occasion they were spotted expressing affection, and when confronted, the couple denied their affair. When Gholamiyan was informed about it, he summoned Panjehshahi to Mashhad and killed him, allegedly with the assistance of Siamak Asadiyan. When the murder was revealed, most members of the OIPFG (fewer than twenty at that time) strongly reacted against the assassination. Mariam Satwat, who was in the newly established second Isfahan team, was told by Abdolrahimpur that Panjehshahi was executed because of embezzlement and stealing OIPFG property (2002). Soon after, Abbas Hashemi heard about the purge through Asadiyan and shared the truth with the rank-and-file members (Hashemi 2008). Sabet was from a Jewish family, a mechanical engineering student who went underground by secretly returning to Iran from her summer vacation in London in 1975. Sabet was disciplined by being sent to live in isolation for three months. At this time many rank-and-file members, including Sabet, had already rejected armed struggle (Satwat 2002). It is not clear what happened to her from this point to the summer of 1978, when she resurfaced in the ranks of the Marxist-Leninist Mojahedin. She was arrested in 1981 and executed in 1982 (Mohajer 2001, 231–34).

Knowledge of this murder, once again, was kept a secret. Panjehshahi's sisters, Nassrin and Simin, both Fadai militants, were also killed during April and May 1976 in street battles. Their mother, Shamsi Ansari, along with two younger sons, Nasser and Khashayar (at the time nine and seventeen years of age, respectively) lived in hiding in a team house with Abdolrahimpur (Abdolrahimpur and Karimi 2001, 39). Until her death in 2001, Ansari did not learn of the tragic fate of her Fadai son.

The details of the three purged members of the PFG are concealed under probably irremovable layers of secrecy. As mentioned earlier, the relations between Setareh and the OPFG abruptly ended when members of Setareh received news about the internal purges within OPFG ranks. According to the available information, OIPFG couriers Khosravi Ardebili and Nurbakhsh first became aware of the "elimination" of Fadai cadres probably in Mashhad under Ja'fari. One of the slain members used the alias Asad. Nurbakhsh broke the news to Masali and Hormatipur, expressing grief and concern, as he had known Asad personally and did not believe he was a "traitor." Dehqani denied the accusations and asked Ashraf about it. The news disturbed Khosravi Ardebili to the extent that he decided to die with honor by committing a suicide attack (unprecedented among Fadaiyan). His comrades convinced him to join the Marxist militants in Dhofar, where he died in February 1976 (Masali 1985, 55–56; OCUA 1987, 122). Dabirifard recalls that one case involved a member who had simply disappeared, and six months later, when Fadaiyan found him working in a company, they killed him. In his recollection, two other members who decided to leave apparently had considerable knowledge about the group (Heydar 2001, 33), and they too were killed. The Fadai leadership treated these cases as security breaches, "indicted" them, and issued their "death sentences" in absentia. The Stalinist manner of condemnation can hardly be exaggerated. It is important to note that there are hints that these individuals left Fadaiyan because of their disagreement with OIPFG policies (Masali 1985, 56).

There are two controversial letters, published by SAVAK in the Persian daily *Ettela'at* (no. 9612, May 20, 1976, and no. 9613, May 22, 1976), allegedly written by Hamid Ashraf and addressed to Ashraf Dehqani about the purges and regarding aid from foreign countries. The letters were obtained from West German police in their raid of Dehqani's temporary residence in Frankfurt. Although the authenticity of these letters remains to be verified (SAVAK tampered with evidence on a regular basis), it is known that SAVAK had knowledge about the internal purges through interrogations (see Naderi 2008, 536). Based on the content of the letter, Asad's assassination must have taken place in 1971 or 1972 because he had already been murdered by Hassan Noruzi and his team (in Masali 1985, 84; in Naderi 2008, 532–34). According to the same documents, another member of the group "was arranging a plan to leave activities and was therefore sentenced to death by Khosrow [Ja'fari]" (in Masali 1985, 83). Fatapour (2001a) was informed that one member had been killed in Mashhad and his body thrown into a well. The identity of the three purged Fadaiyan and the circumstances surrounding their deaths remain extremely hard to obtain.

Aside from the "confirmed" cases of purging, though, there is a rather perplexing disappearance that deserves mention. One case pertains to Manuchehr Hamedi, a member of CISNU and Setareh who was secretly deployed to Iran to join the OIPFG, probably around October–November 1974, as a part of the process of unification (*tajanos*). Some sources report that he was killed by the security forces in Rasht on May 18, 1976 (Naderi 2008, 652–53; Heydar 1999, 262, n.11). However, Cosroe Chaqueri (K. Shakeri) states that Hamedi's father could not find his burial registration after the Revolution, which raised the suspicion that he was never officially buried (Chaqueri 2001). Setareh did not release any information regarding his death either. Given the anti-Stalinist leanings of Setareh, and Hamedi's theoretical knowledge, it remains unknown whether Hamedi was also eliminated because of disagreement with the Fadai leadership or in a shoot-out with the police.

A Disturbing Incident?

As mentioned, in the spring of 1973 the OIPFG was joined by several surviving members of the PDF (see chapter 6). Among those who joined were the mother of the fallen PDF leader Nader Shayegan, Fatemeh Sa'idi, and her two children, Nasser and Arzhang Shayegan. They were transferred to Mashhad, along with Sho'aiyan, under the direction of Ja'fari, and formed a support cell (Sho'aiyan 1976c, 27). Before Sho'aiyan's bitter departure from the OIPFG in February 1974, Sa'idi was arrested while on a needlessly dangerous assignment of checking out a suspicious residence of some team members, despite her (and Sho'aiyan's) reported objection (Sho'aiyan 1976c, 16–18). In her interrogation, though, she mentioned that the assignment was carried out on Sho'aiyan's order (Naderi 2008, 478). With their mother in prison now, the two boys were taken away from Sho'aiyan, with whom they had lived for quite some time, and placed on a team with Saba Bizhanzadeh, Momeni, Ezzat Gharavi, and Heydar (Dabirifard) (Heydar 2001, 29). The children also spent sometime on a logistics team with Zahra Aqanabi Qolhaki who, in prison, told her cellmates that it was truly hard for the children to endure the rigid discipline of a secret Fadai base. Apparently, at some point, it was proposed that the children be quietly released to their aunt, although why the plan never materialized remains unknown (Raf'at 2001).

On May 15, 1976, with SAVAK's tightening grip on the OIPFG, a Fadai base in the Tehran-No District, where the Shayegan brothers lived, came under attack. The team had planned an assassination for the next day and Ashraf was in this base for his last instructions. During the attack, Ashraf managed to break through the police lines, with a bullet in his leg, and escaped after engaging with security forces on two occasions (*Nabard-e Khalq* 1976, 180–81). According to a police report, the six residents of the house (two women and four men) were killed. The report named the Shayegan brothers among the casualties without citing their age (CSHD 2001, 101–2, 104). The fact that the two youngsters (Nasser was eleven, Arzhang thirteen) were in no position to engage in gunfire puts their death under speculation. At this time (1976), SAVAK no longer sought to capture the guerrillas to extract information, as it was confident that security forces would soon liquidate the OIPFG. That is why hardly any cadres were captured during the SAVAK raids between the winter and June 1976. So it is possible that the children were murdered by the security forces. One source attributes their death to Ashraf without providing any evidence (Naderi 2008, 645) because Fadaiyan had strict orders to kill themselves or their comrades should the necessity arise. On the other hand, if the latter had been the case, SAVAK would not have missed this great opportunity to broadcast the brutality of the "saboteurs" as a part of the regime's ongoing propaganda.

Yet who in particular killed the children is sadly beside the point. Nasser's and Arzhang's older brother, Abolhassan, was arrested by SAVAK on a Fadai base at the age of fifteen, and thus avoided a similar fate. The question is, why had the two youngsters been brought into a complex web of events that would have harmed them? Why would the children not have been released to their relatives? The answer is that the children provided great coverage for the teams by deflecting suspicion from neighbors or rental agents. But the two young brothers' deaths show that they must have been the loneliest of all children in Iran: they never "joined" any group and were never even given the choice to stay or leave. The Fadaiyan's instrumental and exploitative use of children is perhaps as tragic as Nasser's and Arzhang's fate. Even after their death, the practice of using children for cover continued, and we do know that at least on one occasion in 1978, the mother of the Panjehshahis and her young son still lived on a Fadai base (Negahdar 2008).

Today the issue is whether the surviving activists have the moral courage to step forward and break their vow of silence about the obscure corners of the OIPFG and redeem those fallen in vain. At this point we must close this book and try to remember the lives of not only those who chose to take the militant path and dedicated their lives to it, but also those who did not choose the path imposed on them and did not deserve to die the way they did.

AFTER THE REVOLUTION

Out of the Revolution, Fadaiyan emerged as Iran's most popular leftist group. The monarchy had been toppled, but Fadaiyan had not succeeded in leading a national liberation movement. After the Revolution, the OIPFG's original mandate had become irrelevant, forcing Fadaiyan to confront, in theory and in practice, the predicament of how to deal with the newly installed populist regime that was no less anti-Left or antisecular than it was anti-imperialist. Fadaiyan were not equipped with a theory sensitive to secular issues for dealing with the religious nature of the new state and thus constantly subsumed the religious character of the Islamic Republic under the anti-imperialism binarism to which they had been uncritically accustomed for years. The new regime perplexed the OIPFG, causing the tormented rebirth of divergent Fadai tendencies in the form of factionalisms and bitter splits. The picture will be complete once we attend to two waves of heavy-handed repressions in 1981 and 1988, each followed by waves of migration of activists. By the end of the 1980s, Fadaiyan were completely removed from the Iranian political scene.

Initially, the postrevolutionary Fadaiyan regarded the provisional government as a precarious alliance between traditional petit-bourgeoisie (represented by radical clerics) and nationalist bourgeoisie (represented by Premier Mehdi Bazargan). This inept class analysis resulted in the OIPFG's treating the former with distrust and viewing the latter as treacherous liberal reformists. On February 20, 1979, the OIPFG called for a march to Ayatollah Khomeini's residence, but he refused to receive them, declaring them "hostile toward Islam" (Kuzichkin 1997, 171, n.1). Contrary to the Tudeh Party that had returned from exile supporting the "national-democratic" Shi'i clerics based on the disastrous theory of the "noncapitalist path" advocated by Soviet theorists (Ulyanovsky and Pavlov 1973), the OIPFG revealed its alienation from the revolutionary government in the referendum of March 30, 1979, that officiated the Islamic Republic of Iran. The OIPFG, along with the National Democratic Front of Iran and the Democratic Party of Kurdistan, abstained from the referendum, pointing out the lack of clarity about the nature of the proposed Islamic Republic.

As the OIPFG transformed from a small cell-based network of a few dozen into a mass movement of hundreds of thousands virtually overnight, it faced the formidable task of organizational restructuring. So an ad hoc committee of five (Negahdar, Fatapour, Mir Moayyed, Abdolrahimpur, and Ghabrai) formed to set guidelines for membership and recruitment. The committee confirmed the membership of about eighty individuals. In a Fadai version of a general membership conference, these members were instructed to elect a new Central Committee of fifteen but only seven individuals—Negahdar, Fatapour, Abdolrahimpur, Ghabrai, Akbari Shandiz, Dabirifard (Heydar), and Amir Mombeyni—obtained the required two-thirds of the total ballots cast. In the next round, those who had gained simple majority (50 percent plus one vote) were added to the CC as well: Mir Moayyed, Anushirvan Lotfi, Naghi Hamidian, Behzad Karimi, and Ali

Tavassoli. The new CC then appointed the alternate members: Gholamiyan, Behruz Soleimani, Akbar Kamyabi (Tavakkol), Jamshid Taheripur, Akbar Sanaye Dustdar, Asghar Soltanabadi, and Heshmatollah Raisi. The executive committee was made up of Ghabrai, Fatapour, and Tavassoli while Mombeyni, Negahdar, Dabirifard, and Akbari Shandiz formed the Politburo (Fatapour 2001a; Heydar 2001, 29). A few weeks after the Revolution, the OIPFG published a weekly, the *Kar* (labor), and then a theoretical journal, *Nabard-e Khalq*. Several provincial chapters also published their publications, often in the region's language. The May Day parade of 1979 showed the extent of Fadaiyan's popularity when a half-million people in Tehran rallied under the OIPFG's banner (Alaolmolki 1987, 218). In the first (and relatively free) parliamentary elections in March 1980, the Fadai candidates received approximately 10 percent of the total ballots (OIPF-M 2001). The *Kar* was published with a circulation of between 100,000 and 300,000 copies each week.

Former Fadai prisoners who had serious doubts about armed struggle now dominated the OIPFG leadership. Even before the leadership election, Fatapour and Negahdar solicited participation from former members (Asghar Izadi, Mohammad Reza Shalguni, Jalal Afshar, and Roben Markarian) who, while in prison, had left Fadaiyan on the basis of rejecting armed struggle. Most of the former members turned down the invitation and instead founded Rah-e Kargar (The Worker's Path) (Fatapour 2001a). However, later Rah-e Kargar proposed joining the OIPFG, but it never materialized because of lack of proper response (Rasul 2003, 19; Heydar 2003, 29).

The new OIPFG directions catalyzed the split of dissenting Ashraf Dehqani in April 1979. The OIPFG spokesman, Fatapour, announced on his own initiative and without the approval of the CC that the veteran Fadai, a celebrity among supporters, was no longer a member (Fatapour 2001a). The announcement provoked a number of contentious exchanges between the OIPFG and Dehqani (see chapter 4). Dehqani, her long-time comrade Hormatipur, and veteran members Rahim Saburi and Fariborz Sanjari formed a pro-Ahmadzadeh faction called Iranian People's Fadai Guerrillas (IPFG), but their split did not have any effect on the OIPFG. The IPFG sustained casualties in 1981 during the suppression of Mojahedin-e Khalq and the militant Left, and it moved to the rebel-controlled parts of Kurdistan and then to Iraqi Kurdistan. Also in 1981, Hormatipur and Saburi took a portion of the IPFG and formed the Iranian People's Fadai Guerrillas–Iranian

People's Liberation Army (IPFG-IPLA) (Same' 1997, 10–11). The group carried out operations in the Caspian region for a year but it disintegrated after Hormatipur's death in March 1982 and its survivors went to Kurdistan. With the Gulf War in 1991, the IPFG left Iraq and became an exile group in Europe.

Several factors led to confrontations between the OIPFG and the new government during the first year after the Revolution: one was Fadaiyan's popularity among students, urban sectors, some workers, and the Kurds and Turkomans, and another was their radicalism, which pushed them to the forefront of defending the people's grievances. The new CC did not have much control over regional cadres, who often made major decisions based on their own judgments while doing it under the OIPFG's name. An early example is the occupation of the U.S. Embassy in Tehran on February 14, 1979, by Fadai supporters. The OIPFG leadership had no knowledge of the incident, and in any case, the occupation was quickly ended with the intervention of the new revolutionary force called the Komiteh. But the most significant case is the war between the Komiteh and the supporters of the pro-OIPFG Cultural-Political Association of the Turkoman People and the headquarters of the Turkoman People in the town of Gonbad Kavus. These organizations represented the Turkoman peasants' demand for the redistribution of land in the vast and fertile Plains of Turkoman, owned largely by the Pahlavis and their affiliates. The war broke out on March 26, 1979, after busloads of Shi'i Komiteh militias from Mashhad were deployed into the town to control the Sunni Turkomans. After a few days of street battles, representatives of the OIPFG and the provisional government managed to broker a ceasefire. About one hundred residents died in the clash. A second war broke out in February 1980 during a march to commemorate the Siahkal operation in Gonbad Kavus. This time the Turkomans received a heavy-handed response from the army. At the same time, four pro-OIPFG Turkoman leaders, who had been negotiating with government representatives on the issues of land and peasant councils, were kidnapped at a checkpoint. Their bodies were found a week later. This war ended the movement of the pro-OIPFG Turkoman peasants (Hamidian 2004, 239–74; Hashemi 2001a; 2001b; Fatapour 2001e).

The summer of 1979 also brought the OIPFG's involvement in the Kurdistan civil war, where the Democratic Party of Iranian Kurdistan maintained the upper hand socially and politically (*Kar* 1979a; *Kar* 1979b). The paramilitary called Hezbollah attacked OIPFG headquarters and meetings across the country. Lasting for a few years, the civil war in Kurdistan is too complex to be discussed here. Until March 1980 Karimi and then Akbari Shandiz headed the Kurdistan branch of the OIPFG. In any case, the first summer of the Revolution brought a precious glimpse into the future of politics in Iran, one that Fadaiyan, blinded by their ideological mandates and radical programs, failed to understand. In fact, as Behzad Karimi (2008) observes, postrevolutionary times faced the dilemma of the "national question," as both ethnic and nationalistic tendencies occurred in ethnically diverse Iran. The Democratic Party of Kurdistan represented the ethnic tendency in Kurdistan, while the OIPFG represented the national one.

The Fateful Schism

The first plenum of the OIPFG, held in September 1979, solidified two factions. It was held in four locations to avoid security risks from the nationwide wave of repression in the aftermath of the civil war in Kurdistan (Mombeyni 2003, 6; Heydar 2003, 31–32). Sixty members participated in the plenum with the goal of reaching an agreement on, first, the past policies and present ideology of Fadaiyan, and second, a policy with regard to the OIPFG's position in Kurdistan (Abdolrahimpur 2003, 43; Navidi 2008). The debates separated a majority from a minority. Out of the twelve members of the CC, only Dabirifard (Heydar) belonged the Minority, but the Minority controlled the editorial board of the *Kar*. Also at this time a small and ephemeral circle of pro-Jazani individuals known as Rah-e Fadai (The Fadai Path) were associated with the Minority-leaning editorial board of the *Kar* (Heydar 2003, 30). As such, dual centers formed around the Majority-dominated CC and the Minority-controlled *Kar*. Three main positions were held with respect to the OIPFG's past: a small group advocated Jazani's theories; a sizable minority defended armed struggle as a tactic; and a clear majority rejected armed struggle altogether (Heydar 2003, 26–27; Abdolrahimpur 2003, 41). With respect to the civil war in Kurdistan, the issue was whether the OIPFG should officially or unofficially defend the rights of the Kurds (Heydar 2003, 30). These two positions on Kurdistan, however, had supporters across the Minority/ Majority divide, so the split cannot be understood in terms of policy (Abdolrahimpur 2003, 43–44; Madani 2003, 56–57) but in terms of the reevaluation of the OIPFG's past (Madani 2003, 51).

The divide increased on November 3, 1979, when a group of Muslim students occupied the American Embassy and took hostages for the next 444 days, placing the new regime in direct confrontation with the United States. A majority of the CC, led by Negahdar, viewed Khomeini and the hostage-taking students as radical anti-imperialists, a position stemming from their past binarism. This position increasingly echoed that of the Tudeh Party (Tudeh Party of Iran 1979), which blamed Fadaiyan for not seeing the anti-imperialist nature of the clerics. The Minority rejected this analysis, citing the CC's failure to offer a class analysis of the new political elite (OIPFG-Minority nd; OIPFG-Minority 1980). These disagreements caused a ten-day delay in OIPFG's announcement of its position, which was to support the radical clerics and the new state.

Soon distrust severed the relations between the two factions. The lack of internal democracy imposed the Majority's positions on the Minority, which accused Negahdar of being in contact with the Tudeh Party. Conflicting views often surfaced in the pages of the *Kar,* confusing supporters, who were kept in the dark about the group's internal crisis. The inner-group relations devolved into such distrust that several pro-Minority members refused dialogue with the Majority.

The Majority tried to bring the Minority's stronghold—the editorial board of the *Kar*—under CC control by gradually delegating Negahdar, Akbari Shandiz, Taheripur, and Mombeyni to serve on the editorial board (Heydar 2003, 30). In protest, Dabirifard and Kamyabi resigned from the board while pro-Minority Mansur Eskandari, Qasem Seyed Baqeri, Manuchehr Kalantari (all three were killed later), and Rasul Azarnush stayed on (Rasul 2003, 21; Tavakkol 2003, 12; Heydar 2003, 35). The Minority insisted on having a section of the *Kar* dedicated to the internal debates. The CC procrastinated, claiming that to do so without the approval of the general membership would be "undemocratic." Eventually, though, in May 1980 the CC yielded on the Minority's ultimatum that they would publish another version of the *Kar.* The CC still attempted to buy time by proposing, to no avail, that such debates should be published in the *Nabard-e Khalq.* The Politburo finally approved the publication of a *Kar Supplement,* but asked the Minority to wait until the CC obtained approval from the membership. Naturally, the Minority refused (Abdolrahimpur 2003, 47–48).

The two factions agreed on June 3, 1980, as the publication date of the issue of *Kar* that contained the debates. But, *seemingly* a typographic error in presenting the debates spelled disaster. Instead of the title "Minority and Majority," the *Kar* that was distributed read "Minority and the Organization." The "error" infuriated the Minority, and in a meeting held immediately following the incident, the Minority leaders agreed to split. The CC representative, Mombeyni, tried to explain the error in a brief meeting with Minority representatives Dabirifard, Kamyabi, Hashemi, and Sheybani, who instead reaffirmed their breaking away from the Majority. The typesetter of the *Kar* tried to explain to Dabirifard and Kamyabi that the error was entirely his fault and that he had prepared a new typeset version of the *Kar* for a new run. Later, Mostafa Madani and Roqiyyeh Daneshgari also met with the Minority leaders to encourage them to stay, but they refused. Reportedly Dabirifard was especially upset about the Majority's negotiation with Ayatollah Beheshti. The Minority remained uncompromising. Within two days, the Minority announced the formation of the Organization of Iranian People's Fadai Guerrillas by publishing a new version of the *Kar* (Abdolrahimpur 2003, 47–48; Mombeyni 2003, 7; Madani 2003, 60–61; Ahmadzadeh 2001).

These events chronicle the crisis that led to the schism, but Madani observes that the split was first perceived, then organized, and that ultimately political reasons were employed to legitimize it (2003, 53). Abdolrahimpur reminisces that Gholamiyan was intent on breaking up with the CC months before these events and points out that Gholamiyan had hidden away cash, printing presses, and weapons caches (2003, 44–45). Gholamiyan, Behkish, and Yadollah Golmozheh (the communications committee of Fadaiyan) organized the Minority (Heydar 2003, 29).

Neither the Majority nor the Minority was homogeneous (Navidi 2008). In the Minority, Dabirifard and Azarnush had disagreements with the others on analytical issues (Abdolrahimpur 2003, 45). Likewise, a small pro-Minority circle led by Mostafa Madani, formed in April 1980, decided to stay with the Majority and publish its positions in the internal bulletin *Be Pish*. In October 1980, Madani and his comrades broke away from the now Organization of Iranian People's Fadai Guerrillas-Majority (OIPFG-M) after Madani was expelled from the CC. This short-lived group split as the Organization of the Iranian People's Fadai Guerrillas–Majority Left Wing (OIPFG-MLW) (Madani 2003, 62). The OIPFG-MLW dissolved itself and joined the OIPFG (Minority) in January 1982 (Same' 1997, 10).

In 1980 the OIPFG (Minority) obtained an internal memo of the Revolutionary Guards indicating the imminent suppression of the militant opposition. Going underground, the group armed its members mainly for self-defense and set up team houses mainly in northern Tehran. Out of distrust for the Majority, the Minority cut off all contacts with them (Ahmadzadeh 2001). The heavy-handed suppression of all militant opposition in the spring of 1981 practically eradicated the Minority's political presence in Iran along with that of the Mojahedin-e Khalq and Peykar. The Minority carried out several operations but was soon forced to move to opposition-controlled regions in Kurdistan.

Further splits, attributable to leadership lusts, fragmented the Minority and plunged it into deep crises. In July 1982, the small, short-lived faction called Revolutionary Socialism broke away. At this time, four of the seven members of the OIPFG (Minority) CC were killed in Tehran (Gholamiyan, Behkish, Golmozheh, and Mohsen Modir Shanechi). In Kurdistan, two of the remaining CC members, Kamyabi and Same', expelled Hashemi. Hossein Zohari and Mastureh Ahmadzadeh were recruited into the CC (now called the High Council). In June 1983, Same' was also expelled over disagreements with Kamyabi. Same' gathered followers and called his faction the Organization of Iranian People's Fadai Guerrillas–Followers of the Identity Platform (which later changed its designation back to the OIPFG). In Europe, Same' joined the Mojahedin-led National Council of Resistance. The remainder of the OIPFG (Minority), headed by Kamyabi, Zohari, and Ahmadzadeh continued their presence in the Iraqi Kurdistan. On January 23, 1986, in an attempt to control the group's radio station (based in a village named Gapilon), a dissenting faction clashed with the militants of Kamyabi's faction, resulting in five deaths. The dissenting leaders were Madani, Hemad Sheybani, and Reza Selahi, who named their group the Supreme Council of the OIPFG and moved to Europe (Ahmadzadeh 2008; OF-Minority 2003, 14–16). They later joined the Fadai Organization and founded the Union of People's Fadaiyan of Iran (UPFI) in April 1994. By March 1987, what remained of the OIPFG (Minority) disintegrated: Kamyabi started his Organization of Fadaiyan (Minority), Zohari continued using the designation OIPFG, and Ahmadzadeh created the Minority Cell before leaving politics (Same' 1997, 12–15).

One small circle stayed in Tehran. It was led by Mahmoud Mahmoudi, a veteran member of the Siahkal teams, who was practically shut out of the OIPFG after the Revolution because of his radical views. After the split, he became the head of the Minority in the Caspian Region in 1981. In 1982, he was stripped of his position and was ordered to undergo a six-month "ideological training" in the Kurdistan headquarters of the OIPFG (Minority). He then went back to Tehran, formed a team, and published *Kar Mahallat*, but was later expelled by Kamyabi, who called him a security risk. Mahmoudi and his team were arrested on April 26, 1985, and he was executed on March 8, 1986 (Prison Dialogue Collective 2003, 15–23).

In the meantime, the Majority began leaning toward the Tudeh Party. The Majority's increasing support for the Islamic Republic grew stronger as the regime tightened its grip on the militant opposition. The OIPFG-Majority did not see the loss of freedom and tolerance and the eradication of secular-Left forces. According to Naqi Hamidian, Negahdar played a key role in rallying the Majority behind the Tudeh and the Islamic state (2004, 404). He was, of course, assisted by an ideological, anti-imperialist, slippery slope. After the suppression of the Mojahedin and the Kurds, the Majority became the largest political organization outside the state orbit with "over half a million reliable supporters" (Behrooz 1999, 105). On the 1981 May Day rally in Tehran, attended by 100,000, the Majority abandoned its old emblem (hammer, sickle, and AK-47) and dropped the word "Guerrillas" from its designation. The Organization of Iranian People's Fadaiyan-Majority (OIPF-M) clearly indicated a move toward a conventional party structure. The May Day celebration was disrupted when Hezbollah thugs assailed the crowd with grenades, knives, and flying rocks, leaving two dead (including nine-year-old Mitra Sane'i) and many injured (including CC member Akbar Sanaye Dustdar, who lost a leg). Still, the OIPF-M clung to its illusions about the nature of the new ruling elite that caused it to attribute violence not to the government, but to such vague elements as fanatic circles, members of SAVAK and monarchists, and the Maoist Ranjbaran Party as the thugs of imperialism (*Kar* [OIPF-M] 1981, 5). While the Majority looked away, Iranian security forces gathered intelligence on them. The OIPF-M capitulated to the increasing state restrictions on individual liberty and political rights, and as such inadvertently facilitated the future disaster waiting for its supporters. Reportedly the OIPF-M and the Tudeh collaborated with the security forces on several occasions. According to Mastureh Ahmadzadeh (2001), on one occasion the Majority disarmed the Minority militants in Kurdistan and buried the weapons of Kurdish Fadaiyan. A similar account holds that the Iranian military sent a letter to the Majority and the Tudeh

Party, commending them for their collaboration in suppressing "counterrevolutionaries" in Kurdistan (Behrooz 1999, 115–16). In the two years between 1981 and 1983, the Majority's policy imposed a curious form of social schizophrenia on thousands of its progressive and secular supporters: they supported the repressive measures of the new state because of the dictates of ideology, while finding such a regime intolerable. By 1981 about 10 percent of OIPF-M members had individually joined the Tudeh (Negahdar 2008), and the OIPF-M leadership was intent on joining the Tudeh, but the Tudeh leaders postponed the plan, citing the precarious status of the Party. Until the arrest of the Tudeh Party leaders in February 1983, all major decisions of the OIPF-M were discussed with the Tudeh leaders (Hamidian 2004, 405; Negahdar 2008).

The prospect of unification of OIPF-M and the Tudeh, pushed by the OIPF-M leadership, sustained a setback when yet another faction broke away from the Majority CC on December 7, 1982. Ali Mohammad Farkhondeh Jahromi (henceforth Ali Keshtgar), Habtollah Mo'ini Chagharvand, Manuchehr Halilrudi, Mehrdad Pakzad, Behruz Soleimani, Heybatollah Ghaffari, and Iraj Nayyeri were prominent members of this sizable splinter group. Calling itself the Organization of Iranian People's Fadaiyan (OIPF), the group published its own *Kar*. The OIPF contained the most learned and professional individuals of all Fadai factions (Rahnema 1997, 29). It derided the Majority leadership as "dissolutionists" and pointed out the undemocratic means used by the politburo to rush into a merger with the Tudeh Party. In any case, both groups were soon forced underground and into exile, following the assault of security forces on the Tudeh and later on the Fadaiyan. Those OIPF members who survived the attacks went into exile, and in June 1988 they joined a Minority splinter group called the Organization of Freedom of Labour (Sazman-e Azadi-ye Kar) and created the Organization of Fadai (Sazman-e Fadai). Founded in September 1985, the Organization of Freedom of Labour included prominent members of the Minority: Parviz Navidi, Azarnush, and Dabirifard. Known as the Mosta'fiyyun, they had walked out of the first Conference of OIPFG (Minority) in December 1981 and left the country in 1983. In March 1990, Keshtgar left the Organization of Fadai and relaunched the OIPF, which eventually dissolved in June 1992 when the few remaining activists of the OIPF dispersed. Later the Organization of Fadai was joined by another Minority splinter group known as the Supreme Council of the OIPFG (led by Madani and Sheybani), and the Union of People's Fadaiyan of

Iran (UPFI) emerged in 1994. The UPFI has been publishing *Ettehad-e Kar* and remains active to this day (Rahnema 1997, 28–29; Same' 1997, 13).

I have already reviewed the contacts between Fadaiyan and the Soviets in the mid-1970s. After the Revolution, Soviet agents approached Fadaiyan in their School of Technology headquarters (Hashemi 2008; Negahdar 2008), and the two parties continued to meet and exchange ideas over issues until the OIPFG office in Tehran (on Meykadeh Street) was shut down. Later the Tudeh arranged a rendezvous between the two parties, but the meeting did not yield any outcome (Negahdar 2008). However, by March 1981, Mombeyni, Abdolrahimpur, and another CC member (Hamidian 2004, 386) secretly slipped into the USSR through the border town of Astara and spent a week as the guests of the Soviet Union Communist Party (Fatollahzadeh 2001, 116). This visit bore fruit in 1983 when the OIPF-M leaders and members fled en masse to the USSR to avoid prosecution and possible death.

On February 5, 1983, Nurreddin Kianuri, general secretary of the Tudeh Party, and 1,500 members were arrested. A week later, the first group of OIPF-M leaders left Iran, followed by the second and third groups within the next two months. Politburo members Taheripur, Fatapour, and Anushirvan Lotfi stayed behind in Iran, but with Lotfi's arrest in August 1983 (he was executed in 1988) the others left the country. Consequently, the OIPF-M no longer had leadership in Iran. In all, some 1,600 refugees fled to the USSR beginning in April 1983. The flow of asylum seekers decreased in 1984 and ended by 1987 (Amir Khosravi and Heydarian 2002, 382).

The Soviets housed the OIPF-M refugees in the Surivostok district in Tashkent (Turkmenistan), where CC meetings restarted in 1983. The Majority joined the Tudeh in establishing the Kabul-based *Radio Zahmatkeshan* (radio toilers) and held a plenum in Tashkent in 1986. Afghan secret agents smuggled ten underground OIPF-M cadres from Iran to Tashkent to attend the plenum and return to Iran. These cadres were tracked down and arrested by Iranian security. All in all, about 1,000 OIPF-M activists were arrested in 1985–86 in Tehran and Mashhad, many of whom were executed in 1988. The OIPF-M stayed in Tashkent until 1989. Disillusioned over Soviet socialism, most Fadai members left for the West through the Red Cross. Stories of discrimination, hard labor, inner-party intrigues, KGB plots, and deportation of dissenting members (including the disappearance of seven dissidents) abound in the USSR. One estimate holds that only one in ten members stayed with the Majority after the Soviet experience (Amir Khosravi and Heydarian 2002, 360–567; Farahati 2006, 450–51; Fathollahzadeh 2001).

All Fadai factions lost hundreds of members and supporters. The recruits of Minority factions and Dehqani's Fadai Guerrillas (as well as Mojahedin-e Khalq and Peykar) comprised the majority of the casualties of 1981–82, while members of the OIPF-M, the OIPF, the Tudeh Party, and the survivors from the early 1980s were executed by the hundreds in July and August 1988. The human loss during the first decade of the Revolution is tragically staggering.

Factionalism, sectarianism, repression, and the disastrous policies of all Fadai factions contributed to the loss of support for Fadaiyan and eventually to their eradication from the Iranian political scene by the mid-1980s. In recent years, though, a new generation of supporters of the major Fadai factions has resurfaced in Iran. The experience of exile has had different impacts on the seven Fadai splinter groups. IPFG (led by Dehqani), OIPFG (led by Zohari), and the Organization of Fadaiyan (Minority) (headed by Kamyabi) are now small Marxist-Leninist circles mostly based in Europe. The OIPFG (led by Same') has stayed with the Mojahedin-led National Council of Resistance. To overcome factionalism, in 1996 former members of the OIPFG, the Minority Cell, and the Organization of Fadaiyan (Minority) formed the Organization of Union of Communist Fadaiyan. They all run Web sites and regular web-conferences, publish books, hold anniversaries, and participate in occasional rallies.

The fall of the "actually existing socialism" brought the resignation of the majority of the OIPF-M membership. In 1990, ten years after the great schism, Karimi, Mombeyni, Mir Moayyed, and Naqi Hamidian, known as the "Left Wing," launched internal critical evaluations of the performance of OIPF-M (Negahdar 2008). To avoid yet another split, the CC resigned to make room for a new generation of leaders (Negahdar 2003, 69; Negahdar 2008). The Majority finally adopted an open and transparent structure, renewing the OIPF-M and facilitating conferences and democratic leadership elections. It is now a Social-Democratic party (in exile) with internal wings within it. Similarly, the UPFI has become a Democratic Socialist party. Both OIPF-M and UPFI maintain Web sites and regularly publish their journals. In 2004 many leftist activists formed the Union of Iranian Republicans, a secular league seeking to influence the future of the country in the aftermath of the decline of the reform movement in

Iran. In 2008, the OIPF-M, the UPFI, and the Provisional Council of Socialists began work on a unification platform (Negahdar 2008). The future of these exile-based groups in their homeland will depend on the political aspirations of the new generation of Iranians, and whether they will be interested in hearing about the experiences that the aging Fadaiyan obtained at a tragically dear price.

THE FADAI GUERRILLAS: A CRITICAL OVERVIEW

By offering a history of the OIPFG, this chapter has shown the significance of Fadaiyan's praxis in the 1970s. Fadaiyan manifested an emergent generation's frustration with the existing political system. Spearheaded by the student movement, this generation was alienated from the regime's repressive development. The inspiring heroism of the Fadai Guerrillas stemmed from the horizons and expectations of the emergent and rebellious intellectuals. The dictatorship and its police state practically deprived this generation of a meaningful sociopolitical future. Therefore and with due caution, it can be argued that *Fadaiyan's struggle was indeed a struggle for democratization of Iranian society*. But the Fadai militants understood this genuine goal, one that was existentially "their own," in the terms they had borrowed from the ideological blueprints that one can only view as imposed. Timid intellectualism and ideological fascination with the working class caused them to lose sight of their own social constituents, and ultimately of struggles for secularism and democracy. As we shall see, the major Fadai theorists tried to bring the needs of their generation in line with imported ideological dictates. Tragically, the imposed ideological categories hindered these theorists from seeking out paths toward democratization. And this feature represents the "constitutive paradox" of the original OIPFG (chapter 9). Moreover, the lack of internal democracy deprived the Fadai activists of having meaningful input in the OIPFG political agendas and yielded tragic internal purges.

3

Bizhan Jazani

En Route to a Democratic Theory of the Liberation Front

> Without being the glowing torch and the symbol of devotion and persever-
> ance, the vanguard won't be able to mobilize the masses towards the revolu-
> tion. What will impress onto the cold steel of the masses during a period of
> inertia is the blazing fire of the vanguard. Self-devotion and self-sacrifice
> [of the vanguard] stems from the sufferings and privation of the masses. It
> is a reflection of the suppressed rage of the masses that blazes out from the
> vanguard. The revolutionary ardour of the vanguard is based on the material
> interests of the masses and that is why it will eventually set to explosion the
> pent-up energy of the masses.
>
> -BIZHAN JAZANI, *Panj resaleh* [Five essays]

WHILE IN PRISON, Bizhan Jazani managed to stay in contact with his group and the PFG, first through his wife, Mihan, who was in touch with Hamid Ashraf (Jazani 1999, 65–67; CSHD 2001, 199) and later via certain younger prisoners whom he had influenced or recruited for Fadaiyan (Negahdar 2008; Navidi 2008). His years of imprisonment, despite periodic interrogations and hunger strikes, proved intellectually fruitful: utilizing the prison circumstances for reflection, he analytically participated in his generation's movement. Jazani began writing intensively by 1972, apparently when he saw the theoretical vacuum within the PFG. Until his death in April 1975, Jazani secretly sent out his later writings to Ashraf by trusted to-be-released prisoners and especially Behruz Armaghani (Negahdar 2008; Navidi 1999, 182; Fatapour 2001a).

Jazani's prison writings can be divided into two clusters: the first group was written in the period between his trial in 1968 and the Siahkal turning point in 1971. Most of these works, which included commentaries, short stories, and paintings, were done in Qom Prison after his comrades' failed escape attempt in 1968. Following the Siahkal operation, he was taken to Tehran for interrogation. The second cluster of Jazani's works were written in and after 1972: in and out of various Tehran prisons, notably in Qasr Prison, Jazani found himself surrounded by enthusiastic followers of Massoud Ahmadzadeh, whose ideas dominated the debates regarding the blueprint for the Iranian revolution. Intense theoretical contentions emerged. An overwhelming pro-Ahmadzadeh majority defended the existence of the "objective conditions of the revolution" (chapter 4), while a handful of prisoners led by Jazani stressed the "pivotal role of armed struggle." The debates led to the isolation of the pro-Jazani prisoners by the pro-Ahmadzadeh majority, which enjoyed the moral support of Mojahedin-e Khalq prisoners led by Massoud Rajavi (CSHD 2001, 47–49; Shalguni 1999, 158; Navidi 1999, 175; Izadi 1999, 111; Ghahremanian 1999, 197–98). Jazani was accused of opportunism, revisionism, or a hidden Tudeh agenda. By 1972 the man who considered armed movement heir to his theory (Jazani 1978, 3) was isolated in a circle of twelve comrades (Same' 1999, 142) and often boycotted by the rest of Fadai prisoners.

The variance between these approaches was an originative one: the PFG was literally founded upon Jazani's and Ahmadzadeh's conflicting views of armed struggle. Because of the exigencies of guerrilla activities, the conflict was never theoretically resolved but only postponed. As Ashraf implies (1978, 10, 24–27, 47–49, 56–57, 66), at times of confusion within the PFG, Ahmadzadeh deployed his charisma and intellectual assertiveness to neutralize the contentions of Ashraf. These originatively discordant ideas continued to haunt Fadaiyan, resulting in the Dehqani split in 1979. Obviously the popularity of Ahmadzadeh's thesis among pro-Fadai prisoners reflected the initial success of guerrilla activities between 1971 and 1973. With the promise of an apparently approaching mass movement, the Fadai activists had little patience for Jazani's theory, and their impatience motivated Jazani to theorize armed struggle in the last two years of his life. His *War Against the Shah's Dictatorship*, arguably his best treatise, went through three revisions from 1972 to 1974, with each newer version sharpening his critique of Ahmadzadeh's theory. The few prisoners who read the first version recall the lack of clarity regarding Jazani's disagreement with Ahmadzadeh (Izadi 1999, 112), whereas the final version contains his distilled criticism of Ahmadzadeh's ideas (Same' 1999, 139).

With the exception of Mostafa Sho'aiyan (chapter 6), Jazani's systematic theorization of national liberation remains unparalleled. His sharp intellect was shown in the perfect grade for his Honors thesis as a student of the eminent sociology professor Dr. Sadighi. His thesis, "The Elements and Causes of the Constitutional Revolution" (Jazani 2009), brought him an academic award as well. Jazani had internalized the rigor and objectivity of the social sciences to the extent that he shunned the Iranian Left's dominant fashion of polemical jargon and accusatory prose. His texts reflect sophisticated conceptualizing with systematic inquiries. His scholarly interests converge with the pressing questions of his generation in his writings. While volumes of his writings were published after his death, many of his works including his children's books, short stories, and other writings were lost in the dark days of 1980 because of the negligence of his wife and the Fadai leaders.

To offer a comprehensive account of Jazani's theory of national liberation, I will employ a discourse analysis of his theory and will identify the pivotal concepts and propositions. I *intentionally* debase ideological justifications to reveal the true contributions of his theory. Mapping his concepts enables us to identify his questions and concerns, and through them, the major thrusts of his theory. Then, with thematic cross-referencing I redefine and revitalize the themes that concern our situation in the post-Communist era, themes that have been silenced, misrepresented, or disfigured by the dominant revolutionary discourses to which Jazani admittedly subscribed.

THE PRAXIS OF THE NATIONAL LIBERATION FRONT

Jazani arrives at the *problématique* of national liberation through historical observation (see Jazani 1980). For him, the theoretical-strategic question of national liberation and the resolution he seeks are in fact the "impositions" that his generation has been burdened with because of the failings of the preceding generation. Jazani refers to the events following the 1941 occupation of Iran by the Allied troops that resulted in the relatively democratic development of social and political forces. He sets himself the task of providing a summation of the struggles of the Iranian Communist movement from its inception as a popular movement (Jazani 1979a, 17), and he records the process that led to the guerrilla movement. His *Thirty-Year Political History* (1979a) is not a researched work and is mainly based on oral history and collective memory. As such, it is riveted by errors, omissions, or prejudices that need to be pointed out (Chaqueri 2000, 43–45; Vahabzadeh 2005). Having lived through the post-1953 period, he assigns himself the unenviable task of completing the unfinished project of Iranian sociopolitical development. At first glance, Jazani's theory seems to consist of responses to unilinear historical events between the 1953 coup and the 1971 institution of the PFG. However, a meticulous reading reveals a theoretical engagement with the issue of sociopolitical development in countries like Iran.

Therefore I should offer a comprehensive account of how Jazani's theory is organized around certain historical-conceptual themes. To stay with his dialectical framework, I will thematize his work around the 1953 coup, the historic failure of the Tudeh Party, his class analysis, his theory of dictatorship, the role of the intellectuals in the liberation war, his conception of armed struggle, and finally his farsighted theory of the hegemonic front.

1. The 1953 Coup d'état

Jazani identifies the 1953 U.S.-engineered coup, which defeated the "anticolonial movement of [the] Iranian People" (Jazani and Group One 1976, 2) led by Mosaddeq, as the turning point in contemporary Iranian history. The Constitutional Revolution (1905–11) represents Iran's uprising against colonial powers Russia and Britain. Because of its bourgeois-democratic character (Jazani 1976c, 12; Jazani 1978, 27; Jazani 1976a, 7), the Constitutional Revolution had to unify the national forces (nationalist bourgeoisie, petit-bourgeoisie, peasants, and working class) against the colonial powers and their Iranian agents in the Royal Court (Jazani 1979b, 39). For Jazani this was the founding moment of the process that led to the armed movement. The anticolonial movement sought to open up the political process to the democratic participation of the masses. Evidently, in his analysis Jazani emulates a well-known Marxist approach to the French Revolution (1789) that marks it as the transition point to modern politics and industrial capitalism. Jazani applies this model without considering the contextual and historical differences between the two events. This application renders his analysis methodologically questionable, but it also reveals that for Jazani, as a Marxist, the Constitutional Revolution is the marker of Iran's entry into political modernity. Although this approach is not original, it allows him to situate his otherwise contingent advocacy of armed struggle within the Marxist canon of historical determinacy.

Jazani identifies several episodes of the rise and fall of the liberation movement by sketching out Iranian history in the fifty years prior to his time. Reza Shah's coup in 1925 brought a repressive regime that dictated laic modernization while denying citizens' input. The twelve years of relative political freedom between 1941 and 1953 allowed an unprecedented growth of the liberation movement. Given the Iranians' heightened nationalist sentiments, the coup both terminated the popular anticolonial front and crushed the hopes and morale of the nation. The wave of repression that followed was briefly challenged in 1961, only to resume after 1963 with an unprecedented wave of inertia (*rokud*) and indifference dominating the country (Jazani 1978, 7–8). Jazani formulates the cycles of the nationalist movement in three periods. First, between 1941 and 1953, the state was weak and mostly concerned with finding strong footholds among world powers and the domestic elite. Then, in the decade following the coup (1953–63), the regime proved to be extremely repressive, but it was slowed down by internal conflicts arising from competing doctrines of development. In the last period, after 1963, the regime reemerged as a mighty police state without serious internal conflicts. It became highly efficient in executing its top-down developmental projects and the required social and political changes (Jazani 1978, 12–13).

The years following the coup saw a reshaping of class composition. The nationalist bourgeoisie, Iran's leading force of liberation since the turn of the century, gradually but decisively disappeared from the political landscape. The coup blocked the growth of the nationalist bourgeoisie in favor of an aggressive "mercantile comprador bourgeoisie" that had lost its influence during the nationalization period. This dominant, parasitic bourgeoisie rapidly developed after 1954, and "the fertile ground that had been provided for the liberation movement was replaced by deterrent and repressive elements" (Jazani 1979a, 108). A similar analysis also runs through Zia Zarifi's works (Zia Zarifi 1995, 21; Zia Zarifi 1996a, 27; Zia Zarifi 1996b).

2. The Historic Failure of the Tudeh Party

Jazani recognizes the Tudeh Party of Iran as the working-class vanguard between 1941 and 1953 (Jazani 1976b, 30; Jazani 1978, 88), despite its docile dependence on Soviet foreign policy, its chronic inaction and hesitance at crucial moments, and its tendency to seek political significance by engaging in unprincipled favoritism. But he also states that the Tudeh must shoulder the blame for the defeat of the people's movement (Jazani and Group One 1976, 2). Although the Tudeh was never a revolutionary party (Jazani 1978, 88), it failed to mobilize its supporters against the coup, and its failure to recognize the necessity of resistance as its historical responsibility hindered Iran's sociopolitical development for at least two decades (Jazani 1976c, 46). This is a serious charge as it holds the Tudeh Party responsible for twenty years of suffocating repression and the tragic loss of some of Iran's brightest minds and dearest souls.

But what exactly caused such paralysis on the part of the Tudeh? We know the Tudeh emulated Soviet foreign policy and Soviet interests in its internal policies. An example is the Tudeh's advocacy of granting the Caspian oil concession to the USSR. Strangely, Jazani does not make the USSR-Tudeh connection explicit in his assessment of the Tudeh. Instead, he raises a subtle point in his explanation of the international context of guerrilla movement in Iran. He notes that after the Nineteenth Congress of the Soviet Union Communist Party, the USSR changed its formerly hostile view of the liberation movements led by "nationalist-bourgeoisie." The new foreign policy, in effect in 1945, was intended to forge new international alliances through the Soviet's support of nationalist movements (1976c, 191). One regretful aspect of this equilibrium, Jazani observes, is how the Soviets (unsuccessfully) pressured Mosaddeq to give them exclusive rights over the Caspian oil explorations (Jazani 1976c, 198). Obviously the new Soviet foreign policy was simply an expansionist effort in the Cold War context.

Despite its intentions, this policy reinforced Soviet relations with various Third World states (e.g., Nasser's Egypt, Assad's Syria, Kaddafi's Libya—interestingly all regimes created through a coup d'état) as well as with many liberation movements led by nationalist forces whose victory seemed imminent. Jazani reports how in Iran this policy ironically translated into the Soviet's friendly relations with the coup regime (Jazani 1979a, 109). The Soviet's honeymoon with the Shah started in the 1950s and quickly grew into a long-lasting relationship in the 1960s after the Soviet's approval of the Shah's land reform (Jazani 1976c, 57–58). In both periods, one witnesses how the Tudeh leadership either withdrew in inaction (after the coup) or made confused assessments (when it supported the land reform as "progressive"). Jazani, and other Fadai authors after him, assessed such Tudeh policies and positions as "opportunism." Fadaiyan's acclaimed policy not to side with such Socialist magnets as the USSR, China, or Albania must be understood in terms of negating this symptomatic trait of the Tudeh Party.

Jazani contends that given its extensive resources, organization, and vast membership, the Tudeh should have initiated armed struggle against the coup regime, and had it done so, the national liberation movement would have formed almost sixteen years before the PFG (Jazani 1978, 56). After 1953, the Iranian Communists were left in disarray and could not return to open political activism because of the dictatorship (Jazani and Group One 1976, 6). The establishment of SAVAK in 1957 enabled the systematic suppression of dissent. Jazani names nineteen major protests or strikes between 1953 and the early 1970s that were crushed by the police, resulting in thousands imprisoned and a dozen executed (Jazani and Group One 1976, 7–8). The Tudeh's failure left Iranian Communists with a permanent scar from these losses, leaving an attitude of unforgiving condemnation toward the Tudeh Party (see Zia Zarifi 1979).

3. The Land Reform

In the aftermath of the coup, the land reform and the events of 1960–63 represent a turning point for Jazani. The reforms provide him with irrefutable evidence about the increased dependency of the Iranian ruling class on imperialism. In tandem with economic restructuring, the 1963 repressive measures tightened the grip of a brutal dictatorship that prevented all legalist opposition, let alone dissent. The Iranian society, then, entered a new era of repressive development, with the alliance between the new ruling elite and a police state choking Iranian sociopolitical life.

Whether or not the land reform transformed Iranian socioeconomic structure becomes a question central to the theory of national liberation. Unlike many of his contemporaries, Jazani contends that the land reform represents a neocolonial push for industrialization as a precondition for Iran's peripheral participation in the capitalist world system. His comrade Zia Zarifi notes that the land reform follows the Kennedy-Fulbright doctrine in the early 1960s, called the "Obstacles of the Revolution" by the U.S. Department of Foreign Affairs. In the context of the Cold War, the purpose of the reforms was to prevent revolutionary changes in peripheral societies. This purpose indicates, in Zia Zarifi's terminology, "compradorism": the emergence of neocolonialism brokered by comprador bourgeoisie (Zia Zarifi 1996a, 27; Zia Zarifi 1996b). "When colonialism stepped into the dominated countries," writes Jazani, "feudalism was the established formation in the most advanced of the assailed [colonized] territories" (1976c, 89). The creation of a new class was not necessary, as colonial powers established economic and political links with the feudal class. Neocolonialism, on the contrary, involves a planned construction of a new capitalist elite in peripheral societies.

According to Jazani, the Shah's White Revolution transformed the dominant mode of production, or in Jazani's terminology, "economic formation" (*formasion-e eqtesadi*), from a "feudal-comprador" (called semifeudal-semicolonial by Maoists) mode into a "comprador capitalist" one. The colonial economy constitutes an "incomplete formation" (*formasion-e naqes*) that is the effect of direct or indirect colonization (Jazani 1978, 3). Comprador or dependent capitalism represents a necessary outcome of the evolution of the feudal-comprador system, which politically began with the Constitutional Revolution. Land reform eventually ended the power of the feudal class and gradually removed it from the ruling circles. I must note that aspects of Jazani's theory are reminiscent of dependency and world-system theories, but it is unknown whether he borrowed this model from theorists like Paul Baran, Andre Gunder Frank, or Immanuel Wallerstein.

The national bourgeoisie can also be theorized as a by-product of feudal-comprador formation. Growing rapidly between 1941 and 1953 at the expense of the comprador bourgeoisie, the national bourgeoisie lost its influence after the coup. The comprador bourgeoisie had sustained three major political defeats since the turn of the twentieth century (the Constitutional Revolution, the 1950s nationalist movement, and the 1960–63 protests). Economically, the comprador bourgeoisie absorbed sectors of the national bourgeoisie (Jazani 1979b, 25). With the land reform, the national bourgeoisie lost its last political stronghold and has only had a shadowy presence on the political map. Consequently, Iran became a comprador-bourgeois socioeconomic system (Jazani 1979b, 11).

For Jazani, the incomplete formation is no less conceptual than it is historical or economic. *As a theoretical construct, the incomplete character of such formations dictates direct political action toward their completion.* Since access to Western capitalism as a "complete formation" (*formasion-e kamel*) is largely denied to the developing (peripheral) societies, the only alternative route to complete formation in developing countries is socialism, which Jazani regards as an alternative complete formation. This analysis reflects his Marxist assumptions. The key point for Jazani is that an incomplete formation can *only* be overcome through political action: this is how Jazani creates the conceptual link between peripheral economic formation and revolutionary praxis.[1]

Jazani defines dependent capitalism or comprador bourgeoisie, and he uses the terms interchangeably (Fayazmanesh 1995), as "a 'class' that can only grow due to its dependency on imperialist monopolies. Therefore, as it grows, in order to accumulate capital, it pours . . . huge profits into the bags of foreign capital. This feature allows imperialists to replace old colonial relations with neocolonial relations without much trouble" (Jazani 1978, 6). He enumerates four characteristics for comprador or dependent capitalism in Iran. First, the "oligarchy of comprador bourgeoisie" has grown into the dominant class as the bureaucratic and mercantile bourgeoisies expanded into financial, industrial, and agricultural sectors (Jazani 1978, 6; for detail see Jazani 1976c, 100–46). Second, comprador capitalism is dependent "upon foreign monopolies which mainly operate through the establishment [*esteqrar*] of neocolonial relations between imperialistic monopolies and society" (Jazani 1978, 7). The result, Jazani observes, is that "our people, including the working class, are not simply confronted by 'the bourgeoisie' but by imperialism and comprador bourgeoisie" as well (1978, 8–9). Third, comprador capitalism involves capitalist production and industrialization of agricultural goods (Jazani 1976c, 100; Jazani 1978, 9). Despite the land reform, or because of it (without a social base and with its top-down approach), the "peasant problem" has remained unresolved in the state's hands (Jazani 1978, 10). The last characteristic of dependent capitalism concerns the disproportionate growth of the service sector and the creation of a sizable consumer (middle) class (Jazani 1976c, 100; Jazani 1979b, 24)—a class that, politically, opts for "bourgeois democracy" (Jazani 1978, 14–15; Jazani 1976c, 93, 135–40).

In addition to these four socioeconomic features of dependent capitalism, Jazani mentions dictatorship as its political feature, making the *necessary* link

---

1. On one occasion, Jazani refers to the two types of economic formation by using the terms "main formations" (*formasionha-ye asli*) such as feudalism, capitalism, and socialism, and "transitional formations" (*formasionha-ye dar hal-e gozar*) like feudal-comprador, comprador capitalism, nationalist democracy, and the people's democracy (Jazani 1976c, 63–64).

between the country's political and economic systems (Jazani 1976c, 100). But wherefrom does this necessary relationship arise? The weak position of the comprador bourgeoisie leads to inefficient production, which necessitates an interventionist (*rentier*) state as the representative of the comprador bourgeoisie. The state develops the country through state-planned and state-sponsored economic and developmental projects (Jazani 1979b, 61). Intensified repression after the reforms shows that *in a political closure* (when people are denied political participation), *the state becomes the sole agent of development.* At the apex of the pyramid stands the royal court and the bureaucratic bourgeoisie, followed by the higher caste (*kast*) of official and military bureaucrats (Jazani 1979b, 32).

The social aspects of the reforms such as women's suffrage rights did not affect the repressive nature of the regime (Jazani and Group One 1976, 8). As regards the relations between classes, the reforms resolved the internal (class) conflicts of the Iranian ruling elite by bringing feudalist lords under the power of the comprador bourgeoisie (Jazani 1979a, 113). On the other hand, the increased relative welfare of Iranians immediately following the reforms makes Jazani conclude that rural proletarians will join the revolutionary movement only as the latter reaches its culmination (Jazani 1978, 12). Jazani's hunch proved right, as peasants and workers trailed the urban poor, students, and intellectuals in the 1979 Revolution.

4. Class Analysis

As a Marxist-Leninist, Jazani seeks to locate the revolutionary potential of different strata according to their presumed class capacity. Nonetheless, he warns against the self-acclaimed Marxists in whose hands "Marxism has been reduced to useless verses," declaring, "Unfortunately . . . the misconstrued, subjectivist, and schoolish [*madreseh-i*] Marxism has become an instrument of confirmation of practice [*govahi dar amal*], instead of a guideline of practice [*rahnama-ye amal*]" (Jazani 1976c, 162). He avers,

> We are always inclined to 'copy' [*olgubardari*] former experiences [of others], while our victory depends on our knowledge about [our] specific conditions, and the necessary prerequisite for our success rests in the application of principles and foundations of M-L [Marxism-Leninism] and the experiences of other peoples' movements and revolutions to [our] specific conditions. (1979b, 6)

Evidently his "difference" with other Marxists must be found in the subtext of his polemical exchanges with various Marxists from the Tudeh to the Maoists. Countering those who dogmatically view political positions as predetermined by class, he points out the complexity of class analysis that does not allow determinism derived from the ownership of the means of production (or the lack thereof) (Jazani 1976c, 162). Notwithstanding, he ultimately yields to the essentialism of conferring on certain classes various degrees of revolutionary potential. The issue is the matter of imposed or inherited frameworks within which an original thinker like Jazani finds himself. We will explore the consequences of this theoretical aporia when Jazani reaches the limits of his class analysis, unable to surpass them, and he remains true to his generation's call.

Interestingly, class analysis does not make up the bulk of Jazani's theory. His writings on classes in Iran are subsumed under a political analysis of revolutionary strategy. It seems that *for Jazani political analysis has conceptual primacy over economic analysis,* as he does not derive politics from economics: the two realms, while interdependent, enjoy relative mutual autonomy. This nonderivative notion of politics allows Jazani to include culture and political heritage as intervening variables in "class analysis."

The working class, the middle class, and the petit-bourgeoisie are the three main social "forces of the people" that Jazani analyses. He asserts that in order to understand the working class, we must understand its "social and cultural state" in relation to other classes (1976c, 167). The "cultural" approach allows him to conceptually do away with demographic and "objectivist" approaches. He adds strata (*qeshrha*) to the standard Marxist definition of "class" as defined in terms of the ownership of the means of production and its role in the social organization of labor. He asks, "But is such knowledge sufficient to understand a social force? Certainly not. Immediately after engaging with the issue from an economic point of view, we should attend to the cultural and social state of the class" (1976c, 163). This passage exemplifies his unconventional approach. Once the demographic presence of the working class is ascertained (e.g., the land reform has transformed peasants into workers migrating to the city), the working class appears in terms of its political expression:

> Wherever the working class is mentioned, it refers to the political groups or
> organized economic moves that are connected with the working class and its

ideology, [and the groups] that are considered the political or economic representatives of this class. . . . Therefore, wherever the working class is referred to, . . . it means the *political and organized manifestations* of this class. (Jazani 1976c, 164; emphasis added)

We can interpret these lines as an attempt at "naturalizing" the relationship between the self-acclaimed working-class vanguards (such as Fadaiyan) and the demographic working class. This assumed representation of the class by the vanguard shows that the actual presence of the working class in the liberation movement is secondary to its political presence as shown through the vanguard's politics. At the same time, Jazani seems to posit that class is not "in itself" of political significance unless it exercises political presence.

Beside its political presence, the working class can be known through its cultural manifestation. The working-class culture does not simply emerge as a result of its material life. Culture cannot conveniently be derived from the class. The working-class culture is rather shaped through a long process of interaction "which is a combination of economic, social, and political processes," and it is formed "in relation to other classes and strata, by touching upon its own class position as opposed to other classes" (Jazani 1976c, 168). The conflictual character of the working-class culture has a subtle historical component that allows Jazani to theorize the absence of the actual working class in the liberation movement. He observes that the rapid industrialization with its resulting expansion of the working class weakened the latter's historical and cultural character. Because the emerging workers lose their contact with previous generations and their histories of struggle, they become susceptible to the popular culture propagated by the mass media (Jazani 1976c, 168). In other words, at times of massive development (Iran in the 1960s), the working-class culture changes (Jazani 1976c, 170) to the extent that it cannot accomplish its "historical [class] mission" (Jazani 1976c, 169). One outcome, especially relevant for us, is that *the working class historical mission falls on the shoulders of its vanguards.* Hence the necessity of the Fadai liberation movement.

In spite of the centrality of the working class in Jazani's theory, he expresses reservations about the appropriateness of the "working class" for revolutionary theory. The Iranian working class is politically dispersed and immature. "Given the particular features of the Iranian working class in the present conditions, we must replace the abstract concept [*mafhum-e mojarrad*] of the working class with a more concrete concept of urban toilers [*zahmatkeshan-e shahr*]; we emphasize that the working class is the most organized and skillful [*zobdeh*] class and force among this vast stratum of toilers" (Jazani nd-b, 15). So he expands the concept of "working class" to include the urban toilers and the poor.

Jazani regards the petit-bourgeoisie as the closest ally of the working class in the liberation movement. He identifies three strata of the petit-bourgeoisie whose "deprived" (*mahrum*) condition or lower stratum has the greatest revolutionary potential (1976c, 176). Yet, remaining true to the Marxist notion, he quickly points out the dual character of the petit-bourgeoisie (as both the owner of means of production and the seller of labor). This dual character indicates that "depending on which side it considers the danger to be arising, the petit-bourgeoisie leans toward the opposite side" (Jazani 1978, 16). From this we can infer that the political position of the petit-bourgeoisie is ultimately determined by the hegemonic formation of social forces. In addition, he notes strong sources of discontent within the petit-bourgeoisie as it is threatened by the growing dependent capitalism. This is why the petit-bourgeoisie inherits and embraces histories of political struggle as instituted by the withering nationalist bourgeoisie (Jazani 1978, 17). While he regards the petit-bourgeoisie as a major political force, Jazani underscores its "dual character." Among other things, this position was a warning against strategic unity with the radical Muslim Mojahedin, a position popular among the Fadai prisoners in the early 1970s.

Jazani differentiates the petit-bourgeoisie from the middle class. His distinction is conceptual because, first, it is not based on ascertainable relationship in the process of production, and second, its purpose is to situate these constructed categories in his analysis of the revolutionary forces. For him, the petit-bourgeoisie (*khordeh-burzhuazi*) consists of the traditional, commercial sectors, while the middle class (*tabaqeh-ye motevasset*) encompasses the bureaucratic or service sectors that expanded because of repressive development. He therefore acknowledges that the middle class generally benefits from bourgeois democracy, which suggests that it can be content with a "mild" repressive state. Surprisingly, Jazani does not interpret such contentment as detrimental to the movement. The middle class is actually inclined toward democratic change because it is only *indirectly* involved in production. That the middle class owes its existence to the developmental projects of the Shah does not necessarily translate into allegiance with the regime. He observes that the middle class may become the nucleus of the revolution under repressive development. Historically, the expanding educated strata, including Jazani and most dissidents of the time, were in fact the moral and intellectual force behind all secular social movements in modern Iran (Jazani 1976d, 21). In his view, the intellectuals comprise the force that will mobilize the masses:

> Presently, the middle society [class] and the deprived society [class] make up the main forces of the people, as in a consumer society, the people have allies in their struggle against the dependent capitalist system. The most revolutionary of these forces, or the real forces of a democratic revolution, are [to be sought] within the twenty-three millions of the masses. But in the current stage of our struggle in which fighting against the regime's dictatorship is the main feature of the liberation movement, *the middle society [class] reveals itself to be better prepared for the struggle. Our mission is to move from this stage of struggle to the people's democratic revolution.* The correct strategy and tactic should be able to reach out for the actual revolutionary forces through the potential forces of today. (Jazani 1976c, 139; emphasis added)

These lines capture the high hopes of a generation of secular intellectuals and activists in Iran.

5. Dictatorship

Jazani views dictatorship in connection with neocolonialism, which implies that dictatorship is a modern phenomenon distinct from premodern despotism. Dictatorship has a specific class character that links it to neocolonialism, as it facilitates the expansion of dependent capitalism through top-down developmental projects. As such, dictatorship signifies both continuity and rupture within Iranian history and culture.

> Familiarity with the history of the past two centuries—the two centuries whose events have influenced our present social conditions more than all the rest of our past—invites us to cut ourselves off from the autocratic apparatus that has been a heavy burden upon the shoulders of the Iranian nation in the emergence of colonialism, as it has been an obstinate obstacle in the path of progress of our

society, and as it has always been a steadfast ally of all the old and new coloniz-
ers. (Jazani nd-a, 7)

Iran's state, however, is not simply the repressive means of class domination;
it is above all a means of the Shah's autocratic dictatorship (Jazani 1976c, 140–41,
143). Dictatorship is central for Jazani, as he believed that the development of
social forces would be best possible under some form of democratic state. He
devotes his most rigorous work, *War Against the Shah's Dictatorship*, to dictatorship. This book also implies his future thoughts on democracy—the thoughts
silenced by his assassination in 1975.

Jazani begins his book by pointing out that prior to the land reform the economic formation of Iran was feudal-comprador (an incomplete formation). The
land reform dissolved this formation into a comprador capitalist one (also an
incomplete formation) to bring the Iranian economy on a par with the capitalist world system. Holding that all incomplete formations are the effects of colonialism, he identifies three such formations: colonial, feudal-comprador, and
comprador capitalist (Jazani 1978, 3). This identification implies that for him
the only complete formations are the two identified by classical Marxist theory:
advanced capitalism and socialism. In other words, *he posits analytical (Marxian) concepts as factual models* and thus measures all other models against these
concepts. Aside from this error, he claims that dependent capitalism represents
a necessary outcome of the "evolutionary" process of the feudal-comprador system, politically symbolized by the Constitutional Revolution, while the economic
transformation was delayed because of the defeat of the Constitutional Revolution and later the Mosaddeq government. The comprador bourgeoisie achieved
its (delayed) victory with the land reform. Jazani claims that feudalism in Iran
does not attest to a feudal-comprador system, and that enables him to identify the
stage of Iranian revolution as a democratic revolution (1978, 5). He borrows these
revolutionary "stages" from Lenin's bipartite theory of democratic and Socialist
stages of the revolution—the April and October revolutions in the Russian case
(Lenin 1935, 18–19; Lenin 1932, 27). Lenin viewed the "bourgeois" character of
the democratic revolution of "*enormous* interest for the proletariat" (Lenin 1935,
38; emphasis in original). While the democratic revolution hinges on the concept
of the "people" (to capture the majority of the masses), the Socialist revolution
has a strictly proletarian character.

Jazani defines the comprador bourgeois class as "a 'class' that considers its own life and growth in its dependency on the imperialist monopolies. Therefore, as it grows, in order to concentrate capital [in its hands], it pours . . . huge profits into the bags of foreign capital" (1978, 6). Therefore, the "people, including the working class, are not just confronted by 'the bourgeoisie' but by imperialism and comprador bourgeoisie" as well (Jazani 1978, 8–9). This means that under dependent capitalism the *basic conflict* (*tazadd-e asasi;* he uses the English word *basic* in his text) is not between labor and capital (a feature of classical, complete formations) but between the people, or *khalq,* which includes workers, peasants, petit-bourgeoisie, middle class, and nationalist bourgeoisie, and the enemies of the people, or *zedd-e khalq* (literally, the "counter-people"), including imperialism, comprador bourgeoisie, and the Pahlavi regime (Jazani 1978, 29; see also 161; Jazani 1976c, 159, 164). "Hence, our society does not fall within the stage of Socialist revolution, and the liberatory character of our revolution determines it to be at the stage of mass democratic revolution" (Jazani 1978, 9).

Jazani asks, "What elements account for the fact that in our system the ruling class cannot appeal to democracy, as is the case with the Western bourgeoisie, without encountering the potential of its own elimination?" (1978, 21) He observes that comprador capitalism owes its victory to dictatorship. Given the basic conflict between the people and its enemy as well as Jazani's distinction between classical and neocolonial capitalisms, he identifies dictatorship as the proper political constellation for dependent capitalism. Interestingly, the political constellation of the classical bourgeoisie is bourgeois (liberal) democracy (Jazani 1978, 19). Repression allows the comprador capitalist class to expand by denying political participation to the people (Jazani 1978, 20). This observation shows that Jazani believes in the relative autonomy of politics and in not subsuming politics under economy, and yet he finds that politics has the potential to affect the economic base. The Iranian society, he submits, has been experiencing a dual stress. One arises from the growth of the working and educated classes, while the other takes place in the detachment of peasants from the land. These stresses necessitate struggles for political participation, but demands for political rights impede top-down development. Thus dictatorship is intensified, so much so that expecting democratic openings from such a regime becomes an illusion (Jazani 1978, 23).

If neocolonialism is impossible without dictatorship, then liberation war against neocolonialism involves fighting against the Shah's dictatorship. The people's demands are essentially anti-dictatorship (Jazani 1978, 30), for they require a participatory model of sociopolitical development. Therefore, in considering the lessons of the liberation movements of his time, he rejects the idea of adopting the strategic slogan of the National Liberation Front of South Vietnam ("Death to American Imperialism and Its Leashed Dogs"). Instead, Jazani transforms it into "Death to the Shah's Dictatorship and His Imperialist Supporters" (1978, 30; Jazani 1976c, 145). In other words, *Jazani shifts from the common strategic slogan of national liberation that targets the foreign enemy, and instead, he adopts one that identifies the enemy within.* This strategy emphasizes the construction of a people's front around a non-class-specific nodal point. Jazani identifies the Fadai movement with this strategy and writes, *"In our opinion the existing movement* [of Fadaiyan] *which is part of the people's liberation movement, is distinguished by the strategic slogan of struggle against the Shah's dictatorship"* (1978, 30; emphasis in original). The proposed strategy will shape all economic demands that reinforce the anti-dictatorship political content (Jazani 1978, 31). As a nodal point that will gather popular forces in a hegemonic front, anti-dictatorship overdetermines other demands with its pivotal political demand. Only the politicization of demands can mobilize the masses toward a democratic revolution (Jazani 1978, 31).

Following a Leninist formula, Jazani understands the democratic revolution to entail a class character. Iran has been standing at the stage of "bourgeois-democratic revolution" since the Constitutional Revolution. This stage could be transformed into the "people's democratic revolution" through a proletarian triumph but that did not happen in Iran. "But does deciding the stage of revolution mean that the necessary conditions for the revolution are at hand? Or, can one claim that in this [recent] era the basic conflict was at the same time the main conflict? We think the answers to both questions are negative" (Jazani 1978, 31). These words refute Ahmadzadeh's point that the "objective conditions" for the revolution are ripe (see chapter 4). But note the nuanced distinction between the basic conflict (between capital and labor) and the main conflict (between imperialism and the people). According to Jazani, only complete formations can produce the melding of the basic and the main conflicts. The struggle against the Shah's dictatorship is a liberation struggle that has a "democratic essence" (*mahiyat-e demkratik*) (Jazani 1978, 32). This means that "there is no reason that struggle against dictatorship should definitely and directly lead to the abolishment of the entire system," Jazani observes. "There is a possibility that in order to preserve itself, the system might make changes in the forms of maintaining its domination, in which case the forces that have imposed these new forms will also continue evolving under the new conditions" (1978, 33). His insight is astounding. The war against dictatorship cannot be deduced solely from the main conflict between people and imperialism; nor can it be assumed that armed struggle will necessarily lead to the collapse of the regime. As Jazani perceives it, armed struggle aims to *institute* social and political opening (1978, 71). And this is yet another point of Jazani's divergence from Ahmadzadeh's theory, one that necessitates a theory of the front, based on a unique political ontology that understands social movements as attempts at social and political reinstitution.

6. The Intellectuals

Jazani does not conceptually reduce the intellectuals to the representatives of different classes: "An intellectual is defined as an individual with acquired education (a capital condensed in education) who works by mental activity and lives off that" (1976c, 181). Informed by his sociological training, not by Marxism, his definition treats the intellectuals as a "human capital" class. The relative autonomy of the intellectuals from class allows them to take positions on issues of sociopolitical development:

> Therefore, the economic definition of the intellectual is bound by the accumulation of education and mental work. The social or psychological definition of the intellectual includes only those professions that necessitate an active and progressive engagement with social issues. According to this definition, only those who directly participate in shaping up the thoughts of society, and whose life and profession make their engagement with culture inevitable, are considered intellectuals. (Jazani 1976c, 181)

The intellectuals, or *roshanfekran* (literally: bright-minded; or the enlightened), are sensitive to social issues because of their education. Thus the "intellectuals have always assumed principal roles in social and political transformations" (Jazani 1976c, 182). Arising from the intellectuals' alternative conceptions of development, the notion of social responsibility is key, because when the intellectuals consciously find themselves responsible for the future of society, they participate in the anti-dictatorship struggles.

Although the intellectuals may come from different class backgrounds, economically they belong to the petit-bourgeoisie. Jazani identifies such intellectuals as "university students, teachers . . . writers, artists, and sectors of the clergy" (Jazani 1976c, 181). The dual character of the petit-bourgeoisie affects the intellectuals as well. In light of this duality, Jazani warns, "in our movement, which is basically an intellectual movement, there are inherent contexts for the emergence of . . . deviations [*enherafat*]" (1978, 106). Yet why should the intellectuals exhibit the petit-bourgeois dual character without actually participating in the process of production? This shows the lack of clarity in Jazani's distinction between the middle class and the petit-bourgeoisie as regards the issue of intellectuals. Obviously his interest in the intellectuals stems from the fact that the militant movement was a movement by the then-emerging "human capital" class. They had their social roots in different urban or rural social classes and obviously held divergent political and cultural views but not dual class character.

The intellectuals are transformed into revolutionaries under imperialism by adopting the revolutionary ideology. Theoretically, the transformation takes place once the working-class ideology replaces the petit-bourgeois essence of the intellectuals. "A significant segment of intellectuals and a part of progressive elements and other petit-bourgeois strata have leaned toward the working-class ideology," Jazani writes. "In the absence of a united and revolutionary vanguard of the working class in our country, these tendencies [reveal themselves] in various groups with varying degrees of ideological purity" (1976c, 184). The degree of "ideological purity," we surmise, will depend on the degree of shaking off of the alleged petit-bourgeois duality. Articulating the experience of his generation, Jazani tries to present the revolutionary intellectuals as representatives of the working class. *The regime's denial of social and political development to the working class necessitates the representation of the working class by the virtually "free-standing" intellectual who can absorb working-class ideology.* A nuanced reading reveals the presumed position of the working class as the sole locus for disseminating national liberation politics. This Marxist essentialism poses a key conceptual problem for Jazani, as we will see shortly. Based on the celebrated messianic notion of the working class among his comrades (especially in prison), Jazani specifically points out that the intellectuals can "represent" but never "replace" the working class. His term, the "worker-stricken complex" (*oqdeh-ye kargarzadegi*), captures an intellectual symptom (which he calls petit-bourgeois) when the militants aspired to "become" workers by mimicking the masses' culture (Jazani nd-b, 16–17). Crucial for Jazani, in the end, is working-class politics as the emancipatory agent and not the working class as a demographic or cultural entity.

7. Armed Struggle

Jazani observes that in a short period following the land reform Iran went through increased industrial production that improved the standard of living, especially among the working and middle classes. He concludes that this situation contributed to the weakening of the national liberation movement (1976c, 87). He therefore attributes the political inertia of the 1960s to Iran's rapid economic growth. But as the reforms began to stagnate, dissent found an expanding niche among the new sectors of society, and that explains the intensification of the regime's repression. "As the pressure of the regime increased, the movement that had failed to accomplish the sought-after objectives found a new path to end the regime's absolute power, and it embarked on a liberation movement to resolve the conflict" (Jazani 1976c, 88). In offering a motivational analysis of armed struggle, Jazani's work resembles the J-curve theory, although it is not known whether he had studied the theory. J-curve theory proposes that rising expectations, resulting from a period of growth, come to a halt because of the feeling of frustration when socioeconomic growth reaches its point of saturation. The theory explains the subjective (expectation) and objective (economic stagnation after growth) conditions of revolution (Foss and Larkin 1986, 10–13; Davies 1962).

By the late 1960s, the regime's counterrevolutionary violence is met by revolutionary violence (Jazani 1978, 35). "Revolutionary violence" (*qahr-e enqelabi*) is a mode of political articulation that defines the boundary between the people and its enemies by neutralizing the regime's repression while exposing the state's violent nature (Jazani 1978, 67). Initially, guerrilla "operations basically have an awareness-building essence" (Jazani 1978, 36), and to this end, the vanguard becomes the catalyst in bringing about the conditions of the revolution. *Launching armed struggle does not mean that the objective and subjective conditions of revolution are ripe* (Jazani 1976d, 18). Given that the regime applies different kinds of pressure on different classes, one cannot justify armed struggle based on the regime's violence, because the Shah's dictatorship indicates the nature of social and political development in Iran (Jazani 1978, 38). This analysis reveals two important points for our study: first, it reports *Jazani's inclination toward democratic development despite his theory,* and second, it speaks of a *faint tendency toward a decentered view of politics.*

So, contrary to the regime's deterrent violence, the violent (*qahramiz*) preparation for the revolution offers the possibility of action as it musters and mobilizes the masses toward an increased opening of political life whose symbolic point of culmination is the revolution. Iran's revolutionary movement goes through three strategic stages: in the first, armed struggle is stabilized; in the second, popular moral and material support is won; and in the third, armed struggle is popularized or "massified" (*tudehi kardan*) (Jazani 1978, 16). Jazani clearly argues that in the first or even the second stage, the people will not join the vanguard (1978, 36–37). Armed struggle is *not* the people's revolutionary war of liberation (Jazani 1978, 68), and its task is not to overthrow the state (Jazani 1976d, 21). As such, *armed struggle is only the beginning of a long process of building a social movement.* He uses the term "armed revolutionary movement" to denote the initial stages of the liberation movement when the vanguard is supported only by those who have already opposed the Shah's autocratic rule (Jazani 1976c, 157). "Overcoming the masses' doubts, suspicions, and disbelief is the heavy burden placed on the shoulders of the armed movement" (Jazani 1978, 11).

Yet even with the centrality of armed struggle, Jazani contends that the vanguard should also utilize peaceful tactics. The guerrillas' military organization and operations must be conjoined with political and labor activities, a method for the vanguard to organize the masses politically (Jazani 1978, 40–41). The liberation movement must therefore have a political movement or wing (*jenah-e siasi*) that functions as the "second leg" (*pa-ye dovvom*) of armed movement (Jazani 1978, 41–42). These ideas are clearly aimed at Ahmadzadeh's followers who regarded any action other than political-military as futile (Jazani 1976b, 20). The guerrillas cannot offer the people a passage to a "Promised Land." Instead, they must provide practical solutions for actual problems if they wish to mobilize the masses (Jazani 1978, 81). So he conceives of an organizational structure of the guerrillas that transmits the struggle (1) from political-military cells, (2) to political-trade (*siasi-senfi*) protest networks led by nonmilitant Fadaiyan, and

(3) to the relatively autonomous support groups that he calls "behind-the-front-line committees" such as publication cells or networks that potentially provide new recruits (Jazani 1978, 18, 22–26).

A subtle point can be found in Jazani's concept of armed struggle: if by virtue of its presence armed struggle politicizes the society, and given the distinction between military and political struggles, then armed struggle is not simply the application of militant methods as opposed to political action. Rather, *armed struggle shows politics as it originates and disseminates through society under repressive development.* This is the moment of defining political boundaries, because insofar as all effective power is concentrated in one single locus (the Shah), there can be no politics. Where there is absolute power, genuine politics as the art of persuasion becomes impossible, the society is atomized, and its atomization binds individuals vertically to the autocratic rule. Under these conditions, political participation is reduced to submission to top-down technocratic programs. Armed struggle is an attempt at inverting this situation by detaching the demands of the people from the programs of the state. *Armed struggle creates an alternative source of power that challenges the center, and by so doing it reintroduces politics into social life.* Jazani's distinction between the militant path and the political path should therefore *not* be regarded as the division between two equals. Rather, militancy allows politics to arise out of its hideout in social discontent and expand socially.

Once this first and crucial step is taken, political and economic tactics will provide what armed struggle cannot supply: organization of the people. In turn, armed struggle provides what political and economic tactics cannot offer under a repressive regime: articulation of the demands of the people. The dialectical relations between the two hinge on one of the most original, and misunderstood, aspects of Jazani's theory: *"armed propaganda" (tabligh-e mosallahaneh).* In Jazani's words, "Although these [guerrilla] groups are extremely small in comparison to the forces of the regime, their militancy and immortality [*fananapaziri*] in the face of the great power of the regime puts an end to the one-sided and absolutist reality of the regime" (1978, 43). What is more, "in adamantly defending the ideals and rights of the people, 'the guerrilla' has been able to overcome the people's . . . distrust and pessimism regarding the political situation" (Jazani 1976a, 58). The revolutionary vanguard shatters the image of an impervious and unassailable state by virtue of its very presence.

Jazani borrows the term "armed propaganda" from Latin American revolutionary literature by drawing the similarities between Iran and Latin America (1976c, 92). In *Revolution in the Revolution?*, Régis Debray, following the Cuban experience, defines armed propaganda as the presence of the guerrillas in the region after an armed operation, which involves lecturing the locals and distributing revolutionary literature (1967, 47). However, Jazani transforms the term into a concept: by taking armed propaganda quite literally, *he perceives armed struggle to be a component of armed propaganda, not vice versa.* In this way, he marks two differences between his theory and that of Debray. First, according to Jazani, armed struggle does *not* intend to overthrow the state, but merely prepares the nucleus necessary to build the people's liberation front, and second, guerrilla warfare cannot transform into the people's war. These positions go against Debray's theory. For Jazani, there are only two conditions under which we can take propaganda away from armed struggle: first, if we believe that we can overthrow the regime through military action; and second, if we believe that we can decimate the military forces and economic foundations of the regime. He categorically refutes both assumptions (Jazani 1978, 44). For Jazani, armed operations can only have political and symbolic significance (1978, 47).

If armed propaganda is central to armed struggle, and if, thereby, armed operations do not contribute to the overall strategy of armed struggle unless each and every operation has a clear propaganda character, then *every operation of the guerrillas must have a metonymic signification.* Missing this point will amount to making great sacrifices for little gain. Jazani therefore warns that "without attending to the concept of armed struggle at this stage, many military moves, sacrifices, and damages that are inflicted upon the vanguard will be in vain" (1978, 44).

The English word *violence* does not capture the connotations of the Persian *qahr:* confrontation, avoidance, negative sanction, and violence. The concept of *qahr* for Jazani, therefore, implies the antagonistic imposition of the repressed demands of the people on the regime—demands that cannot be openly articulated in a police state and in the absence of mutual political relations between the people and the state. Guerrilla operations, therefore, perpetuate the presence of the specific *form* of political action that always signifies the *content* of national liberation. An armed operation bereft of armed propaganda will fall into "blind terrorism," a tendency he sharply condemns.[2] *Terrorism does not involve the mobilization of the people in a social movement,* and it is as repressive as state terror. The elimination of those who commit crimes against the people (such as Farsiu) indicates that the regime is vulnerable despite its gestures to the contrary (Jazani 1978, 36, 45–46). This is a difficult position to choose, considering that at the time when Jazani formulated this idea, the OIPFG under Ashraf's leadership was waging a series of assassinations based on their propaganda effects (chapter 2). Whether Jazani endorsed this course of action is unknown, but we can observe that his luminous idea of the symbolic character of praxis has no strategic or theoretical safeguards against using armed propaganda to justify terror.

Where political organization is banned and the intellectuals are cut off from the masses, "instead of educating the individual worker (*kar-e tozihi-e fardi ba kargar*), through military operations, educational activities, and the public propaganda that accompany such operations, the guerrilla calls upon the masses and above all the working class to protest against the regime and demand their rights" (Jazani 1976b, 18). He is concerned about the repeated repression of spontaneous protests that often occurred in spite of the regime's mighty grip. For him, the realization of liberation depends on the contingent relationship (relations of externality) between the rationally and scientifically planned strategy of the (Marxist-Leninist) vanguard and the masses' spontaneous uprising (Jazani 1976d, 13). Spontaneity longs for consciousness (*agahi*) (Jazani 1976d, 14), and armed struggle will "awaken the revolutionary energy of the masses" (Jazani and Group One 1976, 43). The "educative" practice of armed struggle, as consciousness-raising, tends to contain contingency: it guarantees the presence of the vanguard, should the spontaneous protests of the people turn into mass uprising. As fighting between the two sides intensifies (as in 1974–75 when the OIPFG maintained the upper hand against Iranian security), the regime unmasks its brutal nature. In this "educative" process, the guerrillas become a part of the people's tacit, commonsense knowledge, and soon, Jazani hopes, the people will learn how to respond to the repressive state (1978, 78). The symbolic character of armed struggle transforms

2. In Persian the word terror means assassination. Jazani accepts assassination of important figures of the regime as a part of armed struggle with great propaganda effects, but he condemns the "blind terrorism" of Fadaiyan-e Islam based on the verdicts of Islam to kill (Jazani 1979a, 64).

the military defeats of guerrilla operations (e.g., Siahkal) into victory (Jazani 1978, 47–48). Militants become legends endowed with superhuman capacities, as armed struggle produces "historic individuals" (Jazani 1978, 55–57). "Military strikes constantly attack different targets. The selection of these targets is based on a scientific knowledge of the people's enemy," writes Jazani. "These assaults are a specific *language* that the [armed] movement utilizes to give awareness to the masses, but to [do so] it does not stop at this 'language'" (1978, 35). Once people begin to understand this language, they learn about the extent of repression.

But how does armed propaganda connect to the mobilization and massification (*tudeh-i shodan*) of armed struggle? Through the polarization of society. I have already mentioned how the perseverance of the guerrillas removes the people's political pessimism and connects the armed movement to the masses (Jazani 1976a, 58). The vanguard's defiant presence has a polarizing effect as well. "We can see that . . . the conflict is about the regime's exercise of power and the vanguard's exercise of power and not the elimination of the enemy forces on the battlefields" (Jazani 1978, 46). Guerrilla warfare brings the construction of a contending, shadowy authority exercised in elusive, liberated zones. "The result of this chain of operations is the establishment of some kind of revolutionary control [*hakemyyat*] under the control of enemy and within its field of operation," Jazani contends. "This dual authority [*hakemyyat*] is materialized in such conditions when urban guerrillas reach the apogee of their power and the city is filled with waves of people's protests. This is a prelude to the massification of armed struggle" (1978, 85). The popularization of armed struggle begins with the solidification of the political binary, the "dual authority," in society.

From a Marxist standpoint, Jazani's assertion that the objective conditions of the revolution did not exist in Iran is indeed controversial. Launching revolutionary struggle would amount to adventurism without the presence of the objective conditions. Yet this is precisely Jazani's thesis. In a rather unorthodox way, he changes his earlier view and declares that superstructural elements are key in determining political strategies, and he rejects the claim that Marxists derive politics from economic structure (Jazani 1978, 55). The existence of the objective conditions of the revolution is not a prerequisite for the revolutionary praxis; however, certain conditions are necessary. In an observation that attests to the generational experience of Jazani and his comrades, he identifies three "minimal conditions" (*sharayet-e hadde aqal*): first, the people's discontent with existing conditions;

second, brutal dictatorship; and finally, the existence of young, militant forces (Jazani 1978, 65–66). His conception of armed propaganda suggests a tendency toward "building politics" instead of merely taking positions with respect to economic or social demands. Politics, for him, is therefore proactive and initiative, not reactive and responsive (see Jazani 1978, 76), a conception of politics that goes back to his view of the intellectuals. "The revolutionaries play a great role in completing and catalyzing [*jahesh dadan*] the objective conditions of revolution," writes Zia Zarifi. "The objective conditions of revolution are not separated from the conscious revolutionaries by a Great Wall of China, in the sense that the latter should wait until the former become ripe all by themselves" (1996c, 30).

Jazani was aware of the criticisms aimed at his theory by pro-Ahmadzadeh Fadai prisoners regarding his position on the objective conditions of the revolution (see chapter 4), but he also foresaw another major criticism: that in the absence of the objective conditions and without the presence of an established working-class party, launching armed struggle will further isolate the intellectuals. This position was held by the Tudeh Party and later by the 1977 splinter group, the Monsha'ebin. The Tudeh dismissed armed struggle as a juvenile and adventurist reaction against dictatorship (Javan 1972). Jazani stated that the lack of a working-class party should not impede political action; on the contrary, the workers' party would only emerge out of the process of revolutionary struggle (Jazani 1978, 58–59). "Let us ignore the obvious error of seeking the basis for our choice of peaceful or militant (*qahramiz*) paths in the existence or lack of democracy. The lack of democracy is not by itself determinant of the militant path" (Jazani and Group One 1976, 35). He argues that the tactic of armed struggle may be necessary in certain periods but not in others. In other words, Fadaiyan's inceptive use of armed struggle should not be interpreted as a dogmatic commitment to it. Armed struggle is not an arbitrary choice of tactic; it is rather based on existing conditions. For Jazani, these conditions are not the same as Ahmadzadeh's objective conditions of the revolution (Jazani and Group One 1976, 35), but he does not locate these conditions. His position on the issue, eccentric as it appears for a self-declared Marxist, allows him to offer a theory of the hegemonic front (discussed below), and it exemplifies his refusal to view his surrounding reality merely through ideological screens.

This refusal deserves closer attention, for the stakes are high. Risking the collective recognition of his comrades (which led to his isolation in prison for some time), Jazani nevertheless commits himself to a commendable demonstration of integrity. He repeatedly warns against revolutionary recipes and schoolish (madreseh-i) Marxism (Jazani 1976c, 60, 162–63, 199). He indicates the international conditions that have made armed struggle possible instead of tracing the revolutionary movement to the objective conditions. Jazani writes, "In addition to the experiences that [our] movement had acquired in past periods, the international experiences have also influenced the form of struggle at this historical point in time" (1978, 59). These international conditions signify a new historical period, just as the October Revolution had great impact on Iranian social movements of the time (Jazani 1978, 59). Likewise, the (failed) guerrilla attempts between 1963 and 1970 were inspired by the Chinese and Cuban revolutions. The international conditions offer new strategies for liberation movements, and one can cautiously borrow from them and apply their methods in one's own country.

In the end, Jazani's work remains vague regarding the perceived process of popularization of armed struggle because he assumes repression will push the masses, guided by the guerrillas, toward revolution. That proved to be simply an assumption.

8. The Hegemonic Front

As discussed, the vanguard's praxis is potentially a reinstitution of politics: the "militant method" will give "hope and a sanctuary (panahgahi)" to the masses. Because only the militants can create the working-class party, they alone will decide the future leadership of the "the Iranian people's anticolonial and liberation movement in terms of class belonging and ideology" (Jazani and Group One 1976, 45–46). In a nutshell, the armed movement will lead the fight against dictatorship and neocolonialism, and will move toward the consolidation of the people's forces in a united front (Jazani 1976d, 24). But just how different forces converge under the banner of this front and how they resolve the question of leadership reveal one of Jazani's most fruitful theoretical postulates.

Here a quick recap seems necessary: Jazani insists that neocolonial domination (incomplete formation) will end with a people's democracy as the preparatory stage for socialism (a complete formation). If the liberation movement cannot achieve a people's democracy (also an incomplete formation, borrowed from Mao), then Iran will be left under dependent capitalism (Jazani 1976c, 92).

But the social and political forces capable of ending neocolonial domination were themselves largely in disarray because of eighteen years of repression (from 1953 to 1971). Thus the first step toward the formation of a national liberation front is the unification of each class in society. At this junction, Jazani's main concern is the political development of the working class.

The failure of the Tudeh Party bequeathed to the armed movement the task of rebuilding the legitimacy of the Left. Armed struggle is a tactic, a "preparatory stage" and "the most effective form of organizing progressive elements (*anasor*) that have adopted the working-class ideology" (Jazani 1976b, 36). Only *after* acting, *after* announcing their presence through their practice, can groups such as Fadaiyan win legitimacy from the masses to fight on their behalf (Jazani 1976b, 36). Armed struggle allows the PFG to emerge as the most dedicated and progressive force and to grow into the central dissident force. In just two years of guerrilla activity, Jazani observes in 1973, pessimism had subsided, intellectuals had joined the movement, and there had been a significant increase in the urban and workers' movements (1976b, 37–38).

Brutal dictatorship, though, has deprived the working class of proper political development, and political development requires liberal democracy. "The economic movement of the working class that appears as extensive union activism, as well as strikes and protests, has [always] needed the political condition of bourgeois democracy," Jazani argues. "Under the conditions that dominate our society, despite the growing development of the working class which indicates the growth of objective conditions, [the workers] sustain . . . this lack [of democratic conditions] as do urban toilers" (nd-b, 26–27). The simultaneous processes of economic-demographic development of the working class and its political underdevelopment resulted in a curious situation: in a society where genuine trade unions, federations of labor, cooperatives, and genuine political parties are banned, the task of advancing the interests of the working class falls to the armed vanguard. But such a mutant representation of the working class shows that *no one Marxist group can be the exclusive representative of that class.* In other words, class dispersion also causes the fragmentation of the militant Left. "Although these groups have differences in their understanding of Marxism-Leninism and their policies (*mashy*), together they take on the role of the working-class 'Vanguard' [he uses the English word]" (Jazani 1976b, 30). It should be noted that by the working-class vanguards he specifically refers to intellectuals as the representatives of the working class (Jazani 1976c, 171). The plurality of vanguards, a rather maverick and unorthodox idea in revolutionary Marxism, is an inescapable fact in Iran. The OPFG perceived itself in the role of the unifying force of the diverse Left. Note that while for Jazani the militant vanguards together represent the working class, they cannot function as the working-class party because they are disconnected from the workers' movements (Jazani 1976b, 41). This line of argument implies that *ideological convergence comes from praxis* (Jazani 1976b, 4–5). Already in 1967, he had argued that the conflicts within the international Communist movement (i.e., the Sino-Soviet conflict) should not impede the unification of the Iranian Left or "the appropriateness (*sehhat*) of the militant (*qahramiz*) method of [our] struggle" (Jazani and Group One 1976, 44). This argument shows the unifying effect of armed struggle (see Jazani 1978, 21). However genuine his idea of the unifying character of praxis, based on his observation of the Left's sectarianism, his optimism about a united Left faded away by 1973.

The *primacy of praxis* is arguably Jazani's most significant contribution to political theory, and it allows him to surpass the restrictive boundaries of Marxism-Leninism. He saw that the political development of the working class can only result from a certain mode of practice: armed struggle. *"For Communists, unity is never achieved in closed rooms or by signing unity charters. Communists achieve unity through revolutionary practice* [peratik] *in the streets and* [under the] *arcades and force the right-wing leaders in the movement to accept it"* (Jazani and Group One 1976, 3; emphasis in original). This is the "realistic" strategy and tactic. The unification of praxis only takes place through the right tactic, the "militant tactic" (*taktik-e qahramiz*) (Jazani and Group One 1976, 29). The dispersion of vanguards has not shown many Marxists that armed struggle is necessary (Jazani 1978, 14, 17, 21). "To achieve the revolutionary vanguard, the Marxist-Leninist groups that have adopted armed struggle (and the evident example is the PFG) . . . should try to guide other groups toward the revolutionary program through their practice" (Jazani 1978, 17, 14).[3] Jazani summons militant leftists

---

3. There is an ambivalence in this section of Jazani's writing: while he clearly views Fadaiyan as his own political heir (especially with Ashraf, his virtual pupil, being the uncontested leader of the group), these lines can be read not simply as a call on others to join forces with OIPFG, but also as Jazani's emphasis on the uncontested leadership of Fadaiyan over a prospective alliance of the Left.

to enter into an alliance (1976b, 3). The united working-class party will emerge only after a long process of struggle (Jazani 1976b, 40) through which militant Marxists must overcome their sectarianism by exercising "principled flexibility" (en'etaf-e osuli) (Jazani 1976b, 3).

The centrality of armed struggle, as unifying praxis, yields even more interesting outcomes in Jazani's thought: whoever resolves the problem of political action by engaging in armed struggle will also resolve the problem of leadership of the national liberation movement.

> But one must notice that the selection of this tactic [armed struggle] of the Iranian people's liberation movement is not merely a tactical issue as it bears several crucial strategic values; for, to select or not to select armed struggle depends, in a deep and organic way, on whether we stand in support of (dar jahat-e) the general strategy of the revolution or opposed to it. Choosing militant methods (shiveh-ye qahramiz) is connected to the fate of the revolutionary strategy of Iran. Therefore, to choose or not to choose this method at the same time determines whether we are revolutionary or counterrevolutionary. (Jazani and Group One 1976, 31; emphasis in original)

As it polarizes society into opposing camps, armed struggle will push groups to take a stand regarding the (fomenting) revolution. In Zia Zarifi's words, "any group that is able to instigate and carry on armed struggle today will assume the leadership of all national forces: even if this group is not Communist, it is likely it can attain the leadership of our movement" (Zia Zarifi 1996d, 27). The militant vanguard cannot postpone the formation of the front until after the consolidation of the working-class vanguards. To Jazani, Fadaiyan stood as the backbone of the united workers' movement (1976d, 16; Jazani 1976b, 4).

> At the present, the first steps have been taken toward the establishment of such a Front. But reaching such an evolved configuration of the unity of revolutionary forces necessitates the growth and evolution of the revolutionary movement. It is in the course of struggle that the real content of such a Front and its participating forces will be determined and the character of its leadership will be ascertained. The Iranian People's Liberation Front or any unity with such content will terminate the void of leadership in the society. (Jazani 1976a, 78)

The process of unification of the liberation forces, or the "general unity" (*vah-dat-e amm*), will begin with the unification of the working-class vanguards, or the "particular unity" (*vahdat-e khass*). The "particular unity," Jazani envisaged, will construct a hegemonic core for the future unification of all liberation forces, so long as the practice of armed struggle remains the vanguard's tactic (1976b, 5). Only when the dispersed vanguards are unified can they unify the people (Jazani 1978, 71; Jazani 1976d, 28).

What is more, the leadership of the liberation movement will determine its content. The particular constellation of the liberation front will depend upon the forces that initiate or engage in the front. That is why, according to Jazani, it is theoretically unwarranted to justify action based on (presumed) objective conditions of revolution (Ahmadzadeh's thesis) or to wait for the formation of the working-class party before undertaking action (the Tudeh's and Monsha'ebin's position). The conclusion is interesting: "It is the struggle against the people's enemy and [our] class enemy that determines the content and form of the unity of all progressive forces" (Jazani 1976b, 4). Stated differently, *the constellation and content of the liberation front remain contingent.* Here is how Jazani conceptualizes contingency:

> Presently, preliminary steps have been taken toward the formation of this front. But reaching a developed form of unity of the revolutionary forces necessitates the growth and evolution of the revolutionary movement. It is through struggle that the real content of this front and its formative forces are decided and the essence of its leadership becomes clear.
>
> The Iranian Peoples Liberation Front or any other alliance [*ettehad*] that has such content will remove [read: fill] the leadership vacuum in society. This front will unify the political and military struggles of the revolutionary forces and will employ all forces and resources toward the realization of the strategy of the movement.
>
> The realization of such a front is a crucial objective of the revolutionary movement. In organizing the people's forces and in utilizing all effective means, this front will play a decisive role. The front will be able to issue instructions [*dasturol'amal*] for all people. It will lead under its flag the most conservative individual efforts of a government employee as well as the most revolutionary struggles of a liberation army. (Jazani 1978, 78)

Such contingency assigns the vanguard an ever more difficult task of choosing the best strategic nodal point for an expansive liberation front. Fearful of sectarian slogans that would hurt the formation of his perceived front, he called on the OIPFG for "partnership and collaboration with all nationalist forces," asserting that "any group that struggles against the regime's dictatorship and imperialism should enjoy the support and partnership of the working-class revolutionary forces" (Jazani 1976c, 185). Jazani's proposed strategic slogan, "Down with the Shah's fascistic dictatorship and his imperialist supporters," must be understood as a nodal point for the liberation front (1976c, 145), as the immediate goal of the front is to remove the Shah's autocracy (Jazani and Group One 1976, 29).

While Jazani sporadically uses the term "hegemony" as synonymous with domination (Jazani 1976b, 10), for me "hegemony," à la Antonio Gramsci (1971), always involves the contingent process of articulation of a worldview irreducible to ideology. In this sense, I argue, *Jazani's postulate about the liberation front has an undeniably Gramscian character*, despite the fact that Jazani had not read Gramsci and was quite suspicious, if not ignorant, of Western, existentialist, or New Left Marxisms as evident by his wholesale renouncing of Trotskyism, Fanon, and Marcuse (Jazani 1978, 96).

In a 1973 essay, Jazani argues that because the PFG is the first group to initiate armed struggle, any militant activity inevitably resonates the presence of Fadaiyan. This means that the signifier "Fadai" becomes a metonymy of armed struggle, and "Fadai" no longer denotes an insurgent group. The presence of the PFG has given it the potential to become the "umbrella group" of the Left (Jazani 1976b, 7). So, Fadaiyan must assume the role of the hegemonic core:

> If yesterday none of these [i.e., armed, guerrilla] groups were prepared to accept any group as the pivot and the basis of unity, there is a vanguard (*pishro*) group today that has relatively attained the qualifications to assume leadership and can become the pivot of unity. This group is the People's Fadai Guerrillas. (Jazani 1976b, 5–6)

The OIPM is the other force in the people's front. The group's radical interpretation of Islam as reflected in their eclectic ideology grants it, theoretically speaking, a unifying role among the petit-bourgeoisie and middle class parallel to that of Fadaiyan among the working masses (Jazani 1976c, 183). However, Jazani vigorously refused to minimize the differences between the two groups. The Fadai prisoners' zeal for alliance with the OIPM had alarmed Jazani to the point that at the height of his isolation in prison, he wrote his most theoretically rigid and even dogmatic essay, *Islamic Marxism or Marxist Islam* (winter or spring 1973). Written for internal PFG distribution and not publicized until the mid-1980s, the essay renounces the Mojahedin's ideological eclecticism and provides a hint about Jazani's insistence on maintaining the boundary between secular and religious forces (Jazani nd-c).

Jazani labels the traditional petit-bourgeoisie led by the clerics as a "caste" (Jazani 1979a, 140; Jazani nd-c, 3). The Shi'i clerics advocate religion as an ideology without class content, but in the past they had allied themselves with the ruling classes. Thus they can emerge as a reactionary political force. Jazani assesses the role of Ayatollah Khomeini in 1963 as progressive partly because "the progressive political wings that had religious propensity supported Khomeini" (Jazani 1979a, 140). The Freedom Movement (Nehzat-e Azadi), the Muslim wing of the National Front, was a source of the Ayatollah's unprecedented popularity (Jazani 1976c, 83). As if making a prediction about 1979, Jazani emphasizes that the lack of an effective presence of the OIPFG in the spontaneous movements of the masses would indicate their failure to become the people's vanguard (1978, 104). Indeed, the OIPFG's failure to connect with the popular uprisings of 1978–79 allowed the clerics to fill the leadership vacuum and to have the secular forces reluctantly trail them.

One last look at the nodal point of the general unity: in the *Thesis* of his group (1967), Jazani pronounces the strategic slogan of the front as "toward republic and democracy" (*barqarari-ye jomhuri va demokrasi*) (Jazani and Group One 1976, 30). As a nodal point, the republic allows different people's forces to identify with the strategic goal of the liberation front. Zia Zarifi, too, finds the "republican motto" (*sho'ar-e jomhuri*) to be the unifying slogan for the widest range of the people's forces (Zia Zarifi 1996d, 27). Later in 1974, perhaps because of the success of Fadaiyan, Jazani declared "people's democracy" to be the objective of those engaging in armed struggle, because only a people's democracy could address the existing social and economic problems (Jazani 1978, 81). Overall, Jazani's remarks on the nature of democracy are scarce. However, one can already see the operative dilemma in his thought: even the centrality of Fadaiyan in the liberation front cannot guarantee the realization of the perceived revolutionary stage. *Between the national (bourgeois) democratic revolution and the people's democratic revolution there lies a fissure, one that cannot be totally traversed by the issue of leadership.* The element of contingency that I found in his theory of the front is also at work in his models of revolutionary stages. Thus politics for Jazani seems to be a *terra nullium:* a great lesson, indeed, in democratic politics.

In drafting out a theory of national liberation that would fit the Iranian conditions, Jazani encounters contingency. I will argue below that the element of contingency stems from two aporias in his theory: the theoretical aporia and the democratic aporia.

THE THEORETICAL APORIA

As we saw, by differentiating the basic conflict (capital vs. labor) from the main conflict (imperialism vs. the people), Jazani arrives at a Marxist analysis of incomplete economic formations and postulates armed struggle as the institutive, alternative political practice under repressive development. I argue that *this approach reveals a contingency that permeates the very theoretical juncture that is meant to prove the necessary relationship between armed struggle and economic formation.*

As a Marxist, Jazani uses a dialectical model but he also holds that there are as many conflicts as there are social phenomena. The key conflicts are the ones essential for societal development, which necessitate the analysis of the social forces behind these conflicts (Jazani 1976c, 1). "The basic conflicts are those that stem from the dominant mode of production [*nezam-e tolidi*], grow with it, and their resolution depends on a fundamental transformation of the existing mode of production" (Jazani 1979b, 7). In capitalism, then, the basic conflict is between the collective character of labor and the private ownership of means of production (property relations) (Jazani 1976c, 3), and as mentioned, it pertains only to complete formations (of metropolitan capitalism). In the peripheral capitalist societies (incomplete formations), the conflict transforms into the "main conflict," a concept that allows us to pose the question of social formation as defined by the mode of production (Jazani 1976c, 2).

The main conflict is a conflict that in a specific condition influences all other conflicts; in such conditions all other conflicts function through the channel of the main conflict. In certain situations, it is possible that the main conflict may not exactly be the basic or fundamental (*rishe-i*) conflict of the system, but undoubtedly the primary conflict or conflicts (and secondary conflicts . . .) will influence the [main] conflict and give it momentum and movement. (Jazani 1979b, 7)

In addition, "primary" (*asli*) conflicts define the current system (e.g., capitalism) while "secondary" (*far'i*) conflicts are residuals from former systems or by-products of an existing system (e.g., feudalism) (Jazani 1979b, 7). For the purpose of liberation strategy, "what is important is to distinguish the main conflict [*tazadd-e omdeh*] from, and understand its relationship with, the basic conflict [*tazadd-e asasi*] and other primary conflicts [*tazaddha-ye asli*] in society" (Jazani 1976c, 5).

It is the main conflict alone that has the capacity to shape social antagonisms. Using this framework, Jazani observes a shift in the main conflict resulting from the replacement of feudalism with the comprador bourgeoisie (Jazani 1976c, 50). The basic conflict under the feudal-comprador system was between the people (nationalist bourgeoisie, petit-bourgeoisie, the working class, and peasants) and the colonial camp (feudal class, comprador class, and imperialists). In Iran, though, the conflict between feudal class and comprador bourgeoisie became the main conflict (Jazani 1976c, 64–65), and neocolonialism gave rise to new conflicts within the ruling classes. The regime managed to use land reform to resolve the internal conflicts between landowners and capitalists and so redefined the main conflict as the clash between the people and their enemy, as epitomized by the 1963 wave of repression (Jazani 1976c, 66, 62). The reforms forced the feudal class to join the capitalists (Jazani 1976c, 69).

Here I would like to point out how, conceptually, dependency distorts and deforms socioeconomic structures as perceived by Marxism to the extent that Jazani must digress from the classical Marxist analysis, paradoxically, in order to apply it. Lenin, Mao, and Castro, the leaders of the three victorious revolutions staged in the name of socialism, all *rethought* Marxism in this respect. In my reading, Jazani's approach also entails this process of rethinking: that the basic conflict, which in theory leads to the abolition of capitalism, can only be resolved through the main conflict (Jazani 1976c, 153; Jazani 1978, 16). Stated precisely, *the main conflict is the nexus through which the basic conflict can be resolved in the neocolonial conditions of Iran.* The main conflict dictates the strategy of the liberation movement: "Given that it is led by a conscious actor [*onsor-e agah*], every revolution narrates the general characteristics of the strategy of the movement linked with it. Accordingly, so long as the socioeconomic conditions of a society have not changed, this general strategy does not change either" (Jazani 1979b, 5).

Rereading Jazani for the purpose of reappropriating his thought in our post-Communist era requires exposing the ultimate referentiality of his theory. The distinction between basic and main conflicts indicates Jazani's attempt at linking the particularity of the Iranian dependent capitalism to the assumed universality of the Marxian model of dialectical analysis. In and of itself, the concept of the main conflict represents an excellent example of working one's way through the pregiven Marxist categories. By adhering to the universal blueprint of the revolution, Jazani receives his theoretical warrant to arrive at the mode of analysis that matches his perception of Iranian reality. What is crucial is Jazani's attempting to leave his mark on the Marxist discourse of revolution.

Several assumptions maintain the link between the universal (basic conflict) and the particular (main conflict). The basic conflict provides the Marxist dialectical analysis with a badly needed revolutionary program. The basic conflict is traced back to Marx's theory of revolution as the working class fights out the contradiction between the relations of production and productive forces in the form of class antagonism. Revolutionaries attempted to apply Marx's universal framework to specific conditions that did not exactly meet Marx's analytical criteria. As such, revolutionary intellectuals ended up fighting out the antagonism *in the name of* the proletariat. Each triumphant twentieth-century Socialist revolution (Russia, China, and Cuba) was in fact a particular response to particular conditions, yet each revolution was carried out in the name of the Marxian universal framework. Lenin, Mao, and Castro (and Guevara) each founded the revolutionary "formula" anew based on their own initiatives and each traveled their own path and espoused their own practices in the name of a world-historical Revolution and in response to a mysterious ultimate referentiality called the basic conflict. "Indigenous" and particular, each revolution produced yet another self-acclaimed, universal blueprint immediately after its triumph.

The universality of the basic conflict functions as an ultimacy that holds together diverse revolutions under one umbrella of Marxist revolutionary paradigm. *This ultimate referentiality absorbs each particularity into its universal framework such that the particularity of each revolution does not pose a threat against the universal principles upon which the ultimacy rests.* Rather than undermining the universal, each particular revolution is now interpreted as an "application" of the universal emancipation of humanity. With this view, *concrete particularities* (which make Russian, Chinese, or Cuban revolutions unique) are camouflaged by *abstract universality* (the world-historical revolution). The universal subsumes the particulars under its mantle and the particular gives up its identity in order to attain the legitimacy of universal identity, as if one cannot be "Socialist" without the approval of Marxism. In the revolutionary twentieth century (rising in 1917 in Russia and falling with the Berlin Wall in 1989), there could only be one "authentic" revolution.

Understanding ultimate referentiality leads us to yet another observation. Recall the theoretical phantasm that the resolution of the main conflict in each peripheral capitalist society brings the basic conflict one step closer to the ultimate annihilation of the capitalist economy. If the struggles against repressive development in peripheral Iran have no necessary connections with the struggles against the capitalist system, then the main conflict is practically a construct of the actors who wish to link their particular struggle to a presumably world-historical revolutionary process. This suggests a conceptual gap between basic and main conflicts. In fact, the triumphant Asian and African wars of liberation showed that "resolving" the main conflict in peripheral societies had no effect on the resolution of the basic conflict of world capitalism.

Now we come across a constitutive ambiguity in Jazani: his theory lacks a sophisticated distinction between the terms "contradiction," "conflict," and "antagonism." He indiscriminately uses the Persian word *tazadd* (literally, "opposition") to refer to both basic and main conflicts. In this book, I translate *tazadd* as "conflict." Strictly speaking, the basic "conflict" between labor and capital refers to Marx's logical "contradiction" between the universal (productive forces) and the particular (relations of production). Marx himself trivialized the distinction between contradiction and conflict—that is, between, on the one hand, abstract historical forces, and on the other hand, the political conflicts of concrete social classes that *supposedly* embody the contradictions and fight them out. In Marxian theory, there is an uncrossability between contradiction and conflict, as one does not automatically lead to the other. For Jazani, the practical conflict over the reallocation of resources among different classes leads to the political demands of the liberation movements. To release ourselves from the vicious circle of abstract contradiction–concrete conflict, we need a new term, "antagonism." I define antagonism as the actor's practice of *articulation* of the conflict between "us" and "them" in the moment of hegemonic formation of a front. Antagonistic politics need *not* draw on abstract contradictions to justify existence. The concept of antagonism undoes ultimate referentiality and overcomes the aporetic relationship between contradiction and conflict (Vahabzadeh 2003).

In one singular passage, Jazani records his hunch about the ambiguity of the term *tazadd:* "this conflict [*tazadd* between labor and capital that embodies a contradiction] is transformed into antagonism [*antagonizm* in Persian] and influences other conflicts and necessitates new positionings [*jenahbandi*]" (1976c, 4). Although the term is used in a transient and ineffectual manner in Jazani's writings, "antagonism" seems to apply to a situation in which there is a confrontation (including the antagonism between the Shah and the Americans) (Jazani 1976c, 147). If, in reappropriating Jazani's thought, we extrapolate from his usage of the term "antagonism," we can postulate three meanings of *tazadd:* first, an abstract, *logical contradiction;* second, a *structural conflict* between groups or classes (which presumably correspond to the terms of contradiction); and finally, various *antagonisms at the political level* where the conflict is consciously acted out. In Jazani's theory, the capitalist *basic conflict* is an abstract contradiction (logical), from which the middle term, regional and neocolonial *main conflict* is deduced (social-structural), and of which the particularistic conflict (between the Shah and the people) is the *antagonistic* moment (political). This model would work just fine for a typical 1970s Third World Marxist. But I cannot accept the imposed, normative ultimacy of economy (contradiction) over the social (conflict) and the political (antagonism). The contradiction is only a phantasm, an assumption that cannot readily invoke action to which we do not need to adhere.

By removing this Marxist assumption from our gaze we arrive at a new view: *politics becomes the source of the social and they both stand as domains with relative autonomy from the economy.* As the field of antagonisms, the political becomes constitutive of the opposing social forces, insofar as each of these forces delineates itself from the other around competing hegemonies. Antagonism does not need to moor itself to any form of abstraction. As the field of articulatory practices and antagonisms between "us" and "them," the political shapes society according to its hegemonic terms.

As a Marxist, Jazani assumes the historical agency of the working class, whereas in fact the working class becomes an agent of change only by virtue of Jazani's intellectual articulation of the people's forces ("us") against the Shah ("them"). The working class has no ontological privilege and its centrality in Jazani's theory comes from his search for a unique identity that would keep Fadaiyan in continuity with the Socialist tradition. Likewise, armed struggle has no organic relationship with the forces of the people and it does not guarantee the leadership of the self-acclaimed working-class vanguard. *What armed struggle does is to conceptually resuscitate the political weight, legitimacy, and prestige of the new Iranian Left after the failure of the Tudeh Party. It is an act of redemption.*

While unable to see the operative ultimacies of the Marxist discourse, Jazani shows refreshing efforts in going beyond dully applied theories in order to give a conceptual voice to a new generation of Iranian leftists. So his theory was constantly halted by an otherwise avoidable aporia. *Aporia* refers to a nonpassage, a situation in which one can never know if one has passed over to the other side. The border in an aporia is incapable of setting apart the two domains (see Derrida 1993). Aporetic experiences force theory to seek a point of moorage that will safeguard it against uncrossability. In Jazani's case, the experience of aporia is located in the presumed subsumption of the main conflict under the basic conflict and the attribution of peripheral liberation movements to the world-historical proletarian revolution. Marxism greatly benefits from such aporia, because uncrossability paradoxically allows the Marxist paradigm to transmute the main conflict into a metaphor for the basic conflict.

My nonreferential and deconstructive reading of Jazani's theory for the purpose of reappropriating his thought has so far yielded a lesson: the *primacy of the political as the field of articulatory practices and antagonisms*. The primacy of the political necessitates repudiating all referential appeals to privileged actors (the working class), central structures (world capitalism), or pregiven domains (economy). The primacy of the political does not justify one's action based on some presumed normative history or abstract principles. The political signals the never-ending positionality of different groups that converge to hegemonize their worldviews over society. The question of hegemony conveys us to that of democracy because hegemony requires some degree of political openness, which is denied under repressive development. If we accept the primacy of the political, we find that the national liberation launched by Jazani and his comrades was not, despite their claim, about ending capitalism in Iran but about delivering Iran from repressive development and to democratic-participatory modernization. We should turn to this aporia now.

THE DEMOCRATIC APORIA

The theoretical aporia in Jazani's theory cannot be separated from the aporia that rules over his politics of national liberation—one that I call the *democratic aporia* as it pertains to the difficult nonpassage from liberatory practices to social development under democratic conditions. I conclude this chapter by attending to this fascinating aporia—one that is still decisive for democratic politics today.

Armed struggle is a response to repressive development, a proactive means of mass mobilization and repoliticization of society. Key to Jazani's theory is the postulate that the guerrilla movement guarantees the presence of the secular-Left intellectuals. But to what end does such presence need to be guaranteed? Armed struggle polarizes society, forcing citizens to take sides on the boundary between the people and the regime. Such a polarization does not necessarily lead to political opening (which, in my reading, is the objective of armed struggle). Instead it leads to belligerent divisions, as in El Salvador in the 1980s (Castañeda 1993, 96–104). For Jazani, armed struggle is to open politics through political mobilization. However, a closer reading of Jazani's theory indicates that armed struggle will lead to political closure if it fails to mobilize the people (as in El Salvador) or if it becomes a prisoner of its own strategy (the case of FARC in Columbia). Insofar as armed struggle emerges to open up politics to participation, it cannot take the boundary between the people and its enemies as predetermined because if it does, armed struggle is no longer *genuinely* the reinstitutionalization of politics. A situation in which political boundaries between "us" and "them" are fixed and known in advance—when we are caught in the vicious circle of guerrilla warfare and state repression—only defers the aporia. The aporia reveals its uncrossability when political boundaries shift owing to mass mobilization, in which case the opening of the political field constantly necessitates new boundaries. With an awareness of the aporia, we can radically rethink the relationship between armed struggle, the hegemonic front, and democracy in Jazani's theory.

The purpose of the militant presence of the people's vanguard is to fill the political vacuum at those occasional moments when the regime's exclusionary politics collapse because of internal crises. Note the distinction between the mobilizing effect of armed struggle and the masses' "spontaneous" movements. In all his writings, Jazani allots only one short essay to this issue. His concern obviously arises from the experience of 1960–63, when the absence of an able secular leadership allowed the clergy to seize leadership of the short-lived spontaneous uprising by default (Jazani nd-c, 30): the Second National Front was in disarray, the Freedom Movement was too small to exercise any influence, and the Left did not have an organization. The long-rooted link between Shi'i clerics and traditional classes aside, the leadership vacuum provided a space for the clerics to propagate their reactionary terms, as Ayatollah Khomeini renounced women's suffrage and land reform. Without secular-democratic leadership, the opportunity for political opening had been lost and Jazani did not wish this to happen again. Perforce, his concept of armed struggle involves a leadership initiative: *the presence of the secular-Left intellectuals enables the vanguard to become the leaders of spontaneous movements of the masses should they arise. The hegemonic front is where such initiative takes place.*

As an antagonistic political opening, the front becomes the field in which the intellectuals connect to the people. But, as we saw, if the leadership of the front is determined from the outset, instead of a hegemonic front there would be a bifurcated politics hinging on dual authority. Here is where Jazani and Zia Zarifi implicitly make a quantum leap into our post-Communist times and come close to the "nonessentialist" politics of today's post-Marxist Left. Jazani admits that the vanguard's leadership in the democratic revolution is not pregiven and that it has to be achieved politically (1976d, 27). On the indeterminacy of hegemonic leadership, Zia Zarifi asserts

> [t]hat the political organization of which class will attain the leadership of the movement will depend on *which political organization realizes the needs of society better and quicker* and steps up toward exercising a strategy compatible with the social and political conditions of the country and proves to other forces in the *national, democratic movement* its *actual leadership* in the process of revolutionary practice. (Zia Zarifi 1979, 33; my emphasis)

The first step in attaining leadership is to unify the Left, because only when it is strong and united can the Left invite others under its umbrella. Jazani's concepts of general and particular unifications should be understood in this context. The leadership of the liberation front is not predetermined because the content and form of the front are to be decided through specific articulations of the people's demands. "The unity of these [progressive] forces is realized in a liberation front. The content, form, and thus future direction of this front are not something that could be agreed on by the constitutive forces [of the front] today" (Jazani 1976b, 2). According to Jazani, because its leadership remains undecided in advance, the front may have the content of a bourgeois-democratic or a "new democratic" revolution (1976b, 2, 3). Any political force that receives support from the masses will establish the hegemonic core that allows the liberation movement to challenge the regime. Ultimately, the politics of the hegemonic front remains contested and no class position (the working class included) can play a central role. Nor can any group that constitutes the hegemonic core remain permanently dominant, as it receives its centrality from the hegemonic articulation of experiences that remain forever precarious. While armed struggle is a prerequisite for entry into the "leadership race," it is insufficient to guarantee the leadership of the militant Left. That is why Jazani always warned against an uncritical advocacy of the alliance between the OPFG and the OIPM simply based on the latter's militancy (Navidi 2008). As a caveat, though, it must be noted that Jazani's emphasis on polarization and the unifying effect of armed movement does in fact nullify his warning against Islamists. Perhaps that is why Fadaiyan neglected their secularism.

This line of argument enables us to remove the imposed Leninist framework that Jazani nominally adopted. Jazani does not deduce armed struggle from repression; rather, he intuitively views democratic rights ("bourgeois democratic" in his vocabulary) as essential for social and political development.[4] The difficulty

---

4. Jazani has reportedly spoken at his trial in defense of democratic rights and freedoms: "You consider a few students subversive to the government and endangering your security, while you know well that the one who has taken security and peace away from [our] nation is a regime that does not even allow [students] to have a club or a library in the university. Students are even deprived of [the right] of having their own associations" (quoted in Jazani 1999, 54). "In a country where all

for Jazani lies in formulating a democratic politics within the framework of the Leninist "two-tactic" model. Occasionally he adopts the American sociological view, that liberal democracy originates in the increased living standard of the working and middle classes in the West, as a motivational explanation for the weak class struggle in "bourgeois" democracies (Jazani 1978, 21–22). If it is the democratic revolution that provides the necessary conditions for proper social and political development of classes, then the Socialist revolution, whose precondition is working-class leadership, loses its necessity as a political program of the Left. In other words, the relationship between democratic and Socialist revolutions in the Leninist model is an aporetic one. This uncrossable gap is detectable even in Lenin's own formulation, however transiently (Lenin 1935, 37). If societies are structurally and historically destined to arrive at socialism, then the "natural" development of different classes in democratic conditions will sooner or later lead to socialism, negating the need for a revolution to achieve it. As such, the democratic revolution that liberates the nation from repressive development renders the Socialist revolution redundant. Lenin's theoretical acrobatics reduce the democratic revolution to the supplement of the Socialist revolution. Only by rendering democratic politics as its supplement, as something added on and thus inessential, can Socialist politics retain its centrality in the discourse of the Left. Just where the transference from democratic politics to Socialist politics takes place remains unconceptualizable. I call this the *democratic aporia.*

For Jazani, the threat of neocolonialism appears to be not simply a factual datum but a conceptual construct. He refers to "neocolonialism" to justify the imposition of socialism as a normative objective on democratic politics. To postulate a theory of national liberation, Jazani needed to construct neocolonialism. Therefore, *conceptually, neocolonialism is a by-product of the national liberation discourse, an outside threat* that justifies the Socialist revolutionary imaginary. Jazani failed to see the limit he imposed on his luminous theory of the hegemonic front, a theory of postliberal democracy that emphasizes praxis as the arch principle of entering into the political realm, a field of simultaneous antagonism and alliances. The hegemonic front remains the backbone of today's postcolonial,

---

the doors of democracy are shut and all the venues of freedom are closed down, weapons begin to speak" (quoted in Jazani 1999, 55).

post-Marxist Left, a Left that has gone beyond the limited national liberation politics and the discourse of neocolonialism, despite the ravaging global expansion of neoliberalism. This does not mean that the Left has entirely abandoned its anticapitalist thread today, when former Social Democrats have proved their political impoverishment by racing to become left-of-center Liberal Lites.

Various articulations of a hegemonic front allow us to radically rethink democracy by the expansive participation of the marginalized majority. The democratic front, then, represents an aggregate of different social movements with different agendas and demands, movements that rally together to oppose those forces that have reduced democratic participation to electoral majorities and restricted meaningful input to bureaucratic decisions made by the functionaries incapable of understanding the needs of the marginalized many, let alone addressing them. In the end, if we address the democratic aporia and acknowledge that the democratic revolution need not lead to the Socialist revolution, we transform national liberation into democratic politics. And I think Jazani would agree, as he believed that "[t]he truth is, it is only through practice [*peratik*] that our theories are corrected and completed" (Jazani 1978, 3). He did not live to see how the praxis of a new generation has corrected his theory.

1. Bizhan Jazani (1937–1975), social science graduate, long-time activist, Marxist theorist, cofounder of one of the founding groups of Fadaiyan, assassinated in prison. Photograph, Jazani nd-b.

2. Hassan Zia Zarifi (1939–1975), lawyer, long-time activist, cofounder of one of the founding groups of Fadaiyan, assassinated in prison. Photograph, Zia Zarifi 2004.

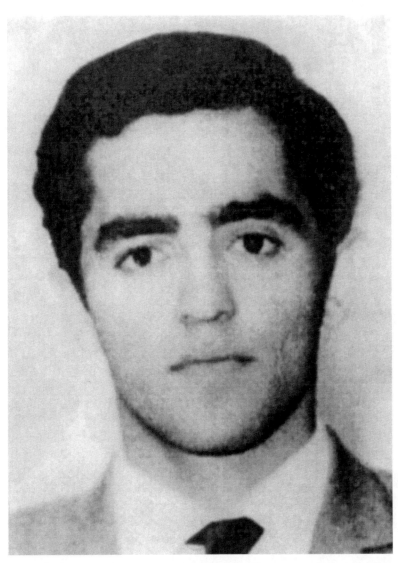

3. Massoud Ahmadzadeh Heravi (1947–1972), mathematics student, cofounder, leader, and theorist of Fadaiyan, executed. Photograph, Naderi 2008.

4. Amir Parviz Puyan (1947–1971), cultural figure, social science student, cofounder and theorist of Fadaiyan, killed in a shoot-out with the security forces. Photograph, Naderi 2008.

5. Hamid Ashraf (1946–1976), mechanical engineering student, cofounder of Fadaiyan and the leader of the OIPFG, killed in a shoot-out with the security forces. Photograph, Naderi 2008.

6. Mehrnoosh Ebrahimi (1946–1971), medical student, the first militant woman and the first Fadai woman to lose her life, killed in a shoot-out with the security forces. Photograph, Naderi 2008.

7. Marzieh Ahmadi Oskui (1945–1974), teacher, poet, writer, activist, member of the People's Democratic Front and later member of PFG, killed in a shoot-out with the security forces. Photograph, Naderi 2008.

8. Mostafa Sho'aiyan (1936–1975, on the left), metal engineer, long-time activist, maverick theorist, cofounder of the People's Democratic Front and a short-time member of PFG, killed by the police. Sho'aiyan stands next to Jalal Al Ahmad, prominent dissident and writer. Photograph, Chaqueri 2007.

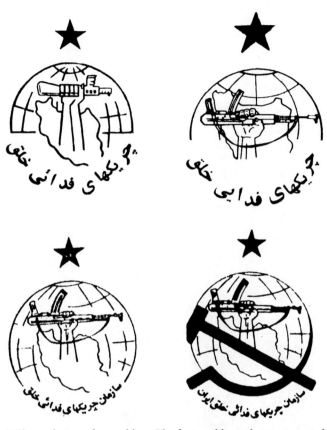

9. The evolution of an emblem: The four emblems that represented the OIPFG in its different stages during the 1970s reveal aspects of Fadaiyan's life. The first, rudimentary, emblem (upper left) probably emerged in 1972 and contains the caption "People's Fadai Guerrillas." It was designed by Faramarz Sharifi. Later, Kiomars Sanjari changed it into the mid-career, artistic emblem of Fadaiyan (upper right, then lower left), as Fadaiyan assumed the title "Organization of People's Fadai Guerrillas," indicating that, at this point, they considered themselves as a political party. Finally, the emblem by which Fadaiyan are best remembered (lower right) probably replaced its precedent around 1975. It is the last emblem before the schisms of the future. With the caption "Organization of Iranian People's Fadai Guerrillas," the hammer and sickle leave no doubt about the ideological position of the group.

4

Massoud Ahmadzadeh

Theorizing Armed Struggle

> Does this not mean that more than anything we need practitioners rather
> than theoreticians?
>
> —MASSOUD AHMADZADEH, *Mobarezeh-ye mosallahaneh:*
> *ham estratezhi, ham taktik* [Armed struggle: Both strategy
> and tactic]

THE FADAI GUERRILLAS emerged as heirs to Ahmadzadeh's theory of armed
struggle, although the new wave of guerrilla movement in Iran originated with
Jazani-Zarifi's Group One, whose loyal survivors launched the landmark "Siahkal
Resurrection." In 1967 the Iranian security forces heralded victory over subversive
groups, which they labeled as isolated, delusional, or agents of an international
conspiracy. What escaped the security forces was that Ahmadzadeh, Puyan, and
Meftahi had in the same year grouped in Tehran and were exploring ways to counter the debilitating effects of the Iranian "police state" (Puyan 1979, 4) on the intellectuals. In actuality, Ahmadzadeh led the largest underground militant network
of 1960s–70s Iran, with some fifty individuals recruited in 1969–70 alone. Above
all, he is the first theorist to bestow upon Fadaiyan a central political role.

What is particularly interesting about members of Group Two is that they
belonged to an entirely different generation of activists: half a generation younger
than Jazani and his comrades, they were children in 1953 and high school students
during the reform years of 1960–63. They had never fully experienced the quasi-
democratic conditions of the intermittent periods of crisis (1941–53) or restructuring (1960–63). Unlike Jazani and his comrades, Ahmadzadeh and his peers did not
learn Marxism in the school of the Tudeh Party. The founders of Group Two originally held religious beliefs before they discovered Marxism on their own and mainly

133

through the literature on the Cuban Revolution (Che Guevara and Debray) or by Brazilian (Carlos Marighella) and Uruguayan (the Tupamaros) urban guerrillas.

In addition, a few major figures of this new generation of leftist activists were cultural figures—writers, critics, educators, and artists. Puyan frequented cultural gatherings and was a critic who published under the pen name Ali Kabiri. Samad Behrangi was a well-known critic and educator who had written a book on critical pedagogy, authored several children's books, and gathered the folktales of Azerbaijan. Behrangi did not live to see the influence of his children's book *The Little Black Fish,* which became Fadaiyan's unofficial manifesto—a book that is believed to have attracted more militants to the Fadai movement than any of the PFG or Marxist texts. Behruz Dehqani and Ali Reza Nabdel were published writers. Belonging to a generation of creative resistance, these future Fadai members had little patience for theory, which they treated as a self-indulging apology for inaction. Mehdi Fatapour, a member of Group Two, captures the spirit of this generation when he describes it as "a force that recognized the Shah's regime as the cause of the backwardness of society, hated America, found the clergy dogmatic, ridiculed the National Front's Patience and Awaiting [Policy], regarded the Tudeh as a force out of action, and considered the students abroad to be so distant from the scene of struggle, it would not even approve of them" (2001b, 6).

While the writings of Group Two are small compared to those of Group One, they capture a generation's untamable spirit and must therefore be taken as a pathfinder's affirmation of élan vital over decay in inertia. To fully capture their works, I offer a reading of Puyan's pamphlet on the rejection of the "survival theory," followed by Ahmadzadeh's treatise on armed struggle—a book that instantly became the official theory of the PFG in its first three years. The theoretical popularity of Ahmadzadeh within Fadaiyan, however, was challenged by Jazani and his followers within the OPFG. The two conflicting views of armed struggle fissured into a schism in 1980. To analyze this conflict, I examine Jazani's criticism of Ahmadzadeh later in this chapter before attending to the internal debates within the OIPFG at the time of the split.

REPUDIATING THE SURVIVAL THEORY

Amir Parviz Puyan wrote *The Necessity of Armed Struggle and the Refutation of the Survival Theory* in the spring of 1970. As a CC member of Group Two, Puyan wrote the twenty-page pamphlet to assert the inevitability of armed struggle for social change in Iran. The text was first distributed internally as a summary of the discussions of the CC, and it harmonized the views of members about the struggle ahead. Soon the pamphlet reached beyond the group and was received by Group One, the People's Ideal, and other activists.

According to Puyan, the roots of the existing political impasse go back to the imposition of the systematic police state after the coup. The repressive conditions made political activism impossible. By removing the slightest democratic conditions, Iran's police state succeeded in isolating the intellectuals (Puyan 1979, 3), leaving them no other alternative except militancy. Echoing Behrangi's *The Little Black Fish*, Puyan writes, "We are not like fish [swimming] in the sea of people's support, but more like small and dispersed fish surrounded by alligators and seagulls" (1979, 4). His concern about the isolation of intellectuals reflects the preoccupation of his generation. Under these conditions, however, some dissidents believed that they must abandon actions that potentially endangered their very existence. Specifically, this was the position of the SAKA (see chapter 2). Puyan calls this position the "survival theory" and traces it to the Tudeh Party. The basic premise of the "survival theory" is that the vanguard cannot develop under dictatorship and can only expect to secretly maintain its rather quiet presence in society.

At first glance it appears that Puyan is making a caricature of the Tudeh, but at the time he was writing his pamphlet, the Tudeh Party was going through a difficult period of damage control after the exposure of the Shahriyari affair (see chapter 2). The Tudeh Party had no choice but to officially announce that it had no organization within the country and to encourage its followers to protect themselves in any way they could against police infiltration. For Puyan, these historical circumstances indicated the irremediable "opportunism" of the Tudeh (1979, 15). After expelling its Maoist wing in 1964, the Tudeh had abandoned its post-1953 strategy to overthrow the regime, once again aligning the Party policy with USSR foreign policy, and it now tried, rather pointlessly, to gain a legal party status in Iran (Dastan 1988, 57). It is in this historical context that urban guerrilla warfare emerged in the works of Puyan and Ahmadzadeh.

For Puyan, therefore, the survival theory means that "in order to survive, let us not assault," and he contends that this tactic only allows police to eliminate dissidents (1979, 14). He argues that followers of this theory (supporters of the Tudeh) eventually end up either joining the revolutionary movements or they are inadvertently forced to collaborate with police, a reference to the Shahriyari affair (1979, 18). The choice for the dissidents seems clear: "Therefore, 'in order to survive, let us not assault' should by necessity be replaced by 'in order to survive, we have to assail'" (Puyan 1979, 21). As such, Puyan puts an end to the dilemma of his generation by preparing his comrades psychologically for armed struggle. Only revolutionary practice (*peratik*) can resolve this dilemma and overcome the atmosphere of distrust and passivity (Puyan 1979, 19). Had the Tudeh truly been the working-class party, it would already be fighting for the emancipation of the working class. Revolutionary action is "to pave the way for the institution of the Communist party and achieving a revolutionary theory" (Puyan 1979, 15). Thus, *revolutionary theory is an outcome of revolutionary practice and not its forebear.*[1]

Revolutionary practice makes the alliance of the working-class vanguards possible (Puyan 1979, 12). If striking the regime makes the vanguards collectively survive the raids of security forces, then the unity of militant vanguards is key to the struggle. Therefore, various militant groups must now join forces for bare survival (*baqa*). This is a loose alliance: "Convergence, even joining together, does not exactly mean unification. The organizational unity of Marxist-Leninist elements (*anasor*) that creates the united organization (*sazman*) of the proletariat is only achieved in the conditions where the exercise of revolutionary force . . . has reached its apogee" (Puyan 1979, 12). Once the guerrillas launch their operations, the enemy will be forced to exercise even more brutality, which in turn will reveal the regime's oppressive nature to the workers (Puyan 1979, 13). Like Jazani, Puyan is hopeful that armed struggle will lead to mass mobilization when political organization is impossible. Therefore, as in theory, the united working-class party cannot precede the revolutionary struggle, because the party is an outcome of the struggle. This argument allows Puyan to neutralize the position,

---

1. In his defense of Ahmadzadeh's thesis, Hamid Momeni argues that the founders of Group Two rejected the primacy of theory over practice but found themselves responding to the theoretical demand of the revolution. Thus they delegated theory to the action of militants: only the praxis of guerrillas can eliminate the theoretical weakness of the Iranian Communist movement by solving, *practically,* the problem of the relationship between the vanguard and the masses (Momeni 1979, 16). The tautology of such an argument should be self-evident.

symptomatic of the survival theory, that the working-class party emerges at the "opportune moment." This "opportune moment," Puyan notes, is a metaphysical construct that will never arrive, and even if it does, we have no way of knowing its arrival (1979, 15–16).

What remains if we remove revolutionary theory and vanguard party as the preconditions for the revolution? The intellectual who will replace the Leninist preconditions. Puyan intuitively grants the intellectuals a vanguard position and thus overlooks the problem of the intellectuals representing the masses. For him, only the intellectuals are able to reverse the banal popular culture used as a means of domination by pacifying workers (Puyan 1979, 8–9). Only the intellectuals are able to rescue Iran's young and backward working class from the effects of cultural brainwashing. The Iranian working-class mentally "lives in the eighteenth century but has the privilege of enjoying the twentieth-century police rule" (Puyan 1979, 6). The intellectuals must sabotage, through armed struggle, the façade of the regime's absolute control in order to disengage the working class from the dominant culture (Puyan 1979, 9). Moreover, the "proletarian intellectuals" should nullify their isolation by engaging in revolutionary practice that allows them to establish an intellectual (or moral or spiritual; *ma'navi* in Persian) relationship with the working class. Over time, this relationship will lead to an organized relationship between intellectuals and the working class. Now the proletariat understands that

> the enemy is vulnerable and learns that the swift breeze that has just started leaves no room for the absolute domination of the enemy. If such "absolute" is threatened in practice, [the working class] can no longer live in [its existing] psyche. From this point onwards, [the proletariat] thinks about the force that has instigated emancipation. Alienation from its vanguards is now replaced by the support that [the working class] finds within itself. From now on, the vanguards are only distant from [the class]. But they are no longer alien to it. (Puyan 1979, 9)

Ironically, *Puyan does away with the two Leninist preconditions for the revolution, while speaking in the name of Leninism.* His pamphlet summarizes the spirit of a generation that sought all justifications to act in a time of inertia. The fast pace of his text represents the actors' lack of patience for building analytical or organizational foundations for their action. Yet in an existential way, this genera-tion understood that political practice cannot be decided in party plenums or platforms. Although this generation had not grown out of the Tudeh Party, once it identified with Marxism it found itself haunted by the Tudeh's original institu-tion of the Iranian Left. Unable to escape the ghost of the Tudeh while the Party was politically absent, Puyan had to hypostatize it through the "survival theory." To the zealous generation of the late 1960s, Puyan gave a reason to rise up, as Ahmadzadeh theorized their strategy and tactics.

A GENERATION'S SAGA

When he wrote *Armed Struggle: Both Strategy and Tactic; An Analysis of the Con-ditions of Iran* in the summer of 1970, Ahmadzadeh probably never expected it to become such a decisive text. The convoluted analytical structure of the text did not impede its warm reception by leftist militants. For the next three years, Ahmadzadeh, who was executed in the winter of 1972, would be the posthu-mous leading theorist of the PFG. *Armed Struggle* is the only published work by Ahmadzadeh, although he had written other works after this seminal text. After the Revolution his sister Mastureh, along with Mehdi Same', uncovered his monographs that had been hidden for years. Mastureh Ahmadzadeh reminisces about two interesting discussions in these monographs: the first was Ahmadza-deh's strong rejection of the Soviet Union, which he found to be "non-Socialist." The second point was on how guerrilla warfare would lead to the formation of the Party: Ahmadzadeh did not view guerrilla activity as a means of captur-ing political power; he argued instead that guerrilla operations would enable the militants to win over the people, and that would lead to the formation of the Party. According to Mastureh, Massoud's newer ideas were never discussed in the OIPFG. These monographs remain unpublished and their fate unknown (Ahmadzadeh 2001).

The spring of 1974 inaugurated a year of heightened guerrilla activities dur-ing which some of Jazani's writings were internally distributed among select Fadai cadres. Later that year these texts stirred an inconclusive debate over the existence or the lack of "the objective conditions of the revolution." Almost four years into armed struggle, critical positions about the viability of militant meth-ods were emerging. Consequently, in 1974 Ashraf ordered that the new reprint of

Armed Struggle not be distributed (Heydar 1999, 251–52), while the OPFG's theorist at the time, CC member Hamid Momeni (1979), had written a long prefatory defense of Ahmadzadeh, which was only published posthumously as a book. In his preface to the first printing of *Armed Struggle*, Abbas Jamshidi Rudbari states that before arriving at the necessity of armed struggle, Group Two had adopted the Chinese model of establishing the Party, which involved working among workers and peasants and engaging in militant action. But in their actual contacts with workers and peasants, their "objective review of experimenting with this [Chinese] approach showed its absolute futility" (in Ahmadzadeh 1976, x).

In accord with other Iranian revolutionaries of the 1960s, Ahmadzadeh traces the rise of the "new Iranian Communist movement" back to the 1953 coup and the failure of the Tudeh Party (1976, 19). He condemns the Tudeh for having defended the Shah's reforms, as the Tudeh believed that with the assistance of the Socialist camp the reforms would distance Iran from dependent capitalism, or to state it in Ahmadzadeh's sardonic tone, it would replace "the Shah's dictatorship with the Shah's democracy" (1976, 25–27). Ahmadzadeh insists that the land reform imposed setbacks on the traditional tie of imperialism to feudalism (1976, 33). Land reform eventually eradicated feudalism and then the nationalist bourgeoisie, reducing all conflicts in society to one "main conflict" (*tazzad-e asli*) between the people and imperialism. In order to implement an "artificial growth" (dependent, peripheral development) in the East, imperialist domination comes with an "organic relationship" with violence (Ahmadzadeh 1976, 43–44). Therefore, "any transformation must resolve this conflict and the resolution of the conflict equals the overthrowing of imperialist domination and founding the rule of the people" (Ahmadzadeh 1976, 45).

Ahmadzadeh reflects that the group he and his comrades founded intended mainly to study Marxism-Leninism and to analyze Iran's socioeconomic conditions. However, "as it grew, the group faced a dilemma: should we establish the proletarian party? Or [should we] start armed nuclei in the country and wage guerrilla warfare?" (1976, 24). As in Puyan's writings, Ahmadzadeh acknowledges that the dilemma was no less generational than it was theoretical. "[W]ithout having been truly convinced that to embark on guerrilla warfare would lead to defeat, not accepting it [guerrilla warfare] meant the lack of revolutionary audacity and fear of action," he recollects. "[O]ur theoretical approach to the present conditions, our evaluation of the claimed transformations of the system, the role of the reforms, etc., did not reject our choice; rather, they approved of it" (1976, 24–25). Once the group found it essential to institute a working-class party, it immediately found itself confronted by the twofold task of training party cadres and working among the masses. This latter task woke up the group to the fact that Iran was indeed different from the revolutionary blueprints of Russia and China, because in Iran no connections existed between the intellectuals themselves, let alone between the intellectuals and the masses.

> In fact, we expected a party that would soon be able to grow into the real vanguard of the masses. Since we also believed in the inevitability of armed struggle, the party should have prepared the conditions for armed struggle, convinced the masses that armed struggle was the only [viable] way, and then engaged in armed operations. (Ahmadzadeh 1976, 53)

The Leninist model called for a long process of organization by the Party—a model for which the zealous generation of Ahmadzadeh had no patience. Besides, in Lenin's time the struggle against dictatorship was basically political, whereas in Iran it is political-military (Ahmadzadeh 1976, 74). The Maoist model initially seemed more plausible because of its militancy. The experiences of China and Vietnam are the proof that armed struggle is the "highest form of struggle" as it would ignite "the historical energy of the masses" (Ahmadzadeh 1976, 77). Nevertheless, the group increasingly moved away from Maoism when it observed that the Maoist ROTPI totally rejected the transformation wrought by the land reform (chapter 1). The ROTPI's position was contrary to the group's analysis that the reforms had prepared the Iranian economy for entering into the capitalist periphery. Consequently, rural Iran lost its revolutionary potential, while the role of the city and the proletariat gained prominence (Ahmadzadeh 1976, 25–27). So, in search of a third way, Ahmadzadeh arrives at the Cuban experience via Régis Debray.

Debray's work, *Revolution in the Revolution?*, left a lasting theoretical impression on Ahmadzadeh, who incorporated a long review of Debray's work into his own book. Although Group Two had initially rejected Debray's thesis, Debray allows the group to understand the changing nature of class struggle (Ahmadzadeh 1976, 72) and to "absorb the profound lessons of the Cuban revolution" (Ahmadzadeh 1976, 84). By studying Debray, *Group Two makes a bold departure from Leninism beyond what they ever acknowledged,* while still identifying itself as Marxist-Leninist, despite the fact that Debray's work is a rejection of Leninism. At one point, Ahmadzadeh insists that his adoption of Debray's work constitutes a critical engagement with Marxist-Leninist parties. He claims that they failed to play the vanguard's role and forced revolutionary Marxist-Leninists to differentiate between the vanguard and the Party (Ahmadzadeh 1976, 88). In this regard he contrasts the Chinese-Vietnamese model, in which the Communist Party led the popular armed struggle, with the Latin American model, in which the Party was not necessarily the vanguard. Ahmadzadeh concludes, "the guerrilla force is the embryo of the party; the guerrilla is the party" (1976, 97–98). *This suggests that Ahmadzadeh uses the dominant revolutionary discourse of Marxism-Leninism merely to justify his own experiential search for the place of the intellectuals in the perceived imminent liberation of the Iranian people.*

Mastureh Ahmadzadeh recalls an incident in the late 1960s when Massoud acted as a "strike-breaker" in his university by attending a final examination that was boycotted by other students. Many students accused Massoud of betrayal. His conduct may be justified as an effort to avoid SAVAK (he led Group Two at this time) (Ahmadzadeh 2001). In the late 1960s dissident Iranian students subscribed to one of the three trends: the first trend opted to work among workers and peasants and to leave the intellectual milieus altogether; the second believed in working among student activists; and a third recognized guerrilla warfare as the only form of struggle. Ahmadzadeh believed in the last method and his aforementioned decision indicates his doubts regarding the "peaceful" methods. In fact, the wholesale rejection of any form of struggle other than militancy was prevalent among the leaders of Group Two (Fatapour 2001a). Ahmadzadeh believed that under repressive "conditions where there is no link between the vanguard and the masses" (1976, 136), only armed struggle is viable (1976, 71). For him the issue was practical, not theoretical: political presence requires action (1976, 102).

Debray provides Ahmadzadeh with the language to articulate his doubts about the Leninist model, all the while claiming allegiance to it: Leninism was central to Iranian Marxism. Ahmadzadeh quotes Debray that to be a revolutionary it is no longer enough to be a Party member (1976, 89). In Debray, Ahmadzadeh finds the way out of the political impasse manifested through the isolation of Iranian intellectuals (1976, 54) and the lack of spontaneous mass movements

(1976, 62). Writing in the aftermath of Siahkal, however, Ahmadzadeh knows that what he wants from Debray is not a prescriptive model but the *essence* of his theory—that revolutionary action is possible without the Party or the presence of the masses. The Latin American experience shows him that the guerrilla *foco* cannot succeed without the support of the city, and this conceptually leads him to the necessity of urban guerrilla warfare (Ahmadzadeh 1976, 138). Once Ahmadzadeh theoretically derives urban guerrilla warfare from Debray, he transposes a range of Debray's concepts into his own theory. The *foco* now becomes the *urban* "motor force of a total war" (Debray 1967, 57). The small motor starts the large motor: the masses can only be motivated into the revolutionary process by the vanguard's exercise of armed struggle (Ahmadzadeh 1976, 136). The metaphor of the "small motor" symbolizes armed struggle as the central form of revolutionary praxis, but it does not exclude other forms of action (Ahmadzadeh 1976, 121). Rural revolutionary action, for instance, is valued as an extension of urban guerrillas. He goes on to reassert armed struggle by detailing the similarities between Latin America and Iran with the problems from repressive development.

Reflecting on Siahkal in his June 1971 preface to *Armed Struggle,* though, Ahmadzadeh acknowledges his initial reluctance to engage in guerrilla operations in the mountains. He acknowledges the Siahkal operation by default and interprets its implications in favor of his own group's conviction of the necessity of urban guerrilla movement.

> In the beginning, the objective of armed struggle is to inflict political strikes at the enemy ... [and] to show the path of struggle to revolutionaries and the people, make them aware of their power, *demonstrate that the enemy is vulnerable* ... show that struggle is possible, expose the enemy ... Launching a guerrilla nucleus in the mountains pursued this objective ... Accordingly [the Siahkal operation] played a decisive propaganda and political role in the development of the Iranian revolutionary movement. (Ahmadzadeh 1976, 6–7; emphasis in original)

For him, the fiasco of the Siahkal operation indicates only a tactical defeat, resulting from the team's lack of mobility and distrust (1976, 9); it does not undermine the plausibility of armed struggle. What matters is the strategic survival of armed struggle: "What is important is that *if a weapon falls out of the hands of a militant, there will be another militant to pick it up*" (Ahmadzadeh 1976, 13; emphasis in original). Just like Jazani and Puyan, Ahmadzadeh points out the symbolic nature of armed struggle, except that for him Fadaiyan, the "vanguard children" of the masses, embody the struggle as "under the present conditions, the vanguard cannot be a vanguard unless s/he is a Fadai Guerrilla" (in Ahmadzadeh 1976, 14). As a strategy, armed struggle unifies revolutionary forces and mobilizes the masses. As a tactic, it launches armed propaganda and leads the liberation movement and the working class (Anonymous 1976a, 37–42).

In line with the Leninist theory of stages, Ahmadzadeh classifies the revolution at the democratic stage, given that the objective is to de-link Iran from imperialist domination. This requires the vanguard's mobilization of the masses and the leadership of the proletariat. For him, the last requirement is crucial because he goes beyond Jazani to propose that bourgeois revolutions in countries like Iran will eventually lead to imperialist domination (1976, 47). His narrow conception of politics impedes him from envisioning class alliances and frontal politics. The working class is reduced to its vanguard and the other classes it cannot represent are almost completely left out of the picture. In national liberation the leftist intellectual groups can represent and lead the working class (Ahmadzadeh 1976, 154), so the *leadership of the proletarian party is not necessary in the democratic revolution*. The revolutionary intellectuals directly represent the demands of the working class and the toiling masses through armed struggle (Ahmadzadeh 1976, 161–62). Thus, *armed struggle, which always remains the practice of small groups of intellectuals, becomes an ontological field that constitutes the "working class"* (and the masses) as the agent of change. The process of forming a revolutionary working class begins with the action of the "working-class intellectuals." For Ahmadzadeh as for Jazani, the working class exists in the normative demands of Marxist theory as the revolutionary agent of history.

Ahmadzadeh's reductionist notion of class heavily limits his conception of the liberation front. Like other Fadai theorists, he perceives the liberation movement as involving a wide range of anti-imperialist classes allied around the node of armed struggle. He believes that all revolutionaries, Communist and non-Communist alike, can participate in the fight against imperialism because they will inevitably realize the advantages of an anti-imperialist front (1976, 162). For Jazani, the particular unity (of revolutionary Communists) would place them at the helm in the general unity (of the front). For Ahmadzadeh, "the unity of all revolutionary and anti-imperialist groups and organizations that have adopted armed struggle"

(Ahmadzadeh 1976, 163) is conceptually prior to the unity of Communist groups (in the working-class party), which is why the pro-Ahmadzadeh Fadai prisoners advocated extensive alliances with the Muslim Mojahedin. Furthermore, the front will be the site for the development of the working class as a political force. Armed struggle, he hopes, automatically propels the working-class vanguards to the center of the liberation front. "Since the working class acquires self-consciousness and organization in the process of a mass armed struggle," argues Ahmadzadeh, "it grows in the womb of the united anti-imperialist front and will only gain its particular form when the issue of maintaining the proletarian hegemony and continuing the revolution in a specific way finds its way in its agenda" (1976, 163). The leadership of the working class is attained through the effective participation of its vanguard in the front (Ahmadzadeh 1976, 145–46).

The theory of armed struggle brings Ahmadzadeh to a major aporia—one that does not escape Jazani and causes a long debate within the OIPFG. Caught in the aporia between voluntarism and necessity, Ahmadzadeh posits revolutionary practice as proactive, but only animated in response to "the objective conditions of revolution." The problem is: are the objective conditions ready for the revolutionary action? If so, then where are the expected spontaneous mass movements against dependency and its political constellation? If the conditions are not ready, then guerrilla praxis only attests to the adventurism of intellectuals—an action, however effective and forceful, that will not lead to a popular revolution. Ahmadzadeh's response to this perceived critique is most interesting:

> But is this an absolutist dictum that spontaneous mass movement reflects the abundance of the objective conditions of revolution [and] that the spontaneous movement indicates that the time of revolution has come, and is this always and under any conditions true? Is its opposite also true? *Should we conclude from the lack of spontaneous mass movements that the objective conditions of revolution are not ripe?* That the time of revolution has not come? I think not. In the present conditions of Iran, one cannot regard the lack of vast spontaneous movements as evidence for the lack of objective conditions of revolution. (1976, 63–64; emphasis added)

One must not, in other words, conclude from the existing political inertia that the objective conditions of the revolution do not exist. Intense repression, state propaganda, and the dispersion of dissidents do not allow these conditions to reveal themselves in a protest movement (Ahmadzadeh 1976, 64). Ahmadzadeh polemically twists the argument in a curious way in order to justify his theory: the *objective conditions of the revolution do indeed exist, but they cannot manifest themselves in popular practice.* This is obviously an aporia, a conceptual nonpassage that haunts Ahmadzadeh:

> But what are our reasons for the existence of the objective conditions of the revolution? . . . The enthusiasm of the revolutionaries, the tireless search for the path to the revolution by progressive and revolutionary classes of intellectuals, the continuing raids of the police, the prisons, tortures, murders. Are these not the subjective reflection of the ripeness of the objective conditions of revolution? Could all these militant circles and groups of all oppressed classes exist, if the objective conditions did not dictate [them] to resolve the problem of the revolution? And finally, are the dispersed sparks of the masses' movements not the reason that the objective conditions of the revolution are ready? (1976, 66)

He suggests that without certain conditions, the existing revolutionary praxis would not have been possible. "Debray does not say that all the conditions are ripe," insists Ahmadzadeh, "but that the necessary conditions for initiating armed struggle exist, and the sufficient conditions for the expansion and popularization of armed operations will grow in the process of action" (1976, 117). Here, Ahmadzadeh commits a logical slide from the necessary or minimum conditions for revolutionary action to the objective conditions of revolution, while the two are indeed different.

This slide serves him well: he mystifies the objective conditions of the revolution in order to legitimize the action on which his generation has already embarked. This generation did not really need theory to justify its activities; it arrived at a global revolutionary theoretical discourse (Marxism) that sought to normatively regulate and universalize action. Overwhelmed by such a legislative discourse, Ahmadzadeh's generation was unable to formulate its social angst in its own generational terms. In a fleeting moment, though, it seems that Ahmadzadeh feels the grip of the imposed theories, and he announces it in all honesty.

> In the Communist movement today . . . we hardly encounter theoretical works such as *Capital, Anti-Dühring,* or *Materialism and Empirio-criticism:* is this not expressive of the fact that from the standpoint of pure theory, the international

Communist movement, faced with direct revolutionary practice, has neither
the time nor the need to engage in [theoretical] work? (1976, 96)

Indeed, action is what is needed, a practice unbound by theoretical limitations,
and this action remains true to its own terms as it finds its necessary forms in
the conditions of its emergence. And this was the true spirit of a revolutionary
generation that rose up in arms in Iran in the early 1970s.

THE CONFLICTUAL RETURN OF DUAL ORIGINS

The PFG uneasily traversed a generational gap: being half a generation older than
Ahmadzadeh, Jazani's roots go back to the Tudeh Party, so he was socialized into
Marxism in his youth. On the contrary, Ahmadzadeh's generation had to work
their way to Marxism and achieve it. As such, Ahmadzadeh carried out the task
of providing the frustrated young activists of the late 1960s with a language to
articulate their grievances. In prison, this gap between pro-Ahmadzadeh and
pro-Jazani Fadaiyan widened.

In the spring of 1971, Ahmadzadeh was injured and arrested in a shoot-
out. During the interrogation, he demonstrated remarkable willpower, endured
unimaginable tortures, and was kept in solitary confinement until his execution in the winter of 1972. He did not live to see the stealthy opposition to his
ideas: over the next three years, conflicting positions on armed struggle dominated the theoretical discourse of Fadaiyan. One can grasp the intensity of this
debate in the introduction to *War Against the Shah's Dictatorship* where Jazani
alludes to the "disagreements between the current factions of the movement on
the issue of the future path of the movement and of strategy and tactics of the
revolutionary movement in general" (1978, 1). He employs nuanced language
to discuss the disagreement: the pro-Ahmadzadeh faction is the *pishgam* (fore-
runner; literally, "forward-stepping") of armed struggle, while the pro-Jazani
faction is the *pishro* (vanguard; literally, "forward-going") (Jazani 1978, 104). In
the third revision to his book, Jazani observes that by spring 1974 most *pishgam*
(pro-Ahmadzadeh) activists were "in retreat" (1976, 107).

While the Fadai guerrillas were intensely engaged in a life-or-death struggle
on a daily basis, the (pro-)Fadai prisoners had time to debate the two positions.
Jazani was at the center of the debate, leading a small minority that challenged

Ahmadzadeh's dominant ideas. He accurately points out the existence or non-existence of "the objective conditions of the revolution" and argues that the "objective conditions" are not the precondition for launching armed struggle. Rather, the vanguard acts as a catalyst to bring these conditions about. Therefore, armed struggle is not the initial stage of the revolution; it is only the initial stage of the people's liberation movement that owing to its propaganda component mobilizes the masses. In due time, the vanguard is able to rise to leadership and ensure working-class hegemony (in this context, "leadership") in the people's democracy (Jazani 1978, 48). Ahmadzadeh assumes, the argument continues, that the objective conditions are ripe and soon the masses will respond to the call of the vanguard. The name of this concept is the "squeezed spring thesis" (*tez-e fanar-e feshordeh*) (Jazani 1978, 99). In the people's democratic revolution the working class plays a central role by bearing the movement's Socialist element. The main conflict is between the people and imperialism (and the comprador bourgeoisie). In Jazani's summary, Ahmadzadeh's position is that armed struggle is the first stage of the people's war, and its slogan should be "the rule of the people under working-class leadership." Armed struggle is pivotal, and all other forms of struggle are used only to reinforce armed struggle (Jazani 1978, 48–49). According to Jazani, Ahmadzadeh called it a "deviation" (*enheraf*) to engage in armed struggle without the presence of objective conditions (1978, 100). Jazani also argues that when Ahmadzadeh's thesis is confronted with facts that do not support it, it can yield either a total rejection of armed struggle or a "left-wing" tendency (*chapravi*) (1978, 49–50). *Jazani's intuitive observation predicts, with cunning precision, the first two schisms of the OIPFG while they were in their embryonic phases:* the "total rejection" came about in 1977 when the Monsha'ebin broke away from the OIPFG and joined the Tudeh Party later (chapter 5); and the "left-wing tendency" emerged in 1979 when Ashraf Dehqani split from the OIPFG over the group's abandonment of Ahmadzadeh's theory (see below). According to Jazani, the difference between his and Ahmadzadeh's position is not tactical; rather, there lies an ideological and analytical difference that cannot be compromised: "This disagreement cannot but lead to two [distinct] paths (*mashy*); they [the two opposite positions] might be both mistaken, but certainly they both could not be correct" (1978, 50). Jazani observes that Ahmadzadeh's thesis of the existence of the objective conditions (a "left opportunism" in Jazani's terms) is an antithesis of the Tudeh's inaction justified by the lack of the objective conditions (or "right opportunism" in Jazani's words) (1978, 98).

Jazani explicates the ramifications of Ahmadzadeh's thought by observing that the popularity of Ahmadzadeh's ideas stems from the optimistic belief that the masses will soon join the struggle (1978, 104). Given that the objective conditions are supposedly ready, now everything depends on the vanguard's initiative. As a form of political action, armed struggle leaves no doubt in anyone's mind as regards its intent, and even the people's indifference cannot debunk this thesis. The pro-Ahmadzadeh Fadaiyan maintain that the lack of mass movements indicates the extent of repression of the regime, not the lack of the objective conditions of the revolution (Jazani 1978, 100). Such a description of Ahmadzadeh's thesis should not be regarded as a distortion on Jazani's part. In his defense of Ahmadzadeh, Momeni makes the same claim, by deducing from Ahmadzadeh the tautological idea that in countries where the objective conditions are ready, imperialist repression and violence do not allow social change. Put differently, the Shah's brutal dictatorship is a sure sign of ripe conditions for the revolution (Momeni 1979, 5).

Thus an undertow gradually destabilized the theoretical dominance of Ahmadzadeh over the PFG. As his theory faded among most Fadai prisoners, Ashraf used his uncontested influence over the OPFG to propagate Jazani's ideas. When Jazani was still alive, Ashraf distributed his writings among select Fadai cadres (*Nabard-e Khalq* 1975b, 6). In 1974, two years after Ahmadzadeh's death, Fadaiyan published *Four Criticisms of "Revolution in the Revolution?"*, implying probably their first move against Ahmadzadeh and his appropriation of Debray's work. The book contains four translated critical essays on the key issues in Debray's book (OIPFG nd-c).

The predicament regarding the choice of a foundational theory for the OPFG reflects the theoretically split CC. Ashraf, on the one hand, had consistently shown his inclination toward Jazani's ideas. On the other hand, Momeni—who had authored books on human social evolution and enjoyed a reputation for his knowledge of theory—clearly defended Maoism and Ahmadzadeh (a strange mélange). Momeni was killed in a shoot-out with the police in February 1976 and the Tehran branch of OIPFG was nearly wiped out in the spring of June 1976. The Fadai Guerrillas were now scattered and in retreat. The rebuilding process consumed the next eighteen months of OIPFG's life.

The OIPFG inaugurated its return with the well-known December 6, 1977, communiqué published in *Payam-e Danshju*. The OIPFG announced a sharp turn, criticizing Ahmadzadeh's theory and declaring Jazani as *the* theorist of the group. According to this communiqué, the original Fadaiyan had committed an error by accepting Ahmadzadeh's thesis of the objective conditions of the revolution. Because Ahmadzadeh's assumption cultivated the expectation that the people would soon join the struggle, Fadai cadres conceived of armed struggle as short-term, as putting "the large motor" in motion. Soon they found themselves engaged in endless tasks that would not let them "critically engage with the early theories" (*Payam-e Daneshju* 1977, 25). According to the communiqué, the (former) "leadership comrades" were the first to face this theoretical predicament, but they did not decisively resolve it. The loss of the OIPFG leadership made the problem clear to the surviving activists while exposing the "left-wing tendency" (*chapravi*) among the Fadai founders. As a result of ideological struggles, Jazani's ideas were found applicable to Iranian conditions. The communiqué regards armed struggle as a "movement against dictatorship as well as a stage in the people's liberation movement . . . [as it] tries to mobilize the people's revolutionary forces and assumes leadership in a people's democratic revolution" (*Payam-e Daneshju* 1977, 51). And this position marks the end of an era in the history of the OIPFG.

THE BELATED SCHISM

Three months after the Revolution, on May 15, 1979, at Sharif University in Tehran, OIPFG spokesperson Mehdi Fatapour announced that Ashraf Dehqani was no longer a member of the OIPFG (Dehqani 1979, 1). Fatapour reminisces that he had spontaneously declared Dehqani's dismissal without prior consultation with the CC, and afterward, his announcement was not even discussed or challenged in subsequent CC meetings (Fatapour 2001a). It was a feature of Fadaiyan that a leading member would make a decision on behalf of the entire group—a survival technique born out of the exigencies of guerrilla life, but at the same time an indication of the lack of internal democracy. In the "Spring of Freedom" (1979), the OIPFG was undisputedly the largest leftist organization in the country, enjoying the support of a growing number of secular students and intellectuals with democratic tendencies. Ashraf Dehqani was a household name among

OIPFG supporters, and her widely read prison memoir *The Epic of Resistance*, written after her legendary escape from Qasr Prison, had earned her celebrity status. Fadai supporters were unaware that the conflict between Dehqani and the OIPFG went back to 1977, and that Dehqani and her colleague Mohammad Hormatipur (the OIPFG delegates in Europe and the Middle East) had published in 1979 the polemical book *On the Objective Conditions of the Revolution*, in which they had criticized Jazani and defended Ahmadzadeh.

Upon her "dismissal," Dehqani insisted that she would "die as a People's Fadai Guerrilla" (1979, 2) and reserved the right to expose the "opportunists who had infiltrated" the OIPFG (IPFG 1983). She did so in a subsequently published and widely read staged interview. Thereafter she embarked on a crusade, calling upon Fadai supporters to help her "cleanse [*tasfieh*] the organization" (Dehqani 1979, 9) through a "smashing [*kubandeh*] ideological struggle" (Dehqani 1979, 76), and she founded her faction by invoking Fadaiyan's earlier designation, Iranian People's Fadai Guerrillas (IPFG). She attracted supporters mainly in the southern provinces of Sistan-va-Baluchestan and Hormozgan, and in the Caspian region and Tehran. Later she published two pamphlets around the issues pertaining to the split (IPFG 1980; IPFG 1983). Fadai supporters did not take seriously Dehqani's charge regarding the group's selective "special recruitment" before the Revolution that led to advancing certain views in the OIPFG (IPFG 1980, 56). Emerging out of the mist of a legendary past, Fadai Guerrillas represented the high hopes of a young, secular mass that believed itself to be the force of Iran's true future. The radiance of a heroic future, however, had blinded OIPFG supporters to the creeping silhouette of an unfolding degeneration.

In her defense of Ahmadzadeh as *the* theorist of Fadaiyan, Dehqani and her followers generally offer unsophisticated analyses, heavily enfolded with polemical (at times emotional and accusatory) statements. Understandably, they frequently attempt to list the flaws of Jazani's theory instead of pointing out the merits of Ahmadzadeh's treatise. As mentioned, the debate hinges on the "objective conditions of revolution," and the works of Dehqani and her comrades (one interview and three books) center on this contested issue. They praise Ahmadzadeh for explaining his position by referring to his own theory instead of using borrowed frameworks and classical texts (IPFG 1983, 23–24). Believing that "a borrowed political theory cannot guide true revolutionary action" (Ahmadzadeh 1976, 94), Ahmadzadeh and Puyan "authored theories that shaped one of the most luminous periods in the history of our country" (IPFG 1983, 1). According to Dehqani, revolutionary wars in Vietnam and China showed Ahmadzadeh that the main conflict of the time was between the people and imperialism. Dehqani and her comrades underline the fundamental relationship between dictatorship and imperialism, legitimizing the necessity of violence (*qahr*) by guerrilla cells and dismissing the possibility of democratic struggle (IPFG 1983, 17). Waiting to institute the working-class party is a waste of time because the organization of the party is external to the method of armed struggle. Aside from the advanced sectors of the population, the masses cannot participate in armed struggle, which gives rise to and shapes the vanguard (see IPFG 1983, 36, 39).

Like Ahmadzadeh and Momeni, Dehqani falls into the tautology intrinsic to the concept of "objective conditions": to assert that these conditions are ripe strangely does not negate the fact of existing political inertia. Armed struggle is premised on the existence of these conditions and will influence the political atmosphere of the country through armed propaganda among the masses (IPFG 1983, 29–30, 31). The abstract concept of the "objective conditions of revolution" (*sharayet-e eyni-ye enqelab*) actually refers to the conflictual relationship between the people and imperialism, and it is different from Jazani's concept of "revolutionary condition" (*vaz'iyyat-e enqelabi*). According to Dehqani and her comrades, the revolutionary condition means that the objective and subjective conditions for the revolution are both in place (IPFG 1983, 32–33). Clearly the centrality of the concept of "objective conditions" lies in its authors' existential tendency to rise up in arms. This firm belief in the militant intellectual as the lone emancipatory savior is in line with the early Fadaiyan's motto "the guerrilla is the party," the belief that even one militant can ensure the survival of the movement (Dehqani 1979, 6–7). Theoretically, though, this tendency deprives Fadaiyan of a clear position on the popular movement.

Dehqani obviously tries to set the context in order to rationalize armed struggle in a manner faithful to Ahmadzadeh. She finds herself confronted by a subtle issue of practical importance for which Ahmadzadeh had neither time nor concern: if armed struggle is necessary to problematize the "theory of survival" of talkative café-frequenting intellectuals (Puyan), and if armed struggle is to ignite the small motor of militant intellectuals in order to overcome the political inertia that defines the masses' social mood and to put in motion the larger motor of the masses (Ahmadzadeh), what method of struggle should be employed once both of the above-mentioned problems are overcome? Stated simply, is not armed struggle an exhausted method in the context of postrevolutionary Iran? Dehqani's unequivocal response is that because Iran is a dependent capitalist society and because the Iranian state is the instrument of subjugation of subordinate classes by the dominant class, then the postrevolutionary government is a dependent bourgeois government that shares power with the petit-bourgeoisie (Dehqani 1979, 25). Her argument that the petit-bourgeoisie is "essentially democratic" is naïve. However, given that the Islamic state suppresses freedom and the people, then (by deduction) the class base of the Islamic government should be bourgeoisie (Dehqani 1979, 31). Yet at the same time, this dependent capitalist state is admittedly threatened by imperialism. Thus "we must prepare all anti-imperialist forces for an armed struggle that will definitely be imposed on us" (Dehqani 1979, 64). Stated plainly, we should prepare for armed struggle, for one reason or another, regardless of the new postrevolutionary conditions.

Defending Ahmadzadeh's theory is one part of Dehqani's strategy. The other part is refuting Jazani, this "free-thinking dualist" (IPFG 1983, 47–48), and his theory that bears "opportunist" elements. In challenging Jazani's theory, Dehqani's objective is to reassert that armed propaganda as a method of mass mobilization must be abandoned, for the militant intellectuals are the only force that can overthrow the state (the Cuban model). Yet in defending Ahmadzadeh, Dehqani moves against the grain of Ahmadzadeh's treatise and abandons the concepts of small and large motors. How paradoxical that in revitalizing Ahmadzadeh's theory, Dehqani succeeds only in dismantling it. What is imaginative in Ahmadzadeh becomes banal in Dehqani, as she offers only a caricature of her bright icon's theory, depriving Ahmadzadeh of the context in which he wrote and of the generational spirit that motivated him. And so, one of the origins that defined the Fadai Guerrillas in the years of steel and fire simply faded away.

THE VANISHING ORIGIN

While the split exposed the vanishing of Ahmadzadeh's influence through ineffectual polemical defenses of his theory, it also demonstrated that the OIPFG leadership had gone beyond Jazani, reaching canonical Leninism. Officially, the OIPFG published an argumentative book in response to Dehqani (OIPFG 1979c), written by Farrokh Negahdar, the future leader of OIPF-M (Negahdar 2008). Ali

Reza Akbari Shandiz probably wrote the other, highly polemical, rejoinder to Dehqani (OIPFG-Kurdistan Branch 1980; see also Fadaiyan-Plains of Turkoman 1980). The main thrust of all OIPFG reflections about its past is class-based critique: announcing the "dialectical negation" of Ahmadzadeh's theory, the leadership criticizes the Fadaiyan's "petit-bourgeois" past and their lack of a distinct working-class position (OIPFG-Kurdistan Branch 1980, 4). The OIPFG rejoinders point out the tautological aspect of the concept of "objective conditions." As well, they expose the way Dehqani's (indeed Ahmadzadeh's) position replaces the masses with militant intellectuals in the revolutionary struggle. Personified by the celebrated Fadai Guerrilla as *the* ' liberating hero," this view of liberation spellbound early Fadai theorists to the extent that they lost sight of economic and class (literally, *senfi* or "guild") interests, which led to their failure to organize the working class or the people (OIPFG-Kurdistan Branch 1980, 11). Jazani had already recognized, five years earlier, that the adventurist and martyrdom-loving tendency of Fadaiyan was symptomatic of their failure to mobilize the masses (1978, 43, 15). This failure explains why the leadership of the 1979 Revolution fell into the hands of the clergy (OIPFG-Kurdistan Branch 1980, 14). Referring to Jazani, the *Rejoinder* argues that the political history of twentieth-century Iran shows that despite endemic suppression, *it has been political struggle that has been the norm, not armed struggle* (OIPFG 1979c, 13).

According to the OIPFG's *Rejoinder,* Ahmadzadeh must be understood in his specific historical and intellectual context. In particular, two situations made Ahmadzadeh's theory successful: first, the stagnation that dominated the Iranian Communist movement in the 1960s, and second, the poor knowledge of Marxism among the intellectuals (OIPFG 1979c, 3–4). The dismissal of the "guerrilla path" (*mashy-e cheriki*) does not automatically amount to an "ideological baptism" (*ghosl-e ta'mid-e ideolozhik*) of a "corrected" working-class politics. "One must deeply recognize that although the former views [of the OIPFG] contain a deviation from Marxist principles, their rejection does not necessarily guarantee a 'proletarian path'" (OIPFG-Kurdistan Branch 1980, 5). The 1977 splinter group Monsha'ebin also renounced armed struggle, but in its stead, it gave in to "right opportunism" and joined the Tudeh Party (OIPFG-Kurdistan Branch 1980, 5). If "left adventurism" and "right opportunism" are so closely intermingled, what should be the measure of Communist practice? According to the OIPFG's new politics, it is Leninism (OIPFG 1979c, 38). Calling the 1979 revolution an "uprising" (*qiyam*), the new leadership states that no *revolution* has actually taken place in Iran because the system of comprador capitalism has not yet been defeated (OIPFG 1979c, 22). The "leadership issue" (*masaleh-ye rahbari*) of the revolution must be resolved in favor of the proletariat (OIPFG 1979c, 25). This position is a rejection of Dehqani's argument, but it also rejects the "noncapitalist path" (Soviet-cooked and advertised by the Tudeh) where revolutionary democrats (nonproletarian, radical national bourgeoisie, or petit-bourgeoisie) would lead the democratic revolution (see chapter 5) (OIPFG-Kurdistan Branch 1980, 43). The petit-bourgeois leadership (i.e., the Islamic Republic) will fail the Revolution because of its dual, unstable class character. So the immediate task of Fadaiyan is to ensure the leadership of the proletariat in the movement (OIPFG-Kurdistan Branch 1980, 25–26).

Interestingly, postrevolutionary Fadaiyan's Leninist class politics was first developed through Jazani's thought, but further explorations of Jazani's ideas soon dissipated in the most dramatic split in OIPFG in 1980. Instead of building the foundations of the social and cultural secular-Left, the Majority quit class politics altogether in favor of populism and the Tudeh's "noncapitalist path" and became submissive to the clerics' leadership, while the Minority tried to appropriate a Leninist reading of Jazani in postrevolutionary Iran, which led it into a violent clash with the new regime. Both of these postrevolutionary strategies, heirs to Jazani's theory, failed, and Fadai factions were soon eliminated from Iranian politics. Looking back into the history of Fadaiyan, one speculates that the two founding groups of the PFG probably would not have merged if Jazani had been free and in charge of Group One in 1971. The specific circumstances that gave the OIPFG its dual origin, indeed its *diverging origins,* burdened Fadaiyan with an identity crisis for years to come.

THE THEORETICAL IMPASSE

Ahmadzadeh's appeal to the "objective conditions of revolution" is an example of a subconscious pretense to act in the name of a theoretical framework, while in actuality being bound by practice. Theory provides Ahmadzadeh with the justifications that allow him to avoid the inescapable fact that politics begins with the articulation of antagonistic relations and *political practice does not need to be subsumed under some mystified theoretical fundament.* However, in a world where claiming allegiance to Leninism and Marxist-oriented national liberation theories qualified one as revolutionary, politics without theory was too bold a step for any Fadai theorist to take. Ahmadzadeh travels a significant distance away from Leninism by adopting Debray's analysis. Yet he and Puyan adamantly claimed to be Leninists. These efforts to assert one's allegiance to normative-theoretical requirements are amazing because Fadaiyan emerged out of a "practical generation" that rebelled against the inaction of its predecessors. Despite the fact that they used theory to justify their action, for this generation theory belonged to the founding ideologues or scholars. As theoretical dilemmas permeated every aspect of their politics, however, Fadaiyan had no solution but to reductively apply these theoretical pillars in the Iranian context. This is how the practice-oriented Fadaiyan lost their fascinating theoretical originality, despite the problems that permeated their theories.

5

Three Failed Interlocutions

Diverging Propensities

> Not visible for the public were . . . the deviations that deepened by the
> moment and gradually eradicated the young tree of hope . . .
>
> This invisible current was the slow and painful process of the impov-
> erishment of the movement. . . . Instead of Marxism-Leninism, Maoism
> showed up and instead of the authority of thought over weapon, militarism
> appeared, and this sad process continued to its final logical conclusion in
> thought and in action: the emergence of Stalinism.
>
> —Group for Communist Unity, *Moshkelat va masael-e jon-*
> *besh* [The problems and issues of our movement]

THE FADAI GUERRILLAS shone on one of the darkest horizons of Iranian
politics, but their shining was not because of their theoretical contributions to
the *problématique* of national liberation. Their works reached activists who did
not need much theory to persuade them to join the movement. They joined the
armed movement for rather existential reasons. Ahmadzadeh's predilection for
practice over theory demonstrates the pervasive mood of this dissident generation. For this generation, Siahkal was a rare but decisive blessing. Students and
youth attempted to contact Fadaiyan, and when unsuccessful in joining the unat-
tainable PFG, they formed guerrilla cells on their own. After sustaining heavy
casualties in 1970–71, Fadaiyan found these cells to be ideal sources of recruitment. So the PFG expanded by continually absorbing these deeply practice-oriented (*amalgara*), self-made militants.

No matter how pathbreaking, Fadaiyan could not avoid receiving their fair
share of debate. The near eradication of the group in 1976 pushed the originative
debate between Jazani's and Ahmadzadeh's positions to the decisive point when,

in 1977, the OIPFG officially adopted Jazani's theory. Before this point, however, Ashraf curbed the originative debate within the group while he was still alive, but that produced a defiant opposition to guerrilla warfare that tore a quarter of the OIPFG away in 1976. The "Fadai *Monsha'eb*" (Fadai Splinter Group), or Monsha'ebin, radically questioned the raison d'être of the Fadai Guerrillas. In actuality, the exchange between Mohsha'ebin and Fadaiyan fell short of a live debate because of Monsha'ebin's lack of original ideas and because of the fact that at the time (1976–77) Fadaiyan were occupied with rebuilding the OIPFG.

As mentioned, Fadaiyan often recruited zealous militant cells, but not all whom they absorbed were theoretically docile. The OIPFG recruited members of the People's Democratic Front (PDF) along with their maverick theorist, Mostafa Sho'aiyan, who single-handedly challenged Fadaiyan with such vigor that it led to his dismissal within a few months (chapter 6). Setareh, or the Group for Communist Unity (GCU), merged with the OPFG in 1973, providing them with much-needed logistics in Europe and the Middle East. Later, in 1975, when the GCU learned in dismay about the secret purging of Fadai members, it broke away from the OIPFG and publicized four theoretical exchanges and other documents about the OIPFG's organizational life. Finally, the Marxist-Leninist Mojahedin-e Khalq, which had violently wrested this Muslim group away from its religious leaders, posed another challenge to Fadaiyan over the issue of the united popular front. Their exchanges show major differences in their understanding of national liberation, differences that made unification impossible.

In this chapter, we focus on the three debates of Fadaiyan: with the GCU, the Marxist-Leninist Mojahedin, and Monsha'ebin. These debates show the specter of Stalinism that haunted the OIPFG, the internal plurality of Fadaiyan, and above all, *the irreducibly paradoxical character of the discourse of national liberation,* a discourse permeated by the aporias of agency and democratic politics. Last but not least, these diverging positions show that the unifying effect of armed struggle that Fadai theorists advocated was simply a phantasm.

OIPFG AND THE GROUP FOR COMMUNIST UNITY

In 1972 the OIPFG was contacted by a clandestine exile group, known as Setareh (Star). Several members of Setareh had worked with the National Front Organization Abroad since its formation in Europe and the United States in 1961 (GCU

1978, 2, 5). Setareh was active under the name National Front of Iran–Middle East Chapter (henceforth NF-ME) (Matin 1999, 352). Setareh emerged in 1970 from the unification of several Communist circles in exile whose members were activists with the CISNU (founded in 1962) (Chaqueri 2001). By this time, two main factions existed in the National Front Abroad and the CISNU: the Worker (*Kargar*) faction rejected both Maoism and guerrilla warfare, while the Star (*Setareh*) faction defended armed struggle and was in contact with Group Two and the OIPM even before their advent. Setareh later left the National Front and renamed itself the Group for Communist Unity (Guruh-e Ettehad-e Komonisti; hereafter GCU) (Matin 1999, 284–85). The GCU official line, however, holds that Setareh was the name the group used for contacting Fadaiyan (1977a, 46, n.1).

The activities of Setareh as the "Communist members of the Front" began in Beirut in 1970 (Chaqueri 2001). The group published *Bakhtar-e Emrooz* without revealing the group's true identity. Setareh had contacted the surviving members of the Palestine Group and the OIPM in the Middle East, but with little consequence. In the autumn of 1970, Setareh had contacted Massoud and Majid Ahmadzadeh and Puyan in Mashhad and sent them the Persian translation of Che Guevara's *Guerrilla Warfare*. The GCU had also translated and published Carlos Marighella's *Minimanual of the Urban Guerrilla*, which Ahmadzadeh had obtained and praised. Apparently Ahmadzadeh had promised to send Setareh the two pamphlets of Group Two, but in 1971 the two sides lost contact (GCU 1977a, 12; see Masali 2001, 152–55). Because Fadaiyan were the founders of the armed movement, the GCU sought to join the PFG, and finally in the fall of 1973 the two groups established contact. After studying the theoretical work of the GCU, *Revolution,* Fadaiyan agreed that there was "no fundamental disagreement between [the two] and the minor differences could be resolved in a process of unification [*tajanos;* literally, homogenization]" (quoted in GCU 1977a, 10). The "minor differences" raised by Hamid Momeni in fact turned out to be anything but minor.

After the merger, Setareh apparently dissolved itself in the autumn of 1974, allocating its resources and passing its precious contacts with the Middle Eastern revolutionary movements to the OPFG. Now Setareh members worked individually under OPFG delegates Ashraf Dehqani and Mohammad Hormatipur. While participating as OPFG members, the GCU individuals also maintained their activities and contacts under NF-ME. A member of Setareh, Manuchehr Hamedi (the organizational secretary of the CISNU in 1971), was secretly deployed to Iran in October–November 1974 to join the OIPFG and was reportedly killed in Rasht in May 1976 (Naderi 2008, 653; Heydar 1999, 262, n.11; Matin 1999, 318; GCU 1978, 40; Masali 2001, 155).

Setareh member Hassan Masali (the CISNU's international secretary in the mid-1960s) closely worked with the Fadai representatives. Setareh members more or less followed OIPFG orders insofar as their individual judgments allowed. As former GCU activists reflect, "Some comrades obeyed the orders of the Fadaiyan Organization, despite their own individual views, while there were comrades who did not even stand [the orders]" (OCUA 1987, 118; see also GCU 1977a, 46, n.3).

Despite the joint activities of the two groups in the Middle East, the unification process did not go smoothly. The OIPFG did not expect Setareh membership to be theoretically competent or have anti-Stalinist tendencies. While working with the OIPFG, the GCU members discovered that Fadaiyan had moved away from Ahmadzadeh's theory and were preparing criticisms of his work (GCU 1977a, 13). Furthermore, they read shocking praises of Stalin and Mao in *Nab-ard-e Khalq* (1974a). The GCU members felt betrayed for having been kept in the dark about the positions of the OIPFG. Now Setareh faced a dilemma: since its formation in 1970 it had refused to recruit Stalinists and Maoists, and now it had literally dissolved itself in a group that displayed Stalinist characteristics. When confronted by Setareh's protest, the OIPFG pointed out that those were the positions of "a certain member," and in no way did Stalinism reflect the OIPFG's politics (GCU 1977a, 15). The article in question was written by Momeni, and Jazani had criticized it from prison (see Heydar 1999, 250–51). The two groups exchanged several theoretical pieces on Stalin and Mao in the next two years, which we shall look at shortly.

In the autumn of 1975, Setareh members received disturbing information that Fadaiyan had purged some nonconformist rank-and-file members. Confronted by the baffled GCU members, the Fadai delegates argued that they had orders not to disclose such information (GCU 1977a, 16; Matin 1999, 353–54, 384). Even before the news about the purges reached Setareh, diverging theoretical and political principles had produced a sombre prospect for unification. According to Heydar (Mohammad Dabirifard), by 1975 the OIPFG leadership, especially Momeni, had decided to terminate contacts with Setareh, but delayed the decision on Ashraf's insistence because Fadaiyan depended on Setareh's logistics support. Seeing the imminent collapse of *tajanos,* Ashraf sent Heydar abroad in early 1976 to create the OIPFG's own logistics niche in the region (Heydar 1999, 262, n.11; Heydar 2001, 27). So despite apparent organizational unity, the relations between the two groups had rapidly deteriorated by the winter of 1976 and they were suspended in April 1976 (GCU 1977d, 131). In a meeting held in July 1976 it was determined that Setareh had fundamental disagreements with the OIPFG and therefore the process of unification had to be terminated (GCU 1977a, 20–21). The GCU did not announce the termination of its relations with Fadaiyan until January 1977, while the OIPFG steadfastly maintained silence about the details of *tajanos* (GCU 1977d, 131). The experience proved to Setareh members that they had "idealized" the guerrilla groups (GCU 1977a, 28).

Setareh's departure from the hagiographized Fadaiyan also led the group to terminate its strained relations with the Marxist-Leninist Mojahedin. In the fall of 1977 Setareh ceased all activities under the designation NF-ME (GCU 1977a, 27; GCU 1978, 1). In 1977 it reemerged as the GCU and published several volumes of documents pertaining to the group's relations with Fadaiyan, the Marxist Mojahedin, and the National Front. The GCU underwent yet another transformation two years later, reemerging as the Organization of Communist Unity (Sazman-e Vahdat-e Komonisti) in the United States.

The uneasy relationship between the GCU and the OIPFG highlights the issue of Stalinism in the life and politics of Fadaiyan. The OIPFG-GCU debates reveal a *tension between ideological justifications and the praxis of national liberation.* The GCU's anti-Stalinism compelled Fadaiyan to formulate their uneasy position on the history of socialism and the rival tendencies within the Socialist camp. Evidently Fadaiyan had no interest in publicizing the debates, and in the only publication addressing the process (published in Germany by pro-OIPFG students in 1977) they eliminated all references to Setareh (OIPFG 1977a, *a*). Among other things, the debate reveals the internal diversity of Fadaiyan. In the rest of this section, I will explore the main themes of the debate over the issue of national liberation.

Exposing the Maoist Hideout

While he was not a founding theorist of Fadaiyan, Momeni's vigorous defense of the Communist powers (USSR and China) and their emblematic leaders left its mark on the OPFG's mid-career theories. His dogmatic defense of Marxist canons somewhat hurt the image of a "new Communist movement" premised on "independence" from Socialist powers. Momeni was the writer of the article in *Nabard-e Khalq* that had angered Jazani, whose criticism from prison stirred up internal discussions (Heydar 1999, 250–51). This pulled Fadaiyan into a difficult debate with Setareh for the next two years.

Momeni's "Turning to the Right in the Foreign Policy of the People's Republic of China" (1974) forces Fadaiyan to face an aporetic question, *in potentio* an ideologically fatal one: "Can a Socialist country choose a policy that is contrary to the interests of other peoples? Our answer is: yes, it can" (OIPFG 1977e, 1). Momeni states that a Socialist state is not a classless society free of class conflicts. He offers China as an example: "Bourgeois dictatorship has transformed into proletarian dictatorship" (OIPFG 1977e, 3–4). This is the case, he argues, of bourgeois infiltration into the Party leadership and government. The Socialist state eliminates the bourgeois class, but certain layers of the bourgeoisie still survive under socialism. These include felons, embezzlers, the "elite" (*momtaz*) sector of the bourgeoisie made up of intellectuals and the working-class aristocracy. His use of the old fictitious "bourgeois infiltration" as an excuse for Socialist failures leads him to defend Maoist garrison socialism (OIPFG 1977e, 2, 5–6, 14). Evidently Momeni theoretically suppresses a fundamental problem of Socialist states in order to prop up his ideological attachment to them.

According to Momeni, the turn to the Right in China results from its antagonistic separation from the USSR (OIPFG 1977e, 21–24). The Chinese had to create a "self-reliant" economy after "boldly criticizing" Khrushchev's revisionism. They failed. An ideological ruse justified China's trade with capitalist countries: by realigning its foreign policy with imperialist countries (like the United States), China claims to be accelerating the internal contradictions among capitalist states, whereas in fact the true purpose of the Chinese policy was advancing its national interest (OIPFG 1977e, 61, 69). Momeni's answer to what went wrong in Chinese socialism appears to be most uncritical: China moved away from the Maoist canon. Interestingly, his solution for correcting the "right-wing deviation" in China is another "Cultural Revolution" (OIPFG 1977e, 129). He does not allow the question to problematize the basics of his ideology.

Setareh wrote two rejoinders to this article. In the first, "Critical Comments on 'Turning to the Right in the Foreign Policy of the People's Republic of China',"

Setareh praises the OIPFG for exposing deviationism in Chinese foreign policy while being critical of Momeni's method: socialism does not simply replace bourgeois dictatorship with a proletarian one. Maoism is not a minor error, the criticism goes, it is a defective system of thought (GCU 1977h, 1–2). Setareh criticizes Momeni's use of the word *error* to address the failures of socialism in order to maintain the notion of the "Socialist family" (GCU 1977h, 11; see also GCU 1977a, 37–38). Setareh states that what Fadaiyan call "turning to the Right" conceals the fact that China was always "right-wing." The OIPFG criticizes the policies of China only to detract from criticisms that target the source of such policies (GCU 1977h, 16, 22).

In the second rejoinder, "Mao Tse-tung Thought: Marxism-Leninism of Our Era?" Setareh addresses Mao's distortion of the Marxist theory of revolution in order to popularize it in China. Prominent among the distortions was the coinage of the terms "semicolonial-semifeudal," or "people's democratic dictatorship," by which Mao has apparently "expanded" the dictatorship of the proletariat (by negating its class character). As a result, Mao failed to see the Marxian concept of class dictatorship as a social project and reduced it to a repressive state's annihilation of classes (GCU 1977i, 1–4, 69). In criticizing Mao, however, the GCU reveals its own bookish understanding of class as defined in terms of private property and labor, as it reduces the complexity of class relations in postcolonial national liberation.

Even while agreeing with the GCU's criticism of Mao's garrison socialism and his violent vernacularization of Marxism, one cannot remain heedless, as does Setareh, of the question of liberation wars against imperialist domination, a phenomenon that challenged the application of Marxist theory to post–World War II reality. In criticizing Maoism, the GCU reverts to a puritan Marxism that has little to offer for the immediate theoretical needs of liberation movements. Setareh holds the position that in national liberation, the liberation of the proletariat will be achieved through victory over imperialism (GCU 1977i, 30–32). This view leads the group to make the predominant assumption of Marxists that national liberation movements are somehow endowed with a historical capacity to partially fulfil the ontologically instituted mission of the proletariat. Meaningful socialization between classes, enabled by joint liberation struggles, remains eclipsed in this essentialist dogma. Therefore, conceptually, fundamental class antagonisms render liberation redundant. But the *conflictual essence* of classes is an effect of Marxist class analysis, which cannot produce a unitary, pregiven field of action.

Unveiling Stalinist Tendencies

The issue of Stalinism was prompted by the phrase in Momeni's words in *Nab-ard-e Khalq* (no. 2) that called Stalin "the great leader of the proletariat" (in GCU 1977a, 20). Setareh reports that around the same time that these words appeared in Fadaiyan's official publication, the OIPFG sent them a critical essay entitled "Stalinism and the Problem of Bureaucracy in the Soviet Society," to which GCU responded in a rejoinder, "The Archer and the People of Wisdom" (GCI 1977g). The debate over Stalinism soon proved fatal to the uni-fication process.

Momeni does not hesitate to praise Stalin as "a great Marxist-Leninist" and "the embodiment of the iron will of the militant proletariat of the Soviet Union" (OIPFG 1977c, 10). He states that Stalin "engaged in a difficult struggle with the left and right bourgeois deviationisms and although he exercised utmost brutality (*khoshunat*) in this battle and achieved great victories, years after his death he was defeated by the deviationists, and the bourgeois deviationism of new revisionism (Khrushchevian revisionism) won over Stalin" (OIPFG 1977c, 9). Stalin's mistakes were rather theoretical, and he remained unaware of the "infiltration" of the bourgeois "elite" in the Soviet bureaucratic system. Momeni uses the same justification for Maoism as we saw above (see OIPFG 1977c, 14, 16). In responding to the intra-Soviet class struggle, Stalin failed to mobilize the Russian masses. Momeni's solution is a Maoist Cultural Revolution as a model for mass mobilization that has recourse to the crushing forces of the state to carry out class struggle (see OIPFG 1977c, 20, 24, 27–28).

Setareh's first criticism of the OIPFG's defense of Stalin, written in a cau-tiously soft tone, opens by reminding that "the duty of every honest Commu-nist is to defend Stalin *against* the [imperialist] plot," while it is also the honest comrades' duty to criticize Stalinism (GCU 1977f, 2–3). Then the GCU poses a valid question: how can a state be Socialist, if thirty-five years into the revo-lution, revisionists (i.e., Khrushchev) can still dominate it without any visible resistance? (GCU 1977f, 9–10). The answer, implicitly, rests on Stalin's conduct. Setareh rejects the idea that Stalin belongs to the status of Marx, Engels, and

Lenin (GCU 1977f, 20). Timid and inconsequential as Setareh's point seems, it nonetheless triggers a heavy-handed response from Momeni.

In his rejoinder to Setareh, Momeni admits that the Soviet proletariat had been defeated by the petit-bourgeoisie when it took over the Communist Party under the guise of revisionism. The "inevitable" failure of the "virgin" (bekr) experience of the Soviet working class, he argues, indicates the extent of the conspiracy by the "world's petit-bourgeoisie" against Lenin and Stalin. After all, Stalin had crushed the Russian petit-bourgeoisie and its intellectuals (e.g., Alexander Solzhenitsyn) (OIPFG 1977d, 132, 135). Clearly Momeni's desperate ruses help him defend his banal Marxism. He suggests that national liberation should follow a tried and tested blueprint. So it is not surprising that Fadaiyan contacted the Soviets in 1973–74 to seek their support (chapter 2). If the contacts yielded no results, it was rather owing to the Soviets' disinterest (Kuzichkin 1997, 264–65).

Elsewhere in his rejoinder, Momeni accuses Setareh of bourgeois-individualist tendencies when Setareh attributes Stalin's brutalities to a personality cult instead of treating the issue using proper "dialectical materialist laws" (OIPFG 1977d, 63). This line of argument leads Momeni to defend Stalin's purging the "carriers of bourgeois ideology" and sending the "perverse intellectuals who pursued a counter-proletarian line" to forced labor camps. The Stalinist tendency within the OIPFG is clearly visible when Momeni advocates "sending perverse intellectuals [he names Jalal Al Ahmad] to physical labor, which imperialists call 'forced labor camp' . . . [as] a method we [i.e., Fadaiyan] should extensively use" (OIPFG 1977d, 135), as if, it seems, he is reflecting on the infamous Fadai purges and disciplinary practices (see chapter 2).

Setareh's frustration spills out more harshly in its second rejoinder to Fadaiyan, showing that the GCU perceived no future in staying with the OIPFG: "More than pertaining to Stalin and Stalinism, the disagreement between the [Fadai] comrades and us pertains to the *method of analysis* and *worldview* (*binesh*)" (GCU 1977g, 1). The GCU calls Fadaiyan the "epic-making Communists of Iran" and "the most determined revolutionaries of [our] era" (GCU 1977g, 3), but it also rightly identifies a tendency toward Maoism that manifested in Fadaiyan's "undemocratic" and accusatory treatment of their critics (GCU 1977g, 4, 5). The OPFG failed, Setareh argues, to condemn Stalin from the standpoint of "proletarian humanism," and so Fadaiyan did not realize that fighting Stalinism means fighting Stalinist methods and views within one's organization (GCU 1977g, 28, 31–32).

Problems of Revolution and Democracy

Aside from "differences in method and worldview," a fundamental theoretical difference on the nature of capitalism and Socialist revolution set Setareh and the OIPFG apart. In the initial stages of their contact, the OPFG expressed a positive view of Setareh's main treatise, *On Revolution,* announcing that Fadaiyan had no major disagreements with Setareh. At the same time, they criticized Setareh's notion of armed struggle as a means of overthrowing the regime, which undermined Jazani's armed propaganda (OIPFG 1977a, 2–3). Momeni, the author of the OPFG commentary, assesses that Iranian conditions do not allow spontaneous movements to develop linearly into mass uprising and the fall of the regime as happened in Russia. This dictates a certain twist on armed movements. In Iran the working-class party will grow out of a political-military organization of intellectuals and workers (OIPFG 1977a, 5–7).

In dealing with Jazani's theory, Momeni introduces a Maoist intrusion. First, he undermines Jazani's armed propaganda as a way of mass mobilization under repressive conditions, which leads him to deny in toto the possibility of organizing and leading the spontaneous movements—yet this was precisely how Ayatollah Khomeini succeeded in 1979. Jazani's notions of armed propaganda and the "second leg" (political wing) do not negate that action. Second, Momeni distorts Jazani's concept of armed propaganda by reading into it the Maoist idea of the people's army. Last, contrary to Jazani's projection about the political apathy of peasants, Momeni reinstates Iranian peasants into his theory of revolution (OIPFG 1977a, 7–9).

In a book published after the end of the *tajanos* process, the GCU asserts that it never believed in the existence of the objective or subjective conditions of the revolution. Revolutionaries should not attempt to seize power but should organize the masses—especially the advanced layers of the working class—into cells, educate them politically, and prepare them for the "opportune moment" (GCU 1977e, 67). The GCU views armed struggle as a prolonged war, rejecting both Puyan's disregard for "survival" and Ahmadzadeh's small-motor theory (GCU 1977e, 61, 70). The expansion of armed movement, the GCU contends, does not even necessarily lead to the development of the workers' movement (1977a, 37).

The GCU not only circumvents the Ahmadzadeh-Jazani virtual debate on the objective conditions of the revolution, it also rejects the Leninist stages of revolution by offering the concepts of the "preparatory stage of revolution" and the "revolutionary stage" (GCU 1977e, 7–8). The GCU holds that in the preparatory stage of the revolution, large-scale workers' movements and protests are virtually nonexistent; revolutionary forces are in rudimentary stages; and public awareness is poor, as people enjoy a relative welfare through economic growth (GCU 1977e, 13). The GCU rightly questions Fadaiyan's assumption that armed struggle leads to the revolution, but the GCU neglects its own assumption: that *the preparatory stage of the revolution does not necessitate armed struggle,* and the people's revolutionary consciousness does not inevitably lead to armed movement. One can observe that armed struggle has no conceptual place in the GCU's theory, and the GCU simply takes the presence of the guerrillas for granted and as inseparable from Iran's revolutionary process. It is as if the GCU is still emotionally attached to Fadaiyan, despite their divorce.

Finally, we can observe how an existing mode of practice (guerrilla warfare) imposes itself upon theory even when theory does not logically need it. If organization and education are the means of preparing for a social revolution (the GCU seems to suggest this), then *democracy becomes the issue,* which reminds us of Jazani. We know that the revolutionary Marxists of the 1970s were highly suspicious of liberal democracy because of its structural link to capitalism, and the GCU was no exception. However, the GCU apologetically recognizes the significance of democracy for political development and contrasts "democratic capitalism," which allows public scrutiny into politics, with "repressive capitalism," where the public is denied such right. The GCU rightly argues that even if "the half-hearted bourgeois democracy" existed in Iran, imperialism would not be able to advance its interests so effortlessly (GCU 1977b, 22, 33). The GCU cautiously advocates a democratic class struggle: "We state that in addition to engaging in class struggle, Communists must also participate in democratic struggles. One must not conclude from this assertion that democratic struggles are separate from class struggle. This is never the case" (GCU 1977b, 61). The point is indeed refreshing.

The interlocution between Setareh and Fadaiyan failed. Two years after the breakup, the OIPFG finally referred to its relations with the GCU by using its usual accusatory tone and trivializing attitude. The failure of the unification, however, exposes the ideological and practical impasses that Fadaiyan faced between 1973 and 1976.

THE MARXIST-LENINIST MOJAHEDIN

Existing literature on the OIPM relieves me from detailing its history here (Abrahamian 1989; OIPM 1979b; Nejat Hosseini, 2000; Haqshenas 2001). Official OIPM literature marks 1965 as the year of its birth. Former Second National Front activists and disillusioned members of the Freedom Movement (Sa'id Mohsen, Ali Asghar Badi'zadegan, and Mohammad Hanifnezhad) agreed on the need for new methods of struggle in the face of escalated repression. But the trainings of Mojahedin did not begin until 1969–70 (Haqshenas 2001, 23), and the Mojahedin actually launched their first operations only after August 1971 when SAVAK raided their networks and secret logistics depots (see Nejat Hosseini 2000, 291–97; OIPM 1979b, 81–87). A total of sixty-nine members of Mojahedin stood trial in 1972, accused of plotting to blast power lines on the eve of the Shah's celebration of 2,500 years of monarchy in Iran (see Abrahamian 1989, 128–29). The OIPM's first operation was the November 1970 hijacking of an Air Taxi flight scheduled to fly from Dubai (UAE) to Bandar Abbas (Iran), demanding the release of the six members of the Organization who were to be extradited to Iran by Bahrain (then a British colony) (see Nejat Hosseini 2000, 131–66; OIPM 1979b, 53–80; Abrahamian 1989, 127–28). The group's first operation in Iran, in October 1971, was the failed attempt to kidnap the Shah's nephew, Shahram Shafiq (Nejat Hosseini 2000, 299–300). In spite of all activities, the group had no name until February 1972 (Nejat Hosseini 2000, 277). Mojahedin joined Fadaiyan as shadow warriors and created a heroic era of Iranian politics, representing the unified action of militant Marxists and Muslims in their war against the Shah's repressive regime.

The publication of *Manifesto of Ideological Positions of Organization of Iranian People's Mojahedin (Marxist-Leninist)* (OIPM [M-L] 1976a) in December 1975 surprised the Iranian opposition. The *Manifesto* declared a major ideological shift in the OIPM, claiming that "in honest efforts to resolve the most basic problems of the revolution, we arrived at the truth of Marxism-Leninism" (OIPM [M-L] 1976a, 11). They had concealed the ideological conflicts within their group, partly because of the Shi'i doctrine of *taqiyyeh*—dissimulation, or in this case, avoidance of ideological debates—to which members were ordered to adhere (GCU 1977d, 24). Moreover, the OIPM members were subjected to highly restricted rules of conduct and ideological training, compared to the OIPFG in which personal attitudes and ideological divergence (e.g., Maoism) were toler-ated to some extent (Fatapour 2001a). According to the *Manifesto,* the members of Marxist-Leninist Mojahedin had been in the ranks of the founding members of the group since 1965. But they had actually adopted Marxism around 1971, and launched their internal "relentless ideological struggle" in 1973 (OIPM [M-L] 1976a, 11). "In spite of all the innovations that our Organization introduced to religious thought and in spite of all the efforts it made to revive and revitalize its [i.e., Islam's] historical content and upgrade its archaic principles and methods to the latest scientific contributions [to the study] of society," holds the *Manifesto,* "since it [the OIPM] was based on idealist foundations . . . it could not provide a convincing explanation about the existing issues of our revolutionary move-ment" (OIPM [M-L] 1976a, 91). To "uncover" and "destroy" idealism "the 'reform and education' movement and the ideological retraining of the cadres from top to bottom began in our Organization" (OIPM [M-L] 1976a, 14). Yet according to the Muslim Mojahedin, during the six years of underground work prior to 1971, the issue of recruiting Marxists was raised only once and the idea was unani-mously rejected. Up until the death of the leader of the OIPM, Reza Rezai, in June 1973, there was no doubt about the Islamic character of the group (OIPM 1979a, 33–34). The loss of several leaders in a matter of two years allowed the promo-tion of (covert) Marxist members to the CC. After August 1971, the CC of OIPM included Reza Rezai, Kazem Zolanvar, and Bahram Aram. Zolanvar's arrest in 1972 brought Majid Sharif Vaqefi to the CC, and Rezai's death in 1973 brought in Taqi Shahram (Nejati 1992, 408–9; OIPM 1979a, 41–42). Apparently at this point the "reforms" began. Aram, Shahram, Hossein Rohani, and Torab Haqshenas played key roles in turning the OIPM into a Marxist group (Haqshenas 2001, 25). According to Shahram, "As soon as we mended the worn-out shirt of Islam in one place, it ripped in another" (quoted in Nabavi 2002). So the new CC tried to get the group a new ideological shirt.

The "ideological struggle" did not go well. Between 1973 and 1975, the "ide-ological training" subjected rank-and-file members to forced labor, flogging, ousting, threats, and even exposing the adamant Muslim members to SAVAK (GCU 1977d, 207–8; GCU 1977c, 2; OIPM [M-L] 1976a, 23; Nejat Hosseini 2000, 361). Those who did not "reform" themselves—about 50 percent of the member-ship—were expelled (OIPM [M-L] 1976a, 18, n.1; see also Abrahamian 1989, 165; Khanbaba Tehrani 2001, 200). In addition, according to the Marxist Mojahedin (henceforth Mojahedin [M-L]), four members refused to "reform" themselves and clandestinely "conspired" against the CC (OIPM [M-L] 1976a, 19–21). Consequently the leadership "sentenced" two of the "traitors" to death: Majid Sharif Vaqefi, the only Muslim in the CC, and Morteza Samadiyeh Labbaf. On May 6, 1975, Aram and Shahram kidnapped Sharif Vaqefi and Samadiyeh Labbaf. They killed Sharif Vaqefi, set his body on fire, and disposed of it in a dumpster, which was later found by SAVAK. But Samadiyeh Labbaf, while injured, escaped, was arrested by the police, and was later executed (Nejati 1992, 424). How many OIPM members were purged is not known but other purges have recently been reported (Haqshenas 2001, 25–26; Nejat Hosseini, 362–64, 423–32; see also Peykar 1979).

The ideological shift in Mojahedin caused resentment among Muslim militants. In the eyes of many, the abhorrent conduct of Mojahedin (M-L) made Marxism equivalent to purging and intrigue, and they alienated Muslim militants from the leftists. Forces of the Left, while surprised by the events, dealt with the issue cautiously. Not one single leftist group endorsed the idea of hijacking a Muslim organization. The representatives of Fadaiyan, Mojahedin (M-L), and Setareh held meetings on the issue (GCU 1977d, 67; see also OIPM [M-L] 1977). Fadaiyan's concerns appear in an issue of the OIPFG *Internal Bulletin*, where they published a communiqué by some of the Mojahedin rank-and-file who did not approve of the group's ideological transformation (*Nashriyeh-ye Dakheli* 1976, 91–103). Reports indicate that Hamid Ashraf had strongly reacted against the assassination of Sharif Vaqefi (OIPM [M-L] 1976b, 164). In any case, Mojahedin (M-L) put the OPFG in an awkward situation, given that Fadaiyan, in prison or outside, always had excellent relations with the Muslim Mojahedin. Given the OIPFG's record of eliminating their defectors, in the purges of Mojahedin (M-L) the Fadai leaders found the haunting reflection of a dark part of their own past.

The United Popular Front

Notwithstanding the initial unease, Mojahedin (M-L) and Fadaiyan found themselves, literally by default, on the way to potential unification. Cassette tapes containing the positions of the two groups were exchanged. The Mojahedin (M-L) initiated the process of debate by proposing their strategic "united popular front" (*jebheh-ye vahed-e tudehi*). The debate was soon lost in an atmosphere of distrust, allegation, and sabotage. The OIPFG responded to the call for the "united popular front" by establishing a special internal *Bulletin,* publishing two issues (OIPM [M-L] 1976b, 21–22). The first issue (April 1976) contained three essays by Fadaiyan and the second (October 1976) presented the rejoinders of Mojahedin (M-L) filled with allegations and distortions. The two groups had agreed to publish the *Bulletin* only internally, but after the death of the OIPFG leaders in June 1976, the Mojahedin (M-L) unilaterally published the second issue publicly, which provoked the retaliatory publication of the first issue by Fadaiyan in July 1977. The Mojahedin (M-L) intentionally terminated their contacts with Fadaiyan by publicizing their allegations against them. They opportunistically hoped to replace the nearly annihilated OIPFG in the landscape of Iranian opposition, and to absorb Fadai supporters and resources.

To this end, no weapon could be as effective as distortions and accusations, the features of hostile divisions commonly attributed to the sectarian tendencies of the Left in Iran (and elsewhere). However, such explanations miss the theoretical aporia that penetrates discourses of class conflict or national liberation, and the debate between the OIPFG and the Mojahedin (M-L) was no exception.

According to Mojahedin (M-L), the "united popular front" consists of "all popular forces involved in the struggle against the traitor Shah's regime and its imperialist masters, and at the top, American imperialism." Specifically, the front will comprise: (1) Marxist-Leninist militant groups; (2) religious militant groups; and (3) political Marxist-Leninists (with the exception of the Tudeh Party). The *Manifesto* argues that the front needs a "healthy ideological struggle" because of its diversity (OIPM [M-L] 1976a, 48–50). The proposal overlooks the distrust of the opposition toward Mojahedin (M-L), and reassures Muslims that the OIPM (M-L) endorses "militant religion" (1976a, 52). The group argues that the united popular front should not be postponed until the formation of the Communist Party (OIPM [M-L] 1976a, 54). The last point became the locus of contention between the OIPFG and Mojahedin (M-L).

The prose and directive character of the first of the three OIPFG essays, "On the Front," suggest that it was probably written by Ashraf, and the article explains why the OIPFG calls the "unification of anti-imperialist forces" a naïve slogan; the author goes on to refute the concept of a popular liberation movement. "The front," he formulates, "is a temporary unity that emerges out of those political forces that, in a specific historical stage, under specific objective conditions and based on the material necessities of struggle, have engaged a common enemy"

(OIPFG 1977b, 2). The necessities of struggle become clear from the class content of the opposition forces, their current-stage objectives, or the form of their struggle. Against the unspecific class character of the "united popular front" of Mojahedin (M-L), the essay insists that without the "class consolidation of social forces" and their mobilization under the leadership of the Party the objective conditions for the front cannot be created. Class tendencies, in other words, must have clear political representations (OIPFG 1977b, 4–5). The Fadaiyan's position, which emphasizes the class character of the liberation front, contains an important delineation that does not exist in Jazani's ambivalent theory of front formation. This new shift indicates that *toward the end of Ashraf's leadership, the OIPFG had already moved not only toward Jazani's theory but also beyond it.* Why should class consolidation of participants in a liberation front become an issue? The answer rests in the problem of leadership: by 1976, the OIPFG has decisively focused its attempts to ensure its leadership as the vanguard of the working class over any possible front. Interestingly, however, the idea is not a theoretical derivation from the canons of Marxism-Leninism. Rather, it is reached at through a pragmatic element: a specific platform and program that should determine who can participate in the front.

> Naturally the stronger political force or forces, which reflect the social force of the main classes participating in the front, will play a decisive role in determining the articles of platform and program of the front, and while they grant the minimum demands of other forces at that stage, they will compose the front's program in accordance with their own overall strategy. It is expected that the leading social forces will play a decisive role in managing and directing the front's subdivisions as well. (OIPFG 1977b, 8–9)

The OIPFG implies that the era of bourgeois-democratic revolution in Iran has passed. "In a bourgeois-democratic revolution the leadership of the front will go to the nationalist bourgeoisie and its party, while in a new democratic revolution the leadership of the front will belong to the proletariat and its party, the Communist party" (OIPFG 1977b, 8–9). Naturally, militant Communists must build the leadership of the working class. The article's use of the Maoist phrase "new democratic revolution" rhetorically reasserts the requirement for Communist leadership in the front, but it implies the Leninist "Socialist revolution." So the term "new democratic revolution" should not be interpreted as a Maoist tendency within the OIPFG (OIPFG 1977b, 17–18). The article also rejects the Tudeh Party for not recognizing the comprador bourgeoisie as the enemy (OIPFG 1977b, 20). The rejection of both Maoists and the Tudeh shows that for Fadaiyan the notion of working-class vanguard is defined primarily through certain political positions, modes of practice, and a common enemy, and not by a pregiven ideological stance. This point can be interpreted as Fadaiyan's limited, even sectarian, idea of the vanguard. And yet it can be interpreted to suggest that being Communist is not sufficient for unity. These two positions, of course, are not mutually exclusive, nor do they really oppose one another: the ambiguity remains an arch character of the Fadai discourse.

The author of "On the Front" names three necessary conditions for the formation of a national liberation front: a common enemy; a common strategy of the existing stage (of revolution); and a common pivotal tactic. These are also the supplementary conditions of unity and popularity (see OIPFG 1977b, 8–12). To the dismay of the Mojahedin (M-L), the essay concludes, "The lack of any of the necessary three conditions will render any 'real' front impossible, but the lack of any of the five conditions above will make the 'united popular movement' impossible" (OIPFG 1977b, 12).

The second essay of the first bulletin, "A Glance at Mojahedin's Plan on the Issue of Unification," demonstrates that the OIPFG's rejection of a non-class-based popular front stems from its intention to hold the pivotal role in the future Iranian revolution. The article makes the assertion that Fadaiyan have now passed the initial phase of armed struggle and are in the process of popularising armed struggle (OIPFG 1977b, 31). The essay predicts that in the next ten years Iran will have a large working class, which "will allow us to believe without hesitation in the Socialist character of the Iranian revolution," in stark contrast to their earlier usage of the term "new democratic revolution" (OIPFG 1977b, 39). The "united popular front" has no place in the prediction because it blurs the imminent labor-capital conflict in Iran (OIPFG 1977b, 41). In consequence, the unification of Communists as a hegemonic core is *the* necessity at this stage of struggle (OIPFG 1977b, 48).

In their rejoinder to these criticisms, the Mojahedin (M-L) declare themselves the crusaders "for the purification (*paksazi*) of the theory and practice of the vanguard's armed movement" (OIPM [M-L] 1976b, 10). Without reservations, they point out that the OIPFG's rejection of their proposed "united popular front" necessitates exposing Fadaiyan's deviationism through "ideological struggle" (OIPM [M-L] 1976b, 13). Interestingly, the Mojahedin (M-L) trace their united popular front back to Ahmadzadeh's vision of unified revolutionary forces. By rejecting Ahmadzadeh's view, the Mojahedin (M-L) claim, the OIPFG exposes its deviationism (OIPM [M-L] 1976b, 166). The Mojahedin (M-L) find in the origins of Fadaiyan their own theoretical foundation as well. But their accusing Fadaiyan of deviationism shows how they were kept in the dark about the OIPFG's major shift toward Jazani.

Moreover, the rejoinder continues, while the front is merely a "temporary organization" composed of anti-imperialist forces, Fadaiyan grant themselves an exclusive role in the revolution as if "the growth of the revolution = the growth of the OPFG" (OIPM [M-L] 1976b, 182n1). To refute the OIPFG's advocacy of the programmatic priority of working-class unity over the popular front, Mojahedin (M-L) assert, unwarrantedly, that the working class will find its unity in the front, leaving other forces without a single political representation (OIPM [M-L] 1976b, 219). This argument of Marxist Mojahedin is flawed because they grant themselves the role of unifying the working-class vanguards, while depriving others of such unity. The OIPFG rightly points out that the hegemonic core cannot be arbitrarily granted to one group. Without the core the front will only put the working-class vanguard at the mercy of other forces, and deprive the working class of its political identity. And this is precisely what happened in the 1979 Revolution.

The "ideological struggle" between the Marxist Mojahedin and Fadaiyan restarted during the first year after the Revolution, but its theoretical significance withered as both groups had changed their ideological positions. As early as 1978, with Fadaiyan still assessing Jazani's theory, Mojahedin (M-L) took the bold step of renouncing guerrilla warfare, calling it detrimental to working-class politics. Paradoxically, with the rejection of armed struggle Mojahedin (M-L) came to hold the very same position they had refuted in 1976: that only the leadership of the working class can guarantee the victory of the liberatory revolution (OIPM [M-L] 1978, 10). In 1979, the Mojahedin (M-L) witnessed how during the Iranian Revolution the working class joined the "united front" without claiming working-class identity, demands, or agenda (OIPM [M-L] 1978, 7). Later they merged with small Maoist groups and formed Sazman-e Peykar dar Rah-e

Azadi-ye Tabaqe-ye Kargar (Organization to Combat for the Emancipation of the Working Class; Peykar) (Abrahamian 1989, 146; Behrooz 1999, 70–74).

Haunting Issues of a Centrist Discourse

Another revelation from the Fadaiyan-Mojahedin (M-L) exchange is the issue of Stalinist tendencies in Iranian Marxism. While the GCU raised issues about the OPFG's Stalinist tendencies, the problem was primarily treated as an intellectual and theoretical one. Haunted by their own covered-up purges before or around 1973, the OIPFG displayed ambivalence about the internal disciplinary measures. Such ambivalence can be justifiably attributed to the adversity of guerrilla existence or to the self-appointed leadership that typified many Third World leftist parties. Still the roots of the issue should be sought in the absence of democratic impulse. Even after the Revolution, when the OIPFG grew into the largest leftist party in Iran, the group still could not free itself of the ideological hold that elevated the party to the status of highest intellects. Purportedly, by 1976, Fadaiyan had already become critical of the practice of repressing internal differences in their ranks. "We believe in criticism and self-criticism as a basic weapon in our organization," a Fadai leader is reported to have told the Mojahedin (M-L). "Through this practice, we build ourselves so that we would not have to resort to methods of purging" (quoted in OIPM [M-L] 1976b, 115).

A postrevolutionary document, by Pishgam, the OIPFG's student organization, intends to continue the exchange with Peykar. In it, the OIPFG lectures Peykar that members should be able to criticize weaknesses and problems, both in theory and in practice. Dissenting members should be challenged "in a healthy way," and "if the weakness is not removed . . . the unhealthy individual or current is expelled (*kenar gozashteh mishavad*)," but, Pishgam asserts, expulsion is not done in a "hostile and irresponsible way, but in democratic ways such that the existing forces [i.e., members] in the movement are not hurt. The traitors that are found inside a M-L [Marxist-Leninist] organization, [however,] are enemies of the movement and will be dealt with belligerently" (Pishgam Student Organization nd, 3–4). This passage reads as if the author is reflecting, obliquely, on the darkest pages of OIPFG history: the purges. The text intends to criticize the bloody emergence of the Mojahedin (M-L), now Peykar. Curiously, the text reflects Fadaiyan's constitutive ambivalence regarding membership issues: the passage both rejects and confirms the purging of members. The text, then, refers to the 1977 OIPFG splinter group (Monsha'ebin) as an example of how ideological differences were dealt with in a "healthy way" even though the members of the splinter group had become "pacifist," "deviationist," and "revisionist" in the aftermath of the June 1976 crackdown on Fadaiyan. The pamphlet, of course, does not mention that the split of the Monsha'ebin took place precisely when Ashraf was killed and the remaining Fadaiyan were unable to make any major decision about the splinter group. The pamphlet subconsciously compensates for the indecision of OIPFG's new leadership and their "general theoretical weakness," a weakness that was shown in not engaging in a debate with the splinter group (Pishgam Student Organization nd, 4).

The Mojahedin (M-L) states, "Marxism-Leninism is not an idea that one can claim to know but does not believe in it" (OIPM [M-L] 1976a, 180). This religious understanding of Marxism resulted in a crusader's view of "ideological struggle" and justified any conduct in the name of "ideological purity." Fadaiyan never quite adhered to such a view, partly because of the diverse social and intellectual background of their constituents and partly because of their constitutive theoretical ambivalence and shifting influences. This ambivalence is reflected in the democratic discourse beneath the hard ideological shell of Fadaiyan. This discourse could only be brought to the surface through the OIPFG's major organizational transformation toward an open and democratic political party. That transformation, of course, did not occur before the Revolution.

On a different ground, the contention over the popular front constitutes a prevalent feature of Iranian politics in the 1970s. The undeveloped nature of secular political forces necessitated the OIPFG's position on the primacy of class consolidation prior to frontal formation. Specifically, the OIPFG acknowledges, there is no "organic relationship" between the masses and their vanguards (quoted in OIPM [M-L] 1976b, 2). Here the OIPFG literally admits the failure of guerrilla warfare in social mobilization. Years after their advent, Fadaiyan were still struggling to find a way out of the rather simplistic visions of their founders—Jazani's "armed propaganda" and Ahmadzadeh's "small motor"—who wished for shortcuts in the long and painstaking road to social mobilization. Ahmadzadeh and Jazani, though disagreeing on many issues, both posited the presumed presence of the masses who were discontent, conscious, willing, and self-organizing and who would then, layer by layer, join the struggle of their vanguards when the roar of the guerrillas' machine guns broke the suffocating silence in society. Before his untimely death, Jazani had already seen the problem of mobilization. Because he had not realized that a guerrilla organization was structurally and politically incapable of mobilizing and organizing the people, Jazani tried to remedy this conceptual shortcoming by adding a "second leg" to the de facto armed movement, but to no avail.

Before the 1976 dramatic assaults on the OIPFG, under the direction of Ashraf and Armaghani, Fadaiyan made attempts at contacting workers and constructing a workers' wing of the Organization. The publication of *Nabard-e Khalq-e Zahmatkeshan* (The toilers' *Nabard-e Khalq*) indicated rudimentary steps in changing the OIPFG strategy (see *Nabard-e Khalq* [for workers and toilers] 1978). Fadaiyan were no longer optimistic or hopeful about the spontaneous support of the masses, so they now embarked on the enormous task of branching out. This course of action explains why in their response to the Mojahedin (M-L) they emphasize that what distinguishes the Party from the front is that the front has internal diversity and thus cannot be treated as a (centralist) party (OIPFG in OIPM [M-L] 1976b, 3).

Finally, the debate between the OIPFG and the Mojahedin (M-L) shows that by separating themselves from Maoism and the Tudeh, and by rejecting the possibility of any unity with the Mojahedin (M-L), the OIPFG exposed its sectarianism, a persistent plague of Marxist tradition. While true, this interpretation overlooks a crucial fact: Fadaiyan were originally bound by certain modalities of practice that arose directly out of their specific historical-cultural context. Because Maoists and the Tudeh had formed within different contexts, so long as they remained true to their originative moments, they could not participate in a "new Communist movement" that had its origins in the revolutionary impulse of a different generation of secular-Left intellectuals. Therefore, it is in fact guerrilla warfare (a modality of practice) that defines one's ideological authenticity in 1970s Iran, despite the claims to the contrary. *So communism is literally only a supplement to revolutionary practice. Ideology is only a justification for a modality of action that is unable to theorize itself.* This is one of the conclusions of this study (see chapter 9).

Setareh once pointed out while criticizing the Stalinism of the Mojahedin (M-L) that the guerrilla movement attracted distressed intellectuals who simply wanted to engage in some kind of visible protest action against the regime's dictatorship without having much concern for ideological positions (GCU 1977c, 63). Setareh was right, but the militant Left of the 1970s understood their constituent secular-Left intellectuals as something other than what they actually were, and as a result, these intellectuals sadly lost their historic chance to lead the prolonged process of building a secular-democratic umbrella social movement for a new, democratic Iran.

THE MONSHA'EBIN

The departure of the Fadai splinter group, or Monsha'ebin, can be attributed to the 1976 SAVAK crackdown on the OIPFG, the loss of leadership, and low morale. Nevertheless, the roots of the discontent of members within Fadaiyan who were disillusioned with guerrilla warfare can paradoxically be traced back to 1974 and the heightened guerrilla presence of the OPFG. Mehdi Fatapour reminisces about instances of reactions by a Tehran Fadai team against the OPFG leadership's espousal of Maoism as advocated by Momeni as early as 1974 (Fatapour 2001a; Heydari Bigvand 1978, g). Monsha'ebin were all members of a major Tehran unit under the command of Mohammad Reza Yasrebi (killed along with Ashraf on June 28, 1976), and they were based in Qarechak, south of Tehran (Heydar 1999, 267, n.34). Most of them were former members of an armed cell of Aryamehr Industrial University students that had joined the OPFG. The group was led by Hossein (Siamak) Qalambor and Turaj Heydari Bigvand, and other members included Fariborz Salehi, Farzad Dadgar, Sima Behmanesh, and Fatemeh Izadi (Fatapour 2001a; Behrooz 1999, 67).[1] Some of the Monsha'ebin members were among the most experienced cadres of Fadaiyan. The splinter group took away about one-quarter of the OIPFG's cadres, about ten of nearly forty, and it split in the aftermath of the 1976 assaults (Satwat 2002; Fatapour 2001a).

With the new leadership in place and with their disagreements over OIPFG's strategy and tactics intensifying, Monsha'ebin demanded the distribution of their

1. In the Seventeenth Plenum of the Tudeh Party CC (March 1981), Khatib, Qalambor, Izadi, and Salehi (from Monsha'ebin) were elected alternate members of the CC (Kianuri 1992, 520). Qalambor, Khatib, Dadgar, Salehi, and Lahijanian were executed in the summer of 1988. Another member of Monsha'ebin, Nader Zarkar, managed to flee to the USSR (Amir Khosravi and Heydarian 2002, 526).

ideas among the rank-and-file Fadaiyan. In response, cassette tapes containing their views were circulated among Fadai members, some of whom were equally discontent with the guerrilla strategy (Satwat 2002). The new leadership asked them to stay with the OIPFG and continue their debate, but Monsha'ebin bitterly refused, citing the earlier purges as well as their ideological discontent (Fatapour 2001a). There is no significant report about the activities of Monsha'ebin until March 18, 1979, when they announced joining the Tudeh Party. The Tudeh's publishing of the only work of Monsha'ebin, written by Turaj Heydari Bigvand, is evidence that they had contacted the Tudeh as early as 1978. According to Behrooz, Monsha'ebin established contacts with the small pro-Tudeh underground cell in Iran known as Navid (1999, 67). Nonetheless, they remained virtually obscure until the days of the Revolution.

The split of Monsha'ebin is yet another proof of ideological diversity within the OIPFG, an origination that was anything but ideologically monolithic. Fadaiyan were distinctive in that they developed with (leftist) ideological diversity, which means the action-oriented Fadaiyan had only a secondary interest in theory and ideology. Practical tasks were their primary concern. There is no evidence to suggest that Ashraf planned to expel Monsha'ebin. The fact that the new leadership encouraged Monsha'ebin to stay while retaining their ideas attests to the need for fresh ideological blood. The much-coveted new ideological base was found in 1978, ironically by making a decisive return to the older ideas—those of Jazani. The OIPFG leadership never bothered to engage in documented debates with Monsha'ebin, although we do know about the exchange of cassette tapes containing the issues raised by Monsha'ebin. While the missed interlocution is usually attributed to the harsh conditions of 1976 when the very survival of the OIPFG was at stake, without theoretically competent cadres, the OIPFG leadership could only be silent. The 1976 events awakened the Fadai survivors to the strategic failure of the armed movement and forced them to face the social and political disabilities imposed on the OIPFG by guerrilla structure.

The Leninist critique of guerrilla warfare written by Heydari Bigvand became Monsha'ebin's "manifesto." Although his critique is tainted with colorful accusations, it sheds light on important aspects of Fadaiyan's life. To reconstruct this missed interlocution between the OIPFG and Monsha'ebin, I examine Heydari Bigvand's critique next.

A Leninist Critique of Armed Struggle

Heydari Bigvand was born in 1955 and killed in a street battle in October 1976. He wrote *Theory of Armed Propaganda: A Deviation from Marxism-Leninism* in May 1976 as the first volume of a larger critique of Jazani's thought. Apparently he had also criticized Ahmadzadeh and was angered by the assassination of Nushirvanpur. He had been reportedly "disciplined" with factory work on account of his criticisms (see Heydari Bigvand 1978, *h*).

In *Theory of Armed Propaganda*, Heydari Bigvand specifically targets Jazani's *How Armed Struggle Becomes a Mass Movement?* He reports that the Fadai Guerrillas had only recently acknowledged "errors of militantism" and their "neglect of theory" (1978, 1). Echoing the Tudeh's opinion of Fadaiyan as a terrorist group, Heydari Bigvand compares economism with terrorism and points out how they both fail to mobilize workers because they neglect the revolutionary activities of the masses. The assassination of a capitalist (referring to Fateh Yazdi) represents damning evidence of the convergence of terrorism and economism (1978, 19).

He submits that Puyan's pamphlet exemplifies the isolation of the revolutionary intellectuals. The originators of Fadaiyan, he argues, erred in accounting for the stagnancy of the masses because they did not use proper methods and attributed political inertia to the prevalence of police surveillance (1978, 11–12), a factually distorted claim (Heydari Bigvand 1978, 49). Contrary to armed struggle, Leninism teaches that to neutralize repression, we must cancel out the police efforts in silencing revolutionary propaganda by taking revolutionary ideas to the masses. As such, the notion of "armed propaganda" (Jazani) was an effort at covering up the OIPFG's conflict with Leninism (Heydari Bigvand 1978, 16). Armed struggle not only detached Fadaiyan from the people, it propagated the group's sectarianism as well (Heydari Bigvand 1978, 30).

Heydari Bigvand clearly treats Leninism in a canonical way and evaluates Jazani's work using Lenin's yardstick, and in the end he calls Jazani's thought "eclectic" and "non-Marxist" (1978, 64). He explicitly rejects the claim made in *Nabard-e Khalq* (no. 6) that Jazani offers a "creative application of Marxism-Leninism to Iranian conditions" (quoted in Heydari Bigvand 1978, 52; *Nabard-e Khalq* 1975b, 6). Rather, he asserts, Jazani's work is "eclectic" as he "moves away considerably from Marxism-Leninism and recedes toward theories that preceded social democracy" (1978, 52), showing that Jazani surrendered to the spontaneous movement of despairing Iranian intellectuals. Interestingly, Heydari Bigvand considers Lenin's strategy and tactic in prerevolutionary Russia as the absolute measure with which to evaluate working-class politics (1978, 52–54). The success of Chinese and Cuban revolutions and the prevalence of the Uruguayan model in Latin America do not attest to the correctness of these models (Heydari Bigvand 1978, 55). These models as well as Jazani's, he concludes, lack a "living knowledge" (*shenakht-e zendeh*) based on practice (*peratik*), and Jazani's emphasis on practice (peratik) is especially criticized as a simplistic notion based on a mechanical understanding of Marxism (1978, 58–59).

Overall, though, Heydari Bigvand is correct when he observes that armed struggle failed to achieve its objectives. He also recognizes that armed struggle in Iran does not arise from the "objective conditions" but from the overzealous intellectuals inspired by the international liberation movements (1978, 82). In his view, this suggests a heretical, and thus an unwarranted, intrusion into the Leninist revolutionary program. What he overlooks, however, is his own *presupposition* of Leninism as an irrefutable canon of revolutionary practice. Leninism becomes an imposition, a justificatory supplement, which serves liberation movements, in our case the OIPFG, to position themselves in the postcolonial international movements in the context of Cold War hostile camps. This international division imposed itself upon movements for national self-determination and economic independence and forced liberation movements into calling on the justificatory paradigm of Leninism, so much so that during the 1960s and the 1970s Leninism became the a priori measure of revolutionary Marxism. Strange as it sounds, in the twentieth century *Marxism was no longer revolutionary without Leninism,* and by the same token, Leninism without Maoism, for Maoists. The OIPFG theories need to be evaluated in this context, and not, as in Heydari Bigvand, by the rigid exercise of the then fifty-year-old Leninist prescriptions.

What an irony of history: the activists whose discontent with undemocratic and Stalinist measures made them break away from the OIPFG in turn became members of Iran's oldest undemocratic and internally conspiratorial leftist party (thanks to Lenin!). It is amazing how Monsha'ebin provided an early glance into Fadaiyan's future when, after the 1980 schism, the Majority arrived at the same conclusion that Monsha'ebin had reached four years earlier, rejected its past from a canonical Marxist-Leninist standpoint, and almost joined the Tudeh Party.

The Virtual Tudeh-Fadai Exchange

The theoretical emergence of Fadaiyan involved exorcising the haunting specter of the Tudeh in the Iranian Left. Most of the major works of Fadaiyan entailed, in some way, attempts at distancing the new Communist movement from any trace of the Tudeh Party (see OIPFG 1978a). Jazani was especially attentive to the importance of ideological struggle against the Tudeh. A Tudeh-Fadaiyan debate might well have been extremely productive for the Iranian Left. Not surprisingly, such a debate never materialized. The OIPFG accused the Tudeh of treason, opportunism, and dogmatic pro-Soviet attitude, while the Tudeh charged Fadaiyan with terrorism, adventurism, Maoism, and at best, juvenile rebelliousness. Siahkal had caught the Tudeh by surprise, and the Tudeh responded to it, with delay, by publishing a pamphlet written by CC member Farajollah Mizani (Javanshir). He renounced the Fadai Guerrillas and anticipated the withering of the PFG, which of course did not happen (Javan 1972). For leftist militants, dialogue with the Tudeh would amount to guilt by association and thereby banishment from the new Communist movement. But the many polemical pamphlets that the two published against each other contained a stealthy "debate" between an original movement (the Tudeh Party) trying to tame a new rebellious generation and a young movement denying its historical origin. Jazani judiciously observes that the Tudeh's initial dismissive attitude toward Fadaiyan (until 1973–74) was owing to the Tudeh's confusion of guerrilla movement with Maoism. Ideology made the Tudeh leaders blind to the fact that the guerrilla movement in Iran was not Maoist (Jazani 1979a, 94). Fadaiyan's resilience plus the Tudeh's gradual assurance about the non-Maoist stance of the OPFG resulted in the Tudeh Party's changing its tone into one of paternal criticism. As late as 1980, the Tudeh still described Fadaiyan, now the largest leftist group in the country, as emotional enthusiasts who were closer to the Tudeh than they were willing to acknowledge (Mehregan 1979; Tudeh Party of Iran 1979).

Several studies on the Tudeh Party relieve me of the need to offer its history (Abrahamian 1982; Behrooz 1999; Behrooz 2001; JAMI Collective 1983; Zabih 1986). However, I must discuss a crucial point here: the Tudeh Party traces its foundation back to the international conditions of World War II, fighting against fascism, and the fall of Reza Shah in 1941. From its inception, writes Iraj Eskandari, the Party's general secretary, the Tudeh founders faced a dilemma:

> Either they should have established the political organization of the working class under the rubric of the Communist Party of Iran and then tried to lead the movement from the outside, or they should have directly assumed the movement's leadership by establishing the united revolutionary organization and prevented the non-proletarian forces from taking over the control of the movement and directed it into another path. (Eskandari 1974, 4)

The Tudeh desired a leadership role and acted as a democratic, anti-imperialist front that intended to unify the masses, and not as a Communist party, while paradoxically it identified itself as the historical offshoot of the Iranian Communist Party (Eskandari 1974, 4–5). The Tudeh's appearance in Iranian politics as a front presents the Comintern-Dimitrov doctrine of united anti-fascist front. Documents retrieved from Comintern archives show that the above official party lines conceal how the Tudeh Party was founded by Colonel Seliukov of the Intelligence Division of the Soviet Red Army under the direct initiative and supervision of Stalin and Comintern (Chaqueri 1999). From its very foundation, the Tudeh Party was torn between a policy of united front and its allegiance to the Soviet Union. *The Fadai theorists negated these two founding characteristics of the Tudeh:* they repudiated the Stalinist-Comintern policy of national popular front without Communist leadership, and they advocated neutrality toward the postwar schism in the Socialist camp. The Fadai Guerrillas were rebellious in more ways than one.

The Tudeh's policy toward Fadaiyan altered radically after December 1975 with the new Party Program. In the meantime, Jazani wrote a pamphlet in prison, *Who Betrays Marxism-Leninism?* It contains rejoinders to the Tudeh's accusations against Fadaiyan; however, unlike other OIPFG literature, Jazani's pamphlet also attempts to start, albeit cautiously, a virtual dialogue with the Tudeh.

Jazani observes a historical rift between the Tudeh and Fadaiyan. Armed struggle, he asserts, is a direct response to the Tudeh Party's failure following the 1953 coup, and therefore the Tudeh is accountable for hindering political modernization for two decades (1976c, 46). Its failure is exacerbated by its inaction and its scant analysis of social and political forces following the 1963 uprising (Jazani 1978, 56). Armed struggle restores the belated national liberation project by "filling the leadership void in society," organizing a liberation army, and unifying political and military revolutionary forces. Armed struggle does not aspire to overthrow the state nor does it "conspire" to do so (Jazani nd-b, 10).

The "leadership" issue caused the OIPFG to reject the Tudeh's call for a "united anti-dictatorship front" (*jebhe-ye vahed-e zedd-e diktatori*). The chief feature of the Tudeh's front is the Party's controversial support for the "realistic" wings of the "ruling elite" (*heyat-e hakemeh*) in the interest-driven conflict with the reactionary wing that includes the Shah. The anti-dictatorship forces should then enter into an alliance with the discontented sectors of the Iranian bourgeoisie. The alliance with the bourgeoisie is short-term but necessary, because no single force in Iran is strong enough to overthrow the regime single-handedly. This tactic, the Tudeh insists, is in line with Lenin's theory of democratic revolution in his *Two Tactics*. The Tudeh, of course, was not serious about the front because it had only a negligible political weight. The proposed front simply showed the Party's bookish understanding of the situation. The Tudeh could not envision that the discontented sectors in the state orbit would prefer the Shah to any of the opposition forces, and under no circumstances would they enter into an alliance with Marxists, nationalists, or Muslims.

The Tudeh's "united front" linked itself to the ill-conceived, Soviet-propagated thesis of the "noncapitalist path." The core of the theory, advanced by Rostislav Ulyanovsky, is actually quite naïve: under the increasing international hegemony of the USSR, nationalist-democratic forces (the petit-bourgeoisie) in Third World countries have the power to lead the democratic revolution to socialism with the technical and financial support of the "actually existing socialism" (see Ulyanovsky and Pavlov 1973). It is a Socialist "developmental" doctrine that encourages Third World peripheral economies to link themselves to the Soviet sphere instead of to capitalist metropolises. The theory does away with Lenin's emphasis on the leadership of the proletariat (Communists) as the irreplaceable precondition for the triumphant Socialist revolution. Based on this theory, the Tudeh never invoked the issue of leadership. Because the OIPFG *did not assume* the global leadership of the Socialist bloc, it sharply refuted the Tudeh's potentially "compromised position" with parts of the Iranian ruling classes when the Revolution was fermenting in 1978. Instead, Fadaiyan emphasized the leading role of the working class in the liberation movement (OIPFG 1978b, 4–6, 12), alluding to the class character of the liberation front against forces of dependent capitalism, and dictatorship as its political expression (a superstructure). This position echoed the one Jazani had advocated some three years earlier (1976c, 157–58).

The missed interlocution between the OIPFG and the Tudeh confirms that Fadaiyan's true challenge was to seek their roots in the liberation movements of the 1960s and 1970s, especially in Latin America and not in the shrine of the Russian Revolution so passionately cherished by the Tudeh Party. The guerrilla movement in Iran should therefore be viewed as an attempt at recovering, after a twenty-year historical-developmental lapse, the aborted project of national liberation. Armed movement tries to invoke this abandoned historical possibility. Yet because of this, a certain ambivalence reveals itself: the Tudeh's failure in 1953 along with the 1960s revolutionary spirit suggest both continuity and rupture with the past. As such, the Fadai Guerrillas reveal their identity crisis as a Communist movement that could not identify with its received Communist tradition. *This alienation from their roots is precisely what makes them original, regardless of their intended political goals, or their achievements or failures.* Nevertheless, the simple negation of the past would ultimately be impossible for a Communist movement haunted by the ghostly presence of its origins. It is probably no accident that Jazani's strategic slogan, "Death to the Shah's Dictatorship and His Imperialist Supporters," sounded to many activists like the Tudeh's "united anti-dictatorship front," despite the OIPFG's assurance to the contrary (Ahmadzadeh 2001; see also Pishgam Student Organization nd, 37). The haunting origins of Iran's popular Communist movement resurfaced every time Fadaiyan needed to justify guerrilla action. Fadaiyan addressed the issue by adamantly denying their origins both rhetorically and ideologically while Monsha'ebin addressed it by returning to and embracing their Communist past.

THE DIVERSE FADAIYAN

The three preceding interlocutions irrefutably illustrate the internal diversity among the Fadai Guerrillas. Enjoying the position of institutive actors of the new Communist movement, Fadaiyan could not avoid the challenges to their perceived unity despite continuous attempts at theoretical and organizational consolidation. *Each external challenge to the OIPFG reflected an internal one.* Setareh invoked the element of "nonalignment" in regard to the Sino-Soviet conflict within Fadaiyan, forcing them to face the covert but pervasive organizational and theoretical tendencies toward Stalinism. No wonder Setareh could not be integrated into the OIPFG! During 1974–75, critical engagement with Stalinism seemed almost fatal to the Organization of the Fadai Guerrillas. Ironically, the Mojahedin (M-L) forced Fadaiyan to critically reflect on their organizational life by criticizing Stalinist tendencies and purges in the Mojahedin (M-L). In their debates with the Marxist Mojahedin and the virtual debate with the Tudeh, the OIPFG insisted on its principle of leadership and refused to endlessly postpone the issue of leadership in the front.

What is important is that these debates display how the OIPFG was haunted by the original institution of the Communist movement in Iran. In addition, the (virtual) debates document the retreat of Fadaiyan from their early Stalinist tendency that placed the Organization over and above the self-sacrificing individual. As a result, a tendency toward a plurality of leftist ideas started to grow, slowly and painfully, in the OIPFG. The OIPFG embodied more than one group or ideology. *This internal plurality was a reflection of Fadaiyan's student constituency and an outcome of Iran's rising secular-democratic sectors.* Fadaiyan's defense of their strategy (indeed their raison d'être) in their debates was oblivious to the undertow that gradually debased the acclaimed principles of Fadaiyan, this embodiment of Iranian secular-militant movement par excellence. Their centrism proved to be a façade, and their ideological claims were only a legitimating ruse. Their apparent outward organizational unity veiled, however partially, their internal diversity.

This brings us to a critical, and potentially fatal, exchange that Fadaiyan engaged in during 1973–74 with one of Iran's most original and singular theorists of the Left, Mostafa Sho'aiyan. His writings showed that Stalinism in the OIPFG arose from the leadership's violent reduction of Fadaiyan as a frontal movement to a political party. I will explore the OIPFG-Sho'aiyan debate next.

6

Mostafa Sho'aiyan

Haunting Return of Plurivocal Origination

> I am partisan and never a nonpartisan. I support the working class, the
> working-class movement, and any movement that disturbs the status quo.
> —MOSTAFA SHO'AIYAN, *Pasokhha-ye nasanjideh be*
> *"Qadamha-ye sanjideh"* [Injudicious replies to "Judicious
> Steps"]

THE YEARS of heightened urban guerrilla activity in Iran witnessed the emergence of a singular and maverick theoretician who not only stood up to the
regime but also challenged the culture of the militant Left for both their ideology
and their organizational order. The works of Mostafa Sho'aiyan must primarily
be treated as the pathology of the scourge that disfigured the Iranian Left. He
has authored some two thousand pages of works on history, theory, criticism,
memoirs, poetry, open letters, reports, and policy reviews—texts written under
unbearable human conditions with utmost dexterity, enjoying an eccentric lexical
system that challenged the normative leftist jargon. Exceptions aside (Vahabzadeh 2007a; Vahabzadeh 2007b), his works have remained virtually unstudied to
this day. Sho'aiyan's saga offers new glimpses into the rebellious generation of the
1970s, revealing the ashes and diamonds, betrayals and intrigues, despairs and
hopes of the militant movement. The study of Sho'aiyan's place in the history of
the Iranian Left goes beyond the scope of this chapter, as does his debate with the
OPFG's theorist, Hamid Momeni, on Sho'aiyan's *Revolution*. Our task here is to
situate Sho'aiyan in terms of his "frontal thinking" and his tormented relationship with the PFG. I will also discuss his insights on the pathology of the Stalinism that defined a period of Fadaiyan's organizational life. Finally, I will look at
the role of intellectuals in the new Communist movement.

186

THE EMERGENCE OF A VOICE

Sho'aiyan was born to a lower-class family in southern Tehran in 1936. He worked night shifts to sustain himself throughout the secondary school years. In 1958 he enrolled in Tehran Technical Institute (now the Science and Industry University) as an engineering student and graduated at the top of his class in 1962, which qualified him for a state scholarship to the United States that he refused. Instead he went to Kashan as a secondary school teacher (Sho'aiyan 1980, 11). In 1966, based on the "medical grounds" his friends facilitated, he was transferred to Tehran, where for the next two years he taught history and social sciences in various secondary schools (Sho'aiyan 1980, 12).

His political activities began when he joined the Pan-Iranist Party. After the July 20, 1952, uprising against the Shah that reinstated Dr. Mosaddeq as the premier, he left the Pan-Iranists and began espousing Marxism (Sho'aiyan 1980, 13). In the late 1950s he joined a circle of former Tudeh members now critical of the Party. The main figure of this circle—known by activists as *Jaryan* (or *Poroseh*; in Persian *jaryan* implies "circle," because the group had no name)— was Mahmoud Tavakkoli, who wrote two critical analyses about the Tudeh Party (see Jaryan Group 1979). While with Jaryan, Sho'aiyan wrote an extended essay criticizing the Society of Socialists (Jame'eh-ye Sosialistha) (Sho'aiyan 1980, 22, n.2) led by Khalil Maleki, who had broken ranks with the Tudeh Party in the aftermath of the defeat of the Autonomous Azerbaijan Province in 1948 (see Katouzian 2004). Sho'aiyan joined the Second National Front in 1960 and met with Jazani several times between 1962 and 1964 (see Lahiji 1999, 234). During these years Jazani gave Jaryan the derogatory label the "American Marxists"—a label that stuck with the circle and discredited them. In his historiography of the Iranian Left, written a decade later, Jazani tried to confound the Tavakkoli-Sho'aiyan circle, Jaryan or Poroseh, with the Poroseh-ye Marxist-Leninistha-ye Iran (The Process of Iranian Marxist-Leninists)—an "underground" group that was part of a SAVAK sting operation to capture the surviving members of the Tudeh Party (Jazani 1979a, 86). While Sho'aiyan confirms that the Process of Iranian Marxist-Leninists was a trap (Sho'aiyan 1980, 24, n.3), Jazani constantly attempted to discredit Sho'aiyan through guilt by association (Vahabzadeh 2005, 174–76). The term "American Marxists," as Sho'aiyan reflects later, is drawn from one of the circle's analyses: Jaryan argued that there was a competition in Iran between American imperialism and the comprador bourgeoisie, on one side, and British imperialism and the feudal class, on the other. Because British imperialism is the older one in the evolution of capitalist development, the victory of American imperialism would provide the socioeconomic structures for the next revolutionary stage (Sho'aiyan 1980, 24, n.3). A decade later Momeni took Jazani's derogatory label further and called Tavakkoli a CIA agent (Momeni 1977, 37) in order to discredit Sho'aiyan's past struggles at the time when Sho'aiyan joined Fadaiyan. In the 1950s and 1960s, Sho'aiyan frequented the Socialist writers around the intellectual journal *Elm va Zendegi* [science and life] (banned in 1962) that was edited and published by Nasser Vosuqi. In the journal, several noted members of the Society of Socialists introduced the ideas of Jean-Paul Sartre, Frantz Fanon, and Aimé Césaire. Jazani and Momeni also used Sho'aiyan's association with *Elm va Zendegi* to discredit him, while his association with the journal gifted him with anti-Stalinist sensibilities and rigorous theoretical analysis.

Sho'aiyan admittedly had not yet made an intellectual departure from his older nationalist sensibilities when, in 1968, he wrote *A Review of the Relations Between the Soviet Union and the Revolutionary Movement of Jungle,* a five-hundred-page study of Mirza Kuchek Khan's 1920–21 movement in the Caspian region. SAVAK seized and destroyed the copies of the book before distribution, but it was later published in Europe. This study prepared Sho'aiyan for *Rebellion (Shuresh),* later renamed *Revolution (Enqelab),* his magnum opus. His exposing of the Soviets' role in the defeat of the Jangali movement prompted him to identify, in *Revolution,* the ideological roots of the Soviets' betrayal.

In 1971 he left his job to become a full-time revolutionary. Along with Reza Asgariyyeh, Parviz Sadri, and Behzad Nabavi, he founded a guerrilla cell. Sho'aiyan and Sadri soon went underground as the group's plan to sabotage the Isfahan steel plant was exposed and members were arrested (Sho'aiyan 1980, 14; Sho'aiyan 1976b, 13). According to Nabavi, Sho'aiyan's group was originally formed in 1970 and was first in contact with Mojahedin and only later with Fadaiyan (Nabavi 2002).

In 1972 Sho'aiyan sent his books *Jungle* and *Rebellion* to the National Front director in Europe, Dr. Hassan Habibi, via his friend Mr. Mofidian in England. Mofidian was terminally ill with cancer and died shortly after his return to Iran. At this time Sho'aiyan wrote under one of his many aliases (especially Rafiq and

Sorkh), and his works were not published abroad. In his "Unveiling," Sho'aiyan claims that the National Front activists sought to identify the author of the books they had received, and as they did, Sho'aiyan reminisces, so did the police (in Sho'aiyan 1976a, 1; article individually paginated). This identification coincided with the exposure of the Isfahan operation (Sho'aiyan 1976b, 13).

Sho'aiyan was in contact with the PFG but had much closer relations with the OIPM, with detailed knowledge about its activities (Raf'at 2001). After the near eradication of the Mojahedin in August 1971, Sho'aiyan was directly involved in rebuilding the OIPM networks, working with and assisting Reza Rezai (Sho'aiyan 1980, 23, n.2). His dedication reflects his belief in uniting Mojahedin, Fadaiyan, and smaller militant groups in a united front.

After the failure of his first group, Sho'aiyan became acquainted in 1972 with Nader Shayegan Shamasbi (henceforth Shayegan), who had organized an underground cell himself. Shayegan's group and the group Sho'aiyan was in the process of organizing at the time unified and created the People's Democratic Front (PDF). Shayegan was reportedly critical of Leninism and the USSR, and after reading *Revolution* he had reportedly proclaimed to find in it what he had been seeking for a long time. In May 1973 the chemical laboratory of the PDF, where the group made explosives, was raided by SAVAK. Shayegan, Hassan Rumina, and Nader Atai were killed and approximately ten others were arrested. SAVAK believed that the members of the group were Shayegan, Atai, Rumina, Bizhan Farhang Azad, Abdullah Anduri, Reza Purja'fari, Aqdas Fazelpur, Sediqeh Serafat, and a few others whom SAVAK had arrested (see Sho'aiyan 1980, 15; Raf'at 2001). Sho'aiyan and the rest of the PDF—at least two teams in Tehran and Tabriz—subsequently joined the PFG. Marzieh Ahmadi Oskui, Saba Bizhanzadeh, and Mitra Bobolsefat were among the noted women from the PDF. Ahmadi Oskui had recruited many for the PDF and acted as the PFG's link with the former PDF team in Tabriz. Bizhanzadeh became the only female member of the CC after the loss of leadership in June 1976 until her death in February 1977. Also joining the PFG along with Sho'aiyan were Shayegan's mother, Fatemeh Sa'idi, and her three young children: Abolhassan (arrested in 1976 at the age of fifteen), Arzhang, and Nasser (killed at a Fadai base; see chapter 2). A year later SAVAK raided the Tabriz team of the PDF and arrested Ahsan Nahid, Hushang Isabeglu, Dr. Mahjubi and his sister, and a few others (Sho'aiyan 1976c, 43; Raf'at 2001; see also Heydar 1999, 263, n.12; Heydar 2001, 33).

Sho'aiyan was destined to experience a painful relationship with Fadaiyan. He joined them on the condition that his *Revolution* be debated in Fadai teams. With the possibility of quickly absorbing a number of competent militants, the PFG leadership opportunistically accepted Sho'aiyan's condition. It was obvious from the outset that the Fadai leaders would never recruit anyone as maverick as Sho'aiyan. The PDF members were placed in various Fadai teams, while Sho'aiyan, Sa'idi, and her younger children Nasser and Arzhang were placed in a team in Mashhad under the gaze of Ali Akbar Ja'fari. Sho'aiyan stayed with the PFG between June 1973 and February 1974, when first he was pressured to transfer the Shayegan brothers (after the arrest of their mother in early January 1974 he had acted as their custodian) to Ashraf (in late February), before he was cut off from Fadaiyan (Sho'aiyan 1976c, 27). Ashraf had already taken in Abolhassan and housed him in a Tehran team (Sho'aiyan 1980, 99–131).

It was no accident that Sho'aiyan was placed under the authority of Ja'fari, the PFG's second in command. Ja'fari's mission was to test Sho'aiyan's loyalty. According to Sho'aiyan, that test resulted in the unnecessary arrest of Sa'idi. Ja'fari had reportedly ordered Sa'idi, a middle-aged woman, to return to a vacated base to collect the "organization's property," while Ja'fari and someone else acted as lookouts. In ordering Sa'idi back into a dubious place, Ja'fari broke a fundamental guerrilla rule. In any event, Sa'idi was arrested after a chase while Ja'fari and his comrade remained passive bystanders (Sho'aiyan 1976c, 16–18). Sa'idi's interrogation documents deny Sho'aiyan's version of the events and place the responsibility on Sho'aiyan instead of Ja'fari (Naderi 2008, 477–78). Sa'idi was severely tortured because SAVAK knew about her connection with two of Iran's most wanted dissidents, Sho'aiyan and Ja'fari, but she managed to withhold essential information (Sho'aiyan 1976c, 29). The incident infuriated Sho'aiyan, as he saw in it the PFG's discriminatory attitude toward him and those deemed to be close to him.

Meanwhile, Jazani heard about Sho'aiyan's recruitment, so he approached the imprisoned members of the PDF, Anduri and Farhang Azad, to find out about the ideological inclinations of the group and Sho'aiyan's *Shuresh,* but the two refused to talk to Jazani (Heydar 1999, 250). In 1973, recently arrested Mehdi Fatapour met Jazani in prison and confirmed the absorption of the PDF by Fadaiyan. Jazani warned that Sho'aiyan's presence in the PFG would be "dangerous" because his "radical and Trotskyist ideas" might overwhelm Ashraf and others, in which case, Jazani predicted, Sho'aiyan would take over the PFG. Later Anushirvan Lotfi and Ashraf informed Fatapour that there were bitter relations between Sho'aiyan and the PFG, and as a result he was expelled from the group. Whether Jazani's warning had anything to do with Ashraf's decision to oust Sho'aiyan remains unknown (Fatapour 2001a).

The antagonistic predisposition of Ashraf, Momeni, and Ja'fari toward Sho'aiyan prompted him to detect manifestations of Stalinism in the PFG, and so he set himself the task of documenting them. He believes that their spite goes back to his *Revolution*—a work so unconventional and inaccessible to the militants of the time that even Momeni had a hard time grasping it. As an observer remarks, "Sho'aiyan's isolation did not simply result from his idiosyncratic language. His style was a symbolic expression of a fighter's dignified distinctiveness who did not wish to succumb to the predominant Stalinism of the Iranian Communist movement at the time" (Dastan 1988, 69). Unable to challenge his work, Fadaiyan accused Sho'aiyan of opportunism, lack of responsibility, and cowardice (Sho'aiyan 1976c, 5). Sho'aiyan had lived long enough in the leftist circles to understand that Fadaiyan were in the process of "dossier-making" (*parvandeh sazi*) to get rid of him. They had pressed Sho'aiyan's former comrades in the PDF, Ahmadi Oskui and Saba Bizhanzadeh, for information on his personality (Sho'aiyan 1976c, 20, 23). According to Sho'aiyan, Ahmadi Oskui's celebrated book *Memoirs of a Comrade* (1974) was originally written on the PFG's order and contained reminiscences of her time in the PDF that never appeared in the published version of the book. Sho'aiyan was denied a copy of the full version despite Ashraf's promise to provide him with one (Sho'aiyan 1976c, 42). According to Ashraf, Ahmadi Oskui claimed that she and Shayegan had already decided to expel Sho'aiyan from the PDF (Sho'aiyan 1976c, 34). As well, the young Shayegan brothers, now in the custody of the PFG, were reportedly asked to write about Sho'aiyan (Sho'aiyan 1980, 133). Sho'aiyan finds these materials to be Stalinist-style internal tribunal documents waiting to condemn him.

In any case, Sho'aiyan was eventually expelled from the PFG, isolated and without proper coverage or resources. The way Fadaiyan treated him highlights their feeble moral stance vis-à-vis a formidable intellectual. So one of Iran's brightest political theorists found refuge in the proverbial abyss of the masses, disguising himself as a vagabond and living in cemeteries from time to time but resolutely continuing to fight, utilizing his vast connections (Chaqueri 2001). He wrote his open letters in the corners of city parks and buried them in remote areas or at the outskirts of Tehran for posterity (Sho'aiyan 1980, 99).

His last meeting with Hamid Ashraf, on September 9, 1974, was arranged by Mojahedin (Sho'aiyan 1976c, 3), and the *Sixth Open Letter to the Fadai Guerrillas* meticulously documents it. In this meeting, Ashraf told Sho'aiyan that those Fadai members "entitled" to read Sho'aiyan's open letters believed that "we cannot be together in one organization. But we are not each other's immediate enemies either. Of course, if things lead to a confrontation—whose day will inevitably come—then we will stand facing each other" (Sho'aiyan 1976c, 5). Sho'aiyan bitterly reciprocated Ashraf's threat (Sho'aiyan 1976c, 5). While it is obvious that Ashraf threatened Sho'aiyan, it is unlikely that the Fadai leadership had any plan to purge Sho'aiyan. By this time, if considered bothersome and eccentric by the leaders of Fadaiyan, Sho'aiyan had "proven" himself to them as a resilient fighter who posed no security threat to the PFG.

Sho'aiyan's life remains obscure between this meeting and his death. At least for a while he was supported by Mojahedin (M-L) and lived in hiding for the next two years. When Sho'aiyan emerged from his hideout on Estakhr Street in central Tehran on the morning of February 5, 1976, he was identified and shot by a police officer. An eyewitness report records that he was alone at the time and unable to use his weapon (Mikailian 2007). His wounded body was tied up and taken away, but he is said to have been dead on arrival at the prison. He must have committed suicide using his cyanide capsule (see Sho'aiyan 1976c). The police took his body to the Anti-Terrorist Joint Task Force prison (known as Komiteh) in central Tehran and brought Sho'aiyan's imprisoned comrades to Komiteh to identify his body (Sho'aiyan 1980, 19).

FRONTAL THINKING AND THE PATHOLOGY OF STALINISM

Sho'aiyan's experience with Fadaiyan prompted him to launch the pathology of Stalinism in the militant Left. This pathology is partly enabled by his "frontal thinking," as his earlier activities show. His admiration for Mosaddeq and his "frontal thinking" come from his experience in the National Front—an alliance of liberal-nationalist parties in the early 1950s. In the early 1960s, Sho'aiyan invited the three most influential ayatollahs of the country, Khomeini, Shari'atmadari, and Milani, to rally their followers behind an economic boycott of the state's financial institutions in an effort to foment socioeconomic crisis. He wrote about this unsuccessful attempt in "Today's Jihad or A Thesis for Mobilization" (in Sho'aiyan 1976a): his plan meant to test the potential for "passive resistance" and to gauge the Shi'i clerics' level of political commitment (Sho'aiyan nd-a, 34).

While critically adhering to hyphen-free Marxism, he did not regard ideology as an impediment to the convergence of militant forces in the liberation front. He argues that the front must include militant Marxists because of the internal plurality of the working class—a plurality that originates from the diverse relations of production of various industrial sectors. The task of the working-class "enlightener" (*roshangar*), the vanguard, is to educate and prepare the class for the revolution (Sho'aiyan 1976b, 62–63). The political enlightener of the class is the "educator of the class, an educator who has previously received [his or her own] education in the school of the life of the [working] class" (Sho'aiyan 1976b, 62). Sho'aiyan's concept of the "enlightener" somewhat resembles Antonio Gramsci's "organic intellectual." Because he rejects the possibility that the revolution is an exclusive task of only one class, Sho'aiyan acknowledges the need for various representations of the "rebellious seeds" (Sho'aiyan nd-b, 7). No party structure can adequately represent this diversity because a party can only speak for the sector(s) it represents. In other words, the "rebellious vanguard [*pishtaz-e shureshi*] in this society does not have a single-organizational profile [*chehreh-ye tak-sazmani*]" (Sho'aiyan nd-b, 5). Thus the front provides the alternative structure where the forces representing various sectors of the people's forces converge against colonialism (Sho'aiyan nd-b, 3–4, 9). The front weaves together and directs diverse forces, increasing from the few to the many (Sho'aiyan nd-b, 10). For Sho'aiyan, advocating the front as a nonideological and supraclass alliance does not override the necessity for the formation of the working-class party: these are simply two distinct tasks (nd-b, 3, 5, 8–9).

Armed struggle and revolutionary consciousness are the two elements that make the frontal convergence possible. As does Ahmadzadeh, *Sho'aiyan maintains the priority of practice over theory.* He perceives armed struggle as the nexus of the front, beginning with the alliance among militant groups like Fadaiyan, Mojahedin, and the People's Ideal (Sho'aiyan 1976c, 39). The line between the people and the people's enemy must be sought in resistance against colonial forces (Sho'aiyan nd-b, 4), Sho'aiyan's plan was that Fadaiyan and Mojahedin form the nucleus of a front by cooperating with one another through their "unified threads" (Sho'aiyan nd-b, 14) and begin by publishing a joint bulletin (Sho'aiyan nd-b, 27). It should be emphasized that Sho'aiyan's inclination toward the praxis of armed struggle places the PFG ahead of the OIPM in organizing and initiating guerrilla warfare in Iran because, unlike the OIPM, the PFG's strategy is founded on mobilizing the masses (Sho'aiyan 1976c, 39–40).

The PFG leadership had reservations about Sho'aiyan's nonideological approach to the front. Recall how Jazani rejected any alliance where the leadership of militant Marxists (read: Fadaiyan) was in doubt. Likewise, Ashraf reportedly refuted the organizational unity of different ideologies (Sho'aiyan 1980, 54). In 1973 Sho'aiyan raised the point to his Fadai interlocutors that the very name "People's Fadai Guerrillas"—the original designation of the group when founded by Ahmadzadeh and Ashraf—implied a *front*, not an organization, so everyone willing to become a revolutionary militant would automatically become a Fadai, regardless of their organizational or ideological connections. Sho'aiyan's observation becomes clear in light of Fadaiyan's recommendation that "[t]he Marxist-Leninist groups that could not contact the People's Fadai Guerrillas should operate under the name 'People's Fadai Guerrillas' (with a suitable addition)" (*Nashriyeh-ye Dakheli* 1975b, 37). Fadaiyan's adhering to ideological puritanism and still asking militant groups to operate under the PFG's name seemed like a contradiction to Sho'aiyan (Sho'aiyan 1980, 55). In any case, Sho'aiyan demonstrates that by retreating into its sectarian-ideological cocoon, the Fadai Guerrillas lost their potential to be the hegemonic core of the people's liberation front (see also Behrooz 1999, 63–64). However, Sho'aiyan's imprudent trivialization of the ideological differences between Marxists and Muslims in favor of his perceived front endangers the Left's potential rise as the hegemonic core, as the events leading up to the 1979 Revolution clearly indicated. This position indicates Sho'aiyan's unjustifiable neglect of the secular aspect of any democratic front and politics.

The organizing concept in Sho'aiyan's *Revolution* and subsequent works is "rebellion," or *"shuresh."* He calls his idea a "rebellious thought" based on the principle of constant and uncompromising revolution by the exploited masses until the world is rid of capitalism. Armed struggle is the ultimate manifestation of the rebellious essence that defines our epoch of advanced capitalism and liberation movements. The praxis of uncompromising militants in the world is the true measure of the "rebellious essence" (*gohar-e shureshi*). The concept of "rebellion" refers specifically to the situation in which social and productive relations are exploitive and repressive while the popular resistances against them are not yet in place. With the same line of reasoning as Jazani, Sho'aiyan believes that the objective conditions for revolution do not exist in Iran and that guerrilla warfare should not be mistaken for the liberation war, although guerrilla warfare will lead to it. The role of the revolutionary vanguards is accentuated because of the lack of popular participation. This is the time the "rebellious essence" provides unity for the frontal diversity of the militant groups (Sho'aiyan nd-b, 8):

> There are conditions in the life history of a class in which the vanguard neither has the freedom to deliver its message to the entire class and society nor can it submit to whining and surrender. And this is a historical condition in which the class intends to militantly shake off its chains, but its organizational solidarity and connections are so shattered that it starts the enlivening battle of armed movement using whatever number of the connecting cords [that are available]; and this is precisely the stage of sowing the rebellious seeds. (Sho'aiyan nd-b, 7–8)

What sharply distinguishes Sho'aiyan from other leftist activists of his generation is his unwavering criticism of Leninism, based on the determinacy of "rebellious essence." The revolution will happen with or without the Party. Being a true revolutionary (i.e., living the "rebellious essence") does not require being a Communist or belonging to the working class, despite its central role. Likewise, being a Marxist-Leninist, writes Sho'aiyan in "Some Pure Criticisms," does not necessarily guarantee that one is a revolutionary, nor does failure to be a Communist automatically make one a counterrevolutionary (in 1976a, 27–28; article individually paginated). Sho'aiyan obviously trivializes ideological differences within the front, as if he reflects on his first and ideologically eclectic group. The war of liberation demands the liberation of consciousness—indeed a complete cultural deliverance: "To deliver the masses, the working class has to elevate the masses to the summit of its own culture and essence. And this is not doable unless in rebellion. A global rebellion! Rebellion is the best cultural school" (Sho'aiyan nd-b, 13). The subjective element, or consciousness (agahi), weaves together different loci of rebellion and creates a front that aims at this global undertaking.

Measured against the essence of rebellion, Leninism is a betrayal of the revolution. Not only did Lenin reject guerrilla warfare as desperate petit-bourgeois terrorism (Sho'aiyan 1977, 16), he betrayed the world revolution through his thesis of "peaceful coexistence" with imperialism, a theoretical fabrication that Sho'aiyan called "socialism in one country" and found it, like the GCU, "counterrevolutionary and [a] treason" of the international working-class movement (1976b, 27). According to Sho'aiyan, Lenin became a counterrevolutionary around 1920 (1976b, 249, n.135), although the notion of "peaceful coexistence" actually originates with Stalin. Sho'aiyan's argument exhibits his attunement to practice: theoretically Lenin worked along the lines of Trotsky's "permanent revolution," while in actuality he betrayed the Jangali movement in Iran to make concessions to the British, who were backing the Russian White Guards as they launched their offensives from Iranian soil. Sho'aiyan ponders whether Lenin's thesis is a revision of the principles of Marxian thought, or if Marx is just as culpable. Pushing the limits of the Marxist canon, he considers the possibility:

> It seems that the criticism made of Lenin's thoughts on the party and the revolution are also pertinent to Marx himself. But for two reasons, I could not start from Comrade Marx. First, I did not have sufficient knowledge in this respect [Marx's thought]. And second, the translated works of Comrade [Marx] shows that his political works are few and especially synoptic compared to his philosophical and economic works . . . In any case, the basic reason why I could not analyze Comrade Marx was because of my negligible knowledge of Marx and his ideas. (Sho'aiyan 1976b, 99)

Contrary to his view of Lenin, Sho'aiyan admires Che Guevara, "the internationalist guerrilla of the proletariat," who acknowledged in his speech on February 26, 1965, in Algeria that just like capitalism, the Socialist camp treats the Third World in an exploitive manner (Sho'aiyan 1976b, 265, n. 204).

The peaceful coexistence policy of the USSR, a "policy clearly arid and undialectical," caused catastrophes for the people of Iran, Algeria, and Greece (Sho'aiyan 1976d, 5). The Soviet Union's disastrous policy toward Premier Mosaddeq can never be justified, and its opportunistic support of national-liberation movements in different Third World countries only came after abandoning the Iranian people (Sho'aiyan 1976d, 6). Adherence to puritan ideological dogmas, in Leninism and Maoism alike, undermines the "rebellious essence" that lives in the praxis of armed uprising by exploited peoples around the world. Sho'aiyan's approach, again, is indicative of the practice-oriented spirit of a certain generation of Iranian intellectuals. As Shayegan has reportedly averred, "The very fact that I carry a weapon and live militantly means the rejection of Leninist methods" (quoted in Sho'aiyan 1976b, 116).

The Leninist digression from the revolutionary path resulted in the faulty policies and opportunistic approaches of the Communist movement. But Sho'aiyan sees another monster child of Leninism besides Stalinism: an opportunistic attitude has now grown out of Leninism, which Sho'aiyan labels "*shoravism*," or "Sovietism." In 1975 Sho'aiyan made his resentment toward Fadaiyan explicit by mapping Sovietism with the Stalinists in the North (the Soviet Union), new Maoists in the East (China), the ancient Tudehists in the West (in exile), and Fadaiyan in the South (Iran). The common denominator of these representations of Stalinism and opportunism is their lack of revolutionary principles as evidenced by their dossier-making practices and purges (Sho'aiyan 1976c, 6–7). Sho'aiyan observes that only by fabricating the equation of the Soviet Union with the working-class movement can one view the Soviets as progressive. He expressly rejects this equation and the claim that the Soviets and the Tudeh are working-class parties (1977, 13). The Tudeh has never been the working-class party, he argues, not even before the 1953 coup (Sho'aiyan 1976c, 13).

The founders of the PFG had seen this subtle point. Fadai theorists, however, believed that the Tudeh was Iran's working-class party before the coup. Zia Zarifi, for example, notes, "If, as the political organization of the working class, the Tudeh Party had carried out its revolutionary duties and led the action against the counterrevolutionary forces, it would have inevitably maintained the leadership of the [Tudeh] Party over the entire movement" (1979, 33). This is precisely what Sho'aiyan rejects: if the Tudeh was at any time the working-class party, it would not have succumbed to the coup or to USSR foreign policy and instead would have staged armed resistance against the coup. For Sho'aiyan, Fadaiyan's failure to detect opportunism in the world Communist movement caused the OIPFG theorists to "contract" Sovietism. On this point, we do know that while Jazani sharply criticizes the Soviet Union, he fails to identify the ideological basis of Soviet policies, and he eventually acquiesces to the international hegemony of the USSR. Similarly, in *The Revolutionary Execution of Abbas Shahriyari* (OIPFG 1975a), Fadaiyan continue to regard the Tudeh as the working-class party prior to the coup. So it is no surprise that Ashraf asked Dehqani to contact the Soviets for support, a decision Sho'aiyan would certainly have called opportunistic. In Sho'aiyan's judgment, an unequivocal position against Sovietism is the precondition for revolutionary action. Challenging the pervasive domination of Sovietism calls for the "weapon of critique." With categorical criticism, one must dislodge all the hidden expressions of Sovietism and Stalinism (Sho'aiyan 1976g). One must not only expose and criticize the Soviets and the Chinese, but also the Tudeh Party and Fadai Guerrillas.

Of course, such a fatal critique of Leninism did not sit well with Fadaiyan, for whom the working-class cause equaled Leninism. Fadaiyan advocated the position that one could not fight for the emancipation of the workers and the masses without subscribing to Leninism (OIPFG 1978b, 20, n.1). The OPFG's knowledge of Marxism was mostly elementary. Fadaiyan espoused ideological and programmatic Marxism and clearly rejected analytical Marxian approaches, which they derided as only for armchair academics (*Payam-e Daneshju* 1975, 28).

With the insight from his experience as a rank-and-file OPFG member, Sho'aiyan was now able to connect the dots: the lack of a firm stance against Sovietism led to Stalinism and sectarianism, both conditions affecting the OPFG by 1974. Conceiving of the OPFG as an ideological party, the Fadai Guerrillas showed their sectarianism and annulled the possibility of a liberation front (Sho'aiyan nd-b, 7). Stalinism also revealed itself in the PFG's undemocratic organization, which Sho'aiyan experienced firsthand. In a debate, Ja'fari is reportedly inclined to postpone organizational democracy until the realization of favorable conditions: "The movement is still very vulnerable. Let us grow to a certain extent and gain some strength. Then, well, anyone will be free to express any view she or he holds" (quoted in Sho'aiyan 1980, 49). Such indefinite deferment of organizational democracy alarms Sho'aiyan, and he sees the "tradition of killing thinking" (1976b, 22) creeping up on the PFG. His reply to his interlocutor is insightful: "Dear comrade, an organization that blocks the opinion it does not approve at the time of weakness, once formidable, will crush any brain that thinks a thought other than what the organization dictates" (Sho'aiyan 1980, 49).

REVOLUTION AND THE INTELLECTUALS

In July–August 1973 the OPFG sent Hamid Momeni to Mashhad for a debate with Sho'aiyan on the concept of the "intellectual." Although polemical at times, this debate has ramifications for understanding the role of secular-Left intellectuals in modernity and in the liberation movement. Formulating the position of the intellectuals in the new Communist movement became a priority because of the fact that the vast majority of activists in the 1970s had higher education or were university students. The debate placed Sho'aiyan on a crash course with the then dominant understanding of intellectuals.

The issue was originally raised by Momeni, who criticized the elitist Persian of the first edition of *Shuresh*, a puritan style of prose proposed by secular reformer Ahmad Kasravi (1890–1946). The writing style and convoluted lexicon were blamed for making the book inaccessible, and the book remains unyieldingly complex even after its author's third revision using a more accessible language. Momeni's reaction against Sho'aiyan's lexical elitism prompts him to investigate the "problem" of intellectuals in the worker's movement. In particular, Momeni rejects Sho'aiyan's nuanced distinction between the popular term *roshanfekr* (or intellectual; literally, "enlighten-minded"), and the new term *roshangar* (literally, "enlightener").

Momeni's and Sho'aiyan's resentment toward one another led them to stop their face-to-face debate (Momeni and Sho'aiyan nd, 10), but fortunately the two documented their major arguments. The exchange was centered on Momeni's harsh criticism of Sho'aiyan's concept of the enlightener (*roshangar*) of the working class in *Rebellion*. Momeni devotes chapter 4 of his *Not Rebellion, Judicious Steps on the Path to the Revolution* to unraveling the flaws of the concept of "supraclass" enlightener and how it deviates from Marxist class analysis of the intellectuals as superstructural. Momeni argues that the term *roshangar* encompasses seven different connotations under one class-free concept (1977, 102–3). Because there can never be a "freestanding" sector outside the existing relations of production, Momeni argues, all intellectuals belong to the exploiting classes (1977, 104). Despite differences in terms of their class origins, intellectuals are nonetheless the products of bourgeois education and so they belong to either the bourgeoisie or the petit-bourgeoisie (Momeni 1977, 105).

> The intellectuals [constitute] a vast stratum in society which belongs to the bourgeois class in terms of class origins because they feed off the "surplus value." But this stratum is internally incoherent and diverse. Some of them [intellectuals] have arisen from the masses and are in continued contact with the masses in

their private lives. Both such and such Harvard professor and Samad Behrangi are intellectuals. Can one use the stereotypical term "intellectual" to refer to both of them? (Momeni 1979, 28)

In his exchanges with Setareh, Momeni reflects on the problem of Stalinism and bureaucracy and discusses the perils that the intellectuals pose for socialism, as they represent the remnants of the abolished bourgeoisie: "The last remnants of the bourgeoisie under socialism are nothing but the intellectuals," writes Momeni. "The dictatorship of the proletariat . . . cannot eliminate intellectuals. The elimination of intellectuals depends on the full automatization of production and the vast and complete reduction of physical labor and this can only be achieved in a Communist society" (1977, 105). That said, however, Momeni admits that because of "their congruity with the masses and reading revolutionary literature, a small number of intellectuals, even under acute repressive conditions, may incline toward the masses, especially the working class and its progressive ideology" (1977, 107). In other words, these individuals become intellectually "influenced by the great reality of their time, i.e., the working class," by witnessing the harsh realities of capitalist unequal distribution of wealth, and subsequently they become revolutionary or proletarian intellectuals. As revolutionary intellectuals, their task is to "resolve the technical leadership of the proletarian revolution" (Momeni in Momeni and Sho'aiyan nd, 2). These intellectuals are not motivated by material hardship but by their intellectual and moral (*ma'navi*) impulses, and they "forfeit their class interests and continue to struggle by dissolving themselves into the aims and interests of the proletariat" (Momeni 1977, 107–8). They must therefore "establish organic relations with the masses" (Momeni 1977, 119). Political commitment sets the revolutionary intellectual apart from other educated sectors. The former constitute a political category while the rest of the intellectuals remain in economic categories (Momeni 1977, 110).

So in what sense does Sho'aiyan use the term *roshangar* or enlightener? First, he expresses his dissatisfaction with the commonplace term *roshanfekr* or intellectual, because while originally a neutral term, it was brought into Persian via political discourse and has therefore acquired a political overtone. The term's political overdetermination in Persian has obscured its philosophical signification. Sho'aiyan's term "enlightener" or *roshangar,* on the contrary, explicitly means the *political intellectual* in a way that is reminiscent of the Gramscian concept of "organic intellectuals" (Gramsci 1971, 5–43). In 1970s Iran, Gramsci was virtually unknown. As such, Sho'aiyan depoliticizes the term "intellectual" (Momeni and Sho'aiyan nd, 19–20). As each social class consists of different layers (*layehha*), the enlighteners, too, make up a layer and each layer of enlighteners has certain characteristics that distinguish it from the class of its origin. Although the "enlighteners are the products of the class and class conflict" (Sho'aiyan in Momeni and Sho'aiyan nd, 6), different from Gramsci on this point, Sho'aiyan argues that the enlighteners differ from the class they represent in two ways: first, they differ in that they "do not directly participate in the process of production," and second, the enlighteners have a political function as the "mentor [*amuzgar*] of the class" (in Momeni and Sho'aiyan nd, 5). Contrary to Momeni's position, he argues, the enlighteners enjoy social mobility, which indicates that the *class essence* [seresht-e tabaqati] *is not determined simply by one's class origins.* Rather, the praxis of a class allows an enlightener to identify with it: "Living the life of a class determines one's class essence" (Sho'aiyan in Momeni and Sho'aiyan nd, 7). Stated simply, *class position determines class belonging,* not vice versa. This position indicates Sho'aiyan's tacit belief in the primacy of the political—a contemporary post-Marxist concept.

Sho'aiyan is not alone in objecting to Momeni's rigid concept of intellectuals. The *Internal Bulletin* of the OIPFG documents a similar position by Fadai cadres, who argue that an intellectual's class belonging is defined by his or her class position and not by class origins, but Momeni categorically places all intellectuals within the exploiting classes (*Nashriyeh-ye Dakheli* 1975b, 58, 60–61). Sho'aiyan exposes the contradiction of Momeni's argument: how can the intellectuals that belong to the bourgeoisie become revolutionary fighters for the proletarian cause (in Momeni and Sho'aiyan nd, 16)? How can the Fadai Guerrillas be working-class intellectuals when even with revolutionary practice they still belong to the bourgeois class?

In response, Momeni accuses Sho'aiyan of confusing three Marxist concepts of the "conscious layer of the [working] class," the "revolutionary vanguard," and "professional revolutionary"—all squeezed into Sho'aiyan's concept of *roshangar,* which according to Momeni simply designates the "revolutionary vanguard" (in Momeni and Sho'aiyan nd, 23). Momeni insists on a strict class analysis of the intellectuals, utilizing the Marxist idea of the dual class character of the petit-bourgeoisie: while a small number of intellectuals transform into the "greatest advocates of the masses," a vast majority of them become "a major obstacle for the revolution and Socialist society" (Momeni in Momeni and Sho'aiyan nd, 26). The working-class vanguard consists of revolutionary intellectuals who are moved by the conditions of the workers and the "proletarian intellectuals" (Momeni in Momeni and Sho'aiyan nd, 29). According to Momeni, "The proletarian intellectuals make up only a small segment of the large layer of intellectuals. The vast majority of intellectuals simply submit to the Socialist revolution without believing it in their hearts" (in Momeni and Sho'aiyan nd, 30–31). If the intellectuals lose contact with the masses, they will betray the working-class cause and return to their class origins. Examples include Trotsky, Tito, Dubcek, and the Soviet leaders of his day (Momeni in Momeni and Sho'aiyan nd, 31). Momeni's strict class analysis of intellectuals leads to naïve populism: the vanguard intellectuals should stay on the path of the masses as seen through the prism of Marxism-Leninism. In his discussion on how to deal with "deviationist" intellectuals, Momeni reveals his Stalinist attitude:

> On the other hand, our intellectuals [in general], [and] deviationist intellectuals in particular, should go and labor through physical work. A sentimental intellectual, for example, who says, "Machinism is evil, it enslaves humans, etc." must go and furrow the land with an ox or dig a well using shovel and pick to understand his mistake. Moreover, the masses' surveillance over intellectuals and especially the cultural revolution of the masses [reference to Chinese Cultural Revolution] can prevent bourgeois tendencies in science, arts, and politics. (in Momeni and Sho'aiyan nd, 33)

Momeni did not live to see the catastrophic consequences of "the masses' surveillance over intellectuals" in Cambodia, but the dismissive and repressive attitude of Momeni toward nonconformist intellectuals is clear in these lines. Disciplinary measures against members who were judged to display "petit-bourgeois" symptoms were implemented throughout the OIPFG's life (chapter 8).

The term "enlightener" is exclusively reserved for the political-public intellectual. Sho'aiyan refuses the populism of his interlocutor, placing the class enlightener above the masses:

> Class enlightener is the guide of the class in its class struggle, in its political battle, in philosophical knowledge, in its rebellious [shureshi] war, etc., as well

as in its assuming of power. *The class enlightener is the mentor* [amuzgar] *of the class.* The party is the guiding organization of the [working] class in class war. Thus the party is the field of organic solidarity of [working] class enlighteners with one another. (in Momeni and Sho'aiyan nd, 36; emphasis added)

Sho'aiyan makes no apologies about the plurality of the vanguard intellectuals, nor does he justify his position by overstretching Marxist class analyses. His observation is an existential one: he looks at his own life as an advocate and activist who fights for the liberation of the masses, and for him this provides sufficient insight into the life of the enlighteners. Without using pregiven (and abused) Marxist constructs, Sho'aiyan tries to give Momeni an awareness about his place in society: if the intellectuals are parts of the exploiting classes (Momeni's point), then Behruz Dehqani (the head of the PFG Tabriz branch who died under interrogation in 1971) must belong to the Iranian dominant class as well (Sho'aiyan in Momeni and Sho'aiyan nd, 44). Rigid categorical analyses neither reflect nor explain the life of militant intellectuals. Sho'aiyan argues that Momeni's thesis is nothing but a "class multiplication table": a simplified, formulaic approach that does not account for the complexity of the issue (in Momeni and Sho'aiyan nd, 46).

THE HAUNTING RETURN

Sho'aiyan's thought is not immune to criticism. His radical notion of the revolution, or *shuresh,* imposes serious limitations on the liberation forces, while his theory of the front requires extensive diversity. His idea of the "rebellious essence" is intended to capture the praxis of intellectuals of his time, but it remains ambiguous for social and political analysis, and instead it reduces long-term activism to eruptive rebellion. His most problematic political point is that his formulation of the front has no provisions for the leadership of the secular-Left. He leaves the question of the front's leadership open, which is always a risky position. On this point we must recall Jazani's warning about the perils of leadership void. In our post-Communist era, only the leadership of secular-democratic forces can guarantee a nonexclusionary formation of the front.

Sho'aiyan's in-group experience caused him to bitterly abandon the Fadai Guerrillas that he had formerly venerated. Shaken out of his idealized view of the OPFG, he increasingly realized that the problems of organizational Stalinism and ideological dogmatism did not actually stem from the alleged "deviationism" of one group or another. These symptoms should not be taken lightly, as if they arise from character flaws. Rather, they accurately record the malaise of canonical belief and semireligious faith that reigned over the Iranian Left. Sho'aiyan was too maverick to subscribe to the formulaic Marxism of Momeni and Ashraf. Because of his criticisms of Leninism and bookish Marxism, Sho'aiyan emerges as an irreplaceable figure in the intellectual history of Iran and remains a diligent activist while rethinking Marxism. He shows that practice should not be derived from theory; it is theory that must submit to the terms of practice, and this needs a fresh theoretical start.

Like most other leftist traditions of the twentieth century, the entire edifice of the Iranian Left has been based on certain canonical interpretations that reduced Marx's critical methodology to revolutionary how-to manuals. From the establishment of the Iranian Communist Party, starting with the maverick challenges of Avetis Sultanzadeh against Leninism that cost him his life under Stalin (see Chaqueri 1984), to the Tudeh Party, and then to the Maoists and Fadaiyan in the 1960s and 1970s, and to the Trotskyists after them: all of these attempts at refounding the Left were based on adherence to one or another offshoot of twentieth-century canonical Marxism-Leninism. Sho'aiyan's significance was his observation that Stalinism arose from all rigid and derivative approaches to revolutionary theory. Sho'aiyan recognized that Stalinism is an offshoot of insecure dogmatism and uncritical, blind belief in one revolutionary cookbook or another. This recognition underscores the plurivocal origination of the Marxian tradition: Leninism, Maoism, Trotskyism, Castroism, Titoism, as well as social democracy and Eurocommunism are all equally heirs to the Marxian critique of capitalist society. Yet each can only rise to the supreme level of "guidebook" when it suppresses the competing narratives in the name of ideological purity. In his search for the roots of Stalinism, Sho'aiyan challenged exclusionary and canonical ideologies of the Iranian Left. So it is no wonder that his work was suppressed, and today no group or school advocates his thoughts. For the most part, the leftist intellectuals appeared unwilling to reconsider the fundamentals of their beliefs. While among Iranian leftists the ideological allegiances have been the variable, canonical belief in their leftist school of choice has been the constant. Sho'aiyan punctured a rupture, however fleetingly, in this constant.

His thought is not entirely free of its own dogmas either. And yet by rewriting the theory to match his experience as a leftist activist, he invoked, for a brief historical moment, the plurivocal origination of the entire Marxist tradition—an origination that predates the foundation of the Iranian Left and precedes the debates that defined it. His main contribution is his ability to consider his existential conditions as a militant activist and to revise theory so that it would match praxis. He did not subsume praxis under theory; *he allowed praxis to rewrite theory.* Whereas the three failed debates between Fadaiyan and other groups represent debates within canonical traditions of revolutionary theory, Sho'aiyan's theoretical engagement with Fadaiyan reports a radical rethinking of the Marxist tradition altogether as he captured the true essence of Marx's thought: "a ruthless critique of everything existing."

7
The Fadai Movement

> The prisons of Iran are packed with young people who are arrested, tortured, and imprisoned simply for thinking, for their thoughts, and for having read books ... When they are released from the prison, they'll leave books aside. They'll pick up machine guns.
>
> —KHOSROW GOLESORKHI, *Bisheh-ye bidar* [The wakeful thicket]

THE TERM "Fadai movement" (*jonbesh-e Fadai*) entered the official lexicon of the OIPFG most likely after the 1979 Revolution. It denoted the social and political influence of the Fadai Guerrillas in the face of the nationwide popular support for the new Islamic state, which sanctimoniously dismissed the role of secular and leftist forces in the fall of the monarchy. Today exile-based splinter groups—from the Social-Democratic OIPF-M, to the Socialist UPFI, the Communist Fadaiyan Organization-Minority, the militant IPFG, and other factions including the OIPFG—use the term in their publications to acknowledge Fadaiyan not only as a political party but as a social movement. Fadai activists originally used the term "Fadai movement" as equivalent to the "new Communist movement," but not as a label for a social movement. In postrevolutionary Iran, the term "Fadai movement" went beyond the intents of its originators, as it pointed at the cohort of thousands of supporters without whom the Fadai Guerrillas simply could not have survived the omnipresent surveillance and effective intelligence of SAVAK. Initially the term referred to the prerevolutionary Fadaiyan, although it was not used in any OIPFG document of the time. It gained popularity within the months following the 1979 Revolution, as Fadaiyan found themselves leading, by default, popular movements in the Plains of Turkomen and Kurdistan; in Tehran and other major cities; and in universities through their student affiliate, the Organization of Pishgam (Vanguard) Students.

206

A meticulous reading of OIPFG history is necessary for examining the social impact of Fadaiyan in 1970s Iran. Mohammad Dabirifard (Heydar) points out that the PFG was at the core of the Fadai movement, as Fadaiyan influenced student movements both inside and outside the country and inspired artists, guildsmen, and intellectuals (Heydar 1999, 246). Almost forty years have passed since the advent of Fadaiyan, and the official histories of the Revolution have consistently omitted the influence of Fadaiyan in the 1970s, while academics and scholars have neglected it. This chapter offers a synoptic review of Fadaiyan's social and political influence on women, students, intellectuals, and workers in order to assess Fadaiyan's success or failure as a potentially secular force.

As shown in chapter 5, Fadaiyan based their policy of the popular front on the precondition of leadership of militant Communists. Principled as it seems, this precondition did not yield any alliance of militant forces and contributed to OIPFG sectarianism. By 1978 the Shi'i clerics had already shown their disinterest in making alliances with secular-nationalist forces, let alone the Left. The clerics' cooperation with the Freedom Movement of Mehdi Bazargan and National Front figures such as Dariush Foruhar in the provisional government does not qualify as alliance because the clerics clearly maintained the upper hand at all times. Nevertheless, *the OIPFG's leadership principle as the precondition for any popular front offered a great lesson: popular support should not be the measure of alliance.* Had the Majority faction of Fadaiyan learned this crucial lesson, it would have saved itself the embarrassment of compliantly endorsing the authoritarian measures of the Islamic Republic between 1981 and 1983.

To explore the various aspects of the "Fadai movement," we need to deal exclusively with the constituents of Fadaiyan and to examine if the OIPFG in actuality built a movement based on the convergence of the interests of its social constituents—in particular women, intellectuals and students, and workers.

THE WOMEN'S QUESTION

Competing discourses regarding "women's issues" have always been a part of political modernity in Iran. Without a doubt, the OIPFG's neglect of women's issues is the greatest indicator of the group's ideologically driven disregard of its democratic duties. It highlights the extent of the Left's indifference to issues pertaining to the secularization of Iranian society. While the Fadai leadership exclusively focused on the organization of workers (inasmuch as their militant views allowed), it completely ignored the organization of women and intellectuals, Fadaiyan's two greatest constituencies. Indeed, feminist scholars have already documented the Left's neglect of women's issues (Moghissi 1994; Sanassarian 1983; Shahidian 1994; Shahidian 1997). In the same way as other Marxist-Leninist parties of the time, all originating in patriarchal cultures, the OIPFG consistently subsumed the questions of gender inequality under its general strategy (Moghissi 1994, 107–38).

Fadaiyan failed to articulate a tangible women's policy other than the ones already sanctioned in their ideology, and even in those cases, their advocacy of women's rights was often highly abstract and thus unintelligible for the OIPFG's public discourse. Based on his research on Iranian women activists and issues, the late Hammed Shahidian writes,

> [the] Iranian left has often and rightly been criticized for its indifference to the multifaceted character of women's oppression. Dominated by men activists, it reduced the oppression of women to a simple 'problem of superstructure,' which would disappear in a socialist Iran, and adopted an ambivalent attitude toward feminist militancy. (1994, 224)

Consequently, Fadaiyan "retained a patriarchal and gender hierarchy and sexual division of labour in politics . . . Male supremacy and the dominance of male values were realities that were unquestioned by revolutionary women" (Moghissi 1994, 116). Yet female participation in the militant Left was an expression of dissent against the Shah by educated, middle-class women (Shahidian 1997, 11). "Despite women's active participation, revolutionary movements have in most cases mainly addressed women's immediate problems, which were related to poverty and class injustices, without replacing male domination with an egalitarian social structure" (Shahidian 1997, 7). Ironically, in the 1960s and 1970s the overall and formal social status of Iranian women had been steadily rising in part because of the regime's social reforms and in part because of the lobbying efforts of legalist women's rights activists. In the absence of a women's movement, women advocates made great achievements in opening education and employment opportunities for Iranian women.

The formative Fadai groups originated in male circles. From its inception in 1963, Group One recruited only men, and it was not until 1970 when the group's first woman, Shirin Mo'azed (Fazilatkalam), was recruited by Farrokh Negahdar and put in contact with Ashraf (Negahdar 2008). Around the same time, the Tabriz circle that later joined Group Two also recruited its first female member, Ashraf Dehqani, who was the sister of Behrooz Dehqani, a prominent member of the circle. Group Two was also all male even when its ranks held some fifty militants. Although it is not clear when Group Two recruited its first female member, Mehrnoosh Ebrahimi, married to Dr. Changiz Qobadi, was one of the first women guerrillas and has the sad honor of being the first Fadai woman killed in a shoot-out, in August 1971.

Precisely because of their gender, women served a great purpose in urban guerrilla warfare, aiding the need to be elusive in the group's activities. Fadaiyan "encouraged women's involvement only when their womanness provided a cover for the real revolutionaries, the men, or when they were needed as revolutionary nurturer, secretary, or relief worker" (Moghissi 1994, 116). It is often said that women had a "covering role" (*naqsh-e pusheshi*) in the ranks of the militants because their presence often diverted suspicion. Women were far more socially mobile and moved around with greater freedom in spite of the cultural curtailment of women's activities in more traditional neighborhoods. They often acted as a newly wedded wife of a young, aspiring man when the teams needed to rent an apartment. Women performed missions of "reconnaissance" with greater invisibility and could carry out surveillance without being noticed. They participated in the OIPFG's operations. In fact, the names of many Fadai women go unnoticed because of repeated emphases on male leaders such as Jazani, Ahmadzadeh, and Ashraf. Except for Ashraf Dehqani and Marzieh Ahmadi Oskui, who became household names among Fadai supporters with their published memoirs, the women Fadai cadres never received the attention they deserved.

Marzieh Ahmadi Oskui (1945–1974) was originally recruited by the PDF. She is known to have been charismatic, and she had remarkable organizational abilities that enabled her to be a great recruiter. She single-handedly set up the Tabriz branch of the PDF (Raf'at 2001; Razmi 2008; see also *Nabard-e Khalq* 1974b). When the PDF joined the PFG in 1973, she moved up quickly within Fadaiyan's ranks, and at the time of her death she was in a team with Ashraf. Ahmadi Oskui was a poet and writer, and her posthumous *Memoirs of a Comrade* was a celebrated text (1974). In her *Memoirs*, there are hints of feminine prose and sensibilities despite the author's attempt at framing her experiences within the ideological ambits of her group. Ahmadi Oskui edited and rewrote parts of Ashraf Dehqani's prison memoirs, *The Epic of Resistance* (Razmi 2008), undoubtedly the most celebrated Fadai text. However, the success of these two books is not owing to their feminine views, but to these two revolutionary women's positions in the ranks of Fadaiyan. These two books reaffirmed the de-gendered and androcentric leftist discourse. "Feminist awareness was not essential for women's absorption into revolutionary organizations," observes Shahidian. "Women guerrillas raised issues concerning women and condemned the bourgeois woman's life-style, but their analyses focused on class without considering the impact of gender. Written works by guerrilla women revolutionaries are limited to a few didactic poems and short sketches which revolve around armed struggle" (1997, 35). Fadaiyan recruited women by eliminating their womanhood.

Other Fadai women did not have such public profile, although the OPFG is not perceivable without them. Nezhatosadat Ruhi Ahangaran (d. 1975) was recruited in Tabriz around 1970. Behrooz Dehqani was arrested in connection with Ruhi Ahangaran as SAVAK monitored Ahangaran's every move. Later Dehqani was murdered under torture. Tormented by her perceived role in Dehqani's death and seeking redemption, she rose in the ranks of Fadaiyan, becoming a remarkable team commander and participating in key operations including the assassination of Fateh Yazdi (Naderi 2008, 554). She was gunned down in Karaj in June 1975 (*Nabard-e Khalq* 1976, 109–11). Likewise Nastran Al Aqa (1950–1976) was a key female militant, a commander of the operational team that gunned down Major Niktab (Naderi 2008, 558), and a member of the team that purged Nurshirvanpur (CSHD 2001, 81). Having been an underground guerrilla for four years, a remarkably long time for any militant at that time when a guerrilla's lifespan was estimated to be about six months, she was killed in June 1976. Similarly, Zahra Aqanabi Qolhaki (1953–1976) was also an able militant who participated in the assassination of Abbas Shahriyari (Naderi 2008, 600) and the bombing of the Soleymanieh gendarmerie post (Naderi 2008, 597). She commanded the OPFG unit in the Caspian town of Gorgan. She was arrested in Babol in January 1976 and executed in December that year (Naderi 2008, 633). As well, Saba Bizhanzadeh (1949–1976) was originally a member of the PDF and joined the PFG in May 1973 along with Sho'aiyan, Ahmadi Oskui, Bolbolsefat, and Nader Shayegan's mother and siblings. She too lived a "long" underground life, surviving until 1977 when she was killed in a shoot-out. Bizhanzadeh was the first woman to serve in OIPFG leadership, but even though she was a capable militant and organizer, her ascension to the CC occurred only after the eradication of the OIPFG High Council, making it a promotion "by default." Fascinating aspects of the lives of these Fadai women and those who survived guerrilla life have been perpetually ignored under the tacit patriarchal indifference to gender by all Fadai splinter groups.

This indifference reports, of course, the Fadai Guerrillas' persistent neglect of their democratic duties. Their lack of vision in incorporating women's demands and input and organizing women is in particular alarming because it resulted in Fadaiyan's withdrawing from addressing gender modernization in Iran. What Moghissi observes about the OIPFG's policy in the 1980s also applies to Fadaiyan before the Revolution: they "deliberately and consciously avoided raising issues affecting women's personal lives" (1994, 122). Yet, strangely, Fadaiyan provided alternatives for women's participation in revolutionary change. The lives of four women Fadai Guerrillas from different social backgrounds demonstrate that Fadaiyan represented the ideal of a free and emancipated society that effectively overcame class differences (see Satwat 2005). As Shahidian observes,

> In a society where women's capabilities were not taken seriously, leftist organizations provided women with an alternative arrangement. There, women were treated equally with their male comrades and were respected for their dedication. Yet, participation in the underground movement also had serious shortcomings. Male activists regarded their female comrades as "desexed revolutionaries," not women activists. Whenever gender identity became a factor, organizations treated female members much more strictly than their male comrades. (1997, 9)

This is how tacit patriarchal notions were implemented within the Iranian Left, and women became "desexed" revolutionaries.

Romantic relationships were banned as detrimental to the revolution (in Hadjebi-Tabrizi 2003, 32). Aside from women like Ghazal Ayati, who had a "boyfriend" within the group (Satwat 2002), Fadai women by and large internalized these patriarchal values. In a way, some Fadai males believed they were the custodians of Fadai women. The love affair of Abdullah Panjehshahi and Edna Sabet, resulting in his murder and her "exile," is an enforcement of medieval cultural beliefs. Certain Fadai cadres from more traditional sectors tried to impose these traditional roles on their modern and westernized comrades. Some of the guerrillas of the time reminisce about the conflict between the two cultures, traditional and modern-urban, and about how value conflicts played themselves out in every aspect of organizational life, especially in the guerrilla bases (Satwat 2002; Hashemi 2008).

These brief sketches of the lives of prominent female Fadai guerrillas attest to the political effects of repressive development that deprived women (like intellectuals in general) of their own voices, on the one hand, and to pull them into the polarized politics of Fadaiyan, on the other. The extraordinary Fadai women had great potential for staging a secular-democratic women's movement for women's rights. These women would have been outstanding organizers and activists for such a movement, and their work would certainly have had more lasting social effects than the Fadai Guerrillas ever achieved.

The publication of Vida Hadjebi-Tabrizi's two-volume *Dad-e Bidad* (2003; 2004) provides the surviving Fadai women with a place for their own voices. These unique volumes document the experiences of women political prisoners in Iran during the 1970s. These women narrate the heroic resistance of female militant prisoners while also reminiscing about how they had to live a de-gendered and ascetic life that eliminated all expressions of femininity. By attributing these practices to their militancy and ideology, the Fadai women failed to see such practices as expressions of patriarchal control of women's agency.

INTELLECTUALS, STUDENTS, AND FADAIYAN

By the late 1960s, a defiant mood had surfaced in Iran. The most visible protest of this time was the mass boycott of public transit in Tehran. On February 21, 1970, Tehran Transit Inc. announced changes to bus routes that doubled, even tripled, the fare for many routes because of subsidy cuts. The next day university students and the urban poor protested against the new fares. University of Tehran students threw rocks at passing buses and set up roadblocks. Police intervention led to a bloody confrontation when they opened fire and killed or wounded several protestors and arrested many students. The protest escalated when the urban poor in front of the central Tehran Bazaar attacked transit buses and damaged over sixty buses in the mayhem. On the same day, on the Shah's order, Premier Amir Abbas

Hoveyda canceled the new transit regulations and returned the fares to normal the next day. To calm the situation, the police released the arrested students on February 27. In retrospect, the protest presaged the advent of Fadaiyan, showing the inextinguishable defiant atmosphere of Iranian universities, the birthplace of the Fadai Guerrillas. Now the students and intellectuals were evidently prepared to participate in the spontaneous movements.

The year 1971 inaugurated a highly politicized Iran. According to Dr. Hans Holdmann, who traveled to Iran on behalf of Amnesty International in 1970, about one thousand people were arrested in 1970 alone allegedly for political reasons (Matin 1999, 302–3). The Shah had been preparing for the ostentatious celebration of 2,500 years of Iranian monarchy (at a cost of US$200 million). Alerted by the exposed underground activities, the State did not take any chances. The Siahkal operation was the last thing the regime wanted.

The Siahkal operation provided the defiant Iranians with a myth of origin. Haloed with gallantry, the Siahkal guerrillas gradually rose to the status of hagiographized liberators in the underground publications of 1971. The surprising chain of events that followed the execution of thirteen guerrillas of the mountain team (March 16, 1971) reinforced their mythic status. The regime declared its conclusive success in eliminating the guerrilla networks in a press release (March 27, 1971), but only ten days later a Group Two team assassinated General Farsiu, shattering the regime's triumphant gesture and leaving the impression of the existence of a large and well-organized underground movement. The regime literally conceded a psychological defeat in May 1971 when SAVAK issued Iran's most-wanted posters with pictures of nine Fadai guerrillas (Jazani 1978, 49). The formation of PFG in April 1971 coincided with several protest movements. That April, the workers of Jahan Chit textile manufacturing plant came out of their factory outside Tehran to march to the Ministry of Labor and demand wage increases. They were joined by workers from other factories and soon numbered around two thousand. At the Karvansara Sangi gendarmerie post, the gendarmes opened fire, killing three protestors and injuring several others. In the spring of 1971, the police raided the School of Technology, University of Tehran, in search of Hamid Ashraf and arrested twelve students. In protest, the students clashed with the police, burned the Shah's effigy, and went on strike. In May the police raided Ariamehr University and arrested 350 students. Reports state that 2,500 teachers were arrested during the teachers' strike that year (Matin 1999, 322).

In May 1971 handwritten leaflets in defense of the Fadai insurgency were distributed for the first time at the University of Tehran during a speech delivered by Dr. Ali Asghar Haj Seyyed Javadi, an outspoken liberal-Left critic of the regime. The speech sparked demonstrations on the campus grounds against the government (Baladi 2001, 5). Given the student background of most of the guerrillas, it was only natural that the student movement in Iran quickly sided with the guerrillas. Up until the 1979 Revolution, there was a positive correlation between the student movement and the activities of Fadaiyan: *the Fadai guerrillas were most active when a vast but clandestine network of students supported them.* No assassination or bombing could make the clandestine Fadaiyan socially and politically so visible as did the student movement. The extent of contribution of this hidden student support has remained obscure, but it is evident that without such a support network a guerrilla movement could not have been possible (see Nejat Hosseini 2000, 346–47). The regime's taunting nightmare was the prospect of the student movement's rising up to a mass movement, as it fleetingly had done during the 1970 transit boycott.

The OIPFG encouraged its student body to cooperate with other dissident student bodies (especially with the OIPM supporters), a common practice for student groups at the time. For the most part, student solidarity ran high in Iranian universities during the 1970s, with supporters of the OIPFG and the OIPM enjoying leadership. Religious student groups, while active, significantly lagged behind in recruiting members. Curiously, however, the attitude of the PFG toward the largest and most organized student body, the CISNU, was completely different: it was intentionally divisive.

The guerrilla movement left a profound impact on the student movement abroad. When in the early 1970s Fadaiyan managed to establish relations with the CISNU through the NF-ME, they found a seemingly inexhaustible source of support within reach. For one thing, Fadaiyan received enough financial support from Iranian students abroad that by 1972 they no longer were forced to undertake perilous bank robberies. Fadaiyan also benefited when the NF-ME established a pro-PFG faction within the CISNU ranks, but the OIPFG's attempt to monopolize CISNU, along with other factionalist efforts, eventuated in the dissolution of CISNU in 1975. In the end, after the failure of *tajanos* with Setareh, the OIPFG successfully created its own student organization abroad (Matin 1999, 354–55, 366). Obviously, a double standard informed the OIPFG's treatment of the student movements inside Iran and abroad.

Fadaiyan regarded the student movement abroad mainly as a logistic resource and a mechanism for international campaigns. The PFG leaders indeed had an exploitive approach to the activists abroad and failed to appreciate the mutual interdependence of the struggles carried out inside and outside Iran. Fadaiyan discounted the great contributions of the CISNU in raising international awareness about the regime's appalling human rights record, which along with other international factors forced the Shah to concede a more open political atmosphere in Iran after 1976 (see Matin 1999, 378). By not acknowledging the contributions of the CISNU, Fadaiyan were responsible for the disintegration of the CISNU in its 16th Congress in 1975. They never admitted that the CISNU was an exemplary model of coalitional-democratic organization of the Left, a body that had lasted fifteen years (Matin 1999, 2–3). Fadaiyan's sectarianism made them disdain participation in coalitional politics, as if it would undermine their supposed ideological rigor (see Matin 1999, 363–71).

Repressive development involved the eradication of all secular institutions— political parties, trade unions, and free associations—that could potentially challenge the Shah's monopoly over power. The Shah's suppression of secular social institutions paved the way for the quiet but decisive expansion of Shi'i institutions, so the Shah's policies inadvertently contributed to the rise of the Islamist movement. The only major secular institution to survive this policy was the university, on which the Shah depended to train a new stratum of experts required for his grandiose development plans. The university became the birthplace of the guerrilla movement precisely because it remained the only secular institution to endure the regime's suppressive measures (Mirsepassi 2000, 71) and because the university was necessary for Iran's development. Without this institutional base, Fadaiyan could not have survived. The pre-Fadai attempts at founding guerrilla warfare in Iran failed because of their lack of live and effective links with the student movement.

Fadaiyan left a deep impression on certain sectors of secular intellectuals as well. The political dichotomization of Iranian society obligated many socially conscious intellectuals to stand against the regime's repressive measures and defend the socioeconomic grievances that the guerrillas articulated. Many journalists, poets, writers, and scholars defended the guerrilla movement, artistically or figuratively, through their writings. Their defense sometimes cost them dearly. Many prominent founders or activists of the Iranian Writers' Association

(or IWA, founded in May 1968) were Fadai sympathizers. Samad Behrangi's accidental drowning was recreated as a political murder partly by Gholam Hossein
Sa'edi, a founder of IWA (chapter 2). A short list of intellectual supporters of the
guerrillas turns up names of such prominent poets as Ahmad Shamlu, Esmail
Khoi, Hamid Mosaddeq, Reza Maqsadi, and Sa'id Soltanpur; leading playwright
Gholam Hosein Sa'edi; and well-known intellectuals, scholars, and critics including Hedayatollah Matin Daftari and Nasser Zarafshan. With their cultural prominence, these figures gave the guerrilla movement social legitimacy. They created
an idealized image of the guerrilla fighter as the selfless liberator crowned with
the halo of prophecy—one who heralds an imminent deliverance of the masses.

One outstanding event that publicized the support of the artistic-cultural
community for the guerrilla movement was the poetry reading nights held at
the Goethe Institute in Tehran, October 10–19, 1977. Unmistakably political,
the event took place during Jimmy Carter's U.S. presidency (which had begun
in 1976) and his advocacy of human rights around the world. The Shah had been
pressured by President Carter to allow moderate social and political openness.
Cleverly, Iranian intellectuals took advantage of the situation. Over the course
of the poetry nights, over sixty poets, most of them secular but some religious as
well, read their poems to an enthusiastic audience. The well-known Fadai-poet
Sa'id Soltanpur, recently released from prison, gave the event a vivid political
tenor (Boroujerdi 1996, 50). The event celebrated the secular-Left inclinations of
the attending poets and writers. The mutual interdependence of the Fadai movement and the secular, intellectual sectors was clearly at work.

All the more intriguing, it was not just poetry and art that morally and socially
supported the guerrillas. For its part, the Siahkal insurgence and the subsequent
guerrilla movement socially and artistically sanctioned a new genre of poetry—
"guerrilla poetry"—a 1970s accentuation of the "political-symbolic" poetry that
had gained popularity after the 1953 coup. Prominent poet Ahmad Shamlu, an
engagé devotee of socially committed poetry, explains this phenomenon:

> *Social poetry* permeates the depths of society through imagery, rhythm, ver-
> satility, and dynamics of the letter. *With the "night," the poet offers an allegori-
> cal image of society* and, using a metaphoric language, reveals the situations
> such that the reader or audience . . . can identify the socially constructive or
> destructive personages or elements behind the symbols and images. While [the

reader] enjoys the unique presentation of allegories, metaphors, or rhythms in the poem, behind them [literary devices] s/he reaches a truth superior to the poem itself. (1968, ii)

In the same vein, poet and critic Khosrow Golesorkhi (1944–1974) writes, "Poets are stranded on the intellectual peninsula; a poet writes for poets and for this peninsula! Consequently, instead of growing among the people, poetry has grown in itself and has gotten so fat that it is now choking" (1996, 112). Advocacy for the social commitment of poetry and art, already dominant in the 1960s, in fact has its roots in the debates on the role of intellectuals in society. Studies credit the origins of the "political-symbolic" poetry to the founder of modern Persian poetry, Nima Yushij. Majid Naficy explains that in the heightened politicization of life between 1941 and 1953, the "nature poetry" of earlier Nima Yushij's work was transformed into what he calls the "night poetry" (*shabaheh*), which is vividly social and political thanks to its allegorical content and lexicon. Interestingly, the "political-symbolic" style in Persian poetry emerged during the time of relative freedom in Iran (Naficy 1997). This style gradually became accepted into the mainstream and brought poetry to a determinate reading of symbols and allegories during the 1960s and 1970s (Karimi-Hakkak 1995). The emergence of the guerrilla movement in the political vista overdetermined the political-symbolic style, so the new genre of poetry known as "guerrilla poetry" appeared. "Guerrilla poetry" is constructed on relatively fixed lexical symbolism in which such signifiers as *forest, deer, red, fire, night,* or *daybreak* are detached from their everyday signifieds to serve as an allegory for the conditions of life under guerrilla insurgency. Poet and playwright Sa'id Soltanpur is credited as the founder of "guerrilla poetry" (Langarudi 1998, 9). Guerrilla poetry succeeded a similar genre known as "jungle poetry," which praises revolutionary figures such as Che Guevara or Mirza Kuchek Khan. Inspired by the Siahkal operations, Siavash Kasrai, Khosrow Golesorkhi, Sa'id Soltanpur, and Ja'far Kushabadi have written in this genre. These genres of poetry enjoyed a short-lived but pervasive influence to the extent that even the poet Shamlu, who rejected guerrilla poetry himself, was moved to write many poems in this genre in the aftermath of Siahkal (Langarudi 1998, 14–19). The rise of the guerrilla movement in Iran provided a tangible social narrative for an otherwise abstract and idealist genre of poetry. Indeed, *the guerrilla movement became life imitating art.*

As regards the influence of Fadaiyan on secular intellectuals, one case stands out. In October 1973 the daily papers reported the arrest of a group of twelve artists and filmmakers on charges of plotting to assassinate or take hostage the royal family. Overconfident about its propaganda victory over the guerrillas, the regime extensively publicized the case, even broadcasting the military court proceedings of the twelve arrestees on national TV. The regime had made a gross miscalculation: while SAVAK had managed to break most of the accused into public recantation, Khosrow Golesorkhi, Karamatollah Daneshian, Teyfur Bathai, Mohammad Reza Allamehzadeh, and Abbas Samakar challenged the regime in their defense statements on national TV. Those who recanted received short prison terms, while these five were sentenced to death. International pressure forced the regime to commute three of the death sentences to life imprisonment, but Golesorkhi and Daneshian paid the ultimate price for their gallant public condemnation of the regime. Having become heroes in the eyes of the public, they were executed on February 18, 1974.[1]

---

1. The arrested twelve were: Khosrow Golesorkhi, Karamatollah Daneshian, Mohammad Reza Allamehzadeh, Teifur Bathai, Abbas Ali Samakar, Manuchehr Moqaddam Salimi, Iraj Jamshidi, Morteza Siyahpush, Farhad Qeysari, Ebrahim Farhang Razi, Shokuh Farhang Razi (Mirzadegi), and Mariam Ettehadieh. The group (called Simorgh by SAVAK) was not really one group but three circles with very different objectives. The only person that connected them was Shokuh Mirzadegi. Daneshian (1946–1974) was a dropout student of Cinema and Television College in Tehran and later a rural teacher. He met Sho'aiyan in 1969 and was influenced by his thought. Daneshian was arrested in 1970 along with three members of his study group and was given a one-year prison term. Upon release, he went to Shiraz to prepare an armed cell following Sho'aiyan's ideas. Mirzadegi was in an intellectual circle with Golesorkhi; her husband, Ebrahim Farhang Razi; and long-time activist and former prisoner Manuchehr Moghaddam Salimi. In March 1974, Moghaddam Salimi and later Golesorkhi were arrested. In the meantime, the graduates of Cinema and Television College, Bathai, Samakar, and Allamezadeh, had a plan to take the royal family hostage during an award ceremony in the fall of 1974. Incidentally, Bathai and Mirzadegi met for the first time in Shiraz, and Bathai introduced Mirzadegi to his old classmate Daneshian in Shiraz. At this time, Daneshian was under the impression that he was linked to the PFG through Amir Hossein Fatanat. By August 1974 all members of the three cells—Golesorkhi's reading circle, Daneshian's would-be armed cell, and Samakar's cell that planned to kidnap the Crown Prince—had been arrested. The group called Simorgh is therefore a SAVAK fabrication. In the final analysis, two aspects of this trial are important: first, it was a success story in SAVAK sting operations (creating fake groups to net activists), because, as it later turned out, Daneshian's cell had been infiltrated by SAVAK. Second, the unprecedented

In particular, Golesorkhi's bold defense statements shook the country as he openly attacked the regime and defended both Marxism and revolutionary Islam. "As a Marxist-Leninist, I first found social justice in the School of Islam and then arrived at socialism," he declared. "I do not haggle for my life here, for I am the child of a courageous and militant people" (Golesorkhi 1995, 199). In his last written statement, he heralded the imminent downfall of the regime, proclaiming himself a Fadai (literally: sacrificial) of the Iranian people (Golesorkhi 1995, 205). The poet's Fadai-style death symbolized the closing of the rift between secular intellectuals and political activism. The poet had lived his guerrilla/jungle poetry and he had become both a poet (*sha'er*) and a martyr (*shahid*). The secular-Left opposition deeply mourned his death and renowned poets wrote poems in his honor. On March 8, 1974, CISNU activists simultaneously occupied Iranian embassies in Brussels, the Hague, and Stockholm to protest the execution of Golesorkhi and Daneshian and six other insurgents (Matin 1999, 360). Despite SAVAK's calculation, the regime was morally in retreat.

Without a comprehensive oral history of the Iranian guerrilla movement, this information gives only a faint outline of the extent of the Fadai movement's influence among Iranian intellectuals and students. Researchers know that *selective approaches inevitably risk exaggeration.* Yet it is clear that Fadaiyan politicized the atmosphere of 1970s Iran. The pro-Fadai intellectuals made one last attempt, however uninformed, prior to the 1979 Revolution to develop a secular political culture. Preoccupied with daily matters of running an underground organization, the OIPFG leaders plainly expected supporters to take their own initiative in joining the rising revolutionary wave. *The OIPFG never had a clear or consistent strategy for the organization of their supporters or for building up the nucleus of a future civil society,* while Shi'i clerics countered secularism and the Shah by expanding religious institutions. The OPIFG was ideologically fastened to an idealized abstraction of the working class, a notion that brought serious

---

television broadcast of a military court was an attempt on SAVAK's part to push back the efforts of Empress Farah and Reza Qotbi—a liberal-minded, Europe-educated intellectual and the empress's appointed director of the state-controlled National Television—in granting freedom to artists and writers. Although the broadcast produced unintended consequences beyond SAVAK's imagination and made Golesorkhi and Daneshian national heroes, it must be acknowledged that it was part of a power struggle among the inner circles of the Iranian ruling elite (Salehi 2002, 185–86).

misconceptions about the potential for secular intellectuals to lead the country. *Had Fadaiyan properly addressed the issue of organizing the secular-Left intellectuals, they might have well gained a more prominent position during the events leading up to the Revolution.*

THE OIPFG AND IRANIAN WORKERS

With so few reports, a fair account of Fadaiyan's relationship with workers is even harder to establish. Fadaiyan's relations with intellectuals are recounted by many activists and supporters, but a picture of Fadaiyan's influence among workers can only be retrieved from the memories of Fadai leaders and the few surviving Fadai workers. Originally the Fadaiyan's policy was to absorb workers into their militant network. Fadai workers were assigned to guerrilla cells, and so they lost their place among workers. Jalil Enferadi was the president of the Ironworkers and Mechanics Union prior to joining the Siahkal team, and another guerrilla, Eskandar Sadeghinezhad, was active in the same union. An early leader of the PFG, Hassan Noruzi, was also a worker. Iraj Sepehri, Ahmad Zeybaram, and Hassan Zarkari came from working-class backgrounds as well. The available evidence suggests that the early Fadai leaders had neither the vision nor the resources to establish a workers' network in tandem with the PFG.

Until recently, various offshoots of the OIPFG have mainly remained silent on the subject, possibly because of lack of information. One rare source of interviews on the subject is the special May Day 2001 issue of *Kar* (OIPF-M). Qorban Ali Abdolrahimpur, a leader of the OIPFG after 1976, recalls that by 1974 ingroup discussions indicated that the OIPFG was able to shift its resources toward organizing workers. The idea of organizing workers was resisted by some Fadai cadres, but some teams sent cadres to establish a foothold among workers. Armaghani, a member of the CC, was involved in this project. The plan to publish a workers' edition of *Nabard-e Khalq* turned out only one issue. According to Abdolrahimpur, when he and others reconnected with the cells they had lost contact with in 1976, they realized that the OIPFG had already established networks among workers in major plants. In Tabriz, at least thirty workers were organized into partitioned cells led by Asadollah Rahimi and Samad Eslami. Similarly, in Isfahan, Fadai activist Mottale' Farahani and other former student activists who began working in Isfahan Steel Plant after their graduation were organizing the steel workers. In Abdolrahimpur's assessment, Fadaiyan won considerable moral support among workers, and as the revolutionary wave heightened in 1977–78, workers' support for the OIPFG multiplied. Most of the workers who affiliated with the OIPFG were not militant but rather unionists who aligned with the OIPFG because of its advocacy of workers' rights (Abdolrahimpur 2001, 7).

The move to organize workers coincided with the OIPFG's turn toward Jazani's theory as supported by Armaghani. Once in leadership, it seems, he advocated fundamental changes in OIPFG policy. Worker-organizer Rasul Mahdizadeh, who joined Fadaiyan in 1977 in Tabriz, reports that in that year as revolutionary protests rippled across the country Fadaiyan recruited many workers and technicians and organized them into partitioned cells without attempting to draw them into militant networks. Mahdizadeh credits Fadaiyan's popularity among Tabriz workers not to their militant strategy but to their social prestige as a dedicated and uncompromising force (2001, 9).

Another Fadai worker-activist, Tahmasp Vaziri, acknowledges Fadaiyan's influence in large urban-industrial areas such as Tehran, Isfahan, Tabriz, and Mashhad. He reports that in many Isfahan factories workers were generally sympathetic toward the OIPFG. After the 1974 change of OIPFG policies, Fadaiyan refrained from recruiting workers into guerrilla cells, but they still lacked the idea of encouraging workers to form unions. But even this strategic move was enabled by pro-Fadai students. Vaziri observes that the OIPFG, as mainly a student group, established contacts with workers through former student supporters. By the mid-1970s, many pro-Fadai students had graduated from universities and had jobs as engineers or technicians in industrial plants. Still in contact with the guerrillas, they provided the OIPFG with news and information about workplaces. In 1973–74, Vaziri himself was hired in the Isfahan Steel Plant and succeeded in forming a secret workers' cell there. Other individual Fadai cadres (e.g., Behnam Amiri Davan) established contacts with pro-OIPFG workers in various factories and directed their activities based on their own personal initiatives and inventiveness (Vaziri 2001, 8). Given the rapid industrialization of the country, the increased presence of experts and professionals in factories was inevitable as new or expanding industries required trained and skilled workers, technicians, and engineers. The success of Tabriz activists in organizing workers into secret workers' cells in plants of all sizes came from the long-established relations between Tabriz intellectuals and workers like Samad Eslami, Habib Soroush,

Aqazadeh, and Keyan who after the Revolution became pro-Fadai *Kargaran-e Pishro* (worker vanguards). They were executed in 1988 (Vaziri 2001, 8).

The extent of these efforts, however, must not be exaggerated. Granted, there had been limited success (see Kargar 2001). Yet Fadaiyan rose from intellectuals and students, and so they remained. The fact that the Fadai theorists tried to forge the OIPFG as the working-class vanguard cannot change that fact. These theoretical pretenses expose the fictitious referent of the so-called historical mission of the working class. Ironically, while this referent propelled the Fadai militancy, it did not change the social character of Fadaiyan as an urban, middle-class, and intellectual group. Fadaiyan could have succeeded in their advocacy of workers' movements if they had accepted their social constituency and their tasks as a secular-democratic alternative and had organized workers in unions or associations as workers, and not as a figment of their ideology.

THE SECULAR DILEMMA

Politics is the realm of possibilities, and genuine politics always involves the reinstitution of society. In Iran, the repressive development under the Shah was followed by the authoritarian rentier state under the Islamic Republic, and they both impeded genuine alternatives that aim for social reinstitution. In the face of the fierce measures imposed on political originality in Iran, failures in actualizing such alternatives cannot undermine the merits of the attempts at social change. The Fadai movement should be viewed in this light: it was an attempt at recreating new political spaces and institutions for secular social sectors. This attempt was paradoxically undermined by the restrictive guerrilla mode of organization. In the end, such efforts submerged under the clerical-led revolutionary tide that led to the Shah's downfall in 1979.

This line of argument contains major ramifications for a study of the OIPFG, and by extension, for any investigation into political institutions. The undeniable fact that university students and intellectuals were the main constituents of Fadaiyan indicates that *from their very inception and regardless of their original intentions or ideological inclinations, Fadaiyan were granted the unenviable task of reconstructing the secular-Left forces in Iran.* The rising political Shi'ism was a formidable force that enjoyed vast social networks and financial support from traditional and bazaar classes, while the national liberation movement followed the path of secular expansion, paradoxically, through political organizations whose daily operations depended upon internal restrictions and closure.

The fact that the OIPFG was entirely dependent on university students indicates that it belonged *not* to the working-class movement, as its theorists claimed, but to a secular *class-free* sector of society. University students were free of class belonging during their education. Class-wise, they were mobile, destined to join the growing sector of middle-class experts and to gain the potential ability to exercise a fluid and flexible presence in a political field that suffered from dictatorial closure. This means that the many appeals to the working class, populism, and other ideologically sanctioned categories served only to provide a façade for the participants in the Fadai movement. Evidence shows that the Fadai movement grew during periods of heightened student movement, in the early 1970s and then in 1976–78. Fadaiyan were the children of the post-1953 repressive development as well as the international youth movements of the late 1960s that did not necessarily have an explicit Socialist component (Fatapour 2001f, 34–37). If one wishes to speak of the failure of the original Fadaiyan, one should not focus on their ideologically imposed mandate of revolutionary action and working-class politics, but on their failure to act upon, and possibly lead, an expansive and secular movement for the democratization of Iranian society. Fadaiyan's failure to bring about a secular-democratic movement should be sought in the OIPFG's ideological blinds and centrist view of political action (chapter 9).

This brings us to the irreducible heterogeneity of Fadaiyan in terms of class, social, and cultural backgrounds. Universal postsecondary education in Iran, particularly during the 1960s, allowed the children of two major sectors of Iranian society to encounter each other in the university. Students from traditional middle-class and lower-class sectors, with firsthand experience of Iran's harsh realities and usually with religious or traditional beliefs, studied alongside students from the urban upper class or the newly emerging middle class of intellectuals and experts with secular and liberal lifestyles. These two groups of students shared the experience of the ambivalence of the Shah's modernization. Once in universities, the prospect of a future career achieved through modern, scientific training brought these two sectors together, and moderately secularized the outlook of the first group.

The versatile, enthusiastic, and open character that defines a student's life practically rendered students class-free while in universities. The Fadai

Organization and Fadai movement provided venues for voicing the grievances of these two sectors. But Fadaiyan could not bridge the differences between the two sectors. Although cultures have irrefutable class components, the difference between these two sectors cannot be adequately understood in class terms. Traditional and modern-secular cultures were agonistically brought together in the ranks of the OIPFG as a microcosm of a developing society where different cultures, religious-traditional and secular-Left, clashed on a daily basis. The tormented encounter of the two cultures impacted the everyday life and political decisions of the OIPFG. This encounter is revealed especially with respect to women's issues. The ideological egalitarianism of the OIPFG gave voice to this ideal, and its language emerged out of the desires of a new generation of Iranian intellectuals in the universities. These two propensities, inner conflict and outward unity, require reading the history and theories of the OIPFG, as well as the possible social impacts of the Fadai movement, in a highly contextualized way and with nuanced sensitivity.

Finally, the emergence of the Fadai movement, discussed only briefly here, should be read as an attempt to ensure the presence of a secular vanguard in the possible event of a popular, spontaneous movement under the conditions of political closure. By looking into the past, Fadaiyan had already seen the future. Their *Internal Bulletin* published a communiqué signed by Industrial University students on the anniversary of the bloody uprising of June 1963 (led by Ayatollah Khomeini) to point out the reactionary nature of that uprising, which would have been avoidable if the intellectuals had had an effective presence (*Nashriyeh-ye Dakheli* 1975a, 21, 26). The effective presence of a secular political force could have prevented history from repeating itself in 1979. For their part, Fadaiyan definitely failed to expand the secular-intellectual movement. They enjoyed moral authority over certain sectors of society and had at their disposal a network they could effectively utilize to organize a nationwide cultural Left. Given the social, cultural, and political prominence of its actors, this cultural Left would probably possess the power to expand civil society and complete the aborted democratic secularism that would potentially put an end to repressive development.

The Fadai Guerrillas overlooked this enormous and subversive social project. Sadly, they were caught in the vicious cycle of guerrilla offensive and retreat. As mentioned, their neglect can be traced to their ideology. But that answer alone is unsatisfactory. Their centrist ideology and organizational fetishism reveal how

Fadaiyan were fascinated with power. Instead of setting themselves the task of creating a democratic alternative and a social-cultural movement, they tried to link themselves to an awaited spontaneous and popular movement that would overthrow the Shah. After the Revolution when Fadaiyan enjoyed massive support, they still neglected their secular-democratic potential, and different factions of Fadaiyan either engaged in futile confrontations against the new popular regime or tried to win legal presence by supporting an antidemocratic state and ignoring its assaults against basic human rights. That is why we still need to investigate the organizational issues of the OIPFG. The next chapter will investigate this aspect of the group.

8

Technologies of Resistance

> The Iranian state is not only a coercive social formation. It came into being
> gradually by integrating individuals into particular social arrangements.
> People passing into the orbit of the state were charged with a new savoir
> faire, whether it was disciplinary, capitalist, tutelary, or carceral rational-
> ity. In this respect the state was a matrix of subjection. Perhaps one is well
> advised to concentrate less on the state and more on the kinds of rationality
> that state officials exercise and count on to govern Iranians.
>
> —DARIUS M. REJALI, *Torture and Modernity: Self, Society,*
> *and State in Modern Iran*

GOVERNMENTALITY, according to the late Michel Foucault, designates the "art
of government" (Machiavelli) in the double movement of "state centralization
on the one hand and of dispersion and religious dissidence on the other" (1991c,
88), and it articulates "a kind of rationality" that will regulate the relationship
between the prince and his subjects through principality (1991c, 89–90). When
governmentality (Machiavelli's *"principality"*) is in place, both the prince
and the subjects know how to conduct themselves. Government is teleological: "the end of sovereignty is the exercise of sovereignty" (Foucault 1991c, 95).
Indispensable for the success of government is the purposive rationalization
of society that necessitates an institutional rearrangement of the subjects in
accordance with the principles upon which the very existence of government is
founded. "On the one hand, we govern others and ourselves according to what
we take to be true about who we are, what aspects of our existence and nature
as human beings. On the other hand, the ways in which we govern and conduct
ourselves give rise to different ways of producing truth" (Dean 1999, 18). As
such, government is the apparatus of *saviors* (Foucault 1991c, 103), regimes of
knowledge and constellations of truth, or episteme (Foucault 1991a, 55). Now,

men govern and are governed by the systems of production of truth (Foucault 1991b, 79).

For the present analysis, the focus is on two intertwined analytical consequences of Foucault's theory: (1) the production of the subject through a network of power relations that overall accord with and produce the epistemic truth, and (2) the technologies that actually regulate the conducts of the subjects.

First, the production of the subject: for Foucault the word *subject* has a double meaning: "subject to someone else by control and dependence, and tied to his own identity by a conscience or self-knowledge. Both meanings suggest a form of power which subjugates and makes subject to" (Foucault 1983, 212). The exercise of power necessitates a subject capable of knowledge for making decisions—that is, free subjects—and this distinguishes power from sheer subjugation and violence (Foucault 1983, 220–21). The subject is connected to power through a network of actions, a dynamic network where the ceaseless exercise of knowledge defines both power and the subject. At any given time, the sum total of such exercise designates the form of government in which the exercise of power on subjects and their responses to power shape the teleological truth claimed by a given society in a given historical period. Capable of acting based on self-knowledge and knowledge of the other, the subject is located in fields of freedom that enable varied, multiple, and unexpected responses to, or resistances against, the regime that power constitutes. These fields are historical and cultural, and they are most immediately visible through the operations of the state, although not exclusively so. The production of the subject, therefore, cannot be reduced to politics, *stricto sensu.* Foucault expressly rejects "the forms of totalization offered by politics" (1984, 375). An analysis sensitive to these processes reveals "the way a human being turns him- or herself into a subject" (Foucault 1983, 208). The subject, however, is situated within a regime of episteme that defines the teleology of government, where the exercise of power attains, in modern societies, the status of science and objectifies subjects by dividing them into opposing categories of conduct (criminal/law-abiding, madness/sanity, etc.).

Second, the technologies that regulate the subject: governing conduct in a heterogeneous field of action (like modern societies) requires certain normalizing practices based on the scientific discourse of truth and the proper disciplinary technologies. While in modern societies the success of normalizing practices depends on the state apparatus, these practices are indeed not reducible to state and its institutions. They involve complex processes and practices that achieve normalized conduct and knowledges out of a field of freedom while retaining the "subjectivity" of the subject as both actor and acted-upon. "Technologies of government are heterogeneous and hybrid assemblages" (Rose 1999, 190). *The state is not unique in exercising normalizing power over the subjects.* The regimes that govern fields of health, sanity, morality, or other social practices existed long before the state system attained the status of the most powerful actor in the nineteenth century. However, "the state's power . . . is both an individualizing and a totalizing form of power. Never, . . . in the history of human societies . . . has there been such a tricky combination in the same political structures of individualization techniques, and of totalization procedures" (Foucault 1983, 213). Arturo Escobar cogently explains the unsettled creation of the *Third World as the signifier of a developmental lack* and as the West's subject of global, developmental governmentality. This has been achieved through the scientific problematization of poverty, acquired substantively through comparative statistics as well as planned, governed, and funded by agencies like the United Nations or the neocolonial International Monetary Fund and the World Bank. The Third World subject is now required to internalize this knowledge and act based upon the courses of normalized conduct to overcome the "problem" of poverty and do away with the developmental "lack" (Escobar 1995).

Therefore, governmentality entails using disciplinary techniques to achieve the desired normalized society with the subjects who have internalized societal epistemic truths. Power cannot be reduced to discipline, and discipline is only one implement of power (Foucault 1984, 380). Disciplinary society designates a field of implementation of techniques that facilitate the transformation of individuals through knowledge (Foucault 1979, 125). The specific techniques used to achieve the perceived ends of government are contextually and historically varied, and any generalization about them would undermine the Foucaultian sensitivity toward localized knowledges. Such localities are the targets of disciplinary techniques because the coercive observation of power in a disciplinary society constantly renders local forms of knowledge and resistance visible to the omnipresent gaze of an overseer power.

The concept of governmentality allows us to rethink *the techniques through which state sovereignty replicates itself in the fields of resistance that escape its surveillance.* "Where there is power, there is resistance, and yet, or rather consequently, this resistance is never in a position of exteriority in relation to power," states Foucault. "These points of resistance are present everywhere in the power network. Hence there is no single locus of Great Refusal, no soul of revolt, source of all rebellions, or pure law of the revolutionary" (1990, 95–96). The "Great Refusal"—Fadaiyan's bifurcating militant action in our case—is never as clear in practice as ideology claims it to be. The Foucaultian insight reveals the similarities between the Iranian state's techniques of molding docile citizens and the OIPFG's technologies of creating resistance subjects. Understanding power in this light offers lessons for the future of political activism and democratic politics in Iran and elsewhere.

CENTRISM AND THE DISCIPLINARY STATE

Iran's disciplinary regime of repressive development elevated the state to the position of the supreme agent in Iranian politics and economy with a level of violence that can hardly be exaggerated at the expense of nearly all secular-Left sectors. The Iranian state became a "matrix of subjection," as Darius Rejali explains. Repressive development involves the indispensable formation of subjects that the state can integrate into its plans and projects and thereby govern. Indeed, development always implies participation. The range of participation, however, is determined by the specific historical and contextual nature of development. In the Iranian case, the repressive component of development necessitated the construction of a certain genus of subject that was encouraged to actively participate in the advancement of developmental plans. With this process, the Iranian state incorporated the newly emerging generation of subjects in the growing military, civil service, and crown corporations into its network of power through a system of simultaneous discipline and reward defined by particular arrangements of tutelary, scientific, and capitalist rationalities. This particular arrangement provided the subject with a realm of freedom in which one could act according to the epistemic regime of desire and fulfillment. Technocrats, civil servants, entrepreneurs, professionals, and military personnel benefited to varying degrees from the developmental plans because they lived and socially behaved in accord with the epistemic rationality of repressive development. At the end of the 1960s, certain sectors of Iranians "suddenly" found themselves valued as *progressive* and *modern* in sharp contrast to the perceived backward and traditional sectors, because their life activity was now connected to a discourse of modernity that concealed a fundamental value, "being modern," behind discursive legitimizations of the *necessity* and *inevitability* of modernization and progress.

This regime enjoyed a particular structural forte that eventually became its Achilles' heel: while the entire network of disciplinary and tutelary techniques was dispersed across a field of exercise of power, it was tied to the Shah's autocratic state. To assert its disciplinary might, the Iranian regime discursively rendered the state the signifier of power—the source, means, and ends of power—that imposed a discursive sociopolitical closure. It achieved the discursive closure by *disarticulating* those sources or relations of power (power localities) not clearly connected to the state function, and by *accentuating* and *articulating* the state's perceived might ad nauseam. *The regime could probably have functioned without a closure of this kind* (in which case it had to make certain provisions and concessions), but that did not happen. Instead, the state imposed the laws based on a (presumed) center of power that drove Iranian politics into a closure. Accordingly, an unprecedented centrism dominated Iranian politics after 1963. As the localities in which the episteme of modernization was received were regularized, so the networks of power in which various ideas of modernity would be negotiated were generalized and thereby silenced. The centrism so fiercely forced on political life had real effects on virtually all aspects of society, but it was merely a façade. As such, the untrained gaze of the militant opposition could not see *the variety of spaces for resistance where power could be challenged through creative initiatives.*

While acknowledging the field of the possible as opened through the revolutionary action that first emerged in Latin America (after Cuba 1959), the militant resistance against the Shah's regime lost sight of how to open up this discursive closure. I have already argued that armed resistance was not simply a reaction against the political domination of dependent capitalism, but rather an attempt at opening Iranian politics to the secular-Left opposition that had been excluded from political participation and institutional presence. Curiously, though, the guerrillas sought political opening mainly by aggravating the political climate, making it ever more difficult for the average citizen to participate in the polity. Fadaiyan's specific notion of *armed propaganda* aims at pushing political closure to its limits, taking it to the point of crisis in hopes that the entire system would somehow implode as a result of massive withdrawal from state-sponsored political activities. These attempts never led to political openness because the guerrillas did not understand that power was not reducible to the state apparatus. Fadaiyan suffered from the same sort of *centrist illusion* as did the regime. This kind of centrism was sanctioned, propagated, and legitimated ideologically: Marx, Lenin, Mao, and various Latin American revolutionary theorists all believed that capturing the state apparatus was the silver bullet. Most revolutionary Marxists disregarded cultural and social realms, which they considered to be superstructural, and instead privileged the state as the only institution capable of transforming the economic base. *The regime and the guerrillas both assumed that the power to transform society would emanate exclusively from the state apparatus.* Thus resistance was organized through a centrist duplication of the state apparatus but separate from the state—a view that caused the OIPFG to ignore the importance of grassroots networks and bottom-up challenges to the state.

Enjoying the distributive power of the state, the regime used various technologies to ensure its perpetual presence in Iranian social life. From subsidized education and training, to the lucrative expansion of the public sector, to the glorified image of a great, historical nation, to punitive measures against political dissidents: they all reveal the subject of governmentality in the late Pahlavi state. The Iranian state utilized a certain amalgam of disciplinary and punitive techniques to construct a specific genus of governable subjects. Combined with strict (almost military type) rules of conduct, public education promoted a fanatical obsession with curricula and performance, while discouraging any extracurricular inquiry into unsanctioned matters, with corporal punishment if necessary. Any Iranian student of the time would recall terrifying experiences with rigid teachers, strict classroom discipline, and unending homework assignments that characterized Iranian public education. The imposed hardship was rationalized by the privileged teleology of entering university through the universal entrance exam called *konkur* (the French *concour*).

But at the same time, postsecondary education offered new horizons of freedom: it promised upward mobility to average young women and men with the possibility of enjoying a modern lifestyle full of social and personal rewards: social prestige, urban dwelling, disposable income, modern recreation, and vacation packages—in short, the average citizen's dream life. The goal of entering university, hard to attain and thus highly desirable, made the difficulty of schools a matter of perseverance. This logic fitted in with the Iranian patriarchal mentality of strict rules of social and individual conduct, total submission to decisions of the head of the household, and acceptance of various forms of punishment by authority figures. In this way, the educational system shaped specific docile subjects that believed it was their duty to accept disciplinary measures, even violence, for the sake of future laurels. Education portrayed the silent endurance of suffering as a precondition for success. *The surveillance of authority was thereby replaced by self-surveillance, as the subjects internalized during the earlier stages of life the existing social and cultural values that enlivened their future.* Folktales, children's games, friendship patterns, and many social relations exhibit this fundamental rationality (Chaqueri 1996) and constitute the social and cultural roots of political closure, as well as the statist and centrist politics.

At first glance, the subject shaped through this rationality and its concomitant disciplinary measures seems repressed. But a meticulous observation reveals the vast extent of freedom and happiness the subject can enjoy. Once the subject becomes the docile carrier of the epistemic logic, every field of action that does not explicitly undermine the governing principles becomes a realm of freedom. This freedom is not restrictive liberty; the exercise of freedom always contains acts of creativity. But the freedom exercised in such realms constitutes fields of *contingency* in which the very principles of government *may either be reinforced or undermined.* To understand this crucial point, recall the paradox within repressive development: segments of the new class of experts, technicians, and educated middle class refused to be mere functionaries of the state plans, and instead they pushed for political participation. The scientific training intended to produce docile subjects of state planning also produced dissidents who adhered to alternative modernization. Interestingly, both conformists and dissidents dwelled in the realms of freedom within the governing principles of the Iranian regime. This implies that, contrary to the claim of militant Marxists of the 1960s and 1970s, the police state in Iran did not originate with, nor was it a prerequisite for, neocolonialism or capitalism, despite the fact that dependent capitalism greatly benefited from state repression (Rejali 1994, 44).

These observations lead to the Foucaultian conclusion that in the Iranian state security meant obedience plus happiness, which would not have been possible without an episteme of expanding life prospects from the promises of modernization (*telos*). I must note that citizenship in Iran was merely formal, as it came without citizenship rights: the basic tenet of citizenship, the citizens' inalienable entitlement to civil and individual rights, is suspended except where there is a proof of loyalty to the police state. This point is crucial: such a formal concept of citizenship divides the society into loyalists and dissidents. As Mehrzad Boroujerdi observes, "The shah's formula for political stability was based on two main pillars: ruthless suppression of the opposition and encouragement of civil privatism. The state used the former to encourage the latter" (1996, 31). In the eyes of the opposition, the two major setbacks within one decade (1953–63) translated into the end of legalist-nationalist and peaceful, reformist change. So in the 1960s and 1970s dissident intellectuals were disillusioned with the idea that citizens' rights can be achieved through legal means. Hence their wholesale rejection of citizenship: if the state is illegitimate and constitutionally illegal, all its institutions and spaces are likewise unacceptable. In the Iranian police state resistance required a constant denial of state ideology, government policies, popular culture, and even citizenship. The Great Refusal resulted in a binary political situation that lasted at least a decade, seriously damaging the prospect of democratic politics.

The situation is curious: while the regime created a secure state in which loyalty (or pretense thereof) and civil privatism were the prerequisites for the gains of citizenship, the increasingly militant resistance denied itself citizenship. Consequently, by the late 1960s, the younger generation of Iranian intellectuals did not struggle to reassert or expand citizenship rights. Hence the OIPFG's handicap in understanding its role as a secular-democratic movement. These young men and women were now intent upon destroying the state that dispensed citizenship. The result was the formation of *two antagonistic centers—the state and the resistance.* Despite the unequal power, resources, and influence of these competing centers, they each constructed a separate sphere of activity and ideology and denied the other's legitimacy. The polarization of society to which I have frequently referred should be understood in this context. Iran's experience of dualistic political closure as a binary of mutual denial—a binary of two estranged sets of *self-referential* principles and objectives—defined Iranian political life in the 1970s and rendered utterly ineffectual all middle-ground efforts at negotiating with the state power on expanding citizenship rights. The fact that the competing rationalities—of control and rebellion—shared similar teleological characteristics prompts us, the children of the postrevolutionary era, to ponder the difficulty of challenging the sources of control without having recourse to the technologies of domination.

Now it must be clear that Fadaiyan and other militants used principles of governmentality and techniques of constructing docile and loyal subjects similar to the regime's principle of security (loyalty plus happiness). The techniques of governing dissident subjects need a new study, but for now let us gain an understanding of the technologies of resistance by referring to selected Fadai texts. Here, though, a caveat is in order. A critique of technologies of resistance cannot be supported by judging the past based on our present political ethics. The study of the past teaches us that militant politics eventually exacerbated political closure, harming many in the process. That said, readings that repudiate the just demands of the Iranian secular-Left middle class in the 1970s either subscribe to universal fiats on human conduct or deny the contexts and horizons that rendered meaningful certain decisions at certain times. After all, the realm of the possible withers with the historical eras within which phenomena were once meaningful, however agonizingly.

TECHNOLOGIES OF RESISTANCE

The OIPFG manuals or publications on various aspects of guerrilla life provide a springboard for our study here. Reminiscent of Ernesto Che Guevara's *Guerrilla Warfare* and Carlos Marighella's *Minimanual of the Urban Guerrilla,* the PFG manuals follow a textual strategy to justify the shaping of a specific subject of resistance. These texts follow a deductive logic by positing the evident and irrefutable just cause (e.g., fighting against the brutal dictatorship) that legitimizes the means (e.g., armed struggle). This logic renders the regime of knowledge and subjectivation for resistance inevitable.

The PFG probably published *Instructions for Urban Guerrilla Warfare* in 1972 as it was recovering from the assaults of 1971–72. The manual argues that the pervasive police control necessitates an organizational network based on a hermetically sealed system of security checks with ceaseless control of the cadres' whereabouts and their activities. The police state necessitates this kind of organization and that in turn justifies the group's undemocratic and centralist policies. In one occasion when the leadership was pressed to explain the rationale behind the rigorously top-down centralist organization, it responded by referring to the "experiences" of certain comrades and the others' lack of such experiences (*Nashriyeh-ye Dakheli* 1975a, 36). Pervasive police control should be self-evident, hence the necessity of tight surveillance and security measures within the PFG. Therefore, the guerrillas were required to uphold these instructions as the highest principles of struggle, for these instructions alone would ensure organizational survival. Chief among the instructions was an impenetrable around-the-clock surveillance system over all its members. Details of members' lives including their relationships, contacts, and movements were minutely planned and placed under surveillance. This required the partitioned cells to maintain a system of checks twenty-four hours a day. The *Instructions* also teaches that members should refrain from writing notes, because "the best place for keeping notes is in the chest of individuals" (OIPFG nd-b, 14). A guerrilla network lives off secrecy. The pamphlet explains that "a guerrilla must know that death is preferable to being captured" (OIPFG nd-b, 17). The death of the individual ensures the perpetuation of the greater whole. While the individual's life is expendable, the organization's secrets are not.

According to the *Instructions,* each individual is required to carry out assigned tasks without hesitation. There is no room for disagreement, and even when an order is perceived to be erroneous, it must nonetheless be carried out, and only then can the members criticize the initial order. Yet the pamphlet specifies that individual innovation is the best element in guerrilla operations. The *Instructions* emphasizes obtaining a minute knowledge of the city and stresses the patient identification and study of targets. A guerrilla team must never choose a target greater than its power and resources, while choosing a target smaller than its resources and capability allows the team to preserve power for unexpected turns of events (OIPFG nd-b).

The *Instructions* reveals guerrillas' obsession with their organization, and for good reasons. Although competent individuals are indispensable in guerrilla insurgency, the cause will endure only if the organization prevails: an organization capable of undermining the police state must survive at all costs. Organizational perpetuation, of course, requires self-sacrifice from militants. The designation "Fadai," literally meaning "self-sacrificing individual," now shows its significance: it is rooted in the Shi'i notion of martyrdom, which goes back to the archetypical martyrdom (*shahadat*) of the Third Shi'i Imam Hossein and his few followers by the Umayyad Caliph Yazid and his army in 680 CE. Like their Shi'i dissident compatriots and following this deep-seated religious tradition, Fadai-yan called their fallen comrades "martyred comrade" (*rafiq-e shahid*). The word *Fadai* can be traced to the period between the eleventh and thirteenth centuries when trained soldiers of the Ismaili Shi'i sect led by Hassan al-Sabbah carried out political assassinations and committed suicide by swallowing narcotics after accomplishing their task. In recent Iranian history, the word *Fadai* gained a left-ist political connotation when the Social Democratic and Armenian forces of the Azerbaijani pro-Constitution militia that significantly contributed to the vic-tory of the Constitutional Revolution of 1905–11 called themselves "Fadaiyan." In 1946 the autonomous province of Azerbaijan, which practically seceded from Iran for almost a year when northern Iran was under Soviet occupation, called its militiamen "Fadaiyan." In many liberation movements of the Middle East (e.g., Palestine or Algeria), the fighters were also called the *Fadaeen*. The collective memory of Iranians was already seeded with the symbol of selfless, self-sacrificial devotees with causes larger than life. The designation *People's Fadai Guerrillas* (said to have been suggested by the Tabriz branch) evoked the collective memory of Iranians. As a culturally rooted semiological aggregate, the very combina-tion of the words *Fadai* and *guerrilla* (*cherik*) was explosively symbolic. This is a case of situating oneself in the lexical particularities of language that promotes one's cause. The revered historical and symbolic presence of words such as *people* or *khalq* (which signified a sharp distance from the neutral signifier *mellat,* or "nation," of state propaganda), *Fadai* (which placed the Fadai Guerrillas in con-tinuity with centuries of struggle against injustice), and *guerrillas* (which con-noted the heroic struggles of the Vietcong, or Cuban or Palestinian guerrillas) allowed the "People's Fadai Guerrillas" to enjoy a metonymic presence.

Fadaiyan built on the existing cultural background before embarking upon certain technologies of government and subjectivation. The docile subjects of resistance were constructed by pointing out the obvious police brutality. The sur-vival of the organization required total submission to organizational surveillance and control. Orders were to be obeyed without question and the recruits had to voluntarily relinquish their individualism and private lives. The oppositional rationality of resistance creates almost the mirror image of the state in its use of technologies of shaping loyal subjects. The competing closures of the state and the resistance required the construction of a certain genus of the self. While the state rewarded loyal individuals through allocation of resources, the guerrillas drew upon age-old traditions of resistance and self-sacrifice to construct militants with superhuman capacities. The moral-spiritual reward of the militant came from his or her perceived contribution to the coveted liberation. The superhuman guerrilla accepted the "inevitability" of casualties in the process of bloody guerrilla warfare (see OIPFG nd-a; Nejat Hosseini 2000, 368–69). The ideal militant *self* was paradoxically *selfless*. The Fadai cadres had explicit orders to commit suicide upon arrest by swallowing cyanide capsules. They had additional orders not to leave their wounded comrades in enemy hands (*Kar* 1980a, 9). In a situation where the symbolic presence of an organization is perceived as the sole marker of an ongoing struggle, the logic of organizational survival makes individuals secondary to the teleological rationality of liberation. At one point Jazani criticized the prevalent view of glorified martyrdom among the Fadai cadres and called it an "adventurist tendency" that replaced action with a desire for martyrdom (1976a, 43), although he never proposed an alternative concept.

In the 1970s the average guerrilla lifespan was often said to be about six months. The perceived short life of the guerrilla strengthened the tendency toward practice and away from reflection. This is a crucial point: the life of a cadre was filled with around-the-clock, minutely drafted tasks with rounds of meetings, rendezvous, surveillance, military training, physical fitness, team discussions, ideological training, making of explosives, carrying out of operations, monitoring of police radio signals, guarding of bases, and smuggling of weapons, in addition to the everyday chores of cleaning, cooking, and shopping. As Sho'aiyan observes in "An Outline on How to Study," this overwhelming routine leaves no time for study. He estimates (generously, in my view) the average lifespan of a guerrilla to be three to five years, during which time, he calculated, he or she would have time to read only ten to fifteen books (1976a, 12–15; article individually paginated). The theoretical poverty of the average militant, therefore, should come as no surprise even though they were some of the brightest young minds of the country. In fact, the OIPFG had very few theoretically inclined individuals (Puyan, Ahmadzadeh, Jazani, Zia Zarifi, and Momeni). The teleological rationality that places organizational survival above individual survival also creates a system of unending tasks that leaves no time for critical, theoretical reflection on everyday practice.

While the police state required that citizens stay neutral, if not loyal, guerrilla life required a full test of loyalty from militant cadres. The state power was both totalizing and individualizing; citizens could find refuge from the political binarism of the 1970s in the hiatus between the two processes. However, the "matrix of subjection" of a guerrilla is almost panoptic, although never totally so. The purging of the former members is an example, but other events also illustrate this point. Ashraf Dehqani reports the predicament of a young member in prison: during interrogation, Roqiyyeh Daneshgari trusted a seemingly sympathetic prison guard and asked him to contact his comrades so they could escape an impending police raid. The guard was in fact an agent and SAVAK immediately surrounded the house, but Daneshgari's comrades had already evacuated their base. When she learned about the events, Daneshgari felt guilty and depressed. In a rare meeting in prison, the legendary Massoud Ahmadzadeh lifted the burden of guilt and redeemed her (Dehqani 1974, 176–78). *In a guerrilla's life, anything short of perfection might amount to treason.* In a saddening example, a cadre named Nayyereh (an alias) was caught asleep on her night watch. She was disciplined and went through "self-criticism," but the continued pressure led her to commit suicide and end the stigma attached to her in the eyes of her comrades (in Hadjebi-Tabrizi 2003, 124).

The source of distribution of duties is also the source of distribution of verdicts. The OIPFG documents contain scattered hints about the existence of internal tribunals. One document honors the heroic death of Nezhatossdat Ruhi Ahangaran, who was earlier held responsible for the arrest of Behruz Dehqani, but "after investigating the situation, the central [cadre] found her not guilty of all the allegations attributed to her in prison or by some circles" (*Nabard-e Khalq* 1976, 127). The four known cases of internal purges (chapter 2) provide additional evidence. Technologies of resistance involve the panoptic regulation of conduct that leaves little leeway for acting outside assigned tasks. From the Fadaiyan's publications, religious phrases such as "faithful Communist" (*komonist-e momen*) or "toward an ever more true belief" (*beh su-ye iman-i har cheh rastintar*) (*Nashriyeh-ye Dakheli* 1976, 111, 113) attest to the higher court of organizational judgment that can redeem or condemn acts of the resisting subjects.

Technologies of resistance require the resisting subject to submit to an indubitable understanding of the logic of survival. Members of the group must recognize the higher intellect of the collective (read: centralized leadership). While the leadership's decisions may not always reveal their supreme logic, it is the responsibility of the subject of this epistemic regime to act in its accord. In cases where the self falls short in acting according to the disciplinary measures of the organization, he or she must surrender to its punishment. In Fadaiyan's case punishment functions as a corrective response to a curious range of transgressions, from breaking the laws of guerrilla life (which always places others in mortal jeopardy) to simply failing to act in certain manners. *The necessity of punishment arises from the fact that the panoptic totalization of the resisting subject is never complete. Localized knowledges always escape the epistemic gaze of panoptic surveillance, because they arise in particular contexts that the dominant episteme has no or little knowledge about.* An issue of the OPFG *Internal Bulletin* contains allusions to discussions about punishment of comrades and protests over them. The issue offers an explanatory guideline (apparently written by Ashraf) for the punishment of comrades for their errors. The guideline reports cases in which members of teams have resorted to flogging for punishment. It also reports how some remorseful members have used self-inflicted burns to punish their own conduct (see Masali 2001, 158). The question was whether corporal punishment is an accepted method of punishment. The leadership's decision, interestingly, is ambivalent: "We are against flogging and similar corporal punishments as the basic solution for reforming ourselves and for the acquisition of proletarian characteristics under present conditions" (*Nashriyeh-ye Dakheli* 1975b, 93). Ultimately, though, the leadership does not reject such punishments either: "The method of punishment with the greatest effect will be preferable." The reason is obvious. The guerrillas must engage in rigorous self-criticism to remove their weaknesses and "should not refuse to accept any kind of necessary and constructive punishment, be it flogging or any other" (*Nashriyeh-ye Dakheli* 1975b, 95). The teleological rationality of organizational survival requires highly disciplined subjects, and punishment is utilized to curb all undesired characteristics, notwithstanding the panoptic structure of guerrilla organization.

Other disciplinary measures to deal with individuality included the confiscation of weapons, supervised and intensive ideological retraining, forced labor, and isolation. These measures represent diluted versions of Stalinist measures. Forced labor was a common punishment, because, as we saw in Momeni's rejoinder to Sho'aiyan (chapter 6), working like a laborer places the individual in touch with the reality of the masses. Manual labor is valued as a magical and cathartic way of purifying the individual's personality and bringing it in line with the life of an organization that fights for the freedom of labor. This is how the intellectuals who fought for their peoples' rights and were fascinated by the idealized masses dealt with their collective inferiority complex.

The guerrilla must be totally dedicated to the cause or he or she is unworthy of the task. The technologies of resistance require a self that is not only totalized but also homogenized. No internal, categorical differences such as gender, class, or ethnicity may separate the individuals from the cause. Moreover, the guerrilla must not have any characteristic or special talent that might distinguish her or him from the marching files of the soldiers of the future, *unless* such talents could benefit the organization. That is why leaders of the guerrilla teams were responsible for inspecting the creative capacity of members and curbing undesired ("petit-bourgeois") tendencies. As regards socioeconomic differences, the promise of a total liberation of a homogenized humanity required the guerrilla to incorporate the new humanity into her or his self. The official OIPFG texts indicate these homogenizing techniques. A nuanced practice like sexuality would undermine homogenizing technologies and thus had to be eliminated from guerrilla life: it cost Panjehshahi his life in 1977 (chapter 2). This is no small matter given that we are speaking of a *secular* organization.

Technologies of homogenization encroach on writing: Sho'aiyan was criticized by Momeni for his puritan Persian writing style. Written works provided leaders or commanders with a window into the personality of the cadres. This method, as is well known, is particularly popular in totalitarian states, and Stalin used it to indict perceived foes among party members. The OIPFG *Internal Bulletin* reports a case in which a member's poetry is criticized for its alleged petit-bourgeois tendencies: a "critic-commander" criticizes a poem called "Poetic" (*Sha'eraneh*) because it reveals a "romantic" view of the guerrillas. The poem confuses emotion (*utefeh*) with romanticism and reveals the member's petit-bourgeois traits that she or he has inherited from her or his class (*Nashriyeh-ye Dakheli* 1975b, 54–56). A reform of the self through study, greater dedication, and "self-criticism," the report holds, will bring this comrade into alignment with the proper perception of a Fadai Guerrilla.

And yet, despite all the techniques used to create homogenized militants, "the strict, guerrilla discipline and the organizational structure of [Fadaiyan] were in conflict with the spirit of the members of the [student] movement," as Fatapour observes. "Among Fadaiyan, discipline and the full submission to leadership were the exception, and division, fraction, and manifest political and organizational disagreements the rule. To cancel out democratic centralism, Fadaiyan just needed a theoretical justification" (2001d). The extent of production of the docile subject greatly depended on how each militant was individually and culturally socialized into docility. In short, if Fadaiyan failed to produce the ultimate docile subject it was not for the lack of trying.

A normalized self becomes an important issue because there were no guidelines for recruiting new members. Ashraf notes that in the inceptive years of the movement the only criterion for recruitment was the individual's agreement with the policies of the guerrillas (1978, 67). Given that unsuitable recruits could jeopardize the very existence of the group, Fadaiyan relied on a deep-rooted social network: the family. At least one-fifth of all Fadai casualties were related through familial ties, and a brief investigation turns up the names of eighty-eight members of the group (both fallen and surviving) between 1971 and 1979 who were siblings, married, or relatives. As a guerrilla organization, Fadaiyan focused on the recruitment of family members because unlike religious dissidents who had extensive support networks in religious institutions, Fadaiyan had no comparable secular networks or institutions such as unions, political parties, or cooperatives. Because Fadaiyan were based in universities and their few cadres had limited contacts with the large student body, a viable course of action for them was to reach out to sympathetic family members (mostly siblings) for support and recruitment. Familial trust was utilized as a political means of expansion and networking. To counter this technique, SAVAK made it a common practice to arrest or hold hostage family members to track down wanted militants.

GOVERNING THE RESISTING SUBJECT

As the self-acclaimed vanguard of the national liberation movement in Iran, the OIPFG was guided by the same genus of centrism and closure that it challenged in the repressive state of the Shah. A Foucaultian approach unveils the teleological rationality that guides all principal institutions and practices under modernity. This rationality guided the opposing narratives of political modernity in 1970s Iran, but it must not overshadow the noble intentions of Fadaiyan. While aspiration for political opening is still relevant today, Fadaiyan's means to achieve it are not. If there are similarities between technologies of disciplinary control and those of resistance, these similarities must be viewed as the stamp of the historical era, the age of national liberations and revolutionary wars in which Fadaiyan emerged. Awareness of the technologies of resistance provides a learning process in transforming the rationalistic and teleological essence of modern politics. Such awareness enables new insights into preparing for future politics that will refuse to naïvely surrender to the normative technologies of the self as a precondition for a successful process of governmentality. The subject of regimes of governmentality is expected to act according to the epistemic principles guaranteed through regulatory measures of conduct (surveillance, control, punishment, security, and rewards). Still, the doors to the exercise of freedom are never shut on the subject: local knowledges and individual initiatives do permeate the realm of governed activities of the subject. In Fadaiyan's case, the *untamable and youthful spirit of a specific generation, its élan vital, ultimately undermined the governability of the resistance subjects, although resistance would not have been possible without these young women and men.* Herein rests the possibility of acting in terms other than those regulatively sanctioned.

The dominance of "functional trust" over "human trust" is at the heart of technologies of resistance employed by Fadaiyan, as Darius Rejali argues. The distinction defines modern politics. "Politics is founded on trust among people, but there is a vast difference between human trust and functional trust. Human trust is the stuff that binds communities together, yet it is also fleeting and fragile," Rejali observes. "By training human beings according to discipline, tutelage, torture, economic incentives, or legal rules, one can indeed make possible new institutions with tremendous capabilities" (1994, 159). The very concept of modern society as an aggregate of sovereign individuals represents a dislocative reorganization of communities by various disciplinary institutions. The logics of goal and efficiency cannot bear the contingencies of human trust. The long twentieth century shows that most visible resistances against teleological and disciplinary regimes succeeded on the basis of an efficient employment of functional trust, of party building, military organization, bureaucratic structure, or economic restructuring. Iran's Fadaiyan were no exception: their shining horizons and heroic presence attracted a fervent and zealous generation of young individuals who, paradoxically, were organized in the centrist-militant structure based on functional trust. This is indicative of the constitutive paradox of the Fadai Guerrillas: their struggle for freedom from repression and for democratic participation was based on a militant-centrist style of surveillance and disciplinary measures.

Fadaiyan emerged in an era of domination of specific teleological disciplinary technologies. The logic of these technologies, justified by ideology and based on security and survival, impeded Fadaiyan from exploring their possible contribution to struggles for the expansion of the democratic and secular socialization and education of Iran. This is the lesson we should take from this study: *the form of struggle we launch today decides what kind of society we will have tomorrow.*

9

Constitutive Paradox

Liberation, Secularism, and the Possibility
of Democratic Action

> When you cannot make plans for the future, you continually brood over the
> past, analyze it, end up by seeing it more clearly in all of its relationships and
> you think especially about all the foolish things you've done, about your acts
> of weakness, about what it would have been better to do or not to do and
> what it would have been your duty to do or not to do.
>
> —ANTONIO GRAMSCI, *Letters from Prison,* vol. 2

FOR THOSE OF US who lived through the revolutionary experience of 1979,
armed movement and national liberation soon turned out to be utterly futile
modes of struggle because they preclude the democratic struggles that function as a means of political education of the people. Armed struggle did not
mobilize the masses toward a revolution, as Fadaiyan had hoped. But even if it
had, the political outcome would not have been significantly different from the
actual outcome of the 1979 Revolution: the leading militants would have probably degenerated into an autocratic and populist regime supported by politically
uneducated masses who were motivated by the frustrations that arose from dire
socioeconomic status. Fadaiyan shone on the dark horizon of Iranian politics
in the 1970s, not so much because of their militantism but more thanks to
their selflessness, dedication, and love of the people. In their certain "historic
moment," they actually left a lasting impression for many Iranians that a better
world was possible.

But although Fadaiyan had noble intentions, they never achieved the self-
confident critical thinking that would have allowed them to break away from the
political and cultural roots of authoritarianism. Even when the sectors of society

that Fadai Guerrillas inspired and recruited from reached out to the OIPFG, Fadaiyan's ideological blinds did not allow them to see their potential place as the cultural critics of society. Fadaiyan had more in common with the dogmatic mentality of the traditional sectors, from which many of them came, than they were prepared to acknowledge. Despite limited attempts by certain leaders to offer a specifically "Iranian" Marxist theory, eventually Fadaiyan's fascination with, and uncritical adherence to, Marxism-Leninism left them analytically and organizationally ill-equipped for the 1979 Revolution. Consequently, soon after 1979 they fractured into endless schisms leading to either embarrassing support for an antidemocratic state or a futile return to militant radicalism. Both of these approaches were tried and failed at great human cost, causing Fadaiyan to lose their postrevolutionary moral and social weight significantly. However, those Fadai supporters who cleverly detached themselves from ideology and organizations and instead adhered to the *unaging spirit of Fadai belief in freedom, dignity, and change* waited out the dark and suffocating 1980s, and then silently and patiently built an influential cultural and social Left that has affected recent movements as the young postrevolutionary generation rises to the leading roles in various social movements in Iran.

Of course, these observations require no brilliance: we can thank the gift of the hindsight, the new, prevalent epochal discourse of pluralism and democracy, and a certain degree of critical thinking. In this concluding chapter, I would like to offer reflections from the study of the People's Fadai Guerrillas that pertain to our post-Communist era and the contemporary situation in Iran, while I also seek to unravel our subtle continuities with the past.

THE PLURALITY OF THE FADAIYAN

The preceding genealogical study of Fadaiyan in their first period of organizational life provides insights into understanding a new politics for today's Iran. In the 1970s, Fadaiyan were propelled by their original mandate of staging a national liberation movement against imperialism and its domestic agent, the Pahlavi monarchy. While they defined an era of Iranian political life, Fadaiyan failed to mobilize the Iranian people toward a social revolution, let alone a secular-democratic political reconfiguration of society. This book shows that at least in the Iranian case, the discourse of national liberation lacked the ability to mobilize the masses. However, and this is critical, it was on the bedrock of the polarization of Iranian society, an outcome of the militant movement spearheaded by the OIPFG, that the revolutionary movement led by the Islamic clerics succeeded. Fadaiyan failed to mobilize and lead the masses as they had wished, but they inadvertently prepared the collective psyche of Iranian society for popular mobilization by the clerics.

We must note, though, that mass mobilization does not necessarily alter the structure of society. The 1979 Revolution did not transform the fabric of Iranian society: it merely replaced the old ruling class with a new one by shattering the limping Imperial ideology of the Shah's rentier-capitalist state apparatus, inserting a religious ideology in its stead, and installing a new political elite armed with endless *ressentiment* (Nietzsche) because of their exclusion under the Pahlavis. This explains why, unlike Theda Skocpol (1994, 240), I think that the Iranian Revolution was *not* a social revolution: it neither altered the "class structure" of Iranian society nor did it transform any other essential social relation in a historical way. As I have demonstrated in the preceding chapters, liberation movements have essential deficits in terms of reshaping society because of their centrist organization and leadership as well as their populism. With the demise of the dominant and totalizing discourse of national liberation in prerevolutionary times, there emerged in postrevolutionary Iran the new social movements of women, ethnicities, urban middle class, youth, students, and workers. These new movements no longer claim to exclusively hold the key to the future of humanity but push for openings in the existing sociopolitical edifice through democratic action. Mind you: the social strata that Fadaiyan represented, those we loosely discussed under the "Fadai movement," were as plural and diverse as Fadaiyan's origins and constituents. Indeed, the word *organization* in the OIPFG's designation was misleading, and Fadaiyan should be regarded as a coalition of zealous militants from diverse ideological, social, and cultural backgrounds, not a political party. As the group's survival became the highest value, Fadaiyan fell victim to the very organization that they had built in order to voice the grievances of their generation.

And this is one of my main theses in this book: *the seemingly ideologically monolithic Fadaiyan were indeed internally diverse and heterogeneous in all respects.* The plurality of the (conflicting) governing ideas within the OIPFG attests to *different generational formative experiences* of the Fadai theorists, and to varied influences ranging from the Tudeh Party, to the 1953 coup, to the 1960–63 National Front movement, and finally to the late 1960s Latin American and international student movements. In effect, these different experiences required democratic organizational life and democratic social action. Fadaiyan provided the possibility of an organizational existence for members and supporters from very different sectors of society. From the most dogmatic and traditional "believers" (who had simply traded Islam for Marxism) to critical thinkers with modern and individualist values, and from the impoverished districts of major industrial cities to the luxurious mansions of the richest, these individuals converged under one organizational roof. Like their counterparts in the rest of the Third World, the Fadai Guerrillas were too ideologically inflexible to appreciate the gift of plurality of constituents and ideas. They could have cultivated pluralism by opening themselves up to democratic action, but in the end they shunned democratic politics in order to remain loyal to ideology. *In the era of national liberation, ideology was the marker of identity,* and it brought perceived international recognition and solidarity. Adhering to Marxism-Leninism made one a proud member of an international family.

Today, on the contrary, recognition comes from the identity claims that demand and deepen democratic politics. This is a lesson for political action: for a nation to liberate itself from dependent capitalism or traditional despotism, it is social pressure for opening the political sphere that holds the key, not the capturing of the state. Democratic politics is not an end in itself, a project one can complete and achieve once and for all. It is an unending project of building secular-democratic institutions, maintaining social and political coalitions, promoting public debates over issues, and undertaking the long-term project of democratic and cultural education of the people.

THE CONSTITUTIVE PARADOX OF NATIONAL LIBERATION

National liberation is informed by a *constitutive paradox*—a term I borrowed from Ian Angus (1998). National liberation strives to emancipate a nation in a developing country from the imposed political closure concomitant with the country's peripheral entry into the capitalist world system. It is a direct political response to the conditions that I called "repressive development." As worked out by the OIPFG theorists, national liberation intends to put an end to the paradoxical condition in which economic development comes in a package with social and political repression. The aim of national liberation is to puncture openings in the political closure. But Fadaiyan tried to introduce openings into politics, *paradoxically,* by imposing a closure of their own—a closure that came from militantism and polarization of society. In Fadaiyan's case, the task of armed struggle was, in theory, *not* to overthrow the state, but to instigate a popular movement toward revolution or liberation war. In other words, the main objective of the OIPFG was to overcome the political closure through a nationwide social movement. While it is possible to enumerate various reasons for the failure of the Iranian Left in achieving this objective, I argue that this failure comes from a conceptual deficit—namely, the *democratic deficit*—of national liberation. Of course, Fadaiyan did not achieve their original mandate. But even such victorious cases as Cuba and Nicaragua (and many others) show this deficit: while the Cuban leadership has consistently denied the democratic aporia and rules authoritatively, the Sandinistas eventually acknowledged it, thus marking Nicaragua as the first revolutionary state to submit democratically to electoral decision, despite the grave human costs of the democratic transition.

The popular front posed a problem that perpetually haunted the Fadai discourse of national liberation. Many of the theoretical works and organizational efforts of Fadaiyan were dedicated to the problem of the front. Fadai theorists and leaders—Jazani and Ashraf (much less Ahmadzadeh), as well as their critics such as Sho'aiyan and Setareh—had rightly arrived at the significance of the front. The issue of the front, in the context of today's radical democratic politics of the new social movements, has been acknowledged in contemporary political theory (Laclau 1996; Laclau and Mouffe 1985). Democratic frontal politics is credited for the unprecedented rise of the Italian Left to power in 1996 and again in 2006. The revival of frontal politics can be partly credited to our post-Communist era. With the receding of the Socialist horizon and the rise of neoliberal politics in the West, and the concomitant neoconservative assaults on the welfare state, social programs, and civil rights, the issue of redefining the boundaries of democratic politics gained urgency. The rise of new social movements added to the complexity of recent social and political transformations. These new movements of "identity politics" entered the political spectrum in the context of the civil rights movement in the United States and the 1968 student and workers' uprising in France. The "new" in the new social movements stems from

(1) their refutation of utopian universalism and emphasis on group identity; (2) their refusal to transform themselves into formal political parties; and (3) their redefinition of citizenship and civil and human rights (Vahabzadeh 2003, 7–39). The gay, environmental, aboriginals' rights, ethnicities, and feminist/women's movements exemplify the new social movements. These movements challenge the existing political edifice, in both liberal democratic or authoritarian contexts. They seek greater political openings based on their ever-expanding visions of civil and individual rights.

In order to explicate the continuity of movements across historical boundaries, I must distinguish the context of national liberation of yesteryear from that of today's democratic politics. Under the condition of repressive development, the state became the sole agent of economic, social, political, and cultural modernization. While economic restructuring attempted to adapt Iran to the labor, production, and market requirements for entering the orbit of global capitalist economic modernization, sociopolitical modernization lagged behind significantly. Thus repressive development economically enlivened the emerging skilled workers sector and the middle class, while socially and politically alienating the rising intellectual and professional sectors. These groups largely identified the state as the culprit for their alienation and with good reason: *the state, representing the oligarchy, was the exclusionary agent of change* and the center of all decisions. *The Fadai discourse of national liberation duplicated the same image* on the opposite side, *as the sole agent of alternative modernization*. Both the Iranian state and the OIPFG acted as the self-acclaimed centers of modernization. In challenging the political, military, and moral authority of the state, the OIPFG appealed to a centrist view that expressly denied the diverse voices of women, students, workers, intellectuals, and ethnic or national minorities in favor of the perceived unified voice of a homogeneous people, or *khalq*: the sole agent of liberation that was intent upon stirring up a nationwide uprising to uproot the conditions of repressive development. The ultimate referentiality of the working class as the privileged agent of change, an ideological and theoretical construct rather than an empirical and demographic category, sanctioned a constant disregard for other actors. Ideological dogmatism and organizational fetishism and sectarianism solidified this self-acclaimed gesture of the proud liberatory Fadai hero. That is precisely why the Fadai Guerrillas failed to recognize, let alone organize, the diverse, secular movements that supported the Fadai cause by the mid-1970s.

Instead of the unified (and ideologically preconceived) national liberation front, a secular-democratic alliance of diverse movements could have emerged in the manner of Mosaddeq's National Front but with wider constituent movements. The OIPFG failed the secular sectors and movements of students, women, urban middle class, skilled workers, and intellectuals that needed, above all, democratization of the Iranian society. The Fadai movement could have led the Iranian society into a new secular-democratic hegemonic alliance. The OIPFG failed a generation precisely because of the democratic deficits in its ideological worldview, organizational premises, and political objectives, which blinded Fadaiyan to the role that the exigency of time had assigned them. Centrism is the plague of democratic action. Should there be any surprise, then, as to why Fadaiyan's armed struggle neither led to a greater political opening nor propagated the secular-democratic values that would hinder the rise of traditionalism?

In the national liberation discourse, adherence to a unified and monolithic "people" (a theoretical construct) is the precondition of liberation. No wonder that national liberation seeks to replace the state and can only lead to the highly centralized and authoritarian "people's democracy," in which all power is concentrated within the state and conferred only upon a homogenous people. In the national liberation discourse, democracy comes only after the referential constitution of a monolithic construct called "the people." The *referentiality of the people* is what differentiates the frontal politics of national liberation from the democratic front. *In a democratic front, the constituents are not pregiven and nor is there a preexisting leading or central actor.* Alliances are temporary and often precarious. The composition of frontal actors and the leadership of the front remain contingent. The documents of Fadaiyan are laden with cases, exemplars, theses, and policies that trivialized, undermined, or simply warded off ethnonational, cultural, or local demands. The same holds for gender discrimination as Fadaiyan and other militants postponed the resolution of the "women's issues" until after the victory of the Socialist revolution. Indeed, the meager number of pages in the OIPFG documents dedicated to women's issues is startling. As for other issues and movements that were mostly local in nature—the 1977 uprising of shantytown dwellers south of Tehran and various workers' strikes—Fadaiyan's populism overdetermined these issues, and through its ideological lens the OIPFG saw in these movements their vision of a popular revolution. The normative *telos* of socialism ultimately justified all forms of homogenization of the popular front. *The liberatory-emancipatory project that intended to open up the polity concomitant with repressive development was already foreclosed unto itself, containing actors within a determinate field of practice.* That, along with ideology, impeded Fadaiyan from democratic practices.

The *conceptual* transition from a liberatory front to a democratic front is achieved through the acknowledgement of the nonreferential conception of the actor. This transition requires the theoretical removal of pregiven and privileged centers, actors, and teleological horizons. Stepping out of the referential and centrist ambits that governed the social movements of the past is what enables us, the inhabitants of this era of radical democratic politics, to depart from the past while acknowledging our indebtedness. This is *the inadvertent contribution of Fadaiyan* to our understanding of contemporary democratic struggles—a contribution the group's originators could not have perceived. Recognizing their contribution, indeed, is enabled by the radical phenomenological method of stepping back from the actual into the possible.

One needs to remove universalism of "national liberation" and referentiality of the "working class" or the "people" from the framework of acting and thinking in the 1960s and 1970s in order to arrive, theoretically, at the democratic movements of our time. At the time, of course, thinking outside the ambit of the era and its constellation of truth hardly seemed possible. Just as we find our democratic era as the ultimate stage in social and political thinking, just as we can hardly think beyond the boundaries of the existing constellation of intelligibility, just as we act according to the requirements of the democratic discourse, so did Fadaiyan in their time: they too acted according to the mandate of the dominant revolutionary discourse of their time. And this is what radical phenomenology holds as our human condition: we are constituted by our historical eras and the truths that our respective eras project upon us as measures for our acting and thinking. That said, however, sober actors are always able to see the openings in their historic era and change their perspective according to new principles of acting and thinking.

DECENTERED STATE, DIVERSE MOVEMENTS

Allow me a quick recap: the discourse of national liberation understands the state as an apparatus of class oppression. As such, the state becomes the unique source of emanation of politics. The anti-imperialist self-affirmation of a nation should therefore aim at overthrowing the state as the agent of repressive development. This is achieved by mobilizing the people through the vanguard's articulation of the popular demands, which allows the vanguard to function as a state-to-be. Herein rest the origins of the political binarism of national liberation. The centrist conception that takes the state as the source of emanation of politics (shared by both repressive development and liberation movement) is flawed. Warren Magnusson and Rob Walker observe that in the Third World, in "the triad of election/government/public policy, 'armed struggle' has taken the place of elections" (1988, 47). This certainly was the case in Iran. But as they also acknowledge (1988, 56), this strange form of "elections" suffers from a monistic notion of imperialism, the state, and the struggles against them, whence arise the conceptual roots of universalization of struggle, unitary notion of the historical subject (the working class), and homogenization of "the people."

Conceptually, though, while the state is arguably the most formidable agent of change, it is not the source of politics. In our Iranian case, development would not have needed to be repressive, because developmental projects—structurally economic but in fact social and political to their core—would have been completed without serious resistance by negotiating and incorporating alternative scenarios of modernization. Hence the centrality of social movements as sources of emanation of alternative social and cultural models, or to borrow a term from Alain Touraine, as the sources of "historicity" (1988). Both authoritarian state and national liberation fail to recognize that politics is the brainchild of social movements. That is why the liberation movement acts like a shadow state, paradoxically, by denying its roots in, and the supports it receives from, a myriad of heterogeneous constituents and social movements.

Democratic-frontal politics is a politics of a decentered state in that it pressures the state apparatus and the ruling elite to submit to the variety of demands of diverse social movements, as it is happening in today's Iran. A front, properly understood, cannot have the characteristics of the state because it is a strategic alliance in which a certain movement can function as a leader on two conditions: first, an unwavering adherence to the secular-democratic principles that govern a coalition, and second, an articulation of the demands of as many social movements as can be represented under the frontal banner. In our case, students, women, writers, intellectuals, urban middle class, and workers could all be considered as the constituents of Fadaiyan, each supporting the OIPFG with the hope that their demands would be articulated and their voice heard through armed struggle. The plurality of Fadaiyan and their origins is a point that necessitates a genealogical critique. The centric notion of politics that informs national liberation, however, deprived these constituents of opportunities to arrive at a secular-democratic society in which they could be heard.

SECULARISM AND DEMOCRATIC ACTION

The removal of state centrism and the referentiality of privileged actor from the liberation front pave the way, theoretically, for the concept of "participatory secularism" that challenges both repressive secularization and theocracy in the Iranian case. We need to recognize state-sponsored secularism as a part of modernization under the Pahlavi shahs. But such superficial secularization was mostly limited to those aspects of Iranian social life involved in the institutions of the state apparatus. Secularization from the above was achieved in two ways: first, by the state's sanctioning of secular institutions and education, and the second through the rise of the new educated middle class that leaned toward a break with tradition. However, the fact that Iranian secular intellectuals uncritically and mostly without serious reservations supported the Islamic revolutionary wave attests to the superficiality of the secularization project of the Shah's modernity. For the most part, various secular individuals and groups took secularism for granted, mistaking the Shah's laic and formal inhibition of religion, however cursory, as a guarantee that the country had undergone an irreversible process of secularization and that Iranians would not support theocratic rule. History proved them wrong.

Secularism cannot be achieved without democratic participation and education. Fadaiyan's fascination with centrist liberation blinded them to the perpetual critical revisiting of all aspects of life, especially a critical reexamination of one's political and theoretical positions. Fadaiyan's lack of critical thinking resulted in their insensitivity toward the secular question, while the *intellectual and social constituency of the Fadai movement yearned for it without being able to articulate the issue politically.* Fadaiyan themselves did not really undergo a *critical* secularization process, and exceptions aside, all militants had understood Marxism in the same way that they internalized religious or traditional values as absolute. Secularization can only be achieved through critical social and political education, or to quote Nietzsche, through "the revaluation of all values."

Reading history "backward" demonstrates that there was no political or structural necessity for the guerrilla movement in Iran: it was the product of the age and a certain referential ultimacy that seized upon actors and directed them into steel and blood and toward a glorified future. The lack of critical self-understanding reduced these noble actors to "the bureaucrats of the revolution," as Michel Foucault once said, who were soon consumed by the mundane and endless chores of maintaining an underground organization. *The guerrilla movement had no organic relationship with Iranian society in the 1970s.* In its stead, patient network building and founding the process of participatory secularization would have resulted in the removal of repressive development in a slow, democratic, viable, and educational way. Iran was, and still is, in need of a profound democratization and secularization to complete the unfinished project that began with the Constitutional Revolution, continued with Dr. Mosaddeq, and was lost to the 1953 coup.

Understanding the past in this way is a gift of our genealogical critique, as this approach reveals what paths the heroic generation of the 1970s did *not* take. Fadaiyan articulated a generation's spirit and aspirations for freedom, self-expression, and participation in a society that repressed both genuine politics and generational ambitions. The generation of young Iranian intellectuals that the OIPFG represented became heir to a nation's post-1960s withering hopes. At the same time, this generation was born into a unique world: a world dominated by the Cold War but also a world that presented "the sixties," a time of shining horizons, boundless visions, heightened expectations, unprecedented activism, and inexhaustible futurity of life, when "everything was possible," as Fredric Jameson described it. From "the sixties" Fadaiyan borrowed defiance but not its pluralism while choosing the puritan binarims of the Cold War!

From the viewpoint of genealogical critique the notion of "failure" must be revisited. In genealogical analysis, failures are understood in terms of lack of insight into the future: Fadaiyan "failed" in that they remained oblivious, because of their ideological fascinations, to the theological-repressive movement that gradually crept up as a populist revolution. Moreover, they "failed" because they neglected to meaningfully take notice of the rise of the democratic-secular movement of writers, intellectuals, and students by the mid-1970s, let alone change their strategy to address the changing conditions. *Failure is a built-in theoretical feature. It dwells in every aporetic corner of inquiry or mode of praxis that the theory prohibits. It stems from inattention toward shifting horizons.* As such, social movements cannot be deemed as success or failure according to the pedantic standards of theory. The success or failure of social movements depends on whether they actually transform with the turn of historical discourses and shifting horizons. In this, Fadaiyan did not fail in their time as they carried out their tasks within the discourse of national liberation that dominated the postcolonial era. But in their transition to the next, democratic era, which was well on the rise by the mid-1970s, and in their not attending to the diverse movements of pro-Fadai students and intellectuals, Fadaiyan did indeed fail. Mesmerized by their ideological truisms, they did not "listen" to the changing praxis of the social movements they inadvertently represented. With unjustified delay, they arrived in the new era of democratic discourse in shaky, confused, and uncertain ways and policies almost a decade after the Revolution. The Fadai activists did not succeed in bringing an opening to society because they did not seize upon the changing essence of time and so missed the moment when they had to shed their old skin.

Fadaiyan tried and tested the "ends of politics" through their militant action—a mode of action that remained irremediably inorganic to Iranian society. For about a decade in Iranian social life, militant actors spoke loudly and shone brightly only to be disillusioned in the end with all forms of centrism and statism and to realize that secular-democratic opening is the only viable alternative for the future of Iran. This book documented the guerrilla odyssey of the 1970s and its heroic sojourn—its departure, adventures, hardships, experiences, as well as its return—in full circle: "participatory secularization" involves the reexamination of all existing social values through social and political education that leads to democratic frontal politics based on the principle of a decentered state and plurality of actors. In today's Iran, women's, student, workers, youth, and ethnic minorities' movements are consciously on this path to change Iran's future.

The originators of Fadaiyan correctly understood that Iran needed to complete the secular-democratic project from Iran's Constitutional Revolution (1905–11), which reached its peak with the nationwide movement led by Premier Mosaddeq, only to be lost by a devastating coup d'état. Yet Fadaiyan understood this project in their ideologically sanctioned way and boldly embarked upon completing it by utilizing militant methods. So they continued the odyssey of the Iranian people. The political life of twentieth-century Iran saw three different efforts at realizing democracy, first through the legal constitutionalism of the Constitutional Revolution, then through the national-democratic struggles of the Mosaddeq era, and later through the national liberation movement of the 1970s. Each era is defined by a specific realm of the possible that enabled these movements to articulate the demands of Iranians and to set the limits of acting and thinking. Now begins the period that many hope will bring fruition: the time of secular-democratic republicanism.

Three decades after the Revolution that derailed this historic project, Iranians are once again intent upon completing the secular-democratic project, and they seem to be doing it the right way this time. Revealing the resilient spirit that vivified the movements of the past—the "Fadai spirit," one might call it paradoxically—the postrevolutionary generation in today's Iran appears to be already embarking upon this long odyssey for the democratic secularization of the country. The difference is that the present generation is no longer in contact with its era-making predecessors, who are aging in exile and separated from the Iranian political scene. This young and aspiring generation may therefore be prone to repeating the mistakes of the past generations. May that repetition never happen!

Fadai Casualties, 1970–1979

The following four tables indicate the number, gender, place, and cause of death of Fadai members who lost their lives between 1971 and 1979. Although it is ultimately impossible to account for each and every casualty because of the secretive nature of the OIPFG, these four tables indicate that the numbers of Fadai casualties are in fact higher than previously acknowledged.[1] The tables are based on various casualty lists (or "martyr lists") provided by Fadai splinter groups. As much as possible, these lists were checked against the original OIPFG sources, various biographical accounts, information retrieved from the Internet, and reminiscences of Fadai activists. In cases of discrepancy, I relied on memoirs or biographies rather than the casualty lists. One must note that two individuals with connections with Fadaiyan actually died before the formation of the group. The most notable is Samad Behrangi, who drowned in River Aras in summer of 1968. The first Fadai actually lost his life about a year before the official formation of the group: Hassan Nikdavudi was killed during interrogation in Tehran in May 1970.

Note that Iranian solar years begin on March 20/21 of each year in the Gregorian calendar.

---

1. Based on resources available to him, Abrahamian (1982, 481) held that 172 Fadai were killed between 1971 and 1979. This figure reappeared in a popular Persian source (Nejati 1992, 377). Ironically, this number resurfaced in *Kar* (OIPF-M): "From February 7, 1971, to the February Revolution of 1979, 341 guerrillas lost their lives. 177 were killed in street battles, 100 were executed, 42 were killed under torture, 7 committed suicide at the time of arrest, and 15 died in unknown circumstances. Out of 341, 306 were identified: 208 (61 percent) were intellectuals, 26 (9 percent) working class, 3 were businessmen, 1 was a clergyman. Out of 306 of them only 10 were above 35 years of age and 39 were women. Out of 341, 172 (50 percent) were Fadaiyan, 73 were Mojahedin, 38 of various Marxist groups, 30 of the Marxist-Leninist faction of Mojahedin (Peykar), and 28 were of small Islamic groups" (*Kar* [OIPF-M] 1995, 8). This study shows that the actual number of Fadai casualties is higher than previously thought.

Table 1. Annual Fadai casualties between 1971 and 1979, in solar years (March 20–March 19)

Year	Number of casualties	Percentage (Year out Total)
1349 (1970–71)	17	7.2
1350 (1971–72)	42	17.7
1351 (1972–73)	11	4.6
1352 (1973–74)	10	4.2
1353 (1974–75)	11	4.6
1354 (1975–76)	46	19.4
1355 (1976–77)	68	28.7
1356 (1977–78)	12	5.1
1357 (1978–79)	20	8.4
Total	237	100

Table 2. Gender distribution among casualties

Year	Number of Casualties	Men (number)	Men (percentage)	Women (number)	Women (percentage)
1349 (1970–71)	17	17	100.0	0	0.0
1350 (1971–72)	42	41	97.6	1	2.4
1351 (1972–73)	11	9	81.8	2	18.2
1352 (1973–74)	10	10	100.0	0	0.0
1353 (1974–75)	11	9	81.8	2	18.2
1354 (1975–76)	46	39	92.8	7	7.2
1355 (1976–77)	68	48	70.6	20	29.4
1356 (1977–78)	12	9	75.0	3	25.0
1357 (1978–79)	20	19	95.0	1	5.0
Total	237	201	84.8	36	15.2

Table 3. Distribution of casualties according to the place of death*

Place of Death	Number of Casualties	Percentage
Tehran**	185	78.0
Mashhad	8	3.4
Tabriz	5	2.1
Rasht	5	2.1
Karaj	3	1.3
Shiraz	3	1.3
Siahkal	2	0.8
Lorestan Province	2	0.8
Ahvaz	2	0.8
Qazvin	2	0.8
Isfahan	1	0.5
Gorgan	1	0.5
Dhofar (Yemen)/Lebanon	2	0.8
Intercity Highways (Motor Vehicle Accident)	3	1.3
Unknown/Undocumented	13	5.5
Total	237	100

* For the purpose of this study, the place of death is based on information provided in casualty lists and checked against other sources.

** Number of casualties in Tehran includes those executed by the military court based in Tehran (forty-seven of Fadai militants were killed by firing squad; see table 4).

Table 4. Fadai casualties by cause of death

Cause of Death	Number	Percentage
Shoot-out with security forces*	129	54.4
Firing squad	47	19.8
Assassinated in prison	7	3.0
Under interrogation	16	6.8
February 1979 revolution	12	5.0
Suicide*, explosion, motor vehicle accident	17	7.2
War in Dhofar and Lebanon	2	0.8
Unknown/Undocumented	7	3.0
Total	237	100

* Upon the OIPFG's instructions, injured militants committed suicide by swallowing cyanide capsules or shooting themselves in order to avoid arrest. As well, Fadai cadres had orders to kill their wounded comrades. As a result, it is often difficult to separate death as a result of shoot-out or suicide.

The Splits of Fadaiyan

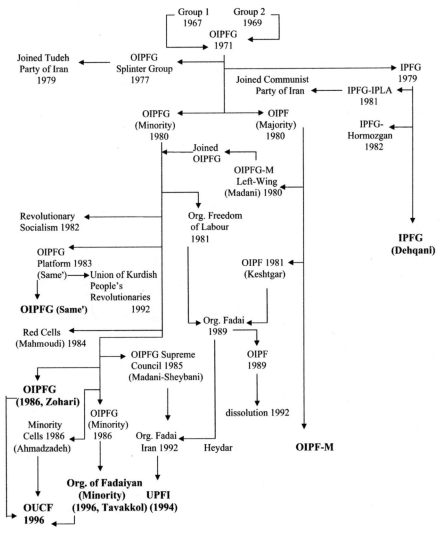

LEGEND

Group 1: The Jazani-Zarifi Group (founding group of OIPFG).

Group 2: The Ahmadzadeh-Puyan-Meftahi Group (founding group of OIPFG).

OIPFG: Organization of Iranian People's Fadai Guerrillas, originally PFG, renamed OPFG, and then OIPFG (the main body of Fadaiyan that, beginning in 1977, gradually split into many groups).

OIPFG Splinter Group: the Monsha'ebin that later joined the Tudeh Party of Iran.

IPFG: Iranian People's Fadai Guerrillas (currently in exile).

IPFG-IPLA: Iranian People's Fadai Guerrillas–Iranian People's Liberation Army (dissolved in 1983).

IPFG-Hormozgan: Iranian People's Fadai Guerrillas, the Provincial Committee of Hormozgan (dissolved).

OIPF-M: Organization of Iranian People's Fadaiyan-Majority, social-democratic, republican (in exile).

OIPFG: Organization Iranian People's Fadai Guerrillas, better known as the Minority, split several times in the 1980s.

OIPFG-M (Left Wing): Organization of Iranian People's Fadai Guerrillas (Majority–Left Wing), split from OIPF-M, later joined the OIPFG-Minority.

OIPF: Organization of Iranian People's Fadaiyan, split from the Majority, later joined other splinter groups (dissolved in 1992).

Organization of Freedom of Labour: Splinter group from Minority (later dissolved).

Revolutionary Socialist Wing: Splinter group from Minority (dissolved).

OIPFG-Platform: Organization of Iranian People's Fadai Guerrillas–Followers of the Identity Platform, later changed into Organization of Iranian People's Fadai Guerrillas (OIPFG) (in exile).

Red Cells: Splinter Group from the Minority, led by Siahkal veteran Mahmoud Mahmoudi, active in Tehran (dissolved in 1985).

Organization of Fadai: short-lived splinter group (dissolved).

Union of Kurdish People's Revolutionaries: Kurdish militants who split from OIPFG-Platform (dissolved).

OIPFG-Supreme Council: Organization of Iranian People's Fadai Guerrillas–Supreme Council, a Minority splinter group (dissolved and formed UPFI).

OIPFG-Minority: Organization of Iranian People's Fadai Guerrillas-Minority, later renamed itself as Organization of Fadaiyan (Minority) (in exile).

Organization of Fadaiyan (Minority): See OIPFG-Minority.

Minority Cells: A short-lived splinter group formed in exile (dissolved).

UPFI: Union of Iranian People's Fadaiyan, formed after many members of the Minority transformed into Democratic-Socialists and Republicans (in exile).

OUCF: Organization of Union of Communist Fadaiyan, formed by disenchanted members of Organization of Fadaiyan (Minority), Minority Cells, and OIPFG (in exile).

Source: Ahmadzadeh 2001, 2008; Fatapour 2001; OF-Minority 2003; Same' 1997; UPFI 2003.

References

Abdolrahimpur, Qorban Ali (Majid). 1996. "Dar bistomin Salgard 8 Tir" [On the twentieth anniversary of June 29, 1976]. *Kar* (OIPF-M), no. 136 (June 29): 8.

———. 1999a. "Cheguneh enqelab ra bavar kardim" [How we believed in the revolution]. *Kar* (OIPF-M), no. 201 (Feb. 10): 7.

———. 1999b. "Tasir-e nazarat-e Bizhan Jazani bar Sazman-e Cherikha-ye Fadai Khalq Iran 1353–1357" [The impact of Bizhan Jazani's ideas on OIPFG 1974–1979]. In CCPWBJ 1999, 275–85.

———. 2001. "Mosahebeh ba rafiq Majid Abdolrahimpur" [Interview with Comrade Majid Abdolrahimpur]. *Kar* (OIPF-M), no. 256 (May 12): 7.

———. 2003. "Mosahebeh ba Qorban Ali Abdolrahimpur (Majid)" [Interview with Qorban Ali Abdolrahimpur (Majid)]. In UPFI 2003, 40–49.

Abdolrahimpur, Qorban Ali (Majid), and Behzad Karimi. 2001. "Goftogu ba Behzad Karimi and Qorban Ali Abdolrahimpur (Majid)" [Interview with Behzad Karimi and Qorban Ali Abdolrahimpur (Majid)]. *Arash* 79 (November): 34–41.

Abrahamian, Ervand. 1980. "The Guerrilla Movement in Iran, 1963–1977." *MERIP Report* 86:3–15.

———. 1982. *Iran Between Two Revolutions*. Princeton, NJ: Princeton Univ. Press.

———. 1989. *Radical Islam: The Iranian Mojahedin*. London: I. B. Tauris and Co.

Ahmadi Oskui, Marziyeh. 1974. *Khaterati az yek rafiq* [Memoirs of a comrade]. Np: OIPFG.

Ahmadzadeh, Massoud. 1976. *Mobarezeh-ye mosallahaneh: ham estratezhi, ham taktik* [Armed struggle: Both strategy and tactic]. Umeä, Sweden: Organization of Iranian Students.

Ahmadzadeh, Mastureh. 2001. Interview by Peyman Vahabzadeh. Aug. 30.

———. 2008. Interview by Peyman Vahabzadeh. July 16.

Alaolmolki, Nozar. 1987. "The New Iranian Left." *Middle East Journal* 41 (2): 218–33.

Amir Khosravi, Babak, and Mohsen Heydarian. 2002. *Mohajerat-e sosialisti va sarnevesht-e Iranian* [Socialist migration and the fate of Iranians]. Tehran: Nashr-e Payam Emruz.

Amui, Mohammad Ali. 2001. *Dord-e Zamaneh: Khaterat-e Mohammad Ali Amui* [Dreg of the time: Memoirs of Mohammad Ali Amui]. Tehran: Nashr-e Eshareh.

Angus, Ian. 1998. "Constitutive Paradox: The Subject in Cultural Criticism." *Continuum: Journal of Media and Cultural Studies* 12 (2): 147–56.

Anonymous. 1976a. "Goruh-e Ahmadzadeh-Puyan-Meftahi pishahang-e jonbesh-e mosalahaneh-ye Iran" [The Ahmadzadeh-Puyan-Meftahi group: The vanguard of armed movement in Iran]. *19 Bahman-e Teorik*, 7 (June).

Anonymous. 1976b. "Goruh-e Jazani-Zarifi pishtaz-e jonbesh-e mosalahaneh-ye Iran" [The Jazani-Zarifi group: The vanguard of armed movement in Iran]. *19 Bahman-e Teorik* 4 (Apr.).

Anonymous. nd. *Tarkhcheh-ye Sazmanha-ye Cheriki dar Iran* [A history of the guerrilla organizations in Iran]. Np: np.

Ashraf, Hamid. 1978. *Jam'bandi-ye seh saleh* [The three-year summation]. Tehran: Nashr-e Negah.

Baladi, Yadollah. 2001. "Negahi beh jonbesh-e daneshju-i dar salha-ye 47 ta 52" [A glance at the student movement between 1968 and 1973]. *Kar* (OIPF-M), no. 252 (Mar. 7): 5.

Behrangi, Asad. 2000. *Baradaram Samad Behrangi: Ravayat-e zendegi va marg-e ou* [My brother Samad Behrangi: A report of his life and death]. Tabriz: Nashr-e Behrangi.

Behrooz, Maziar. 1999. *Rebels with a Cause: The Failure of the Left in Iran*. London: I. B. Tauris and Co.

———. 2001. "Tudeh Factionalism and the 1953 Coup in Iran." *International Journal of Middle East Studies* 33:363–82.

Boroujerdi, Mehrzad. 1996. *Iranian Intellectuals and the West: The Tormented Triumph of Nativism*. Syracuse, NY: Syracuse Univ. Press.

Calvino, Italo. 1985. *Mr. Palomar*. Translated by William Weaver. Toronto: Lester and Orpen Dennys.

Castañeda, Jorge G. 1993. *Utopia Unarmed: The Latin American Left After the Cold War*. New York: Vintage Books.

Chaqueri, C. 1984. "Sultanzade: The Forgotten Revolutionary Theoretician." *Iranian Studies* 17 (2–3): 215–35.

———. 1995. *The Soviet Socialist Republic of Iran, 1920–1921: Birth of the Trauma*. Pittsburgh, PA: Pittsburgh Univ. Press.

———. 1996. *Beginning Politics: The Reproductive Cycle of Children's Tales and Games in Iran*. Florence: Mazdak.

———. 1999. "Did the Soviets Play a Role in Founding the Tudeh Party in Iran?" *Cahiers du Monde russe* 40 (3): 497–528.

———. 2000. "Historiography of the Iranian Left in the Twentieth Century: A Critical Appraisal." In *Conference on the History of the Iranian Left*, June. London: School of Oriental and African Studies.

———. 2001. Interview by Peyman Vahabzadeh. Aug. 28 and 30.

———, ed. 2007. *Mostafa Sho'aiyan, Hasht nameh be Cherikha-ye Fadai-ye Khalq: Naqd-e yek manesh-e fekri* [Mostafa Sho'aiyan, eight letters to the People's Fadai Guerrillas: Critique of an intellectual attitude]. Tehran: Nashr-e Ney.

Che Guevara, Ernesto. 1998. *Guerrilla Warfare*. Translated by Marc Becker. Lincoln: Univ. of Nebraska Press.

CCPWBJ [Centre for Collection and Publication of Works of Bizhan Jazani], ed. 1999. *Jong-i darbareh-ye zendegi va asar-e Bizhan Jazani* [On the life and works of Bizhan Jazani]. Vincennes, France: Editions Khavaran.

CSHD [Centre for Study of Historical Documents]. 2001. *Chap dar Iran beh ravayat-e asnad-e SAVAK: Sazman-e Cherikha-ye Fadai Khalq* [The Left in Iran according to SAVAK documents: Organization of People's Fadai Guerrillas]. Tehran: Centre for Study of Historical Documents, Ministry of Intelligence.

———. 2004. *Chap dar Iran beh ravayat-e asnad-e SAVAK: Konfedrasion-e daneshjuy-an-e Irani dar Orupa* [The Left in Iran according to SAVAK documents: The Confederation of Iranian Students in Europe]. Tehran: Centre for the Study of Historical Documents, Ministry of Intelligence.

Dastan, A. K. 1988. "Seh chehreh-ye Marksism dar Iran" [Three Marxist figures of Iran]. *Kankash* 1 (2–3): 49–85.

Davies, James C. 1962. "A Theory of Revolution." *American Sociological Review* 27 (1): 5–19.

Dean, Mitchell. 1999. *Governmentality: Power and Rule in Modern Society*. London: Sage Publications.

Debray, Régis. 1967. *Revolution in the Revolution? Armed Struggle and Political Struggle in Latin America*. Translated by Bobbye Ortiz. New York: Monthly Review Press.

Dehqani, Ashraf. 1974. *Hamaseh-ye moqavemat* [The epic of resistance]. Np: National Front of Iran Organizations Abroad–Middle East Division.

———. 1979. *Cherik-e Fadai khalq Ashraf Dehqani sokhan miguyad* [Speaks the People's Fadai Guerrilla Ashraf Dehqani]. Np: np.

———. 2002. *Farazha-i az tarikh-e cherikha-ye Fadai-ye khalq-e Iran* [Passages of the history of Iranian People's Fadai Guerrillas]. http://www.siahkal.com/tarikhimages/tarikh.pdf (accessed Jan. 16, 2002).

———. 2004. "Moqaddameh-ye nevisandeh bar chap-e jadid" [Author's introduction to the new edition]. In *Hamaseh-ye moqavemat* [The epic of resistance]. London: IPFG.

Dehqani, Ashraf, and Mohammad Hormatipur. 1979. *Darbareh-ye sharayet-e eyni-ye enqelab* [On the objective conditions of the revolution]. Tehran: Nashr-e Hamid Ashraf.

Derrida, Jacques. 1993. *Aporias: Dying–Awaiting (One Another at) the "Limits of Truth."* Translated by Thomas Dutoit. Stanford, CA: Stanford Univ. Press.

Escobar, Arturo. 1995. *Encountering Development: The Making and Unmaking of the Third World.* Princeton, NJ: Princeton Univ. Press.

Eskandari, Iraj. 1974. "Chand nokteh-ye asasi darbareh-ye bonyadgozari-ye Hezb-e Tudeh-ye Iran va tahavvol-e an" [Basic points on the foundation and development of the Tudeh Party of Iran]. *Donya* 3 (Aug.–Sept.): 2–7.

Fadaiyan–Plains of Turkoman. 1980. *Naghdi bar andisheha-ye rafiq Ashraf Dehqani* [A critique of the thoughts of Comrade Ashraf Dehqani]. Np: Fadaiyan–Plains of Turkoman.

Fallaci, Oriana. 1976. *Interview with History.* Translated by John Shepley. New York: Liveright.

Farahati, Hamzeh. 1991. "Qesseh-ye Raz-e Koshandeh-ye Aras" [The story of Aras's deadly mystery]. *Adineh* 67 (Feb.): 11–12.

———. 2006. *Az an salha . . . va salha-ye ba'd* [Of those years . . . And the years that followed]. Cologne, Germany: Forough Verlag.

Fatapour, Mehdi. 1999. "Sherkat-e Fadaiyan Khalq dar enqelab-e Bahman" [The participation of the People's Fadaiyan in the February Revolution]. *Kar* (OIPF-M), no. 201 (Feb. 10): 8.

———. 2001a. Interview by Peyman Vahabzadeh. Nov. 24, Dec. 8, and Dec. 15.

———. 2001b. "Jonbesh-e daneshju-i dar salha-ye 47–52" [Student movement, 1968–1973]. *Kar* (OIPF-M), no. 248 (Jan. 10): 6.

———. 2001c. "Jonbesh-e daneshju-i dar salha-ye 47–52" [Student movement, 1968–1973]. *Kar* (OIPF-M), no. 251 (Feb. 21): 6.

———. 2001d. "Khizesh-e roshanfekran-e javan-e Iran dar dahe-ye 50" [The revolt of young Iranian intellectuals in the 1970s]. *Iran Emrooz.* http://www.Iran-emrooz.de/maqal/fatapu0113.html (accessed Apr. 3, 2001).

———. 2001e. "Mosahebeh ba rafiq Mehdi Fatapour" [An interview with Comrade Mehdi Fatapour]. *Kar* (OIPF-M), no. 257 (May 16): 4, 11.

———. 2001f. "Goftoguy-e Shahrvand ba Mehdi Fatapour" [*Shahrvand*'s interview with Mehdi Fatapour]. *Shahrvand-e Vancouver* (Aug. 24): 34–37.

Fathollahzadeh, Atabak. 2001. *Khaneh-ye dai Yusof* [Uncle Joseph's house]. Saltsjöbaden, Sweden: np.

Fayazmanesh, Sasan. 1995. "Theories of Development and the Iranian Left (1960s–70s): A Critical Assessment." *South Asian Bulletin* 15 (1): 98–107.

Foucault, Michel. 1979. *Discipline and Punish: The Birth of the Prison.* New York: Vintage Books.

———. 1983. "Afterword: The Subject and Power." In *Michel Foucault: Beyond Structuralism and Hermeneutics,* edited by H. L. Dreyfus and Paul Rabinow, 208–26. Chicago: Univ. of Chicago Press.

———. 1984. *The Foucault Reader.* Edited by Paul Rabinow. New York: Pantheon Books.

———. 1990. *History of Sexuality: An Introduction.* Vol. 1. New York: Vintage Books.

———. 1991a. "Politics and the Study of Discourse." In *The Foucault Effect,* edited by Graham Burchell, Colin Gordon, and Peter Miller, 53–72. London: Harvester Weathsheaf.

———. 1991b. "Questions of Method." In *The Foucault Effect,* edited by Graham Burchell, Colin Gordon, and Peter Miller, 78–86. London: Harvester Weathsheaf.

———. 1991c. "Governmentality." In *The Foucault Effect,* edited by Graham Burchell, Colin Gordon, and Peter Miller, 87–104. London: Harvester Weathsheaf.

Foss, Daniel A., and Ralph Larkin. 1986. *Beyond Revolution: A New Theory of Social Movements.* South Hadley, MA: Bergin and Garvey Publishers.

GCU. 1977a. *Nokati darbareh-ye poruseh-ye tajanos* [Issues concerning the unification process]. Np: Group for Communist Unity.

———. 1977b. *Bohran-e jadid-e siasi va eqtesadi-ye rezhim va naqsh-e niruha-ye chap* [New political and economic crisis of the regime and the role of the Left]. Np: Group for Communist Unity.

———. 1977c. *Masael-e hadd-e Mojahedin ya "Masael-e hadd jonbesh-e ma"?* [The critical issues of the Mojahedin or the "Critical issues of our movement"?]. Np: Group for Communist Unity.

———. 1977d. *Moshkelat va masael-e jonbesh* [The problems and issues of our movement]. Np: Group for Communist Unity.

———. 1977e. *Marhaleh-ye tadarok-e enqelabi* [The revolutionary preparation stage]. Np: Group for Communist Unity.

———. 1977f. "Nokati dar tarh-e masaleh-ye Stalin" [Sketching the outline of the Stalin issue]. In *Stalinism: daftar-e dovvom tabadol-e nazar dar poroseh-ye tajanos* [Stalinism: Second volume of the exchange of ideas in the unification process]. Np: Group for Communist Unity and OIPFG. Article individually paginated.

———. 1977g. "Kamandar va ahl-e kherad" [The archer and the people of wisdom]. In *Stalinism: daftar-e dovvom tabadol-e nazar dar poroseh-ye tajanos* [Stalinism: Second volume of the exchange of ideas in the unification process]. Np: Group for Communist Unity and OIPFG. Article individually paginated.

————. 1977h. "Nazarat-e enteqadi" [Critical comments]. In *Andisheh-ye Mao Tse-tung va siyasat-e khareji-ye Chin* [Mao Tse-tung doctrine and China's foreign policy]. Np: Group for Communist Unity and OPIFG. Article individually paginated.

————. 1977i. "Andisheh Mao Tse-Tung" [Mao Tse-Tung thought]. In *Andisheh-ye Mao Tse-tung va siyasat-e khareji-ye Chin* [Mao Tse-tung doctrine and China's foreign policy]. Np: Group for Communist Unity and OIPFG. Article individually paginated.

————. 1978. *Cheh nabayad kard?* [What is not to be done?]. Np: Group for Communist Unity.

Ghahremanian, Safar. 1999. *Khaterat-e Safar Khan (Safar Ghahremanian)* [Memoirs of Safar Ghahremanian]. Edited by Ali Ashraf Darvishian. Tehran: Nashr-e Cheshmeh.

Golesorkhi, Khosrow. 1995. *Bisheh-ye bidar* [The wakeful thicket]. Edited by Majid Roshangar. Tehran: Entesharat-e Morvarid.

————. 1996. *Dasti miyan-e deshneh va del* [A hand between the dagger and the heart]. Edited by Kaveh Goharin. Tehran: Moassesseh Farhang-e Kavosh.

Gramsci, Antonio. 1971. *Selections from the Prison Notebooks*. Edited and translated by Quintin Hoare and Geoffrey Nowell Smith. New York: International Publishers.

————. 1994. *Letters from Prison*. Vol. 2. Edited by Frank Rosengarten. New York: Columbia Univ. Press.

Hadjebi-Tabrizi, Vida. 2003. *Dad-e-Bidad: Femmes politiques emprisonnées 1971–1979*. Cologne: BM-Druckservice.

————. 2004. *Dad-e-Bidad: Femmes politiques emprisonnées 1971–1979*. Vol. 2. Cologne: BM-Druckservice.

Halliday, Fred. 1980. "Fedayi: 'A Confrontation Between Us and the Regime May Well Be at Hand.'" *MERIP Report* 86 (Mar.–Apr.): 18–19.

Hamidian, Naqi. 2004. *Safar bar balha-ye arezu* [A voyage on the wings of a dream]. Vällingby, Sweden: Arash Förlag.

Haqshenas, Torab. 2001. "Interview with Torab Haqshenas." *Arash* 79 (Nov.): 21–26.

Hashemi, Abbas. 2001a. "Goftogu ba Abbas Hashemi (Hashem)" [Interview with Abbas Hashemi (Hashem)]. *Arash* 79 (Nov.): 41–45.

————. 2001b. "Jang-e dovvom-e Turkoman Sahra" [The second war in the Plains of Turkoman]. *Arash* 79 (Nov.): 45–46.

————. 2008. Written interview by Peyman Vahabzadeh. Dec. 10, 13, 18, and 19.

Hassanpour, Ghasem. 2007. *Shekanjehgaran miguyand* [What torturers say]. Tehran: Ebrat Museum of Iran.

Heydar (Mohammad Dabirifard). 1999. "Rafiq Bizhan Jazani va Sazman-e Cherikha-ye Fadai Khalq Iran" [Comrade Bizhan Jazani and the OIPFG]. In CCPWBJ 1999, 245–68.

———. 2001. "Interview with Heydar." *Arash* 79 (Nov.): 26–34.

———. 2003. "Mosahebeh ba Heydar" [Interview with Heydar.] In UPFI 2003, 25–39.

Heydari Bigvand, Turaj. 1978. *Teori-ye tabliq-e mosallahaneh enheraf az Marksism-Le-ninism* [Theory of armed propaganda: A deviation from Marxism-Leninism]. Np: Tudeh Party of Iran Publications.

IPFG. 1980. *Nokati darbareh-ye "Pasokh be mosahebeh ba rafiq Ashraf Dehqani"* [Remarks on "A rejoinder to the interview with Comrade Ashraf Dehqani"]. Tehran: IPFG.

———. 1983. *Shemai az poroseh-ye takvin-e nazarat-e cherikha-ye Fadai-e khalq-e Iran (46–50)* [A schematic of the process of the development of theories of Iranian People's Fadai Guerrillas (1967–71)]. Np: IPFG.

Izadi, Asghar. 1999. "Goftogu bemonasebat-e bistopanjomin salgasht-e teror-e Bizhan Jazani" [Interview on the twenty-fifth anniversary of the assassination of Bizhan Jazani]. In CCPWBJ 1999, 109–17.

Jameson, Fredric. 1988. *The Ideologies of Theory: Essays 1971–1986*. Vol. 2. Minneapolis: Univ. of Minnesota Press.

JAMI Collective. 1983. *Gozashteh cheragh-e rah-e ayandeh* [The past is a light into the future]. Edited by Bizhan Nikbin. Tehran: Entesharat-e Nilufar.

Jaryan Group. 1979. *Chand maqaleh va tahlil az goruh-e "Jaryan" (1335–1345)* [Selected essays and analyses of the "Jaryan" group (1956–1966)]. Tehran: np.

Javan, F. M. 1972. *Cherikha-ye khalq cheh miguyand* [What do the People's Guerrillas say?]. Germany: Tudeh Press.

Jazani, Bizhan. 1976a. *Cheguneh mobarezeh-ye mosallahaneh tudehi mishavad* [How armed struggle becomes a mass movement]. Germany: OIPFG.

———. 1976b. "Vahdat va naqsh-e estratezhik-e cherikha-ye Fadai-e khalq, 'mashy-e siyasi' va 'kar-e tudehi,' hezb-e tabaqeh-ye kargar-e Iran" [Unification and the strategic role of People's Fadai Guerrillas, "political approach" and "popular activities," The Iranian Working Class Party]. *19 Bahman-e Teorik*, 1.

———. 1976c. "Jam'bandi-ye mobarezat-e si saleh-ye akhir dar Iran" [Summation of the struggles of the past thirty years in Iran]. *19 Bahman-e Teorik*, 5–6.

———. 1976d. "Panj resaleh" [Five essays]. *19 Bahman-e Teorik*, 8.

———. 1978. *Nabard ba diktatori-ye shah* [War against the Shah's dictatorship]. Np: OIPFG.

———. 1979a. *Tarh-e jam'ehshenasi va mabani-ye estratezhi-ye jonbesh-e enqelabi-ye khalq-e Iran; baksh-e dovvom: tarikh-e si saleh-ye siyasi fasl-e avval)* [A sketch of sociology and foundations of the strategy of Iranian People's Revolutionary Movement; Second part: The thirty-year political history, chapter 1]. Tehran: Mazyar Publishers.

———. 1979b. *Tarh-e jam'ehshenasi va mabani-ye estratezhi-ye jonbesh-e enqelabi-ye khalq-e Iran, bakhsh-e avval: Eqtesadi* [Sociological sketch and foundations of the strategy of Iranian People's Revolutionary Movement, Part 1: Economic]. Tehran: Mazyar Publishers.

———. 1979c. *Tahlil-e moqe'iyat-e niruha-ye enqelabi dar Iran* [An analysis of the position of revolutionary forces in Iran]. Np: OIPFG.

———. 1980. *Capitalism and Revolution in Iran.* London: Zed.

———. 2009. *Enqelab-e mashrutiyyat-e Iran: Niruha va hadafha* [Iranian constitutional revolution: forces and objectives]. Paris: The Union of People's Fadaiyan of Iran.

———. nd-a. *Mohreh-i bar safhe-ye shatranj* [A pawn on the chessboard]. Np: Pishro Students Abroad Supporters of Rah-e Fadai.

———. nd-b. *Cheh kasani beh Marksism-Leninism khyanat mikonand?* [Who betrays Marxism-Leninism?]. Tehran: Entesharat-e Nuzdah-e Bahman.

———. nd-c. *Marksism-e eslami ya eslam-e Marksisti* [Islamic Marxism or Marxist Islam]. Np: Danashjuyan-e Pishro dar Kharej-e Keshvar, Havadar-e Rah-e Fadai.

Jazani, Bizhan, and Group One. 1976. *Tez-e goruh-e Jazani* [Thesis of Jazani's group]. Np: 19 Bahman Publisher.

Jazani, Mihan. 1999. "Bizhan: Ma'shuq, rafiq, va hamsar" [Bizhan: Lover, comrade, and husband]. In CCPWBJ 1999, 15–84.

Kamalvand, Farideh. 2002. *Yadha-ye mandegar: khaterat-e man va hamsaram Dr. Hushang Azami Lorestani* [Obstinate memories of my spouse, Dr. Hushang Azami Lorestani]. Tehran: Nashr-e Eshareh.

Kar (OIPFG). 1979a. No. 30 (Wednesday, Sept. 2).

———. 1979b. No. 32 (Wednesday, Sept. 17).

———. 1980a. No. 45 (Wednesday, Feb. 7).

———. 1980b. Special Issue (Friday, Feb. 9).

Kar (OIPF-M). 1981. No. 108 (Wednesday, May 5).

———. 1994. Special Issue Commemorating 7 February (19 Bahman), appendix to Vol. 3, no. 77 (Wednesday, Feb. 9).

———. 1995. No. 102 (Wednesday, Feb. 8).

———. 1996. No. 136 (Wednesday, June 26).

———. 1998a. No. 185 (Wednesday, June 24).

———. 1998b. No. 196 (Wednesday, Nov. 25).

———. 1999. No. 201 (Wednesday, Feb. 10).

Karimi, Behzad. 2001. "Moruri khaterehvar bar jonbesh-e daneshju-i daneshgah-e Tabriz dar dah-e-ye chehl" [A recollective review of the student movement of University of Tabriz during the sixties]. *Kar* (OIPF-M), no. 253 (Mar. 21): 6.

————. 2008. Interview by Peyman Vahabzadeh. July 12.

Karimi-Hakkak, Ahmad. 1995. *Recasting Persian Poetry: Scenarios of Poetic Modernity in Iran.* Salt Lake City: Univ. of Utah Press.

Kargar, Sadeq. 2001. "Sazman va jonbesh-e kargari" [The OIPFG and the workers' movement]. *Kar* (OIPF-M), no. 252 (Mar. 7): 4.

Kashkuli, Iraj. 2001. *Negahi az darun beh jonbesh-e chap-e Iran: Goftogu ba Iraj Kashkuli* [A glance from within on the Iranian Leftist movement: interview with Iraj Kashkuli]. Edited by Hamid Shokat. Tehran: Nashr-e Akhtaran.

Katouzian, Homa. 2004. "The Strange Politics of Khalil Maleki." In *Reformers and Revolutionaries in Modern Iran: New Perspectives on the Iranian Left,* edited by Stephanie Cronine, 165–88. London: Routledge Curzon.

Keddie, Nikki R. 1981. *Roots of Revolution: An Interpretive History of Modern Iran.* New Haven: Yale Univ. Press.

Khanbaba Tehrani, Mehdi. 2001. *Negahi az darun beh jobesh-e chap-e Iran: Goftogu-ye Hamid Shokat ba Mehdi Khanbaba Tehrani* [A glance from within on the Iranian Leftist movement: Interview with Mehdi Khanbaba Tehrani]. Edited by Hamid Shokat. Tehran: Enteshar.

Kianuri, Nurreddin. 1992. *Khaterat-e Nurreddin-e Kianuri* [Memoirs of Nurreddin Kianuri]. Tehran: Didgah Research and Publication Institute.

Kuzichkin, Vladimir. 1997. *KGB dar Iran: afsaneh va vaqe'iyyat* [Inside the KGB: Myth and reality]. Tehran: Nashr-e Hekayat.

Laclau, Ernesto. 1996. *Emancipation(s).* London: Verso.

————. 2005. *On Populist Reason.* London: Verso.

Laclau, Ernesto, and Chantal Mouffe. 1985. *Hegemony and Socialist Strategy: Toward a Radical Democratic Politics.* London: Verso.

Lahiji, Karim. 1999. "Haqq-e dusti" [By friendship's obligation]. In CCPWBJ 1999, 203–10.

Langarudi, Shams (Mohammad Taqi Javaheri Gilani). 1998. *Tarikh-e tahlili-ye she'r-e no* [The analytical history of modern Persian poetry]. 4 vols., 2nd ed. Tehran: Nashr-e Markaz.

Lenin, V. I. 1932. *State and Revolution.* New York: International Publishers.

————. 1935. *Two Tactics of Social Democracy in the Democratic Revolution.* New York: International Publishers.

Madani, Mostafa. 2003. "Mosahebeh ba rafiq Mostafa Madani" [Interview with Comrade Mostafa Madani.] In UPFI 2003, 50–66.

Magnusson, Warren, and Rob Walker. 1988. "Decentring the State: Political Theory and Canadian Political Economy." *Studies in Political Economy* 26:37–71.

Mahdizadeh, Rasul. 2001. "Mosahebeh ba rafiq Rasul Mahdizadeh" [Interview with Comrade Rasul Mahdizadeh]. *Kar* (OIPF-M), no. 256 (May 12): 9.

Marighella, Carlos. 1971. "Minimanual of the Urban Guerrilla." In *Urban Guerrilla Warfare*, edited by Robert Moss. London: International Institute for Strategic Studies.

Martin, Vanessa. 2000. *Creating an Islamic State: Khomeini and the Making of New Iran*. London: I. B. Tauris and Co.

Masali, Hassan. 1985. "Tasir-e binesh va manesh dar mobarezeh-ye ejtemai" [The influence of perspective and character on social struggle]. In *Natayej-e seminar-e Wiesbaden darbareh-ye bohran-e jonbesh-e chap-e Iran* [The outcomes of Wiesbaden Conference on the Crisis of Iranian Leftist Movement], 39–84. Frankfurt: Wiesbaden Conference Organization Committee.

———. 2001. *Seyr-e tahhavol-e jonbesh-e chap-e Iran va avamel-e bohran-e modavem-e an* [The process of transformation of Iranian Left movement and the causes of its continued crisis]. Los Angeles: Dehkhoda Publisher.

Matin, Afshin. 1999. *Konfedrasion: tarikh-e jonbesh-e daneshjuyan-e Irani dar kharj az keshvar 1332–57* [Confederation: The history of the Iranian student movement abroad 1953–79]. Translated by Arastu Azari. Tehran: Shirazeh.

Mehregan, Heydar (Rahman Hatefi). 1979. *Hanuz mashy-e cheriki-ye joda za Tudeh* [Guerrilla strategy, detached from the masses]. Tehran: Tudeh Party of Iran Press.

Mikailian, Vartan. 2007. "Shahed-e eyni" [Eyewitness]. In *Darbareh-ye Roshanfekr: Yek bahs-e qalami* [On intellectuals: A debate], edited by Nasser Pakdaman, 146–53. Cologne: Forough Verlag.

Mirsepassi, Ali. 2000. *Intellectual Discourse and the Politics of Modernization: Negotiating Modernity in Iran*. London: Oxford Univ. Press.

Moghissi, Haideh. 1994. *Populism and Feminism in Iran: Women's Struggle in a Male-defined Revolutionary Movement*. New York: St. Martin's Press.

Mohajer, Nasser. 2001. "Divar-e sokut va badbini-ye doost" [The wall of silence and friend's suspicion]. In *Ketab-e Zendan; jeld dovvom* [The book of prison, vol. 2], edited by Nasser Mohajer, 231–34. Berkeley, CA: Noghteh Books.

Mombeyni, Amir. 2003. "Mosahebeh ba rafiq Amir Mombeyni" [Interview with Comrade Amir Mombeyni]. In UPFI 2003, 2–7.

Momeni, Hamid. 1977. *Shuresh na, qadamha-ye sanjideh dar rah-e enqelab* [Not rebellion, judicious steps on the path to the revolution]. Np: Support Committee for the New Revolutionary Movement of Iranian People.

———. 1979. *Pasokh beh forsattalaban dar mored-e "Mobarezeh-ye mosalahaneh, ham stratezhi, ham taktik"* [A rejoinder to the opportunists on "Armed Struggle: Both Strategy and Tactic"]. Tehran: Entesharat-e M. Bidsorkhi.

Momeni, Hamid, and Mostafa Sho'aiyan. nd. *Juyeshi piramun-e roshanfeker ya roshangar-e tabaqeh-ye kargar* [An inquiry into the intellectual or enlightener of the working class]. Np: Enqelab Publishers.

Nabavi, Behzad. 2002. "Razha-ye Behzad Nabavi" [The Secrets of Behzad Nabavi]. *Hamshahri* 2706 (Apr. 27). http://www.hamshahri.org/hamnews/1381/810207/polig.htm (accessed Mar. 22, 2004).

Nabdel, Ali Reza. 1977. *Azerbaijan va masaleh-ye melli* [Azerbaijan and the national question]. Np: OIPFG.

Nabard-e Khalq (organ of OIPFG). *1974a. No. 2 (Mar.).

———. 1974b. No. 3 (May–June).

———. 1974c. No. 4 (July–Aug.).

———. 1975a. No. 5 (Dec. 1974–Jan. 1975).

———. 1975b. No. 6 (May).

———. 1976. No. 7 (May–June).

Nabard-e Khalq (For workers and toilers) (organ of OIPFG). 1978. No. 3 (Nov.–Dec.).

Naderi, Mahmoud. 2008. *Cherikha-ye Fadai-ye Khalq: az nokhostin konesh ta Bahman-e 1357, jeld-e avval* [People's Fadai Guerrillas: From their first acts until February 1979, vol. 1]. Tehran: Political Studies and Research Institutes.

Naficy, Majid. 1997. *Modernism and Ideology in Persian Literature: A Return to the Poetry of Nima Yushij*. Lanham, MD: Univ. Press of America.

Nashriyeh-ye Dakheli [The internal bulletin of OIPFG]. 1975a. No. 11 (June–July).

———. 1975b. No. 14 (Aug.–Sept.).

———. 1976. No. 21 (Mar.–Apr.).

Navidi, Parviz. 1999. "Yadi az zendegi va mobarezat-e Bizhan dar zendan" [Recollections of the life and struggles of Bizhan in prison]. In CCPWBJ 1999, 167–88.

———. 2008. Interview by Peyman Vahabzadeh. July 17.

Nayyeri, Iraj. nd. "Mosahebeh ba rafiq Iraj Nayyeri" [An interview with Comrade Iraj]. In *Dah maqaleh va mosahebeh as Kar-e aksariyat* [Ten essays and interviews from *Kar* the organ of the Majority], 60–63. Sweden: General Council of Iranian Student Associations in Sweden Supporters of OIPF-M.

Negahdar, Farrokh. 1997. *Demokrasi baray-e Iran: sokhanrani-ha, goftoguha, maqalat* [Democracy for Iran: Speeches, interviews, essays]. London: np.

———. 1999. "Sargozasht-e 'Qiyam ra bavar konim'" [The story of "Let Us Believe in the Revolution"]. *Kar* (OIPF-M), no. 201 (Feb. 10): 10.

———. 2003. "Mosahebeh ba Farrokh Negahdar" [Interview with Farrokh Negahdar]. In UPFI 2003, 67–73.

———. 2008. Interview by Peyman Vahabzadeh. Dec. 7–8.

Nejat Hosseini, Mohsen. 2000. *Bar faraz-e khalij-e Fars: khaterat-e Mohsen Nejat Hosseini* [Over the Persian Gulf: Memoirs of Mohsen Nejat Hosseini]. Tehran: Nashr-e Ney.

Nejati, Gholamreza. 1992. *Tarikh-e siyasi-ye bistopanj saleh-ye Iran.* [The twenty-five-year political history of Iran]. Tehran: Rasa Cultural Services.

Nobari, Ali Reza. 1978. *Iran Erupts.* Stanford, CA: Iran-American Documentation Group.

OCUA [Organization of Communist Unity Abroad]. 1987. "Dar hashieh-ye seminar-e Wiesbaden: pasokhi beh chande ede'a" [On the Wiesbaden Seminar: Responses to claims]. *Andisheh-ye Rahai* 6 (Mar.): 117–27.

OF-Minority. 2003. *Asnad-e komision-e tahqiq va barresi* [Documents of the Joint Research Committee]. Frankfurt: Organization of Fadaiyan-Minority.

OIPFG. 1975. *Edam-e enghelabi-ye Abbas Shahriyari, mard-e hezar chehreh* [The revolutionary execution of Abbas Shahriyari, a man with a thousand faces]. Np: OIPFG.

———. 1977a. *Chahar resaleh az Sazman-e Cherkha-ye Fadai-ye Khalq-e Iran* [Four essays by the Organization of Iranian People's Fadai Guerrillas]. Germany: Support Committee of Iranian Peoples New Revolutionary Movement.

———. 1977b. *Nashriyeh-ye vizheh-ye bahs-e darun-e Do Sazman-e Mojahedin-e Khalq-e Iran va Cherikha-ye Fadai-ye Khalq-e Iran shomareh-ye avval* [The special bulletin of the internal exchanges between the OIPM and OIPFG, vol. 1]. Np: OIPFG.

———. 1977c. "Stalinism va masaleh-ye burokrasi dar jameh'eh-ye Shoravi" [Stalinism and the problem of bureaucracy in the Soviet society]. In *Stalinism: daftar-e dovvom tabadol-e nazar dar poroseh-ye tajanos* [Stalinism: Second volume of the exchange of ideas in the unification process]. Np: Group for Communist Unity and OIPFG. Article individually paginated.

———. 1977d. "Pasokh beh 'Nokati dar tarh-e masaleh-ye Stalin'" [Rejoinder to "Sketching the Outline of the Stalin Issue"]. In *Stalinism: daftar-e dovvom tabadol-e nazar dar poroseh-ye tajanos* [Stalinism: Second volume of the exchange of ideas in the unification process]. Np: Group for Communist Unity and OIPFG. Article individually paginated.

———. 1977e. "Gardesh beh rast dar siyasat-e khareji Jomhuri-ye Khalq-e Chin" [Turning to the right in the foreign policy of the People's Republic of China]. In *Andisheh-ye Mao Tse-tung va siyasat-e khareji-ye Chin* [Mao Tse-tung doctrine and China's foreign policy]. Np: Group for Communist Unity and OIPFG. Article individually paginated.

———. 1978a. *Jonbesh-e khalq va oportunistha-ye ma* [The people's movement and our opportunists]. Np: OIPFG.

———. 1978b. *Jebhe-ye vahed-e zedd-e diktatori va dar-o-dasteh-ye Hezb-e Tudeh* [The United Anti-Dictatorship Front and the Tudeh Party bunch]. Np: OIPFG.

————. 1979a. *Hasht sal mobarezeh-ye mosallahaneh dar ravand-e jonbesh-e khalq (zamimeh-ye 19 Bahman)* [Eight years of armed struggle in the process of people's movements (supplement to 19 Bahman)]. Np: OIPFG.

————. 1979b. *Gerami bad khatereh-ye Fadai-ye kabir rafiq Hamid Ashraf* [In commemoration of the great Fadai Comrade Hamid Ashraf]. Np: OIPFG.

————. 1979c. *Pasokh beh "Mosahebeh ba rafiq Ashraf Dehqani"* [A rejoinder to the "Interview with Comrade Ashraf Dehqani"]. Tehran: OIPFG.

————. nd-a. *Yadnameh-ye razmandegan-e shahid Sazman-e Cherikha-ye Fadai-e Khalq dar sal-e 1351* [Commemorating the martyred warriors of Organization of People's Fadai Guerrillas in 1972–73]. Np: OIPFG.

————. nd-b. *Amuzeshha-yi baray-e jang-e chirki shahri* [Instructions for urban guerrilla warfare]. Np: OIPFG.

————, ed. nd-c. *Chahar naqd bar ketab-e "Enqelab dar enqelab?"* [Four critiques of "Revolution in the Revolution?"]. Np: OIPFG.

OIPFG-Kurdistan Branch. 1980. *Ashraf Dehqani: bazmandeh-ye doran-e kudaki!* [Ashraf Dehqani: A remnant of our childhood era!]. Kurdistan: OIPFG.

OIPFG-Minority. 1980. *Pasokh-e Aqalliyat beh nameh-ye "markaziyyat"* [The Minority's rejoinder to the letter of the "Central Committee"]. Np: OIPFG.

————. nd. *Darbareh-ye bohran-e darun-e Sazman-e Cherikha-ye Fadai-ye Khalq-e va rishehha-ye an* [On the internal crisis of the OIPFG and its roots]. Np: OIPFG.

OIPFG (Splinter Group). 1977. *Elamiyyeh tozihi-ye mavaze ideolozhik-e goruh-e monsha'eb az Sazman-e Cherikha-ye Fadai-ye Khalq* [Explanatory manifesto on the ideological positions of the OIPFG splinter group]. Np: np.

OIPF-M. 2001. "The Organization of Iranian People's Fadaian (Majority): 1971–2001." http://w1.315.telia.com/~u31525377/english/his01eng.htm (accessed Apr. 28, 2009).

OIPM. 1979a. *Tahlil-e amuzeshi-ye bayaniyyeh-ye oportunistha-ye chapnama* [An educational analysis of Left-feigning opportunists]. Tehran: OIPM.

————. 1979b. *Sharh-e tasis va tarikhcheh-ye vaqaye'e Sazman-e Mojahedin-e Khalq-e Iran as sal-e 1344 ta sal-e 1350* [A brief history of establishment and circumstances of Organization of Iranian People's Mojahedin, 1965–1971]. Tehran: OIPM.

OIPM (M-L). 1976a. *Bayaniyyeh-ye e'lam-e mavaze'e ideolozhik-e Sazman-e Mojahedin-e Khalq-e Iran* [Manifesto of ideological positions of the OIPM]. Np: OIPM (M-L).

————. 1976b. *Masael-e hadd-e jonbesh-e ma* [The critical issues of our movement]. Np: OIPM (M-L).

————. 1977. *Zamimeh-i bar masael-e hadd-e jonbesh-e ma* [Supplement to the critical issues of our movement]. Np: OIPM (M-L).

———. 1978. *E'lamiyyehha-i az bakhsh-e Marksist-Leninisti-ye Sazman-e Mojahedin-e Khalq-e Iran, Aban-Azar 1357* [Communiqués of the Marxist-Leninist faction of the OIPM, Oct.–Nov. 1978]. West Berlin: Iranian Student Union in FDR and West Berlin.

Payam-e Daneshju (Student organ of the OIPFG). 1975. No. 1 (Oct. 22).

———. 1977. No. 3 (nd).

Peykar. 1979. *Tahlili bar taghir va tahavvol-e daruni-ye Sazman-e Mojahedin-e Khalq-e Iran (52–54)* [An analysis of the internal transformations of the OIPM (1973–75)]. Np: Paykar.

Pishgam Student Organization. nd. *Qiyam va economistha: tahlili bar "Naqdi bar mobarezeh-ye ideolozhik-e" Peykar* [The uprising and the economists: An analysis of "A critique of ideological exchanges" by Peykar]. Umeä, Sweden: Organization of Iranian Students.

Prison Dialogue Collective, ed. 2003. *Goftoguha-ye Zendan: Vizhenameh Mahmoud Mahmoudi* [Prison dialogues: Special issue on Mahmoud Mahmoudi]. Leipzig: Sonboleh.

Puyan, Amir Parviz. 1979. *Zarurat-e mobarezeh-ye mosallahaneh va radd-e teori-ye baqa* [The necessity of armed struggle and the refutation of the theory of survival]. Tehran: Gam Publishers.

Raf'at. 2001. Interview by Peyman Vahabzadeh. Nov. 6 and 9, Dec. 3.

Rahnema, Saeed. 1997. *Tajdid-e hayat-e sosial demokrasi dar Iran?* [Rebirth of social democracy in Iran?]. Spånga, Sweden: Baran.

Rasul (Azarnush). 2003. "Mosahebeh ba rafiq Rasul" [Interview with Comrade Rasul]. In UPFI 2003, 18–22.

Razmi, Mashallah. 2008. Interview by Peyman Vahabzadeh. July 7 and 21.

Rejali, Darius M. 1994. *Torture and Modernity: Self, Society, and State in Modern Iran.* Boulder, CO: Westview Press.

Rezvani, Mohsen. 2005. *Negahi az darun beh jobesh-e chap-e Iran: Goftogu ba Mohsen Rezvani* [A glance from within on the Iranian Leftist movement: Interview with Mohsen Rezvani]. Edited by Hamid Shokat. Cologne: Mortazavi.

Rohani, Seyyed Hamid. 1993. *Nehzat-e Emam Khomeini Jeld 3* [Imam Khomeini's movement, vol. 3]. Tehran: Centre of the Islamic Revolution Documents.

Rose, Nikolas. 1999. *Powers of Freedom: Reframing Political Thought.* Cambridge, UK: Cambridge Univ. Press.

Safai Farahani, Ali Akbar. 1976. *Ancheh yek enqelabi bayad bedanad* [What a revolutionary must know]. Np: 19 Bahman Publishers.

Salehi, Anush. 2002. *Ravi-ye baharan: mobarezat va zendegi-ye Karamatollah Daneshian* [The spring's narrator: The life and struggles of Karamatollah Daneshian]. Tehran: Nashr-e Qatre.

Same', Mehdi. 1997. *Tadavom: goftogu-i ba Mehdi Same'* [Continuity: An interview with Mehdi Same']. Edited by Ali Nazer. Grigny Cedex, France: OIPFG.

———. 1999. "Bizhan, Marksisti khallaq, rabari mostaqqel va democrat" [Bizhan, a creative Marxist, a democratic and independent leader]. In CCPWBJ 1999, 133–49.

Sanassarian, Eliz. 1983. "An Analysis of Fida'i and Mojahedin Positions on Women's Rights. In *Women and Revolution in Iran*, edited by Guity Nashat, 97–108. Boulder, CO: Westview Press.

Schürmann, Reiner. 1987. *Heidegger on Being and Acting: From Principles to Anarchy*. Translated by Christine-Marie Gros. Bloomington: Indiana Univ. Press.

Satwat, Mariam. 2002. Interview by Peyman Vahabzadeh. Jan. 14 and 28.

———. 2005. "Chahar pari-ye kuchak-e mosallah" [Four armed little fairies]. *Baran* 8–9 (Autumn): 51–54.

Shahidian, Hammed. 1994. "The Iranian Left and the 'Woman Question' in the Revolution of 1978–79." *International Journal of Middle East Studies* 26 (2): 223–47.

———. 1997. "Women and Clandestine Politics in Iran, 1970–1985." *Feminist Studies* 23 (1): 7–42.

Shalguni, Mohammad Reza. 1999. "Jay-e uo khali mand" [His absence is felt]. In CCP-WBJ 1999, 151–59.

Shamlu, Ahmad, ed. 1968. *Khusheh: avvalin hafteh-ey she'r va honar* [Cluser: The first week of poetry and art]. Tehran: Entesharat-e Kavosh.

Shokat, Hamid. 2002. "Naqdi bar do maqaleh darbareh-ye tarikh-e roshd-e komonism dar Iran and konfedrasion-e daneshjuyan" [Critical review of two essays on the history of communism in Iran and on the Confederation of Students]. *Persian Book Review* 11 (37–38) (Fall 2001–Winter 2002): 92–100.

Sho'aiyan, Mostafa. 1976a. *Chand neveshteh* [Selected writings]. Florence: Edition Mazdak.

———. 1976b. *Enqelab* [Revolution]. Florence: Edition Mazdak.

———. 1976c. *Sheshomin nameh-ye sargoshadeh be cherikha-ye Fadai* [The sixth open letter to People's Guerrillas]. Florence: Edition Mazdak.

———. 1976d. *Jang-s sazesh* [A war to compromise]. Florence: Edition Mazdak.

———. 1976e. *Negah-i beh ravabet-e shoravi va nehzat-e enqelabi-ye Jangal* [A review of the relations between the Soviet Union and the revolutionary movement of jungle]. Florence: Edition Mazdak.

———. 1976f. *Pasokhha-ye nasanjideh be "Qadamha-ye sanjideh"* [Injudicious replies to "Judicious Steps"]. Florence: Edition Mazdak.

———. 1976g. *Do enteqad beh Cherikha-ye Fadai Khalq* [Two critical essays on the People's Fadai Guerrillas]. Florence: Edition Mazdak.

———. 1977. *Naqsh-e Esrail va rezhim-e Phalavi dar khavar-e miyaneh* [On the role of Israeli and Iranian regimes in the Middle East]. Florence: Edition Mazdak.

———. 1980. *Shesh nameh-ye sargoshadeh beh Sazman-e Charikha-ye Fadai-e Khalq-e Iran* [Six open letters to the Organization of Iranian People's Fadai Guerrillas]. Tehran: Edition Mazdak.

———. nd-a. "Cheh bayad kard?" [What is to be done?]. Np: mimeographed monograph.

———. nd-b. *Nimgami dar rah: Jebheh-ye rahaibakhsh-e khalq* [Half a step on the way: The People's Liberation Front]. Np: Enqelab Publisher.

Skocpol, Theda. 1994. *Social Revolutions in the Modern World.* Cambridge, UK: Cambridge Univ. Press.

Tavakkol (Akbar Kamiyabi). 2003. "Mosahebeh ba rafiq Tavakkol" [Interview with Comrade Tavakkol]. In UPFI 2003, 8–14.

Touraine, Alain. 1988. *Return of the Actor: Social Theory in Postindustrial Society.* Translated by Myrna Godzich. Minneapolis: Univ. of Minnesota Press.

Tudeh Party of Iran. 1979. *Goftogui ba Cherkha-ye Fadai-ye Khalq-e Iran darbareh-ye masael-e enqelab-e Iran* [A dialogue with the Iranian People's Fadai Guerrillas on the issues of Iranian revolution]. Tehran: Tudeh Party of Iran.

Ulyanovsky, R., and V. Pavlov. 1973. "The Non-capitalist Path as a Historical Reality." In *Asian Dilemma: A Soviet View and Myrdal's Concept,* 152–69. Moscow: Progress Publishers.

UPFI [The Union of People's Fadaiyan of Iran], ed. 2003. *Enshe'ab-e Aqaliyat-Aksariyat* [The Minority-Majority split]. http://www.etehadefadaian.org/bargiaztarikh/Bargi az tarik-Ensheab.pdf (accessed Oct. 28, 2003).

Vahabzadeh, Peyman. 2003. *Articulated Experiences: Toward a Radical Phenomenology of Contemporary Social Movements.* Albany: State Univ. of New York Press.

———. 2005. "Bizhan Jazani and the Problems of Historiography of the Iranian Left." *Iranian Studies* 38 (1): 167–78.

———. 2007a. "Mustafa Shu'a'iyan and *Fada`iyan-i Khalq*: Frontal Politics, Stalinism, and the Role of Intellectuals in Iran." *British Journal of Middle Eastern Studies* 34 (1): 43–61.

———. 2007b. "Mostafa Sho'aiyan: The Maverick Theorist of the Revolution and the Failure of Frontal Politics in Iran." *Iranian Studies* 40 (3): 405–25.

————. 2009. "Ultimate Referentiality: Radical Phenomenology and the New Interpretive Sociology." *Philosophy and Social Criticism* 35 (4): 447–65.

Vaziri, Tahmasp. 2001. "Mosahebeh ba rafiq Tahmasp Vaziri [Interview with Comrade Tahmasp Vaziri]." *Kar* (OIPF-M), no. 256 (May 12): 8.

Zabih, Sepehr. 1986. *The Left in Contemporary Iran: Ideology, Organization, and the Soviet Connection*. Stanford, CA: Hoover Institution Press.

Zamimeh-ye Nabard-e Khalq (Supplementary issue to *Nabard-e Khalq*). 1975. (Feb.–Mar.).

Zia Zarifi, Abolhassan. 2004. *Zendeginameh-ye Hassan Zia Zarifi* [Hassan Zia Zarifi: A biography]. Tehran: Nashr-e Amin Dezh.

Zia Zarifi, Hassan. 1979. *Hezb-e Tudeh va kudeta-ye 28 Mordad 32* [The Tudeh Party and the August 18, 1953, coup d'état]. Tehran: np.

————. 1995. "Chand nevesht-ye montasher nashodeh az shahid-e rah-e azadi Hassan Zia Zarifi" [Unpublished manuscripts of Hassan Zia Zarifi]. *Rah-e Azadi* 42:21, 24.

————. 1996a. "Darbareh-ye siyasatha-ye Amrika, Englis, va darbar" [On the policies of the United States, England, and the Royal Court]. *Rah-e Azadi* 45:8, 27.

————. 1996b. "Eslahat-e arzi: zarbehi bar Peykar-e feudalism-e Iran" [Land reform: A strike against Iranian feudalism]. *Rah-e Azadi* 46:31.

————. 1996c. "Enqelabiyyun naqsh-e bozorgi dar takmil-e sharayet-e eini-ye enqelab darand" [Revolutionaries play a significant role in completing the objective conditions of the revolution]. *Rah-e Azadi* 47:30.

————. 1996d. "Sho'ar-e jomhuri mottahed konandeh-ye niruha-ye jame'eh" [The republican motto unifies social forces]. *Rah-e Azadi* 48:27.

Index